*Innovators*
*and Institutions*
*in Physical*
*Education*

# Innovators and Institutions in Physical Education

ELLEN W. GERBER, Ph.D

Assistant Professor of Physical Education
Department of Physical Education for Women
University of Massachusetts
Amherst, Massachusetts

*Lea & Febiger* • PHILADELPHIA, 1971

*Health Education,*
*Physical Education, and*
*Recreation Series*

Ruth Abernathy, Ph.D., Editorial Adviser
Chairman, Department for Women, School of
Physical and Health Education
University of Washington
Seattle, Washington 98105

ISBN   0-8121-0301-7

*"The history of the world is but the biography of great men."*

**CARLYLE**

# PREFACE

The events and ideas which constitute the history of physical education can be traced back to the individual men and women who helped to formulate them. Insights into the patterns of physical education in the western world can be gained therefore from a study of the people who were primarily responsible for proffering its ideas. This book contains biographical information about the innovators and presents their most important and relevant theories, wherever possible in the originator's own words.

The innovators of this book were chosen because in my view they either introduced, developed or acted as foremost spokesmen for a concept of physical education new in their time. The institutions were selected because they were deemed to have played crucial roles in promulgating physical education through programs for school children, college men and women, or the training of teachers. The objective of providing the reader with information in depth and with details not readily accessible, in a one-volume work of reasonable length, required that I be selective.

Inevitably, the particular people and institutions selected reflect my personal evaluation of their contributions. It is acknowledged that every participant, student, teacher, administrator, or advocator of physical activity has in some measure contributed to the development of physical education. Men and women working in what are sometimes considered related but separate areas, such as the dance, health, recreation, and the world of sport, have often had a special influence on physical education. For that reason Joseph Lee, Gertrude Colby, Margaret N. H'Doubler, Rudolph von Laban, Walter Camp, and many others might have been included in this book. In Parts V and VI, however, which deal with European and American physical educators and institutions, only those who were directly concerned with physical education, per se, were discussed. Living American educators were also excluded since they are part of a generation too close to the present for fair evaluation. Hopefully, a later edition may include the work of these latest innovators.

A particular effort was made to use in the book an extensive number of primary sources. For each innovator, a bibliography of the most significant writings by or about him or her can be constructed from the references made within each chapter. Numbers in parentheses, for example (19:264), refer the reader first to the bibliographical listing with the corresponding number, and second to specific pages within the work. Graduate students can utilize the bibliography to do advanced work on figures in whom they have particular interest. Undergraduates are urged to study the book as a whole, so that they may understand physical education as a developing pattern of ideas.

A work of this scope inevitably requires many acknowledgments. Perhaps most important, the contribution of the innovators and institutions themselves should be regarded with full appreciation. The quality and creativity of their work, often against strong opposition and without help or precedent, deserve acclaim. Similarly, the foundation work of other historians, particularly Edward Mussey Hartwell and Fred E. Leonard, must be recognized. Assistance in researching the early programs at Stanford University and Teachers College, Columbia University, was given by archivists at the libraries of those institutions. Walter Kroll and Guy Lewis shared the fruits of their research on George W. Fitz and the degree program at Harvard University. The Royal Danish Embassy procured information about Niels Bukh and the Ollerup Gymnastic High School. Nicolaas J. Moolenijzer contributed the section on Karl Gaulhofer-Margarete Streicher. Barbara J. Hoepner researched the section on John Swett. Betty Spears assisted in locating facts pertaining to the Boston Normal School of Gymnastics. John F. Spahr and Ruth Abernathy, editors at Lea and Febiger, were unstinting with their patience and assistance.

For permission to reprint copyrighted material I am in debt for the photographs of Elizabeth Burchenal, W. G. Anderson, Ethel Perrin, and C. H. McCloy to the American Association for Health, Physical Education and Recreation. The pictures of Jessie Bancroft and Delphine Hanna are also reproduced courtesy of the AAHPER from the 75th Anniversary Edition of the *Journal of Health, Physical Education and Recreation*. The photograph of Vittorino da Feltre is reprinted from the *Ciba Symposia*, copyright CIBA, formerly published by CIBA Pharmaceutical Company. *The Boston Sunday Globe* has granted its permission to reproduce the illustration from its May 18, 1958 issue of the class of Sargent girls wielding Indian clubs. The IDLA Corporation in Stockholm has allowed me to use the photograph of the Swedish gymnasts performing at an exhibition; this illustration first appeared in the *Report on the Lingiad 1949 and Idla Gymnastics*, edited by Vello Pekomae and Gunvald Hakanson and published by AB Seelig and Company. "The Masks of the Runner" are taken from *Exercise in Education and Medicine* by R. Tait McKenzie and published by W. B. Saunders Company in 1917. Dr. Nicolaas J. Moolenijzer has lent me the photograph of Margarete Streicher, and Walter Kroll supplied the picture of George W. Fitz. The photograph of Catharine Beecher is taken from *Saints, Sinners and Beechers* by Lyman Beecher Stowe, copyright, 1934, by The Bobbs-Merrill Company, Inc., R. 1962, by Lyman Beecher Stowe, and reproduced by permission of the publishers. And lastly, the Philosophical Library Publishers has provided me with the illustrations of

Homer, Plato and his students in the garden of the Academy, Martin Luther, John Calvin, Ignatius de Loyola, Michel de Montaigne, John Amos Comenius, John Locke, Jean Jacques Rousseau, Pestalozzi and his students, Friedrich Froebel, and John Dewey, from *The Pictorial History of Philosophy* (1959) by Dagobert D. Runes.

Finally contributions of a more personal nature are recalled with particular gratitude. Barbara C Hall awakened my first enthusiasm for scholarship and the world of philosophy and history. An innovator in her own right, Eleanor Metheny's intellectual depth and breadth, and generous giving of herself as a teacher and advisor, contributed enormously to my insight and understanding of physical education. It was at Jan Felshin's suggestion that I became involved in the writing of this book. And Pearl Berlin not only used her blue pencil to make numerous, excellent suggestions for improving this manuscript, but her high standards and scholarly integrity were a constant inspiration throughout the writing of this book.

*Amherst, Massachusetts*                                    ELLEN W. GERBER

# CONTENTS

## PART V

### European Physical Educators and Institutions

GERMAN

SWEDISH

DANISH

SWISS

FRENCH

ENGLISH

AUSTRIAN

## PART VI

## American Physical Educators and Institutions

# LIST OF ILLUSTRATIONS

# PART I

*Early Greek Authors*

# HOMER
## ca 850 B.C.

Mycenaean Greece was a land of action. The vitality and vigor springing through Homer's great epics, the *Iliad* and the *Odyssey*, were characteristic of the people and the time. The Mycenaean civilization arose in war when the Achaean invaders entered the country (possibly from the north), dominated the inhabitants and built the first Greek-speaking civilization. And it ended in war when the Dorian invaders in turn conquered them and left behind fire-blackened ruins still visible to tourists. Although the great palaces at Mycenae, Tiryns and Pylos are now rocky ruins, and the bronze armor and delicate golden jewelry exist only in museums, the spirit of the culture was forcefully preserved in the Homeric epic poems so that even today it is alive in literary memory. The siege of Troy is a landmark of the Mycenaean era. The warrior Achilles, hero of the *Iliad,* and the wandering Odysseus, hero of the *Odyssey,* are vital symbols of a period that probably began between 1900 and 1700 B.C. and ended between 1200 and 1000 B.C.

Homer the man might have been a myth. Later Greek tradition considered him a native of Ionia, a community of Greek settlers established on the other side of the Agean Sea on the west coast of Asia Minor. Archeologists today estimate that he lived about 850 B.C.; it may be significant or just coincidental that the Greek alphabet was constructed around the ninth century in Ionia, although there is no evidence to indicate that Homer actually set down his poems in written form. (35:30) The basic phrases were probably molded by Homer from an earlier oral tradition, not before the ninth century B.C., and it was probably around the sixth century B.C. when they were formalized in writing. (78:36) Like the Old Testament Songs of David, the final work under the symbolic authorship of one man is thought to be a collection of stories sung and recited for generations.

It is said that Homer, afflicted in old age by blindness, wandered from city to city reciting his verses. Whether Homer actually lived as the blind minstrel of traditional fame is almost irrelevant in light of Leonard Cottrell's comment that "to the Greeks of classical times Homer was not only their greatest poet, but was revered as historian, philosopher, moralist. . . . [His] two great epics had as profound an influence on the Greek mind as the

Fig. 1.   Homer.

Bible and Shakespeare have had on the Anglo-Saxon world." (78:35) More important is the question of the poems' historical authenticity. Archeologists have found increasing evidence to support the contention that they essentially depict history rather than myth; some passages, however, are reflective of the later Iron Age culture of Homer rather than the Bronze Age of the Achaean warriors.

Because the *Iliad* and *Odyssey* are generally regarded as marking the beginning of western literature, their detailed references to athletic competition are important early sources of the historical development of physical education. The two poems are evidence that by the time of the Trojan War (ca. 1200 B.C.) diversified forms of sport were not only common but an important part of the culture. Contests described in the epics include chariot racing, boxing, wrestling, foot racing, javelin throwing, discus throwing, armed combat with spear and shield, archery, long jumping, and rhythmic ball tossing. With the exception of chariot racing and ball tossing, competition is still held in these events in modern times (if one considers fencing a modern version of the armed combat). It is not surprising that in the virile, active, warrior culture of the Achaeans athletic prowess was highly valued. Homer, recording this idea through the words of Laodamas, son of Alcinous, said: "Come, sir, won't you take a hand with us in our games, if you're good at any sport? You must surely be an athlete, for nothing makes a man so famous for life as what he can do with his hands and feet." (185:Book VIII, 127) Odysseus was insulted when told that he was no *athleter* (winner of prizes) in what was apparently the first use of the word from which the term "athlete" is derived. (304:237)

But it is not the specific expression alone in the epics that indicates the importance Homer attached to sports—it is the weight of constant reference both formal and casual. The funeral games of Patroclus, beloved friend of the hero Achilles, are included in the *Iliad* (Book XXIII) in the form of a polished, detailed explanation of sports customs as is the scene in the *Odyssey* between Odysseus and the Phaeacians. (Book VIII) From those passages specific information can be derived on the organization and conduct of contests, the manner in which certain events were performed, the use of games as a part of funeral proceedings, the attached religious significance, the role of spectators and referees, and the ways in which contestants were regarded and rewarded. The description of the wrestling match between Aias and Odysseus serves as an example:

Losing no time, the son of Peleus brought out and displayed fresh prizes, for the third event, the all-in wrestling. For the winner there was a big three-legged cauldron to go on the fire—it was worth a dozen oxen by Achaean reckoning—and for the loser he brought forward a woman thoroughly trained in domestic work, who was valued at four oxen in the camp. Achilles stood up to announce the contest.... The two ... stepped into the middle of the ring, and gripped each other in their powerful arms.... Their backs creaked under the pressure of their mighty hands; the sweat streamed down; and many blood-red weals sprang up along their sides and shoulders. And still they tussled on, each thinking of the fine cauldron that was not yet won. But Odysseus was no more able to bring down his man, and pin him to the ground, than Aias, who was baffled by Odysseus' brawn. After some time, when they saw that they were boring the troops, the great Telamonian Aias said: "Royal son of Laertes, Odysseus of the nimble wits; either you or I must let the other try a throw. What happens afterwards is Zeus's business."

With that, he lifted Odysseus off the ground. But Odysseus' craft did not desert him. He caught Aias with a kick from behind in the hollow of the knee, upset his stance, and flung him on his back, himself falling on Aias' chest. The spectators were duly impressed. But now the stalwart admirable Odysseus had to try a throw. He shifted Aias just a little off the ground, but he could not throw him. So he crooked a leg round Aias' knee, and they both fell down, cheek by jowl, and were smothered in dust. They jumped up and would have tried a third round, if Achilles himself had not ... interposed. He told them they had struggled quite enough and must not wear each other out. "You have both won," he said. "Take equal prizes and withdraw...." The two men readily accepted his decision, and after wiping off the dust put on their tunics. (184: XXIII, 431–432)

It is equally significant that sport references and metaphors abound throughout the epics.  For instance, while Achilles was lying by his beaked seagoing ships, nursing his quarrel with the Commander-in-Chief Agamemnon, son of Atreus, "meanwhile on the sea beach his people passed the times in archery, in throwing disks and casting javelins. . . ." (184:II, 60) Phoebus Apollo made "a broad and ample causeway, wide as the space that a man covers with a spear-cast when he is testing his strength." (184:XV, 281) These references indicate the integral part that sport played in the daily lives of the Achaeans.  Men who survived and kept their possessions in those days were men of strength and skill and they delighted in testing and exhibiting these qualities.  Furthermore, the gods liked strong, skilled men and winning implied earning their favor.

The prominent and informative aspects of athletics as dealt with in the *Iliad* and *Odyssey* would in themselves make Homer important to those interested in the relationship between men and sport.  But there is another idea associated with the epics which has had lasting effects on the development of physical education itself.  Plato, talking about the immortalization of the hero, commented that the poet "adorning countless deeds done by men of old, provides instruction for posterity." (285:27)  Thus Homer in describing the proper attitudes and attributes of his ancient heroes, instructs by example.  Since he himself was a hero to the Greeks of the classical period, his ideas were influential; memorizing all of Homer was a fundamental part of Athenian education.  Joy in sport and the desire to excel as an athlete, qualities with which Homer endowed Achilles, were fundamental attributes of classical Greek culture.  The Homeric sportsman-hero can be traced as an ideal in Athenian education.

Skill in sports was important to a man whose life was to be lived as a warrior; in addition it was significant in that it marked the nobleman, the man of breeding, the well-born:

> Euryalus now saw fit to interpose and insult him to his face: "You are quite right, sir.  I should never have taken you for an athlete such as one is accustomed to meet in the world.  But rather for some skipper of a merchant crew, who spends his life on a hulking tramp, worrying about his outward freight, or keeping a sharp eye on the cargo when he comes home with the profits he has snatched. No; one can see you are no sportsman." (185:VIII, 127)

Odysseus, *because* he was skilled at throwing the discus and the spear, and boxing and shooting the polished bow, proved to the unfriendly Phaeacians that he was a man of stature.

While enchanting readers with his tales of the heroic Achaean warriors, Homer presented a picture of Mycenaean Greece in which sport activities played an important role in the life and reputation of men who were valued for what they could do with their "hands and feet."  Over two thousand years later, literature describing the life of medieval knights with their tournaments and crusades was strongly reminiscent of the life and values vividly portrayed in the *Iliad* and the *Odyssey*.

# PLATO

## 427-347 B.C.

Plato himself exemplified the ideal of the Athenian citizen. Born in 427 B.C., he was the handsome son of distinguished aristocratic parents. His father was a descendant of an ancient Athenian king and his mother of the family of Solon the Lawgiver, framer of the Athenian Constitution. He had a careful education in music, gymnastics and poetry, especially Homer, and studied under the tutelage of Socrates. Besides being a master teacher and writer, he was an athlete with a reputation as an accomplished wrestler who twice won prizes at the Isthmian Games and was also said to excel as a soldier. The name Plato ("*platy*" means broad-shouldered) was, according to tradition, given to him by his wrestling teacher because of his physical condition, his original name having been Aristocles. (304:125) His natural intelligence and good education were further tempered by twelve years of experience travelling through Egypt, Italy and Sicily, after he had been forced to leave Athens as the result of his efforts to defend his teacher Socrates who was put to death as a threat to the state. By age forty he had written most of his major *Dialogues*, includ ing *The Republic* During his lifetime he made several unsuccessful attempts to put his social theories into action, first in Athens and later in Syracuse. He died in Athens in 347 B.C.

Although today's scholarship classifies him as a philosopher, the modern connotations of the term do not accurately describe the life of a man who was at once a thinker, poet, dramatist, soldier, and statesman vitally involved in the politics of his day. In 387 B.C. he founded the Academy in a sacred wood dedicated to the hero Academos. Not only was it renowned for its intellectual discipline and discussions of seemingly esoteric ideas, but it was also a training ground for administrators of the *polis* (city-state). Plato's well-known idea that states should be governed by philosopher-kings meant that men must acquire wisdom, including understanding such abstract concepts as justice and virtue. There was no dichotomy in Plato's thinking between doers and thinkers.

He seems to have been the first to articulate the idea of education as a means to building a better society. Although some men were destined by their abilities to be guardians, some to be warriors, and some to be business men and farmers, all men could profit by education. In fact, carrying this

7

idea to its logical conclusion, Plato recommended the same education for women, including gymnastic training, because the arts of music and gymnastic were expected to help men and women be "as good as possible." (286:V, 171–181)

> The regulations which we are prescribing, my good Adeimantus, are . . . but trifles all, if care be taken . . . of the one great thing . . .
> What may that be? he asked.
> Education, I said, and nurture: If our citizens are well educated, and grow into sensible men, they will easily see their way through all these, as well as other matters. (286:IV, 134)

Furthermore, Plato insisted that the rulers not be allowed to tamper with the educational system as he both experienced and prescribed it: "This is the point to which, above all, the attention of our rulers should be directed, —that music and gymnastic be preserved in their original form, and no innovation made." (286:IV, 134)

Gymnastic (physical education) was an integral part of Athenian education in classical times. Children began school at about the age of seven and studied in the music school, reading, writing, poetry, singing, and playing the lyre and the flute, and in the palaestra,* games, wrestling, swimming, running, jumping, javelin and discus throwing, and boxing until they were fifteen. For the next three years, those youths expecting to qualify by virtue of their birth and wealth for ephebic training, spent their time at the gymnasium, continuing in a more strenuous manner the formal instruction started in the palaestra. New activities included racing in armor, and horse and chariot racing. Education at the Ephebic College included military gymnastic training and those subjects generally considered part of a liberal education: grammar, rhetoric, philosophy, and mathematics. (383:300–320)

In *The Republic* Plato advocated an education that in general followed existent practices: "And what shall be their education? Can we find a better than the traditional sort?—and this has two divisions, gymnastic for the body and music for the soul." (286:II, 71) Plato elected to explain why he believed in these two divisions of education:

> Neither are the two arts of music and gymnastic really designed, as is often supposed, the one for the training of the soul, and the other for the training of the body.

---

* The palaestra was a building with facilities for wrestling, boxing, dressing, scraping, bathing, massaging, and storing clothes and equipment. In the courtyard was a sports ground, and a running track was located somewhere in the vicinity. The gymnasium, according to some authorities, was similar to the palaestra with the addition of a room for lectures to the ephebes. However, the usage of the terms is not clear; Marrou interprets gymnasium as referring to the whole while palaestra means the building only. (239:180) Men of all ages used the facilities for sport and also went there to enjoy conversing with friends. In the Roman period hot baths were added; they eventually became the most popular aspect of the gymnasium.

Fig. 2.   Plato and his students in the Garden of the Academy.

What then is the real object of them?

I believe, I said, that the teachers of both have in view chiefly the improvement of the soul.

How can that be? he asked.

Did you never observe, I said, the effect on the mind itself of exclusive devotion to gymnastic, or the opposite effect of an exclusive devotion to music?

In what way shown? he said.

The one producing a temper of hardness and ferocity, the other of softness and effeminacy, I replied. (286.III, 118)

. . . . . . . . . . . . . . .

And as there are two principles of human nature, one the spirited and the other the philosophical, some God, as I should say, has given mankind two arts answering to them (and only indirectly to the soul and body), in order that these two principles (like the strings of an instrument) may be relaxed or drawn tighter until they are duly harmonized.

That appears to be the intention.

And he who mingles music with gymnastic in the fairest proportions, and best attempers them to the soul, may be rightly called the true musician and harmonist in a far higher sense than the tuner of the strings. . . .

Such, then are our principles of nurture and education: Where would be the use of going into further details about the dances of our citizens, or about their hunting and coursing, their gymnastic and equestrian contests? For these all follow the general principle. . . . (286:III, 120)

It can be discerned from the preceding quotation that Plato in no way considered education to be mental knowledge and physical development for its own sake. Plato's dream of education's potential was the development of a citizen—a man of character—and all elements of his education fed into

FIG. 3.   Scene in a Palaestra.

the growth of the whole man (as modern educators have come to term him). Sports and games, rhythmic activities, literature, and music were all activities suited to a man of character because they helped to develop harmony of spirit.

This view of the educative function of gymnastic is strengthened, not contradicted, by Plato's collateral views regarding health and gymnastic. It was, at that time, the practice to attempt to prevent poor health by careful attention to diet and exercise.   Plato, who had little patience for immoderation of any sort, was particularly disapproving of those who gorged themselves:

> Well, I said, and to require the help of medicine, not when a wound has to be cured, or on occasion of an epidemic, but just because, by indolence and a habit of life such as we have been describing, men fill themselves with waters and winds, as if their bodies were a marsh . . . is not this, too, a disgrace? (286:III, 111)

But he also railed against athletes because they, like modern faddists, practiced strange methods of eating and sleeping:

> And will the habit of body of our ordinary athletes be suited to them? [the guardians or rulers]
> Why not?
> I am afraid, I said, that a habit of body such as they have is but a sleepy sort of thing, and rather perilous to health.   Do you not observe that these athletes sleep away their lives, and are liable to most dangerous illnesses if they depart, in ever so slight a degree, from their customary regimen? (286:III, 109)

Clearly he considered both kinds of immoderation as deficiencies of character.   Plato recommended the diet that Homer described his heroes as eating on their campaigns:   roasted meats without sauces and no fish. He also disapproved of the "refinements of Sicilian cookery" and of "Athenian confectionery."   He advocated simplicity in all things, saying:

"Simplicity in music was the parent of temperance in the soul; and simplicity in gymnastic of health in the body." (286:III, 110) Nevertheless, he stressed the theme that "He will regard even health as quite a secondary matter; his first object will be not that he may be fair or strong or well, unless he is likely thereby to gain temperance, but he will always desire so to attemper the body as to preserve the harmony of the soul." (286:IX, 359)

Some thirty years after he wrote *The Republic*, Plato completed work on *The Laws*. By then he was about seventy and his work showed the tempering of experience combined with the deteriorating political situation in Athens. Wars between Greek city-states occurred continually, breaking down the strength and morale of all of them. Twenty years after *The Laws* was written the army of Philip of Macedonia, father of Alexander the Great, held Greece helpless; the free city-state was at an end. Thus it is not strange that *The Laws* is a much more practically-oriented work than the utopian *Republic*. In terms of physical education this orientation was expressed in continuous emphasis on training for military efficiency.

The general purpose of education remained unchanged: "The right system of nurture must be that which can be shown to produce the highest possible perfection and excellence of body and soul." (284:VII, 170) But the activities stressed were those of a military nature:

> When the age of six has been passed by either sex, there shall henceforth be a separation of the sexes . . . the boys being sent to instructors in riding, archery, the management of the dart and sling—the girls may share in the instruction if they please—but, above all, in the use of spear and shield. (284:VII, 177)
>
> We are instituting gymnasia and all kinds of military exercises—exercises in archery, the throwing of various sorts of missiles, light skirmishing, infantry-fighting . . . tactical manoeuvres . . . . In fact, there must be public teachers in all these branches, receiving a stipend from the State, and they must have for their scholars not merely boys and men, but the girls and women, who must get knowledge of all this. (284:VII, 199)

The purpose Plato advanced for women receiving instruction in military techniques was their potential need to fight to defend the city while the men's army was engaged elsewhere.

Even wrestling and dancing, two of the activities quite removed from war and most popular as sports or at ceremonial events, were given a warlike countenance in the *Laws:* "The kind of wrestling we have in mind is far more closely connected with military combat than any other sort of movement, and also that it is to be cultivated with a view to this latter. . . ." (284:VII, 200)

> The war-dance—depicts the motions of eluding blows and shots of every kind by various devices of swerving, yielding ground, leaping from the ground or crouching, as well as the contrary motions which lead to a posture of attack, and aim at the reproduction of the shooting of arrows, casting of darts, and dealing of all kinds of blows. (284:VII, 200–201)

Athletic contests were similarly to be directed to military ends: "Those which provide a training for war should be encouraged and prizes instituted for success in them; those which do not may be dismissed." (284:VII, 219) In conjunction with this plan the skills catalogued as being useful for war were fleetness of foot and rapidity in general, body agility, and quickness of hand and foot. Certain races were to take place in full armor; wrestling, one of the popular events then in practice, was to be replaced by fighting in armor between single combatants, pairs, or groups up to ten to a side. Boxing, another event then commonly practiced, was to be replaced by combat with bow and arrows, and darts and stones thrown by hand or slings. Chariot racing and other events calling for skill in horsemanship were also to be included. Events were classified for boys, lads, men, and women. The latter were not to be required to take part, but it was expected that if their earlier training had been successful, they would do so voluntarily. (284:VIII, 219–221) It should be emphasized that Plato's *Laws* is an account of what he believed necessary for the best interests of the state. It was not necessarily representative of common practice particularly with regard to the armored combat and chariot racing.

Children's games were also taken seriously by Plato. He advocated a sort of nursery where children between the ages of three and six would be brought to play together under supervision. "And for their play, there are games which nature herself suggests at that age; children readily invent these for themselves when left in one another's company." (284:VII, 176) But he stressed that children, presumably as they grow older, must not be permitted to change the rules of games or vary them incessantly; this would lead to instability in the state. He said:

> They all suppose, as we were saying, that innovation in children's play is itself a piece of play and nothing more, not, as it is in fact, a source of most serious and grievous harm; hence they make no attempt to avert such changes, but compliantly fall in with them; they never reflect that these boys who introduce innovations into their games must inevitably grow to be men of a different stamp from the boys of an earlier time, that the change in themselves leads to the quest for a different manner of life, and this to a craving for different institutions and laws. . . . (284:VII, 181)

The preceding quotation is further evidence of Plato's belief that physical activity develops the soul as well as the body.

In some ways there is no contradiction between the Plato of *The Republic* and the Plato of *The Laws*. Underlying both works is a conviction that education for citizenship is an important requisite of the city-state. In later years concern for the survival of Athens placed undue emphasis upon military training. Yet the martial activities of *The Laws* were meant to develop the *man* as much as were the gymnastics of *The Republic*. The earlier work stressed harmony and balance in man, the later emphasized courage and fortitude; all were qualities related to the "soul."

Plato at times discussed the body and soul as if they were separate entities.  In particular this occurred when he strove to clarify the necessity for the body's subjugation to the soul.  However, in the context in which he spoke, it is clear that his purposes related to advocating the exercise of control over physical passions, including hunger and lust.*  Such discussions, like those concerning gymnastics in *The Republic*, serve only to underscore his belief in the fundamental interrelationship of body and soul.  The philosopher Plato conceived of a world of perfect forms of which material reality was only an imperfect shadow.  That he regarded the body, a part of material reality, as of secondary importance, did not prevent him from viewing strength, courage and physical ability as essential qualities.  They contributed to the ideal man in whom all the elements of the universe were harmonized into a kind of human nobility.

---

* For a somewhat different interpretation of this point, emphasizing Plato's denigration of the body, refer to the article by John Fairs on "The Influence of Plato and Platonism on Physical Education in Western Culture." (98)  A dissertation by Joseph L. Cahn (70) is also of interest.

# PART II

*Concerned Physicians*

# CLAUDIUS GALEN

## ca. A.D. 130-200

When Claudius Galen was born in A.D. 130 or 131 his home kingdom of Pergamum had been diminished from an earlier time when it covered most of western Asia Minor. Son of a wealthy and learned man, Galen had the opportunity to become well-educated and well-travelled, as evidenced by the hundreds of essays he wrote on subjects ranging from philosophy, rhetoric and medicine, to athletics. While in his teens he studied with teachers of the schools of the Stoics, Academicians, Peripatetics, and Epicureans, and completely rejected the teachings of the latter, but drew on the others throughout his long life and career. When he was approximately seventeen he began the study of medicine and during the next ten years travelled throughout the Mediterranean countries studying techniques for healing, surgery and the compounding of drugs and balms. In Alexandria he practiced as a physician earning special recognition for his treatment and cures of the gladiators; in Rome he served as doctor to Marcus Aurelius, the Emperor and Stoic philosopher. He became a favorite of the wealthy, and once received as much as four hundred pieces of gold for curing the sick wife of Boethus the Consul. Esteemed by many of his contemporaries, copied extensively by later men of medicine, he considered himself the greatest of physicians, saying that "No one before me has given the true method of treating diseases." (130:xxii)

By the time Galen was writing and practicing medicine, participation in sports was limited to two groups of people: the young students who attended the gymnasiums* and the professional athletes. The latter group developed in part because Roman citizens were not interested in sports except as spectacle for entertainment purposes. Roman use of the term *ludi*, meaning games, had no connotation of competition, and in fact a derivative word, *ludiones*, meaning actors, indicated its relation to performance in the sense of shows. This may be contrasted with the comparable Greek word, *agon*, which meant contest. The Roman outlook on sport discouraged common adult participation throughout the Empire. At the same time, the Roman occupation narrowed the potential livelihoods

---

* Evidence reveals that Pergamum contained five gymnasiums which can be compared with the seven in Athens, an indication of the stress placed upon their role in early education.

available to Greek citizens.  Winning in athletics was highly lucrative because contest winners received very liberal pensions (maintenance allowances such as are given to "amateur" athletes today) from their home cities, as well as exemption from taxation and public service for themselves and even for their sons.  Thus the rewards, the economic situation and the Roman disinterest, led to the development of the professional athlete drawn from the class of well-born Greek citizens.  (Professional athletes were not new to Galen's time but they were not previously drawn from the noble class.)  Galen vigorously condemned this practice, for he saw in the professional athlete the antithesis of the healthy citizen.  In his essay entitled *Exhortation on the Choice of a Profession* he inveighed against the professional athlete:

> In the blessings of the mind athletes have no share.  Beneath their mass of flesh and blood their souls are stifled as in a sea of mud. . . . Neglecting the old rule of health which prescribes moderation in all things they spend their lives in over-exercising, in over-eating, and over-sleeping like pigs. . . . They have not health nor have they beauty.  Even those who are naturally well proportioned become fat and bloated. . . . Even their vaunted strength is useless.  They can dig and plough but they cannot fight. (118:115)

Of course the professional athletes engaged in a vigorous conditioning program under the direction of trainers who considered themselves "health scientists," as well as athletic coaches, but Galen said that "their practices are all directly the opposite of his [Hippocrates'] health doctrines." (304: 193) Furthermore, Galen asserted that "athletic training is useless in the real business of life. . . ." (304:196)

Living thus at a time when the populace at large did not engage in sports, and the athletes furnished such poor examples, Galen the physician addressed essays to laymen on subjects such as: *On the Preservation of Health, Whether the Preservation of Health Depends on Medicine or Exercise* and *Exercise with the Small Ball*.  In these he stressed the relationships previously discerned by Hippocrates, between exercise, hygiene (diet) and medicine, and he recommended suitable exercises and diets.  His definition of exercise was similar to that of the earlier Greco-Romans:

> To me it does not seem that all movement is exercise, but only when it is vigorous. . . . The criterion of vigorousness is change of respiration; those movements which do not alter the respiration are not called exercise.  But if anyone is compelled by any movement to breathe more or less or faster, that movement becomes exercise for him. (130:53–54)

And he equated exercise with gymnastic or sport:

> This therefore is what is commonly called exercise or gymnastics, from the gymnasium or public place to which the inhabitants of a city come to anoint and rub themselves, to wrestle, throw the discus, or engage in some other sport. (130:54)

He also stipulated the uses of exercise as twofold:

> One for the evacuation of the excrements, the other for the production of good condition of the firm parts of the body. For since vigorous motion is exercise, it must needs be that only these three things result from it in the exercising body— hardness of the organs from mutual attrition, increase of the intrinsic warmth, and accelerated movement of respiration. (130:54)

In *De Sanitate Tuenda* (*Health*) he indicated which exercises were for the hips, hands, legs, back, chest, or lungs and he classified them as to their intensity and purpose. For example, he specified digging, driving four horses, picking up and carrying heavy loads, climbing ropes, hanging by the arms, resistance-type exercises, and wrestling as being vigorous; that is, they were performed with strength but not speed. He listed running, shadowboxing, sparring, and exercising with the punching bag and the small ball as exercises designed to develop speed rather than strength. He discussed "violent" exercises (those that developed both strength and speed) and gave examples such as throwing heavy weapons or moving quickly while dressed in heavy armor. He also noted that exercises in the vigorous category could become violent if their speed were accelerated. Many of the exercises described by Galen are still familiar:

> Some place jumping weights in front of them about six feet apart, then stand between them, bend over and pick them up; with the right hand they raise the weight on the left; with the left hand, that on the right. Then they replace each weight on its original position, and repeat the performance many times in succession, keeping their feet fixed in one position. . . . The motion mentioned just above exercises the parts which run lengthwise. (304.182)

The essay in which these exercises were classified and described was a scientific treatise on the subject, sufficiently detailed and accurate to rank with those written today. It was the first time that a writer, especially one with the qualifications of a physician, undertook the development of a program composed chiefly of exercises for the maintenance of good body condition, although as early as the fifth century B.C. Hippocrates had stressed the need of men to exercise to attain "long youth." In the first century B.C., Asclepiades had prescribed gymnastics, massage and diet to preserve health. Apparently it was the first time in history that sports had become so separated from the lives of the people that they needed some deliberate, contrived means to preserve their health. The parallel between the situation in the second century and the twentieth century is easily drawn. Galen's excellent treatise has been superseded by later works on medical gymnastics, especially those filling the modern market. Nevertheless, there is little to be found in the newest works that is not, at least in concept, present in Galen's writings.

Today, the most well-known of Galen's essays is *Exercise with the*

Fig. 4.  Exercising with Balls (from Mercurialis' *De Arte Gymnastica*).

*Small Ball.* Although ball playing was a common form of recreation even in the earliest societies, Galen was the first to design a series of exercises with the ball, devised to improve body condition rather than to have fun. He set forth the advantages of playing ball, beginning with convenience: "Ball playing alone is so democratic that not even the poorest person lacks equipment for it, for it takes no nets, no weapons, no horses, no hunting dogs, but just a ball and a small one at that." (304:185)  He may have meant the small hard ball, stitched out of leather and stuffed with hair (*harpastum*), although larger balls stuffed with feathers (*pila*) or air (*follis*) existed.  Then he asserted that "of the other exercises there is none that keeps in motion all parts of the body equally and that can be increased to a very violent one then toned down again to the mildest one; but exercise with the small ball is the only one to accomplish this." (304:186)  After reviewing the advantages to the various muscles he discussed the uses of ball exercises in perceptual training:

> That playing with the small ball trains the eye is readily understood, if you remember that a man will surely fail to catch the ball unless he accurately observes in advance where its weight will carry it. Besides, he sharpens his judgement by planning how not to let the ball slip and how to hinder his opponent. . . . This is no unimportant advantage of an exercise, if it can help both the body and the mind toward the perfection innate in each. (304:187)

Besides being concerned with health, Galen had the Greek appreciation for a beautiful body of harmonious proportions; he saw the two as being interrelated.  Thus he did not approve of running because "it wears a man down thin . . ." and he thought that "exercise is unhealthful exactly to the extent that it develops the parts of the body unequally." (304:188) He said "I heartily commend, then, any exercise which can provide physical health, harmonious development of the limbs, and mental excellence— and all of these are furnished one by the exercise with the small ball." (304:188)  Galen detailed various kinds of exercises with the small ball to be performed by people of all ages.  The art of performing such exercises and the interest in doing them for bodily development has not vanished with the earlier civilization.  Although in the United States the ball is primarily used for playing games, in countries such as Denmark, Sweden and England, it is still used in much the same way that Galen prescribed over seventeen hundred years ago.

The preservation of the written word allowed the first scientific study of medical gymnastics to be passed on to the physical educators who have adopted the physician's concern for the health and physical development of the people.  It is significant that the Greek's good advice and his well-planned exercises were necessary.  Galen's work indicates that people no longer participated in those activities that naturally fostered physical well-being.  Instead artificial means for preserving health had to be contrived.

# HIERONYMOUS MERCURIALIS*

## 1530-1606

During the thirteen-hundred year span which separated Galen and Mercurialis the practice of medical gymnastics was neglected. Physicians, highly skeptical about the use of gymnastics, prescribed them only for cases of indigestion. It was not until the Renaissance brought a revival of Greek ideas and writings that health gymnastics again became popular. Mercurialis, as the author of *De Arte Gymnastica* (*Six Books on the Art of Gymnastics*) (243), was the promulgator of this new interest. The book was printed in Venice in 1569 and went through a second edition and several reprintings, one as late as 1672 in Amsterdam, which is ample testimony to its popularity and influence.

Hieronymous Mercurialis was a physician and since his books contained quotations from philosophers, historians, theologians, poets, and pedagogues (the first edition contained a list of the ninety-six Greek and Latin authors upon whom he drew), it can be assumed that he also received the broad, liberal education of Renaissance times. His reputation was great enough for Emperor Maximilian II to summon him to Vienna to treat him. His career also included service as a municipal physician of Venice and as a teacher at the Universities of Bologna and Pisa. In Forli, Mercurialis' birthplace, a monument was erected in memory of the man who, as well as treating the sick, helped the populace at large to maintain good health.

It must be understood that Mercurialis was not at all interested in athletics; in fact, he believed athletics indirectly injurious to health because they were not performed in moderation. He considered all gymnastics (exercises) only in light of their medical value. Furthermore, he did not write as one physician to another, but in terms understandable to the layman whom he hoped to interest in doing exercises. Thus he tried to demonstrate their value. A quotation taken from Guts Muths more than two centuries later provides an example of Mercurialis' thought and style:

> The ancients had so high an opinion of gymnastics, that Plato and Aristotle, not to mention others, considered a commonwealth as defective, in which they were neglected: and, indeed justly; for if the improvement of the *mind* ought to

---

* *De Arte Gymnastica* is not available in English translation and biographical references to Mercurialis are very limited with the exception of the CIBA Symposia pamphlet (196) from which most of this information is drawn.

be our constant aim, and the mind cannot accomplish anything of worth and importance without the aid of the *body*, assuredly it is incumbent on us, to promote the health and dexterity of the body, that it may be capable of serving the mind, and assisting, instead of impeding its operations.  For this reason, Plato, in Protagoras, calls him a cripple, who, cultivating his mind alone, suffers his body to languish through sloth and inactivity. (146:113)

He classified gymnastics into two kinds:  preventive and therapeutic, and made it clear that the quantity and intensity of each exercise should be individualized according to each person's constitution.

*De Arte Gymnastica* began with a historical description of the ancient gymnastic exercises, proceeded to an explanation of the value of exercise in conditions of health and disease, and then discussed specific exercises and their uses.  The goal of preventive gymnastics was to maintain "harmony of the humours," which was Hippocrates' definition of health.

Mercurialis was enthusiastic about ball playing which was very popular at the time.  Light balls containing feathers or air were available, as well as heavy ones filled with sand.  Florence was already famous for "Calcio," a football (soccer) game played in the principal square of the city, attended by noble ladies and gentlemen, and sometimes used to celebrate as grand an occasion as a Medici* wedding.  He asserted that ball playing strengthened the arms, back, and intercostal muscles and was thus good for "convalescents, weak persons and even for wet-nurses."

He also favored walking with various degrees of intensity.  The mildest he considered useful for stimulating conversation; more intensive walking could work up an appetite or aid digestion.  Mountain climbing was especially recommended for those with paralysis of the legs.  He also advocated running, particularly at night when the sun's heat could be avoided.  Discus throwing as an exercise was recommended for arthritic patients as well as for those with weak legs, arms, hips, and back.  Long jumping was good for men and also for women who were not pregnant.  However, the addition of dumbbells or weights like the *halteres* used by Greeks in the classical period, he considered unhealthy.  Exercises like handsprings were completely rejected because it was thought they pushed the intestines against the diaphragm.  Rope climbing and wrestling caused no such problems and were considered wholesome.

A whole section of *De Arte Gymnastica* was devoted to the care of patients confined to bed.  Mercurialis' recommendations for their exercise, which included the use of a swinging bed to stir the circulation, were novel concepts at that time.  Today a similar idea is seen in beds which mechanically exercise the patient in an attempt to avoid bed sores and atrophied muscles.

The influence of this careful and detailed work by an eminent physician is incalculable.  It has been the basis for all subsequent development of

---

* The Medici family played an important role in Florentine politics in the fifteenth and sixteenth centuries.

FIG. 5.   Exercising with a Discus (from Mercurialis' *De Arte Gymnastica*).

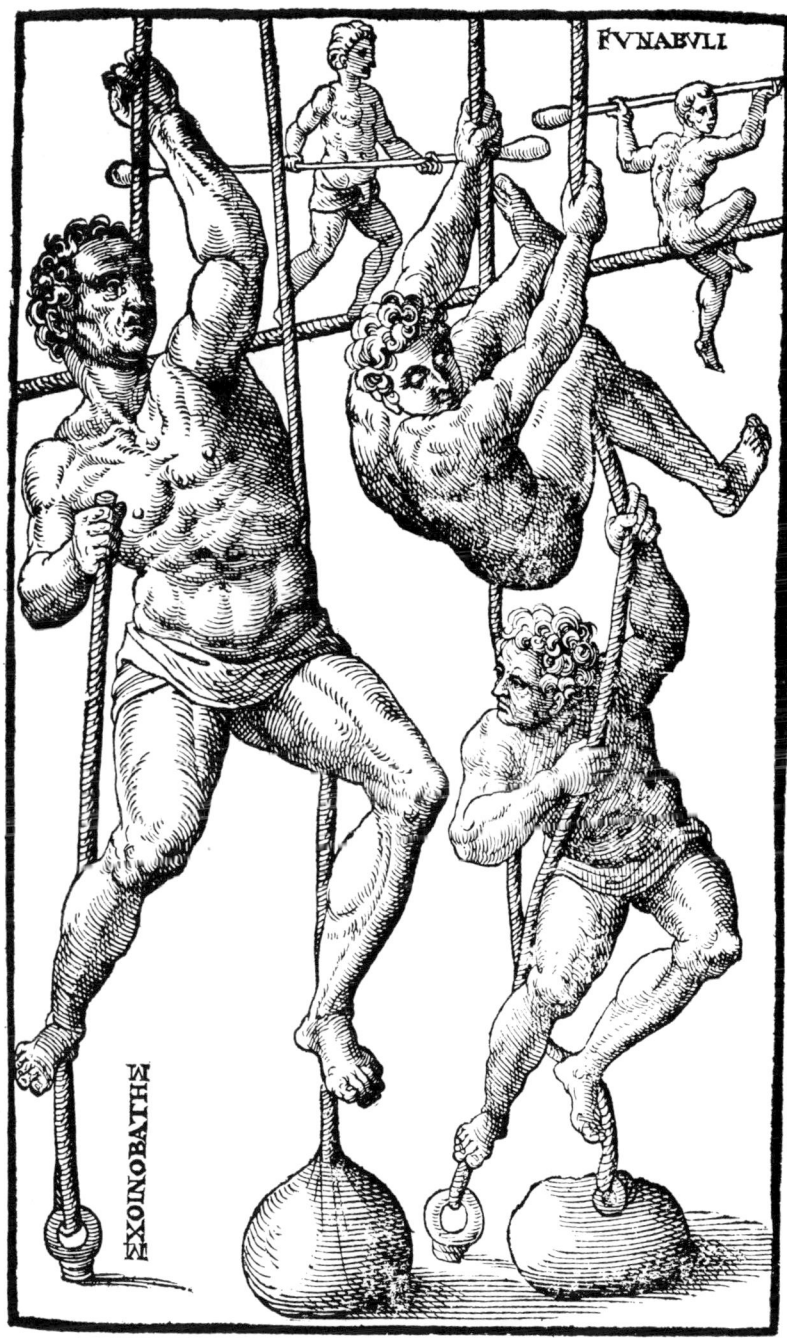

FIG. 6.   Athletes Climbing Ropes (from Mercurialis' *De Arte Gymnastica*).

gymnastics as an important adjunct to the maintenance of health. The Swedish and Danish gymnastic systems of the nineteenth century were based upon this same concept, although the approved activities were in keeping with later anatomical and medical knowledge and, therefore, were not necessarily of the same type. The early American physical educators, such as Dudley Allen Sargent who was also a medical doctor, developed physical education in the United States based on approximately the same interpretation of the needs of the people. To men like Mercurialis the concept of sport for the sake of pleasure, or athletic competition for the purpose of challenging men to fine, even heroic performance, was not an issue. The importance of gymnastics lay solely in its healthful, medicinal aspects. A man exercised, played ball, climbed ropes, even wrestled to strengthen his body, to prevent its degeneration and to ward off disease. This functional concept of exercise is still prevalent in modern day physical education.

# PART III

*Influential Churchmen*

# AENEAS SYLVIUS PICCOLOMINI

## 1405-1464

A *pius* man, according to the Roman usage of the word, connoted a man who was loyal to the three duties of protecting his living family, preserving his ancestry, and propagating his posterity. (311:54-55) It is a clue to the character and the actions of Piccolomini that when in 1458 he became Pope, he chose the name Pius II. Although he was the oldest of eighteen children, the family that he fought to protect was not his natural family, but the Church, particularly the Papacy; the ancestry that he sought to preserve was not the noble Piccolomini family but the literate legacy of thought and learning that had been formulated in earlier times particularly in ancient Greece and Rome. And in his voluminous writings and vigorous campaigning for the use of the vulgate (common tongue) in literature, he propagated his posterity.

Piccolomini was, like Plato, a cultivated citizen capable of both thought and action. He was known to be a man of simplicity and taste, liberal to the poor, forgiving to his enemies, friendly, convivial, and a brilliant orator and correspondent. (311:76,78)

Renaissance Italy was a time of great political intrigue when the Church and various great cities such as Sienna, his birthplace, and Florence, the worldwide seat of scholarship and art, struggled against each other for power. In fact, it was precisely such a war that drove the future pope from Sienna where he had been educated at the University in law and letters, to become secretary to Dominic Cardinal Capranica. As the Cardinal's secretary he attended the Council of Basel and supported its views on reform in opposition to the papal party. Thus he also became involved in church politics and his views eventually caused him some embarrassment when he became Pope, for he recanted his position and himself condemned his earlier writings. He served the Emperor Frederick III of Bohemia as a secretary, and after becoming Bishop of Trieste upon his ordination in 1446, he travelled as an ecclesiastical ambassador on many delicate missions for both Frederick and the Pope.* He became Bishop of

---

* Eugenius IV, who held the papacy from 1431–1447, was well-served by Piccolomini, although for a time he supported the anti-pope, Felix V, when he claimed the throne in 1440. Because of this political maneuvering he was not trusted by Nicholas V who succeeded Eugenius IV. However, his value as a diplomat was great enough to earn for him the cardinal's hat.

Sienna in 1449, Cardinal in 1457, and the next year was elected Pope, a rapid rise in status which was possible only in those days.

Through all these involvements he found time to write a great deal and to pursue his interests in history and geography. He wrote various histories and biographies and a *Dialogue* in which he discussed, among other things, free will, dreams and the chase, predestination, heaven, and history. He also wrote poetry (he was designated poet laureate in 1442), a comedy and treatises on subjects as diverse as the "Care of Horses" and the important ecclesiastical questions of his day. But his philosophy was narrowly and traditionally conceived and he really was not interested in theology except in the historical sense. However he used the power of his papacy to help establish the Universities of Basel, Ingolstadt, Nantes, and Rome as well as to endow those already established. (311:119)

At that time letters were used as vehicles for discussing ideas on a particular subject. Among the letters written by Piccolomini was one to ten-year-old Ladislas, technically King of Bohemia and a ward of Frederick, in which he set forth his ideas on the education desirable for a prince. Woodward included this treatise, known as *De Liberorum Educatione*, in his book on humanist educators. (382) Such an education should develop a man of grace and sensitivity, learned in grammar, rhetoric, history, and music, and since "the body, after all, is but a framework for the activities of the mind," then "both mind and body, the two elements of which we are constituted, must be developed side by side." (283:140, 136) If the end of scholarly study is action, then a man's body must be ready for such action. Therefore:

> As regards a boy's physical training, we must bear in mind that we aim at implanting habits which will prove beneficial through life. . . . A boy should be taught to hold his head erect, to look straight and fearlessly before him and to bear himself with dignity whether walking, standing, or sitting. In ancient Greece we find that both philosophers and men of affairs—Socrates, for instance, and Chrysippus, or Philip of Macedon—deemed this matter worthy of their concern, and therefore it may well be thought deserving of ours. Games and exercises which develop the muscular activities and the general carriage of the person should be encouraged by every Teacher. For such physical training not only cultivates grace of attitude but secures the healthy play of our bodily organs and establishes the constitution. (283:138–139)

Furthermore, a man of morality may be called upon to defend his country or church's honor in actual war. That is why he warned Ladislas that:

> Every youth destined to exalted position should further be trained in military exercises. It will be your destiny to defend Christendom against the Turk. It will thus be an essential part of your education that you be early taught the use of the bow, of the sling, and of the spear; that you drive, ride, leap and swim. (283:138)

Since he is concerned that the child not dislike his studies, he advocated:

> Games, too, should be encouraged for young children—the ball, the hoop—but these must not be rough and coarse, but have in them an element of skill.   Such relaxations should form an integral part of each day's occupations if learning is not to be an object of disgust.   Just as Nature and the life of man present us with alternations of effort and repose—toil and sleep, winter and summer—so we may hold, with Plato, that it is a law of our being that rest from work is a needful condition of further work. (283:138)

Although Piccolomini's viewpoints on education in general followed the Renaissance humanistic tradition which in turn revived classical concepts of education, his beliefs concerning physical education were less in tune with ancient Greece than with earlier Roman writers such as Juvenal, who said: "Pray first for a sound mind in a sound body" (197:x, 131); with Virgil, who insisted that youth be trained in the skills of war in order to defend the state; with Quintilian, who agreed that "some relaxation is to be allowed to all. . . . Boys, accordingly, when re-invigorated and refreshed, bring more sprightliness to their learning. . . ." (295:I, 26)   Later, the great Englishman John Locke expressed Juvenal's idea and developed it so fully and forcefully that he is generally credited with innovating the concept of "a sound mind in a sound body."

Aeneas Sylvius Piccolomini, the man of letters, statesman, sensitive historian, and critic of the Renaissance, who rose from obscure poverty to the throne of Saint Peter, was himself a symbol of the humanist ideal of the cultured and active man.   Coming from such a man, who in one person blended the church, state and scholarly study, his treatise "On the Education of Youth" stands as a representative document of its time reflecting not only education in a noble society but the opinions of the Catholic Church.

# MARTIN LUTHER

## 1483-1546

Like Saint Paul, whom he frequently quoted, Martin Luther's dedication of his life to God and the church began in a singular, spectacular moment of conversion. In 1505, while Luther was taking a walk a summer storm broke over him and a lightning bolt threw him to the ground. At that moment Luther vowed to Saint Anne that if his life were spared he would become a monk, a vow he fulfilled despite very strong parental pressure to finish his law degree. Like Paul, whose ideas and interpretations of Jesus' sayings became the basis for Catholic theology, Luther's ideas and interpretations of the Bible became the basis for Evangelical theology. An even further parallel in their lives exists in that both men were intellectuals whose great strength of character and self-will were entirely focused on one idea: bringing the truth of God to the people.

Luther was born in 1483 at Eisleben in Saxony; his ancestors were peasant farmers although his father had succeeded in establishing himself as a copper miner. Luther took both his Bachelor and Master of Arts degrees at the University of Erfurt preparatory to his studying jurisprudence. As a student he received the usual training in the quadrivium (arithmetic, geometry, music, and astronomy); he also studied philosophy, mathematics, and politics in the light of Aristotelian logic. Later, after two years of preparation in a monastery of the Order of the Hermits of Saint Augustine, Brother Martin took his vows of poverty and chastity and was ordained a monk. He remained at the monastery in Erfurt studying theology until he was sent to lecture and study at the Augustinian monastery in Wittenberg where, in 1512, he received his doctorate in theology. One of his biographers reports that besides the Bible, his first years in the monastery were heavily saturated with studies of Saint Bernard and Saint Bonaventure. (131:44) This is the same Saint Bernard who said: "Always in a robust and active body the mind lies more soft and more lukewarm; and, on the other hand, the spirit flourishes more strongly and more actively in an infirm and weakly body." (365:102) There are many published accounts of Luther's difficulties in subjugating his own body's desires; his attempts to fast for periods up to three days and otherwise deny ordinary bodily needs bear witness to his struggles. It was only later, after breaking with the Catholic Church, that Luther ceased to see virtue in denying the body.  He preached that chastity was unnatural and not demanded by God, and demonstrated his beliefs by marrying a woman who had been a nun.  He believed that "the young must leap and jump, or have something to do, because they have a natural desire for it which should not be restrained. . . ." (216:375)  This was a great change in thought from Luther's monastic days when he was studying Saint Bernard and in a sense it symbolized the general changes prevailing among the people who had begun to break away from the tight hold of the Catholic Church's authority and its moral pontificating.

Education during the Middle Ages had been entirely in the hands of the Church.  Monastic schools meant to prepare youths for lives as clerics were the only kind of schools in existence.  The end of feudalism, the appearance of church reformers like Jan Hus and John Wyclif, and the renaissance of humanist ideas began to sweep through Europe weakening the authority of the Church.  Luther and others preached against the monks' schools

FIG. 7.   Martin Luther.

with their narrow theological education and called for reform. "I should prefer, it is true, that our youth be ignorant and dumb rather than that the universities and convents should remain as the only sources of instruction open to them." (216:362)

By this time, as part of the reaction against a church grown rich from the sale of indulgences and against fat monks and nuns who seemed to have forgotten their vow of poverty, parents had stopped sending their children to school. They saw no reason to educate youths who were not to become monks and nuns and earn their living from the church. For Luther, who sought to bring the people into direct and personal communion with God, an uneducated populace was intolerable. "My idea is that boys should spend an hour or two a day in school. . . . They now spend tenfold as much time in shooting crossbows, playing ball, running, and tumbling about. In like manner, a girl has time to go to school an hour a day . . . for she sleeps, dances, and plays away more than that." (216:376) In his most thorough and important statement on education, "The Letter to the Mayors and Aldermen of all the Cities of Germany in Behalf of Christian Schools," he said:

> But were they instructed in schools or elsewhere by thoroughly qualified male or female teachers, who taught the languages, other arts, and history, then the pupils would hear the history and maxims of the world, and see how things went with each city, kingdom, prince, man, and woman; and thus, in a short time, they would be able to comprehend, as in a mirror, the character, life, counsels, undertakings, successes, and failures, of the whole world from the beginning. From this knowledge they could regulate their views, and order their course of life in the fear of God. . . . (216:375)

In a letter written four years earlier in 1520, "To the Christian Nobility of the German Nation Respecting the Reformation of the Christian Estate," he advocated founding elementary schools for boys and girls in every town and city. At another time he insisted that school attendance be compulsory. Ironically, because he basically was not a humanist in his thinking (in part because he was interested in the masses rather than the nobility on which humanist concerns focused), he demanded that Greek and Latin be taught to all children so that they could read the Scriptures and commentaries in their pure form.

In keeping with his "liberal" view that the body's natural desires to move were not evil, and also in keeping with his sympathy and understanding of the people and their needs, he advocated certain

> . . . honorable and useful modes of exercise to resort to, so that they might not fall into gluttony, lewdness, surfeiting, rioting, and gambling. Accordingly, I pronounce in favor of these two exercises and pastimes, namely, music, and the knightly sports of fencing, wrestling, etc., of which, the one drives care and gloom from the heart, and the other gives a full development to the limbs, and maintains the body in health. (94:176)

Furthermore, Luther believed that "it is the part of a Christian to take care of his own body for the very purpose that, by its soundness and well-being, he may be enabled to labour." (365:155) However, such statements hardly constitute an endorsement of physical education. What they do mark is one change in the thinking of the church, one part of a revolution which culminated in the Reformation itself. Luther was a man of the people in the sense that he spent his life using his scholarly intelligence for their welfare. But he was also a man of the church and he never deviated from his belief that a man must spend his life in the attempt to redeem his sinful nature through faith in the mercy of God and through good works in his name. To these ends he must be credited not only with the founding of a strong Protestant movement, but with the founding of public education. As he believed that chastity was unnatural in man, so he believed that complete subjugation of the body was impossible, and he thus advocated music, games and chaperoned dancing as suitable pastimes. In doing so he made it plain that these were better than gluttony, gambling and rioting, which is not at all advocating them because they are fine activities in themselves. This point of view was carried into America and used to combat the strict Puritan doctrines that regarded all play as inherently immoral.

When Martin Luther died in 1546, he left behind a wife and five children (a sixth child had predeceased him), a great bulk of writings, a movement that had already culminated in the well-established Evangelical Lutheran Church, the beginning of a system of secular education, a Bible written in the German vernacular, and the memory of a man who, despite personal doubts and difficulties, was able to drive all of his adult life to the fulfillment of a single belief.

# JOHN CALVIN

## 1509-1564

At the age of twenty-one John Calvin found God. That is, he experienced a "conversion" in which he regarded his past adherence to the "superstitions of the Papacy" as being in a "deep mire," from which he was "brought out into the light." To espouse openly the cause of the reformers in France in the 1530s was dangerous and after twice being arrested and set free, Calvin left France for Basel, Switzerland, a land that had already experienced Ulrich Zwingli's attempts at reform. Although Zwingli died in battle leading his Protestants against Catholic soldiers, in general the Swiss cantons (states) practiced a certain independence from Rome. While in Basel, Calvin wrote the first of many drafts of his great work: *The Institutes of the Christian Religion.* Later he commented:

> Neither was it then when I published it, the large elaborate work it is now [1558], but it was only a little handbook containing a summary of the most important items; nor was it published with any other aim than that men might know what was the faith held by those I saw cruelly and evilly reviled by those impious and faithless flatterers. (326:34)

Calvin was well-suited to write a book outlining the reformers' beliefs — a book that eventually became the Reformation's most important theological guidebook, having a great influence both in Europe and America. When Calvin was born in 1509 in Noyon, France, his father was a lawyer and a secretary to the Bishop, although his artisan ancestry designated him as being of low birth. The young Calvin seems to have been agreeable to his father's earlier wishes that he prepare himself for the priesthood and his later desire for him to study law. Calvin's intellectual acuity was evidenced quite early and by the age of fourteen he was attending the Collège de la Marche in Paris and later he attended the famous Collège de Montaigu some years before Ignatius Loyola studied there under the same masters. (94:233) At Montaigu, Calvin joined a voluntary association of youths who swore, among other things, to an ascetic life.

> Undernourished, refusing their bodies the superficial attention necessary for even a minimum of cleanliness, they fasted, they meditated, they imposed a rule of silence on themselves, [and] worked from dawn to nightfall. . . . John Calvin . . . found real pleasure in yielding himself to the mortifications which they prescribed

for him, and decided irrevocably that the Christian life, even if it should be cast under happy earthly circumstances, ought to be characterized by unceasing asceticism. (326:11–12)

Besides bodily abstinence, he also learned theology and dialectics at Montaigu where his work culminated in 1528 in a Master of Arts degree.

From there he attended the Universities of Orléans and Bruges, where he studied law and the classical languages and literature.  During this period he continued to mortify his body, which by now was sickly from ill-treatment.  He responded to his ailments by cutting his food down to one small meal a day, a practice he continued throughout his life.  He obtained his law license circa 1530, and then went to Paris where he came under the influence of the reformers, particularly Nicolas Cop.  Thus, by the time of his conversion from the Roman Church to the theories of the reformers, Calvin was a particularly well-educated man; along with his natural intelligence, this made him the right person to try to set forth the guidelines of a Protestant religion.

In 1536 he settled as a pastor in Geneva, a Protestant city by vote of its council, but one in which no firm leader's hand had been applied to codify the various doctrines being preached.  Furthermore, the people were care-

FIG. 8.   John Calvin.

free lovers of pleasure and not learned in Christian doctrine nor suffused with religious piety. Calvin's strong efforts to improve the situation were at first welcomed. But the religion he preached was harsh and joyless and included very strict rules of conduct. According to him most people were predestined by God to eternal damnation, but a few were "elected" for heaven and proof of election could be seen in the strict self-discipline and good deeds performed by the elect. Besides forbidding activities like participating in dances, playing cards or singing frivolous songs, the people were forbidden to take delight in sensual pleasures for "it is clear that this consideration means that licentious abuse is to be curbed, and confirms the rule of St. Paul that we should make no provision for the flesh to fulfill its lusts (Rom. 13:14), which, if they are given too much scope, boil over furiously out of control." (326:142)

He permitted the body just enough care to allow a man to work: "Moreover, may I not sleep to excess, indulging too much to the comfort of my flesh, but only so much as the weakness of my nature requires in order to dispose me for Thy service." (326:57) Not surprisingly, he believed that "this tabernacle of our body which is unstable, defective, corruptible, fading, pining and putrid is dissolved in order that it may be restored in sure, perfect, incorruptible and heavenly glory. . . ." (326:133) After two years of this philosophy, when pleasure had been practically banned from the city, Calvin was himself banished from Geneva. However, the city returned to a disorderly life so Calvin was recalled three years later and he remained there until his death in 1564.

After his return to Geneva, Calvin worked incessantly to weave together the church, the government, the home, and the school into a single unified organism designed to discipline and control the entire citizenry. He reorganized the elementary schools, allowing only those not capable of studying Latin to learn in the vernacular. He organized "colleges" (secondary schools) which largely combined the humanistic curriculum with intensive religious training and he helped to re-establish the University of Geneva. His followers carried on his tradition of education and established schools all over the world, including eight Huguenot (French Protestant) universities.

In accordance with his strict philosophy, attendance at elementary schools was made compulsory. For four days a week the students spent almost nine hours a day studying; on Saturday the week's lessons were reviewed; on Sunday they spent the day in religious worship, as they did on Wednesday morning, after which from eleven to twelve they "debated with restraint. Then recreation shall be allowed till three o-clock, but in such a way that all silly sport be avoided." (94:258) This statement represents the single concession Calvin made to allowing recreation. Although it is said that he loved short walks, "excelled in little games of skill and was quite expert at throwing the quoit . . ." (326:74), it is also true that during his regime in Geneva two businessmen were imprisoned for playing skittles.

"From the point of view of American educational history the most important developments in connection with the Reformation were those arising from Calvinism." (84:175)   This may also be related to physical education; Calvin stands as a sort of negative "innovator" whose ideas are singularly responsible for the retardation of physical education and play in early America.   The Puritans, using the original Calvinist creed as a basis for their thinking, saw to it that laws were passed condemning all amusements. "In New England, where the stern rule of Calvinism condemned idleness and amusements for their own sake, that tradition that life be wholly devoted to work . . . held . . . firmly." (91:5)   Sunday was to be spent in worship, a concept challenged by King James who issued a *Book of Sports* declaring that:

> after the end of Divine Service, our good people be not disturbed, letted, or discouraged from any lawfull Recreation; Such as dauncing, either men or women, Archeries for men, leaping, vaulting, or other harmless Recreation. . . . But withall We doe accompt still as prohibited all unlawfull games to be used upon Sundayes only, as Beare and Bull-baiting, Interludes, and at all times in the meaner sort of people by Law prohibited, Bowling. (91:10)

The Puritans publicly burned the book.  It was not until the 1900s that physical educators began to argue for games and dancing in the school programs over the opposition of those who, like Calvin, regarded idle play as unworthy.

John Calvin's heritage was threefold:  an organized Protestant theology; a firm devotion to education for all children; and a belief in the total suppression of the body and the sinfulness of taking time from work for pleasure through recreation.

# IGNATIUS DE LOYOLA

## 1491-1556

*Omnia ad Majorem Dei Gloriam* (All for the greater glory of God) is the motto of the Society of Jesus, founded in 1540 by Ignatius de Loyola. This date marked a beginning for the Jesuit Order, signified the emergence of the Counter-Reformation, and was for Loyola a landmark in the chapter of his life that included his turning from defender of the city to defender of his church and faith.

Don Inigo Loyola was the youngest son of a noble and wealthy Spanish family. A daring and charming young knight, he loved battles and women and the good life, until the day he was seriously wounded in the legs while defending against a French siege of his native city Pamplona, Spain in 1521. While enduring a long convalescence he read the only books available in his father's library: works on the life of Christ and the lives of the saints. These made such an impression upon him that he decided to become a knight of God and thereafter ceased envisioning himself as a great general and began to dream of becoming a saint. At the monastery in Montserrat where he had spent the traditional night in vigil when dubbed a chevalier by the King of Navarre, he returned to pass a second vigil to become a knight of the King of Heaven. (187:20)

After Loyola meditated in the solitude and poverty of a cave in the mountains near Manresa, for about a year, his first action was to make a pilgrimage to the Holy Land for the purpose of teaching the Turks the beliefs of Christianity. He did get to Jerusalem but Christian leaders fearful of a rebellion prevented him from teaching. He returned to Barcelona where at the age of thirty-three he set himself to learning Latin, thus embarking upon a lengthy career as a student. His age and lack of prior education created great difficulties, but finally after eleven years of study in philosophy, the last five at the University of Paris, he received his Master of Arts and Licentitate in Theology. He then began his theological studies but was disappointed in his desire to earn his doctorate.

While at the University of Paris he became the leader of a small group of men and in 1534 six of them took a vow in Paris in the Church of the Blessed Virgin in Montmartre and pledged to renounce all their goods and either go to the Holy Land or offer their services to the Pope. This moment was the real beginning of the Jesuit Order which was formally sponsored by the Pope in 1540 and which, at the time of Loyola's death in 1556, numbered a thousand brothers and twelve units spread through Portugal, Spain, Italy, France, Germany, India, and Brazil.

Loyola was an exceptional leader.   His earliest writing, started in the cave at Manresa, was a book of *Spiritual Exercises* which advocated personal suffering until the sufferer reached the understanding that he was a sinner.   Only then could he embark on a new life:  one of obedience to the laws of the Church.   Loyola, like the good soldier he was, taught that strict obedience to God meant strict obedience to all his officers on earth; a man must be ready to believe that what seems white to him is really

Fig. 9.   Ignatius De Loyola

black if the Church says it is black. (195:645) His leadership was such that he was able to convince people to follow these beliefs in a time when Rome was a city of chaos in which invaders and poor leadership had left the Church literally and figuratively in ruins. At the same time Europe was being conquered ideologically by the Calvinist reformers whose discipline and training made them intellectually superior to churchmen who had spent their lives collecting gold and fine art and books, while paying little attention to spiritual matters. Considering the quick success of the Reformation, the Counter-Reformation was a Jesuit miracle. Loyola and his followers not only helped to save the southern half of Europe for the Church, but they helped to institute church reform; by the time the Council of Trent, convened for the purpose of discussing reform, closed in 1563 after seventeen years of bickering, Loyola's theories had become the rules of the Church and were influential for centuries afterward.

The method Loyola employed to accomplish these tasks was education. However, the Jesuits were not particularly interested in education for the masses—that was only thought important by men like Calvin who believed in it as a means to personal salvation. After ten years of "experimentation" during which time brothers of the Order organized not only some schools but also homes for orphans and unprovided for women as well as helped the poor and sick, it was decided to put in writing the *Constitution* under which they had been acting. The *Constitution* (which was not finally and totally approved until after Loyola's death) has ten parts; the fourth part, which is about one quarter of the whole, is devoted to studies and is known as the *Ratio Studiorum*. It is a systematic, practically based and highly organized system of education which has proven so successful that with minor modifications it is used today by Jesuit schools. The *Ratio* made provisions for colleges (secondary schools) which were usually attended by children of nobility although, since no tuition was asked, other apt boys had a chance to enroll in them and the universities. The colleges were usually well-endowed institutions including classrooms, dormitories and *playgrounds*; they averaged three hundred students, although some enrolled as many as three thousand at one time. One hundred and fifty years after Loyola's death there were 769 colleges and universities existent, enrolling 200,000 students. (187:70–74)

The curriculum in the lowest order of the colleges began with grammar, humanities, rhetoric, and moral theology; languages (Latin, Greek, Hebrew), scholastic and positive theology, philosophy, and natural and allied sciences were studied in the highest orders. Nowhere was physical education or physical training included in the curriculum per se.

The philosophy of Loyola and the Jesuits called for rigid obedience to external authority; this differed from Calvinist theology which demanded self-discipline as a means to salvation. Thus Calvin regarded the body as a constant temptation from the devil, while Loyola admonished:

Let your mind be filled with the thought that both soul and body have been created by the Hand of God: we must account to Him for these two parts of our being; and we are not required to weaken one of them out of love for the Creator. We should love the body in the same degree that He could love it. (294:62)

The *Ratio* advised that "the bodily health also was to be carefully attended to. The pupils were not to study too much or too long at a time. Nothing was to be done for a space of from one to two hours after dinner." (294:48) That is, nothing of a studious nature, for that was the time specifically designated for recreation; hence playgrounds were constructed. The masters (teachers) and their students enjoyed playing games and one of the Jesuits noted that "games and manly exercise outside develop physical strength." (187:92)  This idea of the renewing or re-creative aspects of sports and games, although not new (refer to p. 31), was for the first time systematically programmed into a school system. Since the Jesuit schools invariably enforced their *Constitution*, attention to recreation became a standard practice all over the world, for Jesuit schools were widely scattered.

Jesuit education ultimately declined.  In remaining true to Loyola's precepts it had emphasized rigid obedience to God and considered the Church and the Jesuit Society his representatives and interpreters.  Their leader was (and is) called the General and he directed the organization in such a way that the individual was sacrificed to become a link, a soldier in God's army. Eventually people came to hate the Jesuits; their political power came in conflict with various rulers and in some lands they were banned.  However, they recovered and today still maintain a number of schools throughout the world.  Modern Catholic education, even in non-Jesuit schools, is reminiscent of Loyola and the Society of Jesus.  In such schools physical education is often omitted from the curriculum or offered in an extremely limited amount, but after-school sports are encouraged and well-supported.  Thus Loyola's influence remains in evidence today.

# PART IV

*Educational Protagonists and Institutions*

# VITTORINO DA FELTRE

## 1378-1446

"The first modern schoolmaster" is the title given to Vittorino da Feltre by William Harrison Woodward, the famous scholar of Renaissance education. In making this designation, he was at once recognizing the genius and the personality of a man whose reputation was built on his greatness as a teacher, and the turning in the road of educational theory which began with the new humanism of the Renaissance.

Vittorino was born in 1378 in the town of Feltre, located on the southern slope of the Alps. The Rambaldoni family from whom Vittorino descended was respectable but poor, his father earning his living as a clerk. When Vittorino left home at age eighteen to begin his studies at the University of Padua, he was forced to support himself by teaching grammar. Thus began an illustrious teaching career which ended with his death in 1446. In 1396, when Vittorino enrolled at Padua, the Arts (grammar, dialectic, rhetoric, and moral philosophy) occupied a relatively prominent place and were taught with appreciative critical spirit quite different in tone from that of medieval scholasticism. Padua, a well-respected university with fine faculties* in medicine and canon law, eventually came to be regarded as the leading university in the Latin revival. (382:4) Petrarch, the earliest of the Renaissance writers and scholars, was associated with Padua, as was Vergerius whose *De Ingenuis Moribus* delineated the basic ideas upon which humanist education was built.

The study of antiquity had its formal beginnings, however, at Florence, a city responsible for initiating the study of Greek learning. In the same year that Vittorino began his university career, the Studium of Florence extended an invitation to Manuel Chrysoloras, at Constantinople, to accept the Chair of Greek Letters; thus he became the first western professor of Greek language and literature.

Vittorino remained at Padua for close to twenty years as both a teacher and student. He received the degree of Doctor of Arts but never wore either the ring or the gown which symbolized the degree. Instead he continued studying, taking up mathematics which he then became proficient at teaching. When he was thirty-six he went to Venice and began the

---

* The word as it was used then and now in Europe implies both the teachers and the course of study.

3

study of Greek under Guarino da Verona, the foremost Italian scholar of Greek and a man whose reputation as a teacher and schoolmaster ranked with Vittorino's.  By 1420 he was back at Padua as a Latin scholar and teacher.  By then the University was becoming famous for its humanist sympathies which were very much in vogue and therefore when Vittorino accepted the Chair in Rhetoric in 1422, he assumed an important position in the world of scholars.

This position did not suit him however.  Woodward conjectured that the undisciplined, even decadent, life of the university town was disappointing to Vittorino who strove to live as a man of Christian virtue.  As was the custom with great teachers of his time, he had several students boarding with him, in *famulus*, which Vittorino considered a responsibility as well as a means of additional revenue.  Control of their moral behavior in the bacchanalian setting of a university town must have been difficult.  Possibly it was for this reason that Vittorino resigned his position less than a year later and left for Venice.

In Venice he took the sons of Venetian patricians as boarders in his house and conducted a school for them.  But shortly after he began this work he was invited by Gianfrancesco Gonzaga, the Lord of Mantua, to join his court as tutor to his children.  In this situation, Vittorino had an opportunity to do what Plato had dreamed of doing:  to mold the character and guide the education of young princes so that they would rule with wisdom and justice.  Vittorino's goals, like those of humanist education in general, were similar to those of ancient Athens:  the creation of a citizen.  " 'Culture'—not in the sense of something active and preparational like education, but in the sense that the word has for us today—of something perfected:  a mind fully developed, the mind of a man who has

Fig. 10.  Vittorino da Feltre.

become truly man. . . ." (239:142) To educate a man in this manner required a combination of ancient learning and Christian morality; giving such an education is what Vittorino agreed to attempt when he accepted Gonzaga's offer. (Refer to chapter on La Giocosa.) "He brought with him to Mantua a desire to combine the spirit of the Christian life with the educational apparatus of classical literature, whilst uniting with both something of the Greek passion for bodily culture and for dignity of the outer life." (382:27)

Vittorino himself exemplified this idea of the fully developed man. Besides his fine education in Greek and Latin literature, under some of the most renowned scholars of his day, he was known for the dignity and purity of his own life. Although he never acted upon his desire to enter the monastery, he lived the monk's disciplined kind of life. He was slight, possibly frail, but he exposed his body to cold and exercise and took care not to over-indulge in eating or drinking; he was never sick until his final illness. Apparently he was pious and religiously sincere, going to Mass daily and to confession regularly. Thus the man from Feltre was well-suited to serve as an example to his students.

The Italians in their private "court schools," supported by wealthy patrons, strove neither to create new things nor develop new ideas: they attempted to emulate and repeat the style and language of the old. Classical literature, a subject eliminated from medieval church schools because of its pagan concepts and immoral content, was brought back to the curriculum and studied for style, good taste, and eloquent expression. Of course it was expected that the study of such qualities would lead to their corresponding development in the young students. Grace of carriage was the mark of the educated man as well as grace of expression:

> No Humanist disregarded the advantages to a boy of dignified carriage in society, exhibited in walking, sitting or standing with ease and grace. Vittorino was probably the first to teach, with this end in view, gymnastics as an art, deserving of perseverance for its own sake, apart from military training or mere recreation; and after his time it became incorporated into Italian education of the higher type. (382:246)

At the Giocosa, Vittorino, "applying the full *antique conception* of training for the first time, devised systematic methods of physical instruction." (382:245, italics added) The idea of doing this in schools has been credited to Vittorino by most scholars writing on Renaissance education. Since he appears to have elevated physical education to an important place in the curriculum, beyond tradition and contemporary practice, it might be assumed that he was emulating ancient education, particularly Plutarch whose *Education for Boys* was translated by Guarino in 1411 and was very influential in Renaissance Italy. Like the writers of the classical period, Vittorino stressed the importance of intellectual, moral and physical development for the individual to live a complete life as a citizen.

Vittorino's concern for the health of his students was clearly expressed and his regimen of physical training was in part devised to insure the development of strength and hardness.  He even devised exercises for an invalid student.  Furthermore, he had a responsibility to his future rulers to train them in the military skills which they might need when defending their hegemonies.  Martial exercises were a definite part of the training of his students and skill in archery, fencing and riding was held in high esteem.  But above all Vittorino believed that the aim of education was the creation of the complete citizen, and to this end physical education was valued for its contribution.

Vittorino's influence extended not only throughout northern Italy where he was an educator, but wherever and whenever the concepts of humanism prevailed.  His writings were slim and limited to a few personal letters.  He never indulged in the popular habit of writing treatise-type letters for the purpose of setting down his ideas on any subject.  Most of what is known of his life and work is therefore surmised from the writings of other men; fortunately for history he was well-discussed.  His influence can still be detected amidst the surviving remnants of humanist education, and of all his ideas, perhaps the ones currently most popular are those he held about physical education.

# LA GIOCOSA

La Giocosa was one of the new schools established in Italy as a result of the revival of ancient learning. The renaissance (rebirth) of Greek and Roman ideas was the characteristic feature of humanism which brought with it a demand for a new type of education. Until the Renaissance the monastic schools had offered the only formal, academic education, and youngsters generally were enrolled in them only if they planned to serve the Church. Universities had begun to expand their curriculums and the new humanism greatly affected the speed of this process. Religiously-oriented, medieval education had been more interested in the world to come than the world as it existed; humanist education reversed that and endeavored to prepare youths for an intelligent life of public service or commerce.

New schools, headed by famous Italian scholars, were forerunners of the modern education which eventually prevailed over most of Europe. One of the most famous of these schools was La Giocosa in Mantua, established in 1423 under the mastership of Vittorino da Feltre. La Giocosa was a court school, so-called because it, like others of the same designation, was established by a wealthy lord and considered to be part of his court. Such schools were established primarily for the children of the patron and his upper class friends, but bright children with no standing or wealth were also accepted as students. The wealthy lord of La Giocosa was Gianfrancesco Gonzaga, head of the family which held the Lordship of Mantua. Having school-age children of his own, he persuaded Vittorino da Feltre to leave Venice and join his court as the resident scholar. Besides allowing Vittorino to set his own salary, the Marquis apparently gave him a free hand in matters pertaining to the school.

Three of Gonzaga's sons were ready for school, the oldest being nine years old (a daughter and another son born later also attended the school), and Vittorino was permitted to take as pupils a few of the sons of leading Mantuan families. Later he also accepted sons of personal friends from all over northern Italy, including promising boys who were unable to pay. He covered the expenses of the latter boys by charging others high fees, varying according to the position of the parents. The school had a high reputation; some of the greatest scholars of the time, including Guarino da Verona, head of another famous court school, enrolled their own sons in La Giocosa. The ages of entering students varied from four to five years of age to twenty-one, but this was by accident of application rather than design.   The school's fame in northern Italy and even across the Alps in the rest of Europe, was such that sixty or seventy students attended at one time.

Vittorino did not have to design the boys' education entirely from his own ideas and intuitions.   Plutarch's *Education of Boys* (translated by Guarino in 1411), Quintilian's *Institutio* (the complete manuscript discovered in 1417), and Cicero's *De Oratore* (the entire text discovered in 1422) were causing great excitement among Italian scholars and insights thus available into the methods and content of ancient Roman education were important factors in shaping the school in Mantua.

La Giocosa was located in a villa near the Gonzaga family residence.   It had been built in 1388 and named "La Gioiosa" or "the Pleasure House," the connotations of which did not appeal to Vittorino who renamed it La Giocosa, the Pleasant House.   *Giocosa*, or *jocosa*, was derived from *jocus*, a synonym for *ludus* (sport); it was sometimes used by the Romans as an informal name for school.*   It was a spacious, airy house with broad, tree-lined walks, decorated at Vittorino's direction with frescoes of children at play, and bounded on three sides by a large enclosed meadow bordered by a river.   When the enrollment grew too large to board all the students in La Giocosa, a second nearby *casa* took up the overflow, but all lessons took place in the main school.   Luxuries and decorative ornaments were taken from the house because Vittorino regarded these as a temptation to idleness and softness.   He also forbade artificial heat even during the cold Mantuan winters.

Classroom work occupied about seven or eight hours of a student's day. In the early morning he would attend classes and in the evening Vittorino conducted tutorials with individual students.   The arts were studied in such depth that a student had the equivalent of a university education; thus schools like La Giocosa eventually forced the universities to upgrade their curriculums.   Latin and Greek language and literature were studied in a new way.   "To Vittorino Grammar and Rhetoric, combined, implied the critical scholarship of Greek and Latin, a facility in composition in either language, and a power of entering into, and absorbing, the spirit of the literature, history, and thought of the ancient world. . . . The essential foundation of education was Letters; the rest was subsidiary." (382:38) Since textbooks were not available and studies were often undertaken from a single manuscript copy, oral recitation was common and students memorized long passages of the great writings.   Vittorino was particularly careful to allow time for individual instruction.   His attention to the progress of each student was probably one of the chief reasons for the success and fame of his school.   He planned the work to insure variety within the classroom and he also insisted that study be alternated with games and exercises.

---

* Similarly, *gymnasium* is the designation for secondary schools in Europe.

The grassy meadows were an important adjunct to education at La Giocosa because Vittorino considered skill in games as second only to literary power. He regarded regular exercise in all types of weather as necessary for good health. Thus for a minimum of two hours daily, the students at La Giocosa had an organized program of outdoor activity, including games, riding, running, leaping, fencing, and ball games, carefully conducted by specially selected teachers. There were also long walks, and in the summer, when the heat caused the health-conscious Vittorino to transfer his school to the Castle of Goito, they took trips of several days' climbing the Alps above the Lake of Garda. Love of the open air and development of a hard, disciplined body were characteristic parts of Vittorino's teaching.

There were many reasons underlying the deliberate inclusion of a program of physical education at La Giocosa. First and most important, education of the body, like education of the mind and spirit, was regarded as necessary to the development of the citizen, which was the aim of the school. Secondly, training in the martial arts was still important for many students were future political leaders who would be forced to take up arms and go to war. Thirdly, Vittorino was convinced of the importance of variety and wanted his students to have a rest from their studies by turning their attention to vigorous games. And lastly, proper exercise was regarded as necessary to good health and ruggedness of spirit as well as body, which in turn was considered fundamental to good mental discipline.

La Giocosa, with Vittorino da Feltre as its leader, was one of the powerful formative influences of the Renaissance. Not only was it a seat of learning where the finest scholarship took place, but it delineated by its example a new style of education. Basic to this style was the importance attached to physical education as an integral part of the life of a student. This precedent, which established systematic gymnastic instruction as an art to be learned apart from its recreational and military usefulness, was copied in the schools of the humanists. It largely disappeared in later developments in public secondary education but it remained a part of the education in good private schools in England and America (refer to Round Hill School). The concept is returning to favor in mass education in contemporary United States, but the spirit of it has not yet been totally recaptured.

# FRANÇOIS RABELAIS

## ca. 1495-1553

François Rabelais, creator of Gargantua and Pantagruel, stood astride the humanism of the Renaissance and the realism of the seventeenth century. Like the classical humanists, he studied and appreciated the wisdom of the ancient writers, particularly Pliny and Galen and the Greek philosophers. This was demonstrated in a variety of ways: he published a commentary on treatises of Hippocrates and Galen; translated one of the books of Herodotus; was known to be a highly accomplished scholar of both Greek and Latin; composed Greek elegiacs, and of Eudemon, a model student, said appreciatively: "All this was by him delivered with such proper gestures, such distinct pronunciation, so pleasant a delivery, in such exquisite fine terms, and so good Latin, that he seemed rather a Gracchus, a Cicero, an Aemilius of the time past, than a youth of this age." (297:35)

Although Rabelais had Gargantua learn the early authors by heart, it was the substance, not the form that he deemed important: "He himself said them by heart, and upon them would ground some practical cases concerning the estate of man. . . ." (297:49) Education was to be put to use in a practical way. Furthermore, the content of education, as proposed by Rabelais, was "realistically" based. The trivium (grammar, logic, rhetoric), which was an essential part of education since the Middle Ages and formed part of the Seven Liberal Arts, was ignored in favor of an almost total emphasis on the other part, the quadrivium (arithmetic, geometry, astronomy, and music). These were subjects with a basis in the material world and therefore could be studied in a more interesting and natural way. Thus "they brought him cards, not to play, but to learn a thousand pretty tricks and new inventions, which were all grounded upon arithmetic. By this means he fell in love with that numerical science. . . ." (297:49) Or: "In returning they considered the face of the sky, if it were such as they had observed it the night before, and into what signs the sun was entering, as also the moon for that day." (297:49)

It was for practical purposes that Gargantua's education included intense lessons and practice in physical education. For instance:

> He wrestled, ran, jumped, not at three steps and a leap [the triple jump or hop, step and jump used in ancient Greek and modern competition], nor at the hare's leap, "for" said Gymnast, "*these jumps are for the wars altogether unprofitable, and of no use;*" but at one leap he would skip over a ditch, spring over a

hedge, mount six paces upon a wall . . . swim in deep waters on his belly, on his back, sideways, with all his body, with his feet only. . . . Coming out of the water he ran furiously up against a hill, and with the same alacrity and swiftness ran down again. . . .

He did cast the dart, throw the bar, put the stone, practice the javelin, the boar-spear, or partisan, and the halbert; he broke the strongest bows in drawing, bended against his breast the greatest cross-bows of steel. . . . They set up a great pole, fixed upon two trees, there would he hang by his hands, and with them alone, his feet touching at nothing, would go back and fore along the aforesaid rope . . . and then, to exercise his breast and lungs, he would shout like all the devils in hell. . . . (297:51, italics added)

Furthermore, the Esquite Gymnast, a young gentleman of Touraine, taught him the art of riding:

He rode a Naples courser, a Dutch roussin, a Spanish gennet . . . then a light fleet horse . . . made him go the high saults, bounding in the air, free the ditch with a skip, leap over a stile or pale. . . . He was singularly skillful in leaping nimbly from one horse to another, without putting foot to ground . . . he could likewise, from either side, with a lance in his hand, leap on horseback without stirrups, and rule the horse at his pleasure, without a bridle, *for such things are useful in military engagements.* Another day he exercised the battle-ax, which he so dexterously wielded both in the nimble, strong, and smooth management of that weapon, and that in all the feats practiseable by it, that he *passed knight of arms in the field,* and at all essays. (297:50, italics added)

And he learned to handle all the other weapons of his day: he "tossed . . . the pike, played with the two-handed sword, with the back-sword, with the Spanish tuck, the dagger, poniard, armed or unarmed, with a buckler, with a cloak, with a target." (297:50)

The purpose of this education was obviously to prepare the young gentleman for war. The knightly exercises of the medieval days were still considered necessary in the sixteenth century, although the boy was also expected to learn the Seven Liberal Arts as well. Boys living in the middle ages had been educated only in one or the other, to be either scholars of the church or knights of the fief.

Perhaps because of the influence of Galen's writings, Gargantua's education also included some attention to exercise for the body's health and for diversion:

Then, for the strengthening of his nerves or sinews, they made him two great sows of lead, each of them weighing eight thousand and seven hundred kintails,* which they called *alteres;* those he took up from the ground, in each hand one, then lifted them up over his head, and held them without stirring, three quarters of an hour or more, which was an inimitable force. (297:52)

Then for three good hours he had a lecture read unto him**: this done, they went forth . . . either unto a field near the University, called the Brack, or unto

---

* Or quintals, each the equivalent of one hundred pounds—obviously a gross exaggeration.

** The printing press, although invented, had not yet begun to turn out books in great numbers, and manuscript copies were traditionally studied in this oral manner.

the meadows, where they played at the ball, tennis, and at the piletrigone, most gallantly exercising their bodies, as before they had done their minds: all their play was but in liberty, for they left off when they pleased, and that was commonly when they did sweat over all their body, or were otherwise weary. (297:49)

In summary, Rabelais believed that the purposes of physical education were primarily to learn skills useful in the art of war, but also to strengthen the body, and to play games for pleasant diversion. The latter were not taken so seriously that they were formally structured but were done "in liberty," when the participants wanted to. In actuality, Rabelais expressed opinions quite different from those held by the humanists who thought physical education was important in the development of the whole man (refer to p. 49).

Rabelais' ideas, especially those about education, did not influence his contemporaries. He was not an educator, but a physician and was also known to have studied law. Ordained a monk at about age twenty-five, in the Franciscan Order, known for material and intellectual poverty, Rabelais renounced his vows in later years in order to regain his civil rights and thus his inheritance. His father, who was a lawyer and district administrator, owned property at la Devinière, near Chinon, where Rabelais was born. He probably went to a school run by the Benedictine monks for the early part of his education and received his Bachelor of Medicine from the University of Montpellier in 1531. He rose to eminence as a physician and his scholarly abilities earned him a place in the inner circle of the intellectual humanists. Two things, however, occurred to mar his reputation: first, humanism became identified with the growing protestant movement, to the point that in 1523 the Sorbonne proscribed the study of Greek as irreligious, and the Franciscans destroyed all the Greek books Rabelais owned. To be a humanist was not only unpopular but even dangerous for Rabelais and others. Secondly, Rabelais wrote his books not in Latin but in the vernacular and not with attention to grace and elegance but with bawdy peasant expressions and a running stream of vulgarity. This disgraced him in the eyes of the humanists. The first part of *Pantagruel* appeared in 1532 and *Gargantua* in 1535. The latter was a character from folklore, a kind of giant, with an appetite and prowess on a gigantic scale. (Note the physical feats quoted earlier.) Both books were good, lusty tales of the kind people love to read; they were actually part of the earliest literature written for the common man, who naturally could not read Latin. Rabelais' writings gave him great popularity with the people, if not with the intellectuals.

The education of Gargantua was a bridge between the humanists and the education of Émile; and the use of objects in nature and learning by observation and demonstration, rather than by rote memory, was influential in the development of the educational theories of later thinkers like Montaigne, Locke and Rousseau.

# MICHEL DE MONTAIGNE

## 1533-1592

Michel Eyquem de Montaigne had the advantage of receiving the kind of education described in his *Essays*, and as a result was one of the most learned men of his time. The eldest of eight, he was born in 1533 in the Château de Montaigne, situated in Périgord about thirty miles east of Bordeaux. He spent most of his life there on the ancestral property. Although the first of his family to drop the ancestral surname, Eyquem, he acknowledged the strong influence of his heritage "having had the best father that ever was, and the most indulgent, even in his extreme old age, and being of a family famous and exemplary. . . ." (112:15) His father

> sent me from the cradle to be brought up in a poor village of his, training me to the humblest and commonest way of life. . . . And this was the reason why he also had me held over the baptismal font by people of the lowliest class, to bind and attach me to them. (246:844)

This rather unique tactic is recounted by Montaigne in his essay *Of Experience*, in which he attempted to demonstrate that experience, like reason, is a way to knowledge. Experience also taught him that "what cannot be done by reason, and by wisdom and tact, is never done by force. I was brought up that way." (246:281) Therefore he concluded that "education is to be carried on with severe gentleness, not as is customary. . . . Away with violence and compulsion!" (246:122)

When very young he was put in the care of a German who spoke to him only in Latin, as did his family, with the result that "without artificial means, without a book, without grammar or precept, without the whip or tears, I had learned a Latin quite as pure as what my schoolmaster knew. . . ." (246:128) He was also taught Greek, not "artificially, but in a new way, in the form of amusements and exercise." (246:129) However, he never learned Greek well. In part it was these experiences that caused Montaigne to repudiate slapping grammar and rhetoric "into our memory with all their feathers on, like oracles in which the letters and syllables are the substance of the matter. To know by heart is not to know. . . ." (246:112) He used physical education as a further example of this concept:

> I wish Paluel or Pompey, those fine dancers of my time, could teach us capers just by performing them before us and without moving us from our seats, as those

people want to train our understanding without setting it in motion; or that we could be taught to handle a horse, or a pike, or a lute, or our voice, without practicing at it, as those people want to teach us to judge well and to speak well, without having us practice either speaking or judging. (246:112)

Despite his background of learning by active methods, Montaigne was, by his account, a poor student with an unretentive memory. Nor was he adept at sports:

Adroitness and agility I have never had; and yet I am the son of a very nimble father. . . . He scarcely ever found a man of his condition who was his equal in any bodily exercise; just as I have scarcely found any who did not surpass me, except in running, in which I was just fair. . . . At dancing, tennis, wrestling, I have never been able to acquire any but very slight and ordinary ability; at swimming, fencing, vaulting, and jumping, none at all. . . .

My bodily qualities, in short, are very well matched with those of my soul. There is no liveliness . . . if I am not lured to it by some pleasure, and if I have any other guide than my own pure free will, I am good for nothing. (246:487)

Fig. 11.  Michel de Montaigne.

Montaigne's lethargy and slow learning caused his father to doubt the wisdom of his methods; finally he sent him to the Collège de Guyenne in Bordeaux, a fine school with distinguished humanists on its faculty who leaned toward Erasmus' ideas on religious reform.    The latter did not affect Montaigne who remained a Catholic all his life, although one sister and one brother became Protestant.*    Later he studied law, probably in Toulouse and became a magistrate in the Bordeaux Parlement.    At age thirty-eight he retired to spend his life in "freedom, tranquillity, and leisure."

Montaigne lived the life of a sixteenth-century French country gentleman, maintaining his inherited estate, carrying out business transactions in land and its products, caring for his peasants, and writing his *Essays*. Volumes I and II appeared in 1580, and III in 1588, during which period he also served as Mayor of Bordeaux.    The sixth and last edition of the *Essays* was published in 1595, after his death in 1592.

The first to use the term "essay" to describe that particular literary form, Montaigne communicated a wide-ranging evaluation of human thought and behavior in a graceful and friendly manner.    Of particular interest to physical educators are his views on education, specifically expressed in two essays: *Of Pedantry* and *Of the Education of Children*.    In these he set forth the opinion, totally opposite to the views of education prevalent in his time, that the purpose of education is to develop a man of wisdom, judgement, taste, virtue, and manners and not to fill him with knowledge.    "For it seems to me that the first lessons in which we should steep his mind must be those that regulate his behavior and his sense, that will teach him to know himself and to die well and live well." (246.117)    He moved the focus of education from the learning of subject matter to the development of the child's human qualities.    The function of the tutor was to "teach him this new lesson, that the value and height of true virtue lies in the ease, utility, and pleasure of its practice. . . ." (246:120)    Education was to prepare a gentleman to live well, to enjoy the blessings of life with moderation and, if necessary, to lose them with fortitude.    Furthermore, "he owes to education only the first fifteen or sixteen years of his life; the rest he owes to action." (246:120–121)

Mind and body were to be educated simultaneously:

Even games and exercises will be a good part of his study: running, wrestling, music, dancing, hunting, handling horses and weapons.    I want his outward behavior and social grace and his physical adaptability to be fashioned at the same time with his soul.    It is not a soul that is being trained, not a body, but a man; these parts must not be separated.    And, as Plato says, they must not be trained one without the other, but driven abreast like a pair of horses harnessed to the same pole.    And to hear him, does he not seem to give more time and care

---

* In 1544, during the time that Montaigne was at school in Bordeaux, men were executed for Lutheranism.

to exercises of the body, and to think that the mind gets its exercise at the same time, and not the other way around? (246:122)

However, Montaigne showed no evidence of respecting games as suitable pursuits.  In the same essay he suggested strangling a child or apprenticing him to a pastry cook if, among other poor choices, "he does not find it more pleasant and sweet to return dusty and victorious from combat than from tennis or a ball with the prize for that exercise. . . ." (246:120)  Nevertheless, his basic conviction that body and soul are equal was unusual.  He regarded the body as simple and earthy and, unlike the learned churchmen, found great pleasure in satisfying its needs, although moderation was always the guideline in this as well as in rational pursuits.

The gentleman Montaigne, for all he talked of "action," did not mean that men should be doers but that virtues such as valor, temperance and generosity, must be practiced rather than read and talked about.  Thus he said:

> Our life, Pythagoras used to say, is like the great and populous assembly at the Olympic games.  Some exercise their bodies to win glory in the games, others bring merchandise to sell for gain.  There are some, and not the worst, who seek no other profit than to see how and why everything is done, and to be spectators of the life of other men in order to judge and regulate their own. (246:117)

Perhaps that statement was meant to justify his own kind of existence and the importance of the *Essays*, which in some ways were a spectator's sympathetic commentary on the activities of others.  Thibaudet, quoted by Frame, noted:

> Montaigne, more than anyone else, created that public of *bonnêtes gens* capable of judging and testing, constituted outside of the learned, and against them. (17th century, Descartes, Pascal.) . . . One of the main effects, on the 17th century, of reading Montaigne will consist precisely in emphasizing these human personal values, in substituting authentic humanism for the humanism of erudition. (112:315)

Montaigne's contribution was a plan of education designed for independent moral living which stressed thinking rather than memorization; the need for both physical and mental education; the use of subject matter to develop personality; learning by doing; developing a whole man, and education that prepares the student for life.  Following Montaigne, Comenius, Locke, Rousseau, and others advocated some of these methods, but it was John Dewey, in the twentieth century, who welded almost all of them into a coherent educational theory; therefore modern educational practice can be traced to Montaigne.  But as Robert Ulich said, "more important than all specific educational suggestions is the fact that Montaigne represents the first great personality in the history of educational thought to have a completely autonomous and secular concept of man." (364:161)

# RICHARD MULCASTER

## ca. 1531-1611

Richard Mulcaster lived in England in the exciting time when Elizabeth I occupied the throne (reigned 1558–1603), and the plays of William Shakespeare (1564–1616) were entertaining the populace. He was an "esquier borne" in the border district of Cumberland. He attended Eton under the headmastership of Nicholas Udall, writer of the first English comedy, and was elected a student of Christchurch, Oxford in 1555. His reputation for knowing Hebrew as well as Greek and Latin must have helped him to secure the position of first headmaster at the Merchant Taylors' School when it opened in 1561, with 250 students and three assistant masters. During its time the school produced one of England's most famous writers, Edmund Spenser. Mulcaster received as salary the munificent sum of ten pounds sterling a year plus a dwelling, which caused him to live in "straightened circumstances" when he resigned twenty-five years later. In 1596, he became headmaster of St. Paul's School, a position he held until, at age seventy-seven, poor health forced his retirement. Despite the fact that he received a yearly pension of sixty-six pounds sterling as well as a living from the rectorship at Stanford Rivers granted him by Queen Elizabeth, he died impoverished and debt-ridden. This reluctance to pay adequate salaries and pensions to teachers is somewhat indicative of their status in his time. This may have been partially due to the fact that teacher training was unheard of (Mulcaster himself made the first suggestion for a college to train teachers) and therefore those who taught were not always knowledgeable or capable.

While at Merchant Taylors', Mulcaster published in 1581 the *Positions* and in 1582 what he called the *First Part of the Elementarie*, though the completion of the latter was never accomplished. Besides these two works on education, he wrote poems in Latin; *Catechismus Paulinus*, a catechism for his students, and a work called *Cato Christianus*, which has been lost.

Although he was one of the most famous teachers of his time, Mulcaster's educational theories were not popular and his writings, despite his own conceit about them (he thought them a model example of the best the English language could offer), were never considered good literature. He was largely a forgotten figure until the late nineteenth century when R. H. Quick "discovered" him and reproduced the *Positions* because he recognized their value to modern education. Quick believed that:

There is good reason why Mulcaster should not be forgotten. When we read his books we find that wisdom which we are importing in the nineteenth century was in a great measure offered us by an English schoolmaster in the sixteenth. The latest advances in pedagogy have established (1) that the end and aim of education is to develop the faculties of the mind and body; (2) that all teaching processes should be carefully adapted to the mental constitution of the learner; (3) that the first stage in learning is of immense importance and requires a very high degree of skill in the teacher; (4) that the brain of children, especially of clever children, should not be subjected to "pressure"; (5) that childhood should not be spent in learning foreign languages, but that its language should be the mother-tongue . . . ; (6) that girls' education should be cared for no less than boys'; (7) that the only hope of improving our schools lies in providing training for our teachers. These are all regarded as planks in the platform of "the new education," and these were all advocated by Mulcaster. (294:92–93)

In 1903, Oliphant published *The Educational Writings of Richard Mulcaster* (268) which is essentially a rewritten version of both books so that the ordinary reader can understand them and apply the valuable educational theory contained within. A new edition of the *Elementarie* came out in 1925 (249), but since it is a copy of the original it is exceedingly difficult to read.

Mulcaster's significance to physical education is no less than his importance to education. Throughout all of his writings he expressed great interest and concern about the body, a position almost unique among educators in his time. Current practice completely abjured physical activity.* Yet the *Positions* dealt with the principles to be observed in the training of children, "either for skill in their book or health in their body," and a third of the volume was devoted to the physical side of education. Chapter headings (slightly altered and condensed) included: Chapter 4, That exercise must be joined with the book, as the schooling of the body; 6, The importance of exercise and physical training (as an agent of health); 7, The order followed in the present treatment of the subject; 8, Definition and varieties of exercise (athletics, martial exercise, exercises for health); 9, Choice of exercises; 16–27, Dancing, wrestling, fencing, top and scourge, walking, running, leaping, swimming, riding, hunting, shooting (archery), ball games; 28–34, Circumstances to be considered in exercise, nature and quality of exercise, the bodies which are to be exercised; place, time, quantity, and manner of exercise.

Mulcaster had a dualistic conception of the mind and body:

As in setting a child to school we consider the strength of his body no less than the quickness of his mind, it would seem that our training ought to be twofold, both body and mind being kept at their best, so that each may be able to support the other in what they have to do together. . . . The exercise of the body should

---

* For an excellent discussion of Mulcaster's position regarding physical training, refer to Dennis Brailsford, *Sport and Society* (Toronto: University of Toronto Press, 1969), pp. 44–51.

always accompany and assist the exercise of the mind, to make a dry, strong, hard, and therefore a longlasting, body, and by this means to have an active, sharp, wise, and well-learned soul. (268:14–15)

He pointed out that "it is not enough to say that children are always stirring of their own accord, and therefore need no special attention in regard to bodily exercise" (268:15); since educators insist upon keeping children more still than their natures dictate, exercise must be regulated. He assigned a teacher to this function and, because he questioned that a man, "whose work has to do with the body alone" could "judge well of the soul," he asked how such a man could "perceive what is best for the body, who having the soul only committed to this care, hands over the body to some other man's treatment." Consequently he assigned "both the framing of the mind and the training of the body to one man's charge." (268:16).

In general, his writings exhibited a strong naturalistic tendency. In *Elementarie* he said: "Is the bodie made by natur nimble to run, to ride, to swim, to fense, to do anie thing else, which beareth praise in that kinde for either profit or pleasur? And doth not the Elementarie help them all forward by precept and train?" (249:39) He believed that "the proof of a good Elementary Course is, that it should follow nature in the multitude of its gifts, and that it should proceed in teaching as she does in developing." (268:45)

His recommendations for exercise suitable for children with detailed discussions on their value, particularly physiological, seemed to have been closely based on *De Arte Gymnastica* by Mercurialis (243). The following passage from his discussion on football is a good example of his advice:

> Football could not possibly have held its present prominence, nor have been so much in vogue as it is everywhere, if it had not been very beneficial to health and strength . . . though as it is now commonly practiced, with thronging of a rude multitude, with bursting of shins and breaking of legs, it is neither civilized, nor worthy the name of any health training. And here one can easily see the use of the training master . . . who can judge of the play. . . . By such regulation, the players being put into smaller numbers, sorted into sides and given their special positions, so that they do not try to meet with their bodies so boisterously to try their strength, nor shoulder and shove one another so barbarously, football may strengthen the muscles of the whole body. By provoking superfluities downwards it relieves the head and the upper parts, it is good for the bowels, and it drives down the stone and gravel from the bladder and the kidneys. The motion also helps weak hams and slender shanks by making the flesh firmer, yet rash running and too much violence often break some internal conduit and cause ruptures. (268:17–18)

But despite Mulcaster's great interest in exercise, he never considered it as subject matter. Elementary school children were to learn reading, writing, drawing, and music, the doing of which would *nurture* the hand, ear and eye with which they had been endowed by *nature*.  His understanding of this process was remarkably modern:

> Nature has . . . given us for self-preservation the power of perceiving all sensible things by means of feeling, hearing, seeing, smelling, and tasting.  These qualities of the outward world, being apprehended by the understanding and examined by the judgement, are handed over to the memory, and afterwards prove our chief— nay, our only—means of obtaining further knowledge.  Moreover, we have also a power of movement, either under the influence of emotion or by the enticement of desire, either for the direct purposes of life, as in the action of the pulse and in breathing, or for outward action, such as walking, running, or leaping.  To serve the end both of sense-perception and of motion, nature has planted in the body a brain. . . . (268:48)

Nevertheless, physical education was not important in the training of these sense organs but was necessary because "many people of high spirit, notable for their learning and skill in the highest professions, have failed, owing to want of attention to bodily health . . . [;] it is needful . . . especially for those who use their brains, such as students [who] should eat very moderately, and their exercise should also be moderate, and not vary too much, and their clothing should be thin . . . that the flesh may become hard and firm." (268:16–17)

Two works of Roger Ascham, a well-known English contemporary, seemed to have influenced Mulcaster.  Certainly both men's concepts of physical education were similar.  *The Scholemaster* published in 1570, two years after Ascham's death, was one of the earliest works in English on the theory and practice of teaching and it contained the injunction to "joyne learning with cumlie exercises."  The other, *Toxophilus*, was a manual of instruction on archery, although by the end of the sixteenth century the English army had adopted guns and skill in bow shooting was no longer a military necessity.  Ascham's work was more famous and better accepted in its time, but neither he nor Mulcaster really was able to influence practice in Elizabethan schools.

Mulcaster, like other Renaissance thinkers, accepted the body as a significant factor in human endeavors.  Consequently, he developed pedagogical theories which urged that children be trained in practices beneficial to health.  His innovative ideas were ignored in his own time but have formed a cornerstone for modern practice.

# JOHN AMOS COMENIUS

## 1592–1670

THE GREAT DIDACTIC

Setting forth

The whole Art of Teaching
all Things to all Men

or

A certain Inducement to found such Schools in all
the Parishes, Towns, and Villages of every
Christian Kingdom, that the entire
Youth of both Sexes, none
being excepted, shall

*Quickly, Pleasantly, & Thoroughly*

Become learned in the Sciences, pure in Moral,
Trained to Piety, and in this manner
instructed in all things necessary
for the present and for
the future life. . . . (74:17)

A portion of the title page of *The Great Didactic (Didactica Magna)* is reproduced here because it set forth the framework of Comenius' theories of education. When compared with the practices of his day it can be discerned how advanced were his ideas. He was concerned with the "art of teaching" in an age when men were barely beginning to understand that pedagogy entailed special skills and methods. He talked of "teaching all things to all men" when Latin, Greek, the classical authors, and the Bible were the only subjects considered fit for study, and when very few children, usually boys, had the privilege of attending school. Universal education for both sexes, "none being excepted," was at least 250 years away from being realized in any part of the world. He talked of learning "quickly, pleasantly, and thoroughly," when the few schools that existed were dreary, dull and distinctly unpleasant—the more so because of the crude, even vicious, forms of discipline thought necessary to subdue the children.

He wanted children to become "learned in the sciences" when twenty years earlier Galileo had been forced by the Inquisition to recant his heretical belief that the sun was the center of the universe. Finally, in an era when religion's emphasis on the future life had not yet died away, and when education was viewed as diversion for the idle rich or preparation for a scholarly career, rather than as a way to teach useful, vocational skills, Comenius sought to instruct "in all things necessary for the present and for the future life."

Unlike Montaigne, Comenius was not fortunate enough to live a life of quiet reflection, promulgating principles based on idealistic theories. Born Jan Komensky in 1592 in Nivmitz, Czechoslovakia, the son of a miller who was affiliated with the Moravian Brethren, his life was oppressed by the Catholic-Protestant fight for domination of Europe. Both his parents died when he was still a child, and due to his guardians' neglect he was ten years older than most when he entered, at age sixteen, a school that taught Latin. He prepared for ordination as a minister in the Moravian Church by studying at Herborn, Heidelberg and Amsterdam and was ordained in 1616, the year Shakespeare and Cervantes died. After two years as rector in a Bohemian school at Prenau, he was appointed Pastor of the Moravian community at Fulnek. The following year troops of the strongest power in Europe, Spain, plundered the community and Comenius lost everything he possessed, including his manuscripts. Within the next two years his wife and child died. In 1624 all Protestant ministers were sent from Bohemia, followed three years later by the banishment of all Protestants. For a time Comenius was able to hide out in the mountains where he did some teaching and writing, but when the persecution continued to grow he left permanently in 1627, a victim of the Thirty Years' War which made Europe an uncomfortable place for Protestant reformers. Many of the banished Bohemians settled in Leszno in Poland, where Comenius was appointed assistant and later headmaster of a long-established Brethren school.

The next years were devoted to teaching and writing, during which time in 1631 he published the *Janua Linguarum Reserata* (*The Gate of Languages Unlocked*), and *The Great Didactic*. The former contained parallel passages in Latin and the vernacular which progressed from simple to complex sentences to make learning easier by using the mother tongue. This method may be contrasted with the direct method advocated by Montaigne and Locke. In 1641 he was invited to London by a group of learned men (whose efforts later led to the founding of the Royal Society) to join in their Parliament's efforts to open a universal college for the advancement of science, but once again war, this time the Irish Insurrection, intervened and the plans never materialized. Comenius next accepted an invitation to Sweden where he spent six years writing textbooks, a task he disliked, at which point he was appointed the Bishop of the Moravian Brethren. Their difficulties led him to return to Leszno where he was soon confronted

Fig. 12.   John Amos Comenius.

with the Peace of Westphalia, granting religious tolerance to Protestants in
general but not to the Moravians, whose exile was thus made permanent.
Hungary drew him next and for four years he worked to establish a model
school at Saros-Patak.   During this time he wrote his most famous book,
*Orbis Sensualium Pictus*, which was the first children's picture book ever
printed when it was published in 1657.   The illustrative engravings, named
both in Latin and the vernacular, attempted to motivate learning by ap-
pealing to the child's senses.   In response to the needs of his Brethren, he
returned once again to Leszno where his support of Protestant Sweden led
the Poles to attack his house and burn all of his possessions including a
Latin-Bohemian dictionary on which he had worked for forty years.
Finally with his family (he had remarried), he went to Amsterdam and remained until his death in 1670.

His theology was influenced by the Czech martyr Jan Hus, who was burned for his heretical views.  His educational theories strongly reflected the then-popular writings of Francis Bacon who advocated an empirical, experimental method known as induction (inducing the general from the specific).  His outlook on knowledge, which he termed "pansophism" or universal wisdom, reflected his world viewpoint; in fact, he viewed education as the key to world peace.  Comenius' advanced views could be explained perhaps by his supra-national citizenship and his need to deal with the misfortune that befell him and those for whom he was responsible as the Moravian Bishop.

His two most famous writings, the *Janua* and *Orbis Sensualium Pictus*, were translated into more than a dozen languages and used as textbooks in Europe for over a hundred years.  An American edition of the latter was published as late as 1810, because people found that learning through pictures was a good method.  But today it is *The Great Didactic* which is studied by educational historians because it represents Comenius' attempt to state a comprehensive methodology for teaching all subjects.

One of his earliest works, *The School of Infancy* (75), was first published about 1630 in the Czechoslovakian language and later translated by Comenius into German (1633), Polish, and twenty years later into Latin. Predating Froebel, the creator of the kindergarten, it dealt with teaching very young children, which is probably the reason it is seldom referred to when Comenius is discussed.  However, it contained several insights particularly relevant to physical education.  Typical of most churchmen, Comenius expressed a dualistic concept of body and soul in terms somewhat similar to Locke's discussion of the mind-body relationship.  He said:

> The first care therefore ought to be of the soul, which is the principal part of the man, so that it may become in the highest degree possible beautifully adorned. The next care is for the body that it may be made a habitation fit and worthy of an immortal soul. (75:64)

Therefore, when listing the things in which infants should be instructed during their first six years, along with sound knowledge of "things, in labor and in art, and in speech," in morals, virtues and piety, he included health. However, unlike the rest of the list, he explained *why:* "Inasmuch as life and sound health constitute the basis of all things in relation to man, instruction will be given on how by diligence and care parents may preserve infants sound and healthy." (75:75)

Chapter V of *The School of Infancy*, entitled "Health and Strength," instructed that "children must also have daily exercises and excitements" and that "the more a child is active, runs about, and plays . . . the more quickly does it grow and flourish both in body and mind. . . ." (75:83)  He observed that "*a joyful mind is half health*" and urged that "one should provide some little convenient occupations that please its eyes ears or other senses. These will contribute to its vigor of body and mind." (75:84) He also advocated that children's playthings be in the form of such things as horses or little carriages, for "these both amuse and promote their knowledge of things. For this way is to teach children according to their own way. . . ." (75:89)

In *The Great Didactic* he said that "children should also be taught to occupy themselves continually, either with work *or with play* . . ." (74:208, italics added) because "much can be learned in play that will afterwards be of use when the circumstances demand it." (74:184) It was natural for Comenius, an incessant worker, to believe that *all* time should be usefully spent: "Finally, it will be of immense use, if the amusements that are provided to relax the strain on the minds of the scholars be of such a kind as to lay stress on the more serious side of life, in order that a definite impression may be made on them even in their hours of recreation." (74:142)

Prior to Comenius the play of children was at best regarded as not sinful. He was the first educator-cleric in the Christian era to regard play as an important part in the life of the growing child, performing the useful function of insuring a healthy, vigorous body as well as providing a pleasant method *through which children could learn* to distinguish objects in their environment by exercising their senses. Later thinkers such as Pestalozzi, Froebel and John Dewey developed the concept of learning through play as an important aspect of their educational theories, but the innovator of the idea was Comenius.

# JOHN LOCKE

## 1632-1704

> A Sound Mind in a sound Body, is a short, but full
> Description of a happy State in this World.

These words, perhaps one of the most famous statements ever made relevant to the development of physical education, opened Locke's essay: *Some Thoughts Concerning Education* (1693). The phrase "a sound mind in a sound body," was representative of the Cartesian (from Descartes) dualistic philosophy, in which mind and matter within a single human being are considered separate. According to Descartes,

> The mind and the body are really distinct. . . . But we clearly perceive mind, that is, thinking substance, without body, that is to say, without any extended substance (by Postulate II); and conversely, body without mind (as all readily admit). But the mind and the body are substances (by Definitions V, VI, and VII) which can exist independently of one another. . . . (86:124)

Locke basically agreed; he felt that the "same happens concerning the operations of the mind, viz. thinking, reasoning, fearing, &c, which we, concluding not to subsist of themselves, nor apprehending how they can belong to body, or be produced by it, we are apt to think these the actions of some other substance, which we call spirit. . . ." (213:383)

This statement was an outgrowth of Locke's basic theory of ideas delineated in the work which first made him famous as a philosopher, *An Essay Concerning Human Understanding* (1690). In it he sought to show that all ideas come either from sensation or reflection: "External objects furnish the mind with the ideas of sensible qualities, which are all those different perceptions they produce in us: and the mind furnishes the understanding with ideas of its own operations." (213:356) He expounded this philosophy in which the mind could function separately from body, although by noting that ideas come also from sensation, he gave the body its own role to play. He did not attempt to place greater value on the one sort of idea as being of a higher quality than the other. On the contrary, Locke commented:

> If it shall be demanded, then, when a man begins to have any ideas? I think the true answer is, when he first has any sensation. . . . It is about these impressions made on our senses by outward objects, that the mind seems first to employ

Fig. 13.   John Locke.

itself in such operations as we call perception, remembering, consideration, reasoning, &c. . . . In time the mind comes to reflect on its own operations, about the ideas got by sensation, and thereby stores itself with a new set of ideas, which I call ideas of reflection. (213:357)

In connection with this he expounded the *tabula rasa* theory in which the mind is pictured as a "blank tablet" waiting to receive impressions. This theory directly opposes Plato's belief that the soul comes into the world carrying within itself true ideas which have been planted there before birth. Whereas Plato attempted to demonstrate that sense impressions could not give true knowledge, Locke said:

Thus, the first capacity of human intellect is that the mind is fitted to receive the impressions made on it, either through the senses, by outward objects, or by its own operations, when it reflects on them. This is the first step a man makes towards the discovery of any thing, and the ground work whereon to build all those notions which ever he shall have naturally in this world. (213:358)

Thus, when Locke said that all men's ideas come from experience, he meant by that term sensation and reflection—a position that both influenced and reflected the eighteenth-century empiricist epistemology rampant in Britain.

It would be totally inconsistent for a man who believed that the senses were a primary source of knowing, to be unconcerned with the condition of the body.  Locke's natural acceptance of the body's value, was intensified by his own personal and permanent condition (from about age forty) of poor health.  In his letters he frequently referred to the wretched health which forced him to decline several opportunities to serve as an ambassador. "What shall a man do in the necessity of application and variety of attendance on business to be followed there, who sometimes after a little motion has not breath to speak, and cannot borrow an hour or two of watching from the night without repaying it with a great waste of time the next day?" (214:xxxvii)  It is not surprising, then, when he ruminated on life's pleasures:  "Let me then see wherein consists the most lasting pleasure of this life, and that as far as I can observe is in these things:" he topped his list with "1st. Health,—without which no sensual pleasure can have any relish" (214:xxvi).  In *Some Thoughts*, after his opening *mens sana in corpore sano* statement, he went on:  "He that has these two, has little more to wish for; and he that wants either of them, will be but little the better for anything else." (214:1)

Locke's essay on education, like Montaigne's, began as a series of letters to his friend Edward Clarke, who had solicited advice on the education of his child.  Biographers of Locke noted there was no indication that he had ever seriously studied educational theory, except by reading Montaigne's essay which apparently influenced him to a certain extent.*  The entire first part of *Some Thoughts* is devoted to advice on the development of a healthy body.  He summarized:

> And thus I have done with what concerns the Body and Health, which reduces itself to these few and easy observable Rules:  Plenty of *open Air, Exercise,* and *Sleep,* plain *Diet,* no *Wine* or *strong Drink,* and very little or no *Physick,* not too warm and strait *Clothing,* especially the *Head* and *Feet* kept cold, and the *Feet* often us'd to cold Water, and expos'd to wet. (214:20)

Mixed in with his advice about washing the feet in cold water every day, and sleeping on a hard bed, is a passage advocating swimming:

> I shall not need here to mention *Swimming,* when he is of an Age able to learn, and has any one to teach him.  'Tis that saves many a Man's Life; and the *Romans* thought it so necessary, that they rank'd it with Letters; and it was the common Phrase to mark one ill-educated, and good for nothing, That he had neither learnt to read nor to swim:  *Nec literas didicit nec natare.*  But, besides the gaining a Skill which may serve him at need, the Advantages to Health by often *bathing in cold Water* during the Heat of Summer, are so many, that I think nothing need be said to encourage it. . . . (214:6)

---

* Like Montaigne, Locke believed that children should be brought up by tutors rather than in schools, and that the best way to learn a language was to speak it colloquially as a young child.

His mention of the need to acquire the skill of swimming was a rare digression from his main theme that the purpose of exercise was health. He did, however, undertake to discuss those activities which were then commonly accepted as part of a future gentleman's education. "Besides what is to be had from Study and Books, there are other *Accomplishments* necessary for a Gentleman, to be got by Exercise, and to which Time is to be allowed, and for which Masters must be had." (214:174) Of dancing he said:

> *Dancing* being that which gives *graceful Motions* all the Life, and above all things Manliness, and a becoming Confidence to young Children, I think it cannot be learned too early, after they are once of an Age and Strength capable of it. But you must be sure to have a good Master, that knows, and can teach, what is graceful and becoming, and what gives a Freedom and Easiness to all the Motions of the Body. (214:174)

Similarly, he regarded fencing and riding as essential adjuncts to a gentleman's education, though he was personally interested only in their health benefits:

> *Fencing*, and *Riding the Great Horse*, are looked upon so necessary Parts of Breeding, that it would be thought a great *Omission* to neglect them; the latter of the two being for the most part to be learned only in great Towns, is one of the best Exercises for Health, which is to be had in those places of Ease and Luxury: And upon that Account makes a fit Part of a young Gentleman's Employment during his Abode there. And as far as it conduces to give a Man a firm and graceful seat on horseback, and to make him able to teach his Horse to stop and turn quick, and to rest on his Haunches, is of use to a Gentleman both in Peace and War. But whether it be of moment enough to be made a Business of, and deserve to take up more of his Time than should barely for his Health be employed at due Intervals in some such vigorous Exercise, I shall leave to the Discretion of Parents and Tutors. . . . (214:175)

> As for *Fencing*, it seems to me a good Exercise for Health, but dangerous to the Life; the Confidence of their Skill being apt to engage in Quarrels those that think they have learned to use their swords. (214:176)

Actually he favored wrestling but recognized the cultural benefit of knowing how to fence and ride:

> I had much rather mine should be a good *Wrestler* than an ordinary Fencer, which is the most a Gentleman can attain to in it, unless he will be constantly in the Fencing-School and every Day exercising. But since Fencing and Riding the Great Horse are so generally looked upon as necessary Qualifications in the breeding of a Gentleman, it will be hard wholly to deny any one of the Rank these Marks of Distinction. (214:176)

But despite his preoccupation with the education of a gentleman* his

---

* He wrote a separate work on the education of poor children called *Working Schools*, which was in part responsible for the establishment of the awful British workhouses that Dickens later attacked so vividly.

overriding concern was that "Due Care being had to keep the Body in Strength and Vigour, so that it may be able to obey and execute the Orders of the *Mind.* . . ." (214:20)

Locke advocated one other principle of specific interest to physical educators:

> *Recreation* is as necessary as Labour or Food. But because there can be no *Recreation* without Delight, which depends not always on Reason, but oftner on Fancy, it must be permitted Children not only to divert themselves, but to do it after their own Fashion, provided it be innocently, and without Prejudice to their Health; and therefore in this Case they should not be deny'd, if they proposed any particular kind of *Recreation.* (214:87)

Recreation was a serious business meant to relieve the monotony of one's usual activities; he thought that ideally recreational pursuits should be useful and "produce what will afterwards be profitable." (214:180) "For you must never think them set right, till they can find Delight in the Practice of laudable Things; and the useful Exercises of the Body and Mind, taking their Turns, make their lives and Improvement pleasant in a continu'd train of *Recreations*, wherein the weary'd Part is constantly reliev'd and refresh'd." (214:88) He also said that "recreation belongs not to People who are Strangers to Business, and are not wasted and wearied with the Employment of their Calling." (214:180)

Locke's interest in education and in health stem in part from the activities of his life. Born in Wrington in Somerset in 1632, he came from a middle class family. His lawyer father supervised his education until the age of fourteen when he was sent to the Westminster School, where Latin, Hebrew, Greek, and Arabic were the chief studies. Like Montaigne he noted how quickly such learning is forgotten and his essay on education reflected his belief that an empirical method of education would be of better use in preparation for life. At twenty he took a Junior Studentship at Christ Church, Oxford; in 1656 he received his Bachelor's degree and later also completed his Master's Degree. He became Tutor of his college and the College Reader in Greek and in Rhetoric and in 1664, Censor of Moral Philosophy. He began the study of medicine and occasionally practiced it, although he never formally completed his degree. It was the practice of medicine, though, that originally won him an appointment with Lord Ashley, later the Earl of Shaftesbury, whom he served for many years as physician, secretary and advisor, as well as overseer of the education of his sons and grandson. Shaftesbury, deeply involved in the political revolution then taking place in England, drew Locke into politics. When, as Lord Chancellor, Shaftesbury fell from power in 1675, Locke withdrew to France where the warm climate enabled him to nurse his bronchial condition; he returned when the Earl's fortunes improved and he became the Lord President. However, in that time of plots and counterplots, the overthrow of James II forced both Locke and Shaftesbury to flee to Holland where the Earl soon died and Locke remained in exile for six years.   Locke was born in a time of great national turmoil:   the struggle between Parliament and King Charles I, which began only ten years after Locke's birth, ended in the king's being beheaded (1649) while Locke was still at Westminster School.   During Locke's Oxford days Cromwell controlled England, followed by the Restoration kings, until finally in 1689 William and Mary of Orange began their joint reign.   Locke's *Two Treatises of Government* at once justified the Glorious Revolution of 1688 and helped establish the throne.   Parliamentary supremacy clearly won, England finally achieved stability, and Locke was able to settle down in the home of the writer Ralph Cudworth, with whom he lived until his death in 1704.   During these later years he held offices such as Commissioner of Appeals, and membership in the new Council of Trade and Plantations, thus continuing his interest in politics.

Locke was an unusual man in that he earned a reputation in several fields:   as a philosopher his ideas "exercised undisputed sway over the ideas of the entire eighteenth century" (16:30); as an educator he was considered one of the great writers and reformers; as an author his works were considered exceptionally well-written, though sometimes inconsistent; as a politician, his influence extended even to the framing of the American Declaration of Independence and Constitution which incorporated his idea that government was instituted to protect the natural rights of individuals, particularly life, liberty and property.

His ideas on the development of the healthy body as a primary function of education, and his dualistic separation of the mind and body were concepts of great influence in the thinking of physical educators.   In fact, the phrase "a sound mind in a sound body" became the motto of physical education, where it remained supreme until twentieth-century psychology irrevocably demonstrated the unity of mind and body.

# JEAN JACQUES ROUSSEAU

## 1712-1788

In 1762 Rousseau's *Émile* was published. In the same year it was condemned by the parlement of Paris and the Archbishop of Paris who forbade its being read:

> We condemn the said book as containing an abominal doctrine, ready to subvert natural law and to destroy the foundations of the Christian religion, setting up maxims contrary to the morality of the Gospels; tending to trouble the peace of states, to cause subjects to revolt against their sovereigns. (36:586)

This was an amazing reaction to a book which was a greatly exaggerated, sometimes fanciful, romantic work; moreover, its main ideas on educational reform had already been expressed in England by John Locke.

Rousseau had evidently studied Locke; he made frequent references to him such as "Locke's great maxim was to reason with children . . ." (309:95), or "Locke . . . falls into a contradiction . . ." (309:124) because he advised against drinking cold water when warm, which is contrary to the *natural* desire to do so. But where Locke's work was a closely reasoned, formally written essay by a respected philosopher whose own status as a gentleman helped him to structure *reform* around the needs of a society whose continuation he desired, Rousseau's was a passionate condemnation of his society, with the aim not of reform but of *revolution*. One of the most famous passages in *Émile* is its opening in which he launched his attack on civilization with the declaration:

> Everything is good as it comes from the hands of the Creator; everything degenerates in the hands of man. He compels one soil to nourish the products of another and one tree to bear the fruits of another; he mingles and confounds elements, climates, and seasons; he mutilates his horses, dogs, and slaves; he defaces everything, he reverses everything; he delights in deformity and monsters. He is not content with anything as Nature made it, not even his fellow-man. Even his offspring must be trained up for him like a horse in his stable, and must grow after his fancy like a tree in his garden. (309:55)

The eighteenth century was an era of contradictions. On the one hand Europe was swept by the rise of empirical science, and by the writings of Galileo, Bacon, Descartes, Newton, and the English philosophers John Locke and Thomas Hobbes. Eighteenth-century France had its own group of *philosophes* such as Voltaire, Diderot, Montesquieu, and Condorcet, all of whom were formulating new social theories which redefined the traditional role of kings, parliaments and citizens. On the other hand in France the actual social and educational structures had remained, to a large extent, unchanged. France was still a Catholic country; the power of the monarchy and clergy and, by extension, the noble class was undiminished; the educational curriculum in most secondary schools and colleges was under the control of the Jesuits and consisted of classical Latin and Greek, plus orthodox religion, taught in a strictly disciplined atmosphere. On Jesuit education Rousseau commented: "We are still further mistaken in wishing to make them attend to considerations which can in no degree affect them, such as their future interest, or their happiness and reputation when they grow to manhood. . . . Thus all the studies which are imposed on these poor unfortunates relate to aims entirely foreign to their minds." (309:110) "True education lies less in knowing than in doing." (309:63) *Émile* was not Rousseau's only "revolutionary" work. Like the other social critics of his time, he sought to rally the populace against the established order, apparently convinced that new ideas could flourish only in a society radically different from his own. Their success, of course, was evident in the French Revolution that took place in 1789, which resulted in the founding of the First Republic. But Rousseau's books were burned, the order for his arrest issued, and his last years spent fleeing from place to place to avoid persecution.

Fig. 14.   Jean Jacques Rousseau.

Rousseau was born in 1712 in Geneva, Switzerland. His Swiss mother died a week later and he was alternately spoiled and neglected by his French father who finally abandoned him completely at the age of ten. He was taught by his father to read, and his early education consisted of his reading everything from Plutarch and Ovid to trashy romantic novels. An uncle who cared for him entrusted his education to the Pastor of Boissy under whom he "completed" his elementary studies. He was apprenticed first to a notary and then an engraver, but in both instances he failed, ran away, and finally became the lover of an older woman, Madame de Warens, who encouraged him to study literature and philosophy. For the next twenty years he wandered; he became a Catholic and studied for the priesthood; he held various jobs such as a lackey, a secretary and a tutor; he learned to know the miseries of the peasants—an understanding which in large part influenced the direction of his social theories. In 1741 he went to Paris, became friendly with the leaders of the Enlightenment (e.g. Voltaire, next to whom his body now lies in the Panthéon in Paris), and lived with Thérèse Le Vasseur, by whom he had five children, all of whom were placed in a foundling home where their lack of education destined them to become workers and peasants.

After this inauspicious beginning, in 1749 he entered and won a contest sponsored by the Academy of Dijon for the best essay on the subject "Has the Progress of the Arts and Sciences Contributed to Corrupt or Purify Morals?" In this essay which first set forth his ideas on the corrupting influence of civilization, he formulated a hypothetical prayer for men of the future to utter: "Almighty God! Thou who holdest in Thy hand the minds of men, deliver us from the fatal arts and sciences of our forefathers; give us back ignorance, innocence and poverty, which alone can make us happy and precious in Thy sight." (257:229)

A second essay written in 1755, *Discourse on the Origin of Inequality*, like his *Discourse on the Arts and Sciences*, continued and expanded the theme by condemning the artificiality and evil of social inequality as the inevitable result of civilization's development. During this time, at Diderot's request, he wrote a *Discourse on Political Economy* which appeared as a chapter in the *Encyclopédie* in 1755.

Then he worked on *Julie or The New Héloïse* (after Héloïse and Abélard) which prefaced *Émile* in describing the early education of children by a wise parent in total isolation, away from the corrupting influences of eighteenth-century society. In this work the heroine (mother) emphasized that "the duty with which I am charged is not the education of my sons but to prepare them to be educated." (309:46) The child is only prepared for education because "reason begins to develop only after some years, when the body has reached a certain stage of development. Nature's intention is to strengthen the body before exercising the mind." (309:28)

Along with *Nouvelle Héloïse*, which appeared in 1761, Rousseau worked on *The Social Contract* which was published in 1762 and is still regarded as a classic statement of the contract theory of government. This work, which was one of the single greatest literary influences on the French Revolution, was predicated on the belief that the will of the people, bound loosely together in a "general will" (social contract) is the basis of society. Its opening words were a clarion call against existing conditions: "Man is born free, yet everywhere he is in chains." Like Locke's *Two Treatises of Civil Government*, *The Social Contract* strongly influenced the formulation of democracy, especially the framing of the documents of the American Revolution.

*Émile*, also published in 1762, was Rousseau's specific treatise on education. But all three works, written in the same period, must be considered together, because if *The Social Contract* dealt with an ideal social structure, Julie and her family and Émile with his tutor were to live and be educated as *individuals* in that society. The chief difference between Locke and Rousseau was the former's formulation of the education of a citizen, contrasted with the latter's education of an individual. Locke's citizens did their duty in society; Rousseau's society was an expression of the individual who grew up in perfect freedom. *Émile*, therefore, should probably be studied only in the context of *The Social Contract* because that was the kind of social structure in which he could have flourished.

In general, *Émile* was a straightforward description of the education Rousseau deemed ideal for both boys and girls (the last section is about the education of the ideal girl: Sophie). It was divided into periods beginning with children under five, and continuing until after fifteen. The idea of a continuous education from birth to adulthood was unusual and was one of Rousseau's real contributions to educational theory. "We begin to learn when we begin to live; education commences with life, the nurse is the first teacher." (309:63) "The education of man begins at birth; before he can speak, before he can understand, he is already learning. Experience anticipates lessons. . . ." (309:79) He stressed the value of free physical activity during this early education:

> Children are always in motion; quiet and meditation are their aversion; a studious or sedentary life is injurious to their health and growth; neither their minds nor their bodies can bear constraint. Always confined in a room with books, they lose all their vigour; they become frail, delicate, and unhealthy, stupid rather than reasonable: their minds suffer all their lives from the enfeeblement of their bodies. (309:28)

> .    .    .    .    .    .    .    .    .    .    .    .

> The body should be vigorous, in order to obey the mind, just as a good servant should be robust. . . . The feebler the body, the more it rules: the stronger, the more it obeys. The sensual passions all lodge in effeminate bodies. (309:76)

He advocated that children be sent to live in the country. "Cities are the graves of mankind . . . . Send your children therefore to renew their

4

strength in the country, and to recover in the open fields that vigour which is lost in the unwholesome air of popular cities." (309:77)

Besides developing physical strength during these early years, the child should have sense experiences:

> His sensations are the raw material of his ideas; by supplying sensations in the right order we therefore prepare his memory to present them in the same order to his understanding. . . . He wants to touch and handle everything which he sees: do not check this restlessness. . . . It is by movement that we discover the existence of external objects, and by our own movements that we acquire the idea of extension. (309:81–82)

As the child grows older, Rousseau specifically wished to train the senses through physical activities, as well as through drawing and music. "It is only by walking, touching, counting, and marking the dimensions of objects, that we learn to make estimates of them. . . ." (309:132) He made it clear that his encouragement of physical activities for the growing child was for benefits derived from participation other than strength:

> Some exercises are purely physical and mechanical; they serve to strengthen the body, without taking the least hold of the judgement; such are swimming, running, jumping, whipping a top, or throwing stones. These are excellent; but have we only arms and legs? . . . Exercise therefore, not only your strength, but all the senses which direct it; make the best possible use of each, and let the impressions of one confirm those of another. (309:127)
>
> When a child plays at battledore and shuttlecock, he exercises his eyes and arms; when he whips a top, he acquires strength by exerting it; but in neither case does he learn anything. I have often asked why children are not encouraged to play the same games of skill as men, such as tennis, fives, billiards, archery, and football, or to play on musical instruments. . . . To spring from one side of a tennis-court to the other, to judge of the rebound of a ball while it is still in the air, and to return it with a sure and steady arm—these are not so much games for the amusement of men as means to make men. (309:137–138)

He believed that "the more his body is exercised, the more is his mind enlightened; his mental and bodily powers advance together, and mutually improve each other." (309:123) This must be so because as the child "is perpetually in motion, he is obliged to observe much and to note a variety of effects; he acquires an early and extensive experience, though his lessons come from Nature and not from men." (309:123) He also hoped that "by accustoming my pupil to bodily exercise and manual work, I insensibly give him a taste for reflexion and meditation. . . . The great secret of education is always to make mental and bodily exercise serve as a relaxation to each other." (309:172) It was this principle of relaxation that probably led to his statement that "the exercises of which I approve must not be confounded with those of an ancient gymnasium. The latter constituted a regular occupation, almost a trade; ours should be only a relaxation, a holiday. . . ." (309:70)

In one of his lesser quoted works, *Treatise on the Government of Poland*, written in 1772 but not published until after his death, he urged the development of Polish nationalism as a solution for the nation's disunity and emphasized the use of games to build character, cooperation and competition:

> A gymnasium for physical exercise should be established in every college. This neglected side of education is, I hold, its most important branch, not only as the basis of a sound and healthy physique, but still more as a training of character. . . . The very fact that they enjoy them will make them beneficial outside the purely physical sphere.
>
> They should not be allowed to play separately according to their fancy, but all together and in public, so that they always have a common aim involving cooperation and competition . . . for the function of games is not merely to occupy children, and to give them a strong physique or free and agile movements, but to accustom them early to discipline, equality, fraternity, and co-operation. . . . (309:66–67)

One last point of interest was made by Rousseau in his description of the education of girls. Although he thought both sexes should receive physical training, the purposes of such education, he admitted, were different: "This priority of bodily training is common to both sexes, but it is directed to a different object. In the case of boys the object is to develop strength, in the case of girls to bring out their charms. . . . Women need enough strength to act gracefully, men enough skill to act easily." (309:221)

Rousseau enjoined the parents to bring up their child "healthy, to make him reasonable and wise." (309:122) A child's physical training should include attention to developing a strong body; training the senses through physical activity; providing good nourishment, fresh air, loose clothing, and frequent baths, all in nature and away from the unwholesome cities; and developing a taste for the relaxing recreational effects of activity as well as a spirit of cooperation through group games.

Although Rousseau's ideas were actually banned in France until after the Revolution which he never lived to see (he died in 1788), they were eagerly accepted by the Prussians who were in the process of trying to reform their schools. The whole philanthropic movement, known especially to physical educators because of the work of Basedow and Guts Muths, was founded on Rousseau's theories. Later reformers such as Pestalozzi, Froebel and Herbart were directly influenced and stimulated by him. American physical education, especially the "new physical education" of Thomas Wood (refer to p. 377), had some of its philosophic roots in Rousseauian naturalism. (113) In addition, his political theories have been credited with being the spark that ignited the French revolution.

Rousseau helped to set off two revolutions—one political and the other educational. Although his ideas may not have been eminently practical and no one may actually have attempted to educate children in the image of Émile, the noble savage, nevertheless his focus on the individual and his will—even the child and his desires—which previously had been almost universally disregarded, was an enormous innovation in the western world.

# THE PHILANTHROPINUM

Founded in 1774 by Johann Bernhard Basedow, the Philanthropinum had the distinction of being the first of the neo-humanist schools developed upon the principles outlined by Rousseau in *Émile*. The humanist schools had become artificial and narrow attempts to assimilate a dead culture by imitation rather than by inspiration. The seventeenth-century "age of reason," with its scientific spirit, was followed by the eighteenth-century "age of enlightenment," with its clear intellectual power and love of truth. German intellectuals were searching for a means to establish a new aristocracy of worth in a country which was still a collection of small states lacking any national leadership and heavily influenced by French writers, philosophers and fashions. *Émile*, in fact, was more influential in Germany than in France because its doctrine of the dignity of man and the rightness of nature provided a rallying point for a new national feeling. Thus in 1768 when Basedow wrote an *Address to Philanthropists and Men of Property on Schools and Studies and Their Influence on the Public Weal*, delineating a plan for a non-sectarian school which put Rousseau's ideas into practice, it was enthusiastically received and financial support was readily made available. The Duke of Anhalt, Prince Leopold Franz, invited Basedow to Dessau where he opened his private academy and named it the Philanthropinum, although it later became known as the Dessau Educational Institute.

Basedow (1723–1790) was an experienced and educated pedagogue. The son of a wigmaker, he attended school in his native Hamburg and later studied theology in Leipzig. After working as a private tutor, he was for eight years professor of moral philosophy and belles-lettres in the school for young noblemen (Ritterakademie) at Soröe, Denmark. The Ritterakademie, in the tradition of the sixteenth and seventeenth centuries, had teachers not only for literary studies but for riding, fencing, dancing, gymnastics, and even a special teacher of various ball games. Thus Basedow observed at first hand a school in which physical and mental training were combined. After leaving Soröe he taught for seven years in Altona, near Hamburg, during which time Rousseau's *Émile* was published (1762).

In the six years following his resignation from Altona he must have devoted his time to studying educational methodology for coincidental with the opening of the Philanthropinum, he published two books on teaching. The *Book of Method for Fathers and Mothers of Families and of Nations* out-

Fig. 15.    Johann Bernhard Basedow.

lined a plan of education for boys and girls. Combining the ideas of Bacon, Comenius and Rousseau, he advocated following nature, learning through the senses, learning languages by a natural (conversational) method, using natural objects to learn, and dealing with children as children. The latter was a real innovation since children were usually treated as young adults; they dressed with formal coats, powdered their hair, and wore rouge and swords. Children at the Philanthropinum, however, dressed in sailor-type uniforms which were simple and allowed freedom of movement. The second book, *Das Elementarwerk (The Elementary Work)* was a four-volume work; it included a hundred copper-plate illustrations, by means of which children were to be taught to read more easily and also to gain a knowledge of morals and social usage as well as the scientific subjects. The book was widely used throughout Germany.

Two years later Basedow and three associates started a newspaper stressing the wisdom of Rousseau's principles and their feeling for nature. Basedow's influence was further extended through the number of visitors who went to see his methods in action. In 1776 a public examination of the students was given, before a large audience, with the intention of demonstrating the effectiveness of his teaching methods.*

The Philanthropinum opened in 1774 free from sectarian distinctions; it intended to offer instruction in the natural sciences (geography, natural history, physics), mathematics, Latin, German, French, music, drawing,

---

* A detailed description of the day was published by Herr Schummel of Magdeburg. Entitled *Fred's Journey to Dessau*, it purports to be written by a twelve-year-old boy. Lengthy extracts are published in Quick's *Educational Reformers*. (294: 282–285)

and physical education.  According to its prospectus, five hours a day were to be alloted to studies, three hours to recreation in fencing, riding, dancing, and music, and two hours to manual labor (each student was to learn a handicraft such as carpentry).  Basedow promised that if he had enough students of the proper ages there would be drill in military positions and movements and frequent marches.  He also planned to have the students live in the field in tents for the two summer months, which would make it possible to do hunting, fishing, boating, and swimming.  (207:68)

Although there was widespread interest in the experimental school, Basedow had trouble making it a success.  A year and a half after it opened there were only fifteen children enrolled, including Basedow's daughter, and only three of these were over eight years old.  Basedow himself was an impractical man, described as being coarse, arrogant, argumentative, vulgar in his language, and given to drunkenness.  (84:296)  It is amazing that a school could be entrusted to such a man.  He resigned in 1778 but others succeeded in keeping the school open until 1793.  It apparently reached its greatest fame between 1781 and 1784 when fifty-three students were enrolled from all over Europe.

The physical education of the students was first entrusted to Johann Friedrich Simon who taught there for a year and a half and consequently is regarded by some as the first modern teacher of physical education.  The earliest program consisted of the "knightly exercises" which included weekly lessons in dancing, instruction in fencing for the older boys, six lessons a week in the Duke's private riding-school, and instruction in vaulting the living horse.  Taking into account the youth of his students, Simon introduced what he termed "Greek gymnastics."  These consisted of contests in running, wrestling, throwing, and jumping, similar to the activities of the Greek palaestra.  For the long jumping he used ditches, dug approximately eight feet across the middle, tapering almost to a point at either end.  The student started at whatever width he could clear and gradually worked his way to the middle.  For the high jump two vertical poles about five feet high were set in the ground about two and a half feet apart; wooden pegs were set at any desired height into holes bored at intervals of one inch; a stick resting across the pegs completed the device. Simon also placed a long round beam raised about four feet from the ground, fastened at one end and in the middle, with the smaller end left unsupported.  The students used this "balance beam" by starting at the supported end with assistance (a spotter) and working up to the small, swaying end unassisted.  They also practiced crossing ditches on a narrow plank.  Besides these gymnastic activities the teacher supervised games including shuttlecock, tennis, skittles, and playing with a large, air-filled ball. For the younger children there were also hoops and a seesaw. (207:68–69)

In 1778 Simon was succeeded by Johann Jakob Du Toit who remained at the school until it closed.  Under his direction other varieties of play were added, such as swimming, skating, shooting with the bow and guns, marching in time and playing soldier, hikes into the surrounding country, and walking up the rounds of a ladder set obliquely, without using hands, or swinging from its underside and climbing hand-over-hand. He also devised an exercise in which a teacher counted aloud while students walked carrying bags of sand with their arms stretched out horizontally at the sides; they noted the number at which fatigue caused them to stop and were thus able to measure the daily increase in strength. (207:69)

It is interesting to note that the activities described above were performed outdoors using equipment made, in large part, from natural materials. This was in keeping with Rousseau's "naturalism," which was the guiding spirit of the institution. The flavor of the outdoors added a dimension that could not be sustained when the same activities were brought indoors and performed, as they are today, in a gymnasium. In the setting of the Philanthropinum, jumping seemed so natural that it appeared to be an "instinctive" activity. In the gymnasium, or even outdoors, using metal high jump standards and the latest jumping style the activity appears more artificial and therefore is regarded as less imperative in a program. When the "natural movement" in American physical education faded away into the team sports program, the activities of the Philanthropinum were easily relinquished; only today are they again incorporated in school physical education programs.

Despite the relatively short existence of the Philanthropinum, or Dessau Educational Institute, it was very influential. Interest in educational ideas and experimentation spread throughout Europe, particularly in Germany. Schools such as the Schnepfenthal Educational Institute were modeled after it. In particular, the inclusion of regularly scheduled physical education classes taught by a full-fledged instructor (rather than a specialized master who was not an educator) became an accepted practice. Since Salzmann, the founder of Schnepfenthal, spent three years as an instructor at the Philanthropinum, an immediate and direct succession was established. Basedow might not have been a success as a headmaster of a school, but his educational theories had a profound influence on German education.

# JOHANN HEINRICH PESTALOZZI

## 1746-1827

Of all the educational reformers Johann Heinrich Pestalozzi was the most influential. His school at Yverdon was a place of pilgrimage for educators from all over the world; he was cited from the date of his first writing, *Leonard and Gertrude*; most important, his ideas formed the cornerstone of modern educational theory. He was greatly affected by Rousseau and there are those who believe that to be Rousseau's most enduring accomplishment. In turn he influenced subsequent reformers like Froebel, Herbart and John Dewey; the German physical educator Jahn taught in a Pestalozzi-inspired school. Ballin stated his importance to physical education in an article for *Mind and Body*: "Pestalozzi . . . is one among the first of educators who drew the attention of the world to the necessity of physical training." (27:222)

It was a long road from Zürich, Switzerland, Pestalozzi's birthplace, to the fame of Yverdon. His father, a surgeon, died when he was five years old, and Pestalozzi was brought up by a self-sacrificing mother and a faithful servant. His biographer Guimps described the effect of his childhood: "The boy, puny from his birth, always indoors, brought up entirely by women, deprived of a father's influence, of all contact with boys of his own age, and of outdoor games and interests, remained all his life small and weak, shy and awkward, changeable and impressionable." (134:6) His schoolmates shunned him, dubbing him "Harry Oddity of Foolborough." Although in later life he was successful in working directly with children, he never developed the ability to deal with problems in a practical manner. He attended the reputed Collegium humanitatis in Zürich where, having been inspired by Rousseau's *Social Contract*, he was active in social reform; this resulted in his imprisonment for a short time. At that time he wrote in the *Memorial*, a student publication, that "I would that some one would draw up in a simple manner a few principles of education intelligible to everybody. . . ." (134:14) From his early interest in theology he turned to law and finally to farming, the latter probably due to his interest in the naturalistic movement of Rousseau. As a farmer he was unsuccessful and in 1774 converted his house into an institution for providing poor children with work and education. Within five years he became bankrupt and for eighteen long years lived at Neuhof under conditions of poverty and despair.  During this period he began writing again.  (He had published during his student days.)  *The Evening Hours of a Hermit* appeared in installments in a periodical during 1780, reflecting his belief in the natural capacities of man and the need for unfolding their potential:

> The pure and beneficent powers of mankind are not the gifts of art or of accident.  In our inner nature they lie bound up with our fundamental tendencies and capacities.  Their development is the fundamental need of mankind. . . .
> Nature develops all the powers of mankind through exercise, and their growth results from use. (13:18)

While *Evening Hours* was ignored, *Leonard and Gertrude* published a year later was highly successful.*  This book about a humble peasant woman who transformed the life of her village through her devotion and lofty purpose expressed the essence of Pestalozzi's convictions and made his name known throughout Europe.  In it could be seen his profound knowledge of peasant life and the method whereby its condition could be improved.  The key was education of a unique kind in which knowledge was valuable only if it had a basis in action.  Gertrude's method of instruction was described:

> Although Gertrude thus exerted herself to develop very early the manual dexterity of her children, she was in no haste for them to learn to read and write.  But she took pains to teach them early how to speak; for, as she said, "of what use is it for a person to be able to read and write, if he cannot speak?—since reading and writing are only an artificial sort of speech."  To this end she used to make the children pronounce syllables after her in regular succession. . . . This exercise in correct and distinct articulation was, however, only a subordinate object in her whole scheme of education, which embraced a true comprehension of life itself. . . .
> The instruction she gave them in the rudiments of arithmetic was intimately connected with the realities of life.  She taught them to count the number of steps from one end of the room to the other. . . . Above all, in every occupation of life she taught them an accurate and intelligent observation of common objects and the forces of nature. (13:25–26)

In the next years Pestalozzi continued writing; although he became famous and made the acquaintance of such men as Goethe and Fichte, and was declared a "Citizen of the French Republic," he still lived in great poverty, far from fulfilling his dreams of bettering the world. (294:310)

In 1798 Switzerland was taken by the French who created a unified government under the leadership of five directors.  Since citizens of great towns like Geneva and Zürich, which had prospered under the canton system, were privileged classes, while the rural peasants lived in poverty, Pestalozzi aligned himself with the new government.  He was "rewarded"

---

* Three parts were later added to the first edition but none of these was acclaimed

by being sent to Stans to take charge of children orphaned or made desti-
tute by the war.   He accomplished wonders in the five winter months of
1799 when he was cloistered with them, much of the time in one room.   The
work ended when the French commandeered his building for a hospital.

His next appointment was as schoolmaster of the lowest class in the
school for burghers' children at Burgdorf.   The Burgdorf School Commission gave him his first official commendation:   "By your method of teaching
you have proved how to lay the groundwork of instruction in such a way
that it may afterwards support what is built on it. . . ." (294:335)   In 1800
they made him master of their second school and Pestalozzi established his
celebrated Institute at Burgdorf.   A training class for teachers was added
in 1801 and elementary level teachers were sent there to learn Pestalozzi's
method.   He was highly successful, the President of the Council of Public
Education in Bern declaring that "Pestalozzi has discovered the real and
universal laws of all elementary teaching." (294:342)   However, reaction
to the Government of United Switzerland forced the restoration of the
cantons and the Institute lost its castle.

In 1804 Pestalozzi and his devoted assistants settled in the Castle of
Yverdon near the lake at Neuchâtel and established the most celebrated
institute in the history of education.   In the years at Yverdon Pestalozzi
experimented with his ideas, communicating them in writings and by
spoken word to the numerous visitors, some of whom were quite distinguished, who came to learn with the master.   Students from all over
Europe were sent to study at Yverdon.*   That the school ultimately failed,
torn apart by internal dissension within the ranks of his assistants, was the
mark of Pestalozzi's great weakness.   He was unable to organize and administer, unable to oversee the practical requirements of a situation.   Perhaps it was recognition of his own difficulties that led him to place such an
emphasis upon this aspect of education.   In 1825 he was forced to leave
Yverdon.   The last two years of his life were spent in Neuhof where half a
century earlier he had begun his task of transforming education.

In the years following the publication of *Leonard and Gertrude* Pestalozzi
explicated his theories in several other works, none of which achieved the
popularity of the first because of their more direct, de-fictionalized accounts
of educational method.   The most important of these was *How Gertrude
Teaches Her Children* (1800) in which he enunciated his beliefs: sense impression is the absolute foundation of all knowledge, and therefore children
must be taught to observe accurately; education must proceed from the
simple to the more difficult; the subject matter should correspond in
difficulty to the child's level of development; the child's interest in the
lesson is an indication of his ability to understand at that level; the objects
of sense impression call forth the exercises of judgment and skill, and

---

* The most complete account in English of this important and interesting school
may be found in Guimps (134), Chapters XIII–XV.

FIG. 16.    Pestalozzi and His Students.

exercising the natural capacities is a central purpose of education.   This
was his version of psychologizing the instruction of mankind.   One paragraph in the work stated the heart of his theory:

> The purpose of leading men, with psychological art and according to the laws
> of their physical mechanism, to clear ideas, and to their expression, definitions,
> demands a gradation of statements about the physical world before definitions.
> This gradation proceeds from sense-impressions of separate objects to their names,
> from their names to determining their characteristics, that is the power of describ-
> ing; and from the power of describing to the power of *specializing*, that is, of
> defining.   Wisdom in guiding sense-impression is obviously the beginning-point
> on which this chain of means for attaining clear ideas must depend; and it is
> obvious that the final fruit, the end of all instruction, the clearness of all ideas,
> depends essentially on the complete power of its first germination. (13:76)

Intellectual education, according to Pestalozzi, was one of three basic
aspects of education, the other two being moral and practical.   Moral education was the foundation of the other aspects; all were essential but it was
the most important.   To Pestalozzi it was bound up with religion and the
mother whom he regarded as the child's first teacher:

Moral education is nothing more than the simple development of the human will through the higher feelings of love, of gratitude, and of trust in the ideal of perfection as these feelings reveal themselves in their first emergence from the pure relationship between mother and child. The aim of this education is perfection in thinking, feeling, and action. (167:62)

Pestalozzi's views on practical education were most significant to physical education. In general, he shared Fellenberg's views* on the necessity of coordinating vocational training with education. From his first experience at Neuhof Pestalozzi was convinced that education to manhood, the development of the capacities of the whole human being, must include agriculture, domestic training and industry with a "commensurate cultivation of the head and the heart." (13:102) Thus he promoted development of the physical capacities of man through physical labor. However, he believed in the importance of gymnastic and game experiences as well. He specified that the aim of gymnastic exercises "is to bring back the body of the child into the full unity and harmony with his intellect and heart which originally existed." (167:66) He perceived several advantages accruing to physical education besides the development of strength and dexterity:

If the physical advantage of gymnastics is great and uncontrovertible, I would contend that the moral advantage resulting from them is as valuable. I would again appeal to your own observation. You have seen a number of schools in Germany and Switzerland of which gymnastics formed a leading feature; and I recollect that in our conversations on the subject you made the remark, which exactly agrees with my own experience, that gymnastics, well conducted, essentially contributes not only to render children cheerful and healthy, which for moral education are two all-important points, but also to promote among them a certain spirit of union and brotherly feeling which is most gratifying to the observer: habits of industry, openness and frankness of character, personal courage, and a manly conduct in suffering pain, are also among the natural and constant consequences of an early and a continued practice of exercises on the gymnastic system. (13:172)

.   .   .   .   .   .   .   .   .   .   .   .

But the greatest advantage resulting from a practice of those exercises is the natural progress which is observed in the arrangement of them, beginning with those which while they are easy in themselves yet lead as a preparatory practice to others which are more complicated and more difficult. There is not perhaps any art in which it may be so clearly shown that energies which appear to be

---

* Phillip Emanuel von Fellenberg's school at Hofwyl was a prototype of the manual-labor school. It combined academic pursuits with agriculture and later extended its subjects to printing, lithography, handicrafts, and other mechanical skills. Its curriculum brought together in one institution children of all classes. Fellenberg's ideas were very popular in America and an important influence on American education for about two decades, 1820–1840. For a brief period in 1804 Pestalozzi joined forces with Fellenberg at Hofwyl but their personalities clashed and they could not endure a working relationship.

wanting are to be produced, as it were, or at least are to be developed by no other means than practice alone. (13:170)

. . . . . . . . . . . . . . . . . .

Physical education ought by no means be confined to those exercises which now receive the domination of gymnastics. By means of them strength and dexterity will be acquired in the use of the limbs in general; but particular exercises ought to be devised for the practice of all the senses. (13:172)

To accomplish these purposes was the responsibility, first of all, of the mother: "I consider it essential that mothers should make themselves acquainted with the principles of gymnastics, in order that among the elementary and preparatory exercises they may be able to select those which according to circumstances will be most likely to suit and benefit their children." (13:171)

He did not believe that mothers did this, particularly the rich who had the leisure time. If one physical skill was practiced it was to the neglect of the others: "Nothing is more common in higher society than the dancer who cannot even walk properly, equestrians who cannot swim, fencers who cannot fell a tree with an axe." (167:66)

Practicing what he preached, he included physical exercise in the Yverdon program. In fact, gymnastics was actually a part of the daily lessons and a great deal of time was allotted to playing Prisoner's Base and other games. Hiking, swimming, sledging, and skating were popular activities and there were dancing and fencing lessons for children whose parents desired it. Military drill was also practiced. In a report on the Institute made on the basis of a six-day inspection in 1809, Father Girad of Fribourg described the graded series of exercises which they had attempted to work out:

The institute pays special attention to physical exercise and has also established its own elementary gymnastics according to certain principles. They begin with the head which the boys move in various directions; then, in order, come the arms, the feet, and finally the whole body. The essential aim here is to proceed from the simplest movements to the most complicated without missing any out. (167:68)

The kind of physical education done at Yverdon under the direction of Pestalozzi was not particularly well-developed or unique. What was accomplished at Basedow's Philanthropinum was far advanced. The significance of the work at Yverdon lies in its connection with the great educational reformer. Founding new theories of education which influenced both the new and old worlds, he included as part of the course of study, gymnastic exercises. Pestalozzi's "imprimatur" gave an important impetus to the general progress of physical education as a school subject which has a part in the fulfillment of educational goals.

# FRIEDRICH FROEBEL

## 1782-1852

Comenius, Rousseau, Pestalozzi, and Friedrich Froebel had a singularly important life circumstance in common: the loss of one or both parents in early childhood and, except for Pestalozzi,* the subsequent neglect by the other. Their early formal education was therefore irregular, but more important, their early lives were lacking in normal affection and security and each developed into a rather lonely, introspective child. The life of Comenius, perhaps sustained by his early developed faith and membership in the Moravian Brethren, was earlier and more clearly focused than the lives of the other three "reformers," all of whom tried numerous vocations before accidentally discovering their proper roles in life. Each then became famous for his educational theories, but lived a life marked by great practical difficulties, especially financial problems. Rousseau was infamous for his despicable personality, while the others were known to be loving and generous; ironically it was Rousseau whose activities had the most immediate and direct effect (through the French Revolution) of ameliorating the lives of the poor classes. The theories of Pestalozzi and Froebel were of unparalleled importance to modern education—especially in the nineteenth and early twentieth century—but both, although wholly successful when able to work alone and on a personal level with their students, were equally unsuccessful as organizers and administrators of a new educational system. The life parallels of all four are striking and it is tempting to think that their childhoods sensitized them to the needs of youths and to the great importance of early experiences; certainly the three schoolmasters lavished on their students the kind of love they lacked and for which they must have yearned.

In Froebel's *Autobiography*, written in 1827 as an unsent letter to the Duke of Meiningen, he commented on another aspect of his early life which probably had great influence on the development of his educational theories:

> Deeply humiliating to me were the frequent slights I received in our play, arising from my being behind boys of my age in bodily strength, and more especially in agility; and all my dash and daring could not replace the robust,

---

* Pestalozzi enjoyed the loving care of his mother and servant, but lacked the identification with a father.

steady strength, and the confident sureness of aim which my companions possessed. Happy fellows! they had grown up in continual exercise of their youthful boyish strength. I felt myself exceedingly fortunate when I had at length got so far that my schoolfellows could tolerate me as a companion in their games. But whatever I accomplished in this respect by practice, by continual effort of will, and by the natural course of life, I always felt myself physically deficient in contrast with their uncramped boyish powers. (114:18)

Thus in *The Education of Man*, published in 1826, he stressed that:

The plays of childhood are the germinal leaves of all later life. . . . If the child is injured at this period, if the germinal leaves of the future tree of his life are marred at this time, he will only with the greatest difficulty and the utmost effort grow into strong manhood; he will only with the greatest difficulty escape in his further development the stunting effects of the injury or the onesidedness it entails. (115:55–56)

Friedrich Wilhelm August Froebel was born in 1782 in Oberweissback, a village in Thuringia, Germany. His father was pastor of the district and ruled his family in the strict, orthodox Protestant, old-style religious manner. When he was ten Friedrich went to live with his uncle in Stadt-Ilm where life was more relaxed and pleasant. At fifteen, he was apprenticed to a forester, an experience which was unsuccessful except that the sustained time alone in the woods enabled him to develop a communion with nature. Following that were two glorious years at the University of Jena, the center of Germany's intellectual life, where Froebel was influenced by the fruits of the Teutonic Renaissance which produced Goethe, Schiller, Kant, Fichte, Schelling, Hegel, Mozart, and Beethoven, among others. Unfortunately his education there ended with imprisonment for debt. In the next four years he changed locations and vocations at least six times, until in 1805 he arrived in Frankfurt to study architecture. It was there Froebel met Anton Gruner, a disciple of the Swiss educator Pestalozzi, whose methods Gruner was using in the Model School of Frankfurt which he directed. At Gruner's insistence he became a teacher there, and wrote his brother that he had at last found his true calling. However, his life continued to have a wandering quality: after about a year with Gruner, including two weeks spent observing Pestalozzi at Yverdon, he became a private tutor in the manner of Rousseau, living alone in the country with his three charges whom he later took to Yverdon for two years. During this time he "studied the boys' play, the whole series of games in the open air, and learned to recognize their mighty power to awake and to strengthen the intelligence and the soul as well as the body. . . . The games, as I am now fervently assured, formed a mental bath of extraordinary strengthening-power. . . ." (114:82) He attended the Universities of Göttingen and Berlin, supporting himself in Berlin by teaching in Plamann's School where he met Jahn and got caught up in the Teutonic uprising of 1813. He

FIG. 17.   Friedrich Froebel.

enlisted in Baron Von Lützow's corps and became a member of the Black
Hunters, led by Jahn who marvelled at his ability to make wonderful
observations from stones and cobwebs.

The death of his brother in 1816 prompted him to found the Universal
German Institute in Griesheim, in Thuringia, with five nephews as his
students.   About a year later the school was moved to Keilhau, where
Froebel stayed for more than twelve years.   Along with Wilhelm Midden-
dorf and Heinrich Langethal, friends he met during the War of Liberation,
and the former's nephew Barop, who later directed the Keilhau Institute, a
real educational community was established based upon Froebel's ideas.
Although the number of students ultimately increased to sixty, Froebel's
inability as an administrator, coupled with total intransigence, kept the
school in a constant state of financial stress.

In 1826, *The Education of Man* was published.   It attempted to set forth
Froebel's theories on the education of children and reflected the influence
of Kant's "new" philosophy as applied by Schelling and Hegel.   Stressing
the oneness in all things, Froebel sought to have his students come to
appreciate the unity of life through self-activity—observing, discovering,
creating—exercising all the faculties.   "The *school* endeavors to render the
scholar fully conscious of the nature and inner life of things and of himself,
to teach him to know the inner relations of things to one another, to the
human being, to the scholar, and to the living source and conscious unity

of all things—to God." (115:129)  A great deal of time was spent in exploring the natural world, in constructing objects and doing forms of manual labor, as well as in learning lessons with an emphasis on the underlying principles rather than on isolated facts.  At Keilhau, and in the written work, occurred the beginning formulations of his theory of play:

> *Play* is the highest phase of child-development—of human development at this period; for *it is self-active representation of the inner—representation of the inner from inner necessity and impulse.*
>
> Play is the purest, most spiritual activity of man at this stage, and, at the same time, typical of human life as a whole—of the inner hidden natural life in man and all things.  It gives, therefore, joy, freedom, contentment, inner and outer rest, peace with the world.  It holds the sources of all that is good.  A child that plays thoroughly, with self-active determination, perseveringly until physical fatigue forbids, will surely be a thorough, determined man, capable of self-sacrifice for the promotion of the welfare of himself and others.  Is not the most beautiful expression of child-life at this time a playing child? . . .
>
> Play at this time is not trivial, it is highly serious and of deep significance. . . . To the calm, keen vision of one who truly knows human nature, the spontaneous play of the child discloses the future inner life of the man. (115:54–55)

Because Froebel believed in the efficacy of play he advocated that "even the plays of this age should be under special guidance," and he categorized them as "physical plays, either as exercises of strength and dexterity, or as the mere expressions of buoyancy of spirits; sense plays, exercising hearing, sight, etc.; or intellectual plays, exercising reflection and judgement." (115:304)

Two of Froebel's most original and enduring ideas, those on the theory of play and the kindergarten, were fully developed after his leadership at Keilhau was ended.  By 1837, after unsuccessful attempts to found a second Institute, a teacher-training school and an orphanage, all in Switzerland, Froebel had become convinced of the importance of education for very young children.  He opened the first kindergarten in Blankenburg, near Keilhau.  Although the grandiose plans concocted for the place were never realized, it lasted about seven years, during which time children were taught, some teachers were trained, play materials were manufactured, and a printing press produced Froebel's famous *Sunday Journals*.  Some of the essays which appeared in the *Journal* were collected and published in 1861 by Richard Lange in a volume called *Pedagogics of the Kindergarten* (117). In this work Froebel established his theory that play was an essential aspect of the education of young children.  He saw play as a natural expression of life:

> Child's play strengthens the powers both of the soul and the body provided we know how to make *the first occupation* of a child a freely active, that is, a creative or productive one. (186:122)

Therefore, the first voluntary employments of the child, if its bodily needs are satisfied and it feels well and strong, are observation of its surroundings, spontaneous reception of the outer world, and *play, which is independent outward expression of inward action and life.* (117:29, italics added)

Froebel developed the concept of the five gifts, or playthings, to be given the child in a progressive order.* The idea is a fantastic philosophical and symbolic projection of Froebel's deepest understandings. The first plaything is the ball which "has in itself such an extraordinary charm, such a constant attraction for early childhood, as well as for later youth, that it is beyond comparison the first as well as the most important plaything of childhood especially." (117:32) But the ball was not to be conceived of as a mere plaything,

for the ball itself, being the representative of all objects, is the unity and union of the essential properties of all objects. Thus the ball shows contents, mass, matter, space, form, size, and figure; it bears within itself an independent power (elasticity), and hence it has rest and movement, and consequently stability and spontaneity; it offers even color, and at least calls forth sound. . . . Therefore the ball . . . leads to the consideration of the most important phenomena and laws of earth-life and the life of Nature. . . . (117:53–54)

He explained what the child would discover from playing with the first gift:

As the child's first consciousness of self was born of physical opposition to a connection with the external world, so through the play with the ball the external world itself began to rise out of chaos and assume definiteness. In recognizing the ball the child moved from the indefinite to the definite, from the universal to the particular, from mere externality to a self-included, space-filling object. In the ball, especially through the movement, through the opposites of rest and motion, through departing and returning, the object came forth out of general space as a special space-filling object, as a *body*; just as the child, by means of his life, also perceives himself, his corporeal frame, as a space-filling object, as a *body*. . . . He feels and perceives *himself* as *life*; so he may and does perceive the ball at least, outside of himself in motion and as *motion*. (117:171–172)

The ball was placed in still another light when Froebel designated it as "a bond of connection between mother and child . . . in general a bond of connection between the child and Nature. . . ." (117:54) As with each of the other gifts, detailed instructions were presented for use of the plaything in a progressive way. In many ways the writing is similar to modern texts on movement exploration and in fact he has a chapter on "Movement Plays."

The work is unique because of the wide significance Froebel attached to play: "The universal qualities of material objects are thrown into relief. . . .

---

* The second gift was the sphere and the cube. The other three gifts consisted of increasingly complicated divisions of the cube into a series of rectilinear solids, oblong prisms and obliquely divided component cubes. Like the ball, the other geometrical gifts were intended to teach concepts such as space and mass.

In the structure of the ball he recognizes form, size and number in undi-vided unity—a three in one. Thus the ball becomes a key to the child's environment, and a guide to and interpreter of nature both as regards her outer manifestations and her inner life." (117:199) It is because of such ideas that the Froebelian concept of play was such an innovative contribu-tion to the development of physical education. The previously discussed "innovators" noted the value of play for health, or for recreation, or be-cause of the useful skills that could be learned, but Froebel's conception was educatively more extensive and appreciative. In a section of *The Education of Man*, where he talked of cultivating an active, vigorous body, he echoed Plato and Vittorino da Feltre when he said: "Without such cultivation of the body, education can never attain its object, which is perfect human culture." (115:250) But he moved beyond them when he added that "bodily exercises have yet another important side: they lead the human being (here the boy) subsequently to a vivid knowledge of the inner structure of his body; for the boy feels with special vividness the inner mutual connection in the activity of his members." (115:250) Froebel used all aspects of school, including play and exercise, to bring the child to realize the inner and external unity of the world, an understanding he re-garded as the aim of education. Furthermore, he recognized that:

> It is by no means, however, only the physical power that is fed and strengthened in these games; intellectual and moral power, too, is definitely and steadily gained and brought under control. Indeed, a comparison of the relative gains of the mental and of the physical phases would scarcely yield the palm to the body. Justice, moderation, self-control, truthfulness, loyalty, brotherly love, and again strict impartiality—who when he approaches a group of boys engaged in such games could fail to catch the fragrance of these delicious blossomings of the heart and mind, and of a firm will; not to mention the beautiful, though perhaps less fragrant, blossoms of courage, perseverance, resolution, prudence, together with the severe elimination of indolent indulgence? (186:122–123)

His work with the kindergarten continued in the form of lecturing, teaching teachers, founding and writing a *Weekly Journal of Education*, and publishing *Mother Play* in 1844, a book of songs and games for the mother to use with the child; the latter was translated into almost every language and used in kindergartens everywhere. Froebel believed that when students and teachers joined together in the plays and games, the child would begin to understand the world of humanity through self-activity. Like the play with the gifts, the games and songs were meant to be true learning experiences for the children, as well as exercises for develop-ing various parts of the body and the senses.

After Froebel's death in 1852 his disciples carried on his work and helped to establish his concepts of kindergarten and education through self-activity on a worldwide basis. The former idea flourished and developed in the United States and Britain, the first private kindergarten in America being established in Wisconsin in 1855 and the first public one in Saint Louis in 1873.   In Europe where education despite attempted reforms largely remained highly structured and formal, the ideas of kindergarten and self-activity never really had widespread adoption.   In fact, in 1851 the Prussian government, fearing that their "revolutionary" quality was a threat to a stable, organized society, actually banned kindergartens.   But the work of Froebel as a whole was carried on most distinctly by John Dewey who built on his ideas a whole new philosophy of education for the American society.

# JOHN SWETT*

## 1839-1913

The early leadership of John Swett in the field of physical education qualifies him as an innovator, and his subsequent reputation as the "father" of the public school system in California places him in the category of educational protagonists. His most far-reaching contribution to physical education is the 1866 Revised School Law for the state of California, the first law in the nation requiring physical exercise in the schools on a state-wide basis. It represented the culmination of Swett's persistent efforts to secure legislation as the foundation of a public school system. Section 55 of this law, signed by Governor Low on March 24, 1866, stated:

> Instruction shall be given in all grades of schools, and in all classes, during the entire school course, in manners and morals, and the laws of health; and due attention shall be given to such physical exercises for the pupils as may be conducive to health and vigor of body, as well as mind; and to the ventilation and temperature of school rooms. (357:265)

This was a broad requirement which has allowed for a great deal of flexibility in its specific implementation over the more than one hundred years that it has been in effect. In addition, this law gave to a State Board of Education the power to adopt a course of study as well as rules and regulations for all public schools in the state. Physical education was not considered a part of the course of study. However, after a detailed description of the courses for grades one through six, there was a statement concerning "General Exercises" which suggested that the whole school, in a mass, engage in "physical exercises daily, such as free gymnastics and other exercises, according to Lewis' or Watson's handbooks." (357:291) More specific information regarding physical education was given in the Rules and Regulations for the Public School. Section 18 stated that in "all primary schools exercises in free gymnastics and vocal and breathing exercises, shall be given at least twice a day, and for a time not less than five minutes for each exercise." (357:283) These same items regarding physical exercise

---

* The basic research and writing of this section was done by Dr. Barbara J. Hoepner of the University of California at Berkeley.

remained in the law after the new state constitution was adopted in 1879 and can be found in nearly identical wording through 1909.*

The Revised School Law of 1866, written by Swett who was then Superintendent of Public Instruction, was introduced into the California State Senate on February 15, sent to the State Assembly on March 8, and approved within two days. The 1860s was a period in American history when many people were concerned about preparing youth to bear arms; the physical deterioration of youth was an issue of the times. Yet California, in existence as a state only sixteen years, was the only one to pass legislation requiring physical activity in its schools.

That they choose to require gymnastics rather than military drill was at least in part the result of Swett's efforts. In 1862 he had become the Superintendent of Public Instruction for the State of California. A year later, when a resolution was adopted at the Teachers' Institute stating that "the history of the present war has demonstrated the necessity of having military tactics taught in Public Schools wherever it may be found practicable" (293:6), Swett in his official capacity pleaded eloquently for gymnastics rather than military drill:

> Any experienced military man . . . will doubtless declare that the first great requisites for a good soldier . . . are sound health, stamina, activity, and power of endurance. The mere manual and tactics can be learned by the rawest recruits in a few weeks; but muscles of iron and sinews of steel cannot be fastened upon them like knapsacks. We must begin at the foundation with the three millions of boys in the public schools, by training them, during their whole school life, to gymnastic exercises . . . to games of ball, leaping, wrestling, boxing, and all other athletic out door exercises. . . . This war is teaching us some useful lessons at the point of the bayonet, and nothing less effective will ever reach the minds of those who think the sole object of the Public Schools is to teach arithmetic, reading, and writing. (358:111–112)

Whether Swett convinced educators to conduct gymnastic programs rather than military tactics is hard to say; however, there were few instances of military training in the public schools of California in the 1860s.†

---

* It has been believed that this law went out of existence in 1879 when the State Board of Education's authority to create a statewide curriculum was taken away by the new state constitution. However, since physical education was not considered to be part of the "course of study" it was not affected by the constitutional change. The identical wording can be found in 1901, listed as Constitution Article IX, Political Code, Part III, Title III, Chapter III, Article X, Section 1668 (formerly Section 55).

† In 1864 the Massachusetts Legislature was also considering two bills intending to introduce military drill into the public schools. Dio Lewis, author of *The New Gymnastics* (210) was among those who appeared before a committee of the legislature to argue the superiority of gymnastics over drill. The bills were never passed but this issue has arisen in state legislatures throughout the country whenever the nation was at war. The *Proceedings* of the early AAAPE conventions show this topic to have been of great concern to physical educators.

Fig. 18.   John Swett.

Swett's dedication to this cause was remarkable in that he had no partic-ular identification with physical education or sport.   Born on his father's homestead in New Hampshire, he was brought up in Pittsfield, New Hampshire where his father was in charge of a corporation boarding house connected with a cotton factory.   His education in the district school and Pittsfield and Pembroke Academies was meant to prepare him for Dart-mouth College, but a youthful attack of scarlet fever had left him with delicate health and weak eyes.   His only formal higher education consisted of the six months in 1851 in which he attended William Russell's Normal Institute at Reeds Ferry, in New Hampshire.   The next fall he sailed for California to try his luck mining the gold fields and when that proved unsuccessful he became a farm worker, picking vegetables for a living.

In September, 1853 he began his career in California education when he was elected to the position of principal in San Francisco's Rincon School at a salary of fifteen hundred dollars per year.   As a young man attending the Pembroke Academy he had supported himself by teaching in the Buck Street School; he had also taught in the District School No. 1 in West Randolph, Massachusetts but had not planned to make a career in teaching. However, he accepted this opportunity and went on to make education his life's work.   The California public schools of the 1850s consisted of three departments:   primary, intermediate and grammar; the principal taught the highest grades and maintained authority over all the classes in the school.   San Francisco had no high school in the early 1850s and young men sixteen to nineteen years old commonly attended Swett's Rincon Grammar School. (72:6)

In the 1850s the "gymnasium" of the Rincon School consisted of a yard in which were swinging rings, a parallel bar, a rotary swing, oblique ladders, a horizontal ladder, a horizontal bar, and parallels used with a string for "high leaping." For indoor use there were four-pound to ten-pound dumbbells, Indian clubs, calisthenic rods, boxing gloves, and footballs. The precise date of the beginning of the physical education program is obscure, but two newspaper reports of the semi-annual public examination at the Rincon School, held in the spring of 1855, stated that a gymnasium had been added to playgrounds for boys and a piano had been added for the amusement of the girls. Money for the school piano, all the gymnastic apparatus and equipment, and a school library as well, was raised at the annual May Festivals of the Rincon School held at Russ' Gardens in San Francisco, beginning in 1855. The Festival also provided occasions for the students, parents and friends to play games, picnic and dance in celebration of the term examinations.

In the earliest stages of the physical education program, girls devoted recesses to dancing and boys exercised daily in the gymnasium, led by John Swett. His recollections of those days indicate the extensiveness of the program:

> The pleasantest recollections of my earlier years of teaching are connected with gymnastic classes of active boys who could, with me, kick foot-ball, play baseball, lift dumb-bells, swing clubs, climb ladders, vault bars, walk twenty miles on Saturday, and roast a beefsteak on a pointed stick. . . . I know . . . that they think of me, not as a mere schoolmaster, but as the friend who shared their sports and entered into the spirit of their boyhood. (355:28)

He also spoke of his experience in a girls' high school where he became convinced of the value of calisthenics for girls.

In *Methods of Teaching* he described the activities he thought should be part of a physical education program; probably those of the Rincon School were similar:

> In every school, whether in city or country, there should be given a daily drill of five or ten minutes in free gymnastics. Without apparatus and without music, a skillful teacher can secure very good results from what may be termed "free-arm movements," executed by counting in time. To these may be added "breathing exercises," and concert exercises in vocal culture or in singing.
>
> Both wands and dumb-bells can be used in any schoolroom. . . . If there is a piano in the schoolroom, the light gymnastic drill can be made quite varied and thorough with no other appliances. If there is a hall, wooden rings should be added for girls.
>
> For the larger boys, there should be some inexpensive gymnastic appliances in the yard. A movable horizontal bar, a circular swing, hanging rings, parallel bars, iron dumb-bells, and Indian clubs. . . .

> The man who understands boys will either join with them or will encourage and direct them in their games of ball and foot-ball; in skating, coasting, and snowballing; and will take an interest in their games of marbles, in kite-flying, and top-spinning. . . .
>
> The games of the primary children must not be forgotten. By a little attention to the playground, their sports may be regulated and made delightful. Marbles, tops, kites, balls, and hoops are all a part of educational apparatus. (355:28–29)

Conscious of the monotony of drills, he supported the use of play in education and reminded his readers that "school drill is designed not to supersede, but to supplement, the natural games and plays of children." "Teachers should give attention to the encouragement of games, plays, and amusements, in addition to calisthenic drill." (355:26, 24)

John Swett apparently had a strong belief in the value of physical education and its appropriateness as a school activity. It is difficult to know how or why he developed this commitment, but there is some evidence that he became interested through the efforts of Frank Wheeler who had a private gymnasium in San Francisco where Swett sometimes worked out. The *turners* were also active in that city and may have exerted some influence on him. At any rate, as editor of the educational pages of the *The Bookseller*, a monthly advertising journal, Swett stated in the first edition (1860) that one of the purposes of the publication was to "urge the necessity of gymnastic and calisthenic training as a vital element in the education of boys and girls." (353:4) In another issue of this publication Swett made a "Plea for Amusement and Physical Culture" in which he gave further insight into his beliefs concerning the importance of physical education:

> Who can read Miss Beecher's startling array of facts about deformed spines, and round shoulders, and ruinous habits in American boarding schools and not feel the urgent demand for reform? . . . Any education purchased at the expense of health, is a loss . . . too many of the little misses in our schools were never girls. They are simply little old ladies, who never romp, never play, never know anything of the rich sensuous life of a rude country girl. (356:131)

Two underlying positions pervaded his writings. One was a conviction similar to that expressed by the English educational protagonists such as Mulcaster and Locke, that "the best results in intellectual training can be secured only by a correlative physical development." (355:25) Or: "By thinkers and educators the necessity of a trained body as the instrument of a trained mind is fully recognized. . . ." (355:23) His other position, that play is an important part of a child's development and can be a means of his education, was similar to the position of Froebel, whom he often quoted on the subject. In *The Bookseller* Swett pointed out that "the direct lessons of the playground are often more important than the studied teaching of the classroom; and the kind word of social intercourse will be remembered when geography and grammar shall have faded from the mind." (356:133)

John Swett made a significant contribution to the enactment of the first physical education law in the nation. Crucial to his actions was his experience as a principal and teacher and his observations of the young students in his charge. Because of his belief in the importance of legislation for education, his commitment to the necessity of supervised and structured exercise programs, his progressive ideas of the value of play in education, and his opposition to military drill, he gave early and vocal support to the cause of public school physical education programs.

# JOHN DEWEY

## 1859-1952

Probably the single most influential figure in American education, John Dewey was the son of a storekeeper from Burlington, Vermont. After a brief interlude teaching in local schools upon graduation from the University of Vermont, he enrolled in 1882 in the graduate school of Johns Hopkins University. Founded in 1876, Johns Hopkins was the first American institution to be a university in the German tradition of disciplined scholarship and research. Darwinism, empiricism and pragmatism came to power in this school and the long standing tradition of *a priori* philosophy began to fade. Dewey's experience in that exciting milieu; his teaching at the universities of Michigan, Minnesota and Chicago; his leadership of the University of Chicago Laboratory School which he helped found in 1896, and which provided the first real testing ground for his experimental ideas; his twenty-six years (1904–1930) as professor of philosophy at Columbia University—all provided a rich atmosphere for the development of his innovative concepts.

It was during his tenure at the Laboratory School that his first essay on education was written. *My Pedagogic Creed* (89), published in 1897, was a charming and simply written personal manifesto, considered to be a prime force behind the progressive movement. It contained the essential ingredients of his educational philosophy, particularly the idea that the child should view himself from the standpoint of the welfare of the group. Two years later in an attempt to rally support in defense of his Laboratory School (which was considered subversive), he published three lectures under the title *The School and Society*. Translated into almost every European language as well as Arabic and Japanese, these were meant to justify his ideas of social reform through an experimental, child-centered education. But it was *Democracy and Education* (87) published in 1916 when he was well-established at Columbia, that presented his comprehensive philosophy of education. *Experience and Education*, published in 1938, was written to correct some of the misinterpretations and misapplications of progressive education which plagued the movement from the beginning. The full list of his books and articles contains over one thousand titles, including many on political and social situations in which he had a deep interest. As a man he was said to be extraordinarily energetic, unpretentious and quite

Fig. 19.   John Dewey.

absent-minded.   He remained productive until he died in 1952 at the age
of ninety-three.

Dewey's contribution to American philosophy exceeded the bounds of
his influence on educational theory.   An astute student of philosophy, he
believed that ignoring the traditions of the past makes present thinking
thin and empty; therefore he studied earlier thinkers, particularly Kant
(about whom he wrote his doctoral dissertation) and Hegel.   Although
there were exceptions, one of the characteristic features of philosophical
thought prior to the twentieth century was its willingness to consider the
world and its occupants in terms of dichotomies.   For example, there was
God and man, idea and matter, society and government, thought and
action, school and real life, the practical and the theoretical, the natural
and the supernatural, man and animal, work and play, and mind and body.
In this century there has been a movement within all disciplines to regard
the world as a unified whole with seeming disparities on either end of a
single continuum.   As an educator John Dewey helped develop the latter
trend when he evolved a philosophy of unity, of interrelationship, where
action demanded thought (and vice versa) and individuals and society
were indistinguishable; school days were real life for the child; the mind
and the body could under no conditions be expected to act separately.
Dewey fashioned a theory wherein all artificial *distinctions between* things
were replaced by focusing on their *unity*.

His belief in the unity of mind and body had particular importance to physical educators. Preceding philosophers grappled with the problem of connecting mind and body, or intellectual thought with perceptual knowledge. Even William James, the theorist of pragmatism (the philosophy underlying Dewey's educational theories), stated that "the ideal of the well-trained and vigorous body will be maintained neck by neck with that of the well-trained and vigorous mind as the two coequal halves of the higher education for men and women alike." (192:135) Dewey, however, defied this tradition. In *Democracy and Education*, Chapter 25 began with a section called "Continuity *versus* Dualism," in which Dewey described several dualistic concepts espoused by others and commented:

> All of these separations culminate in one between knowing and doing . . . theory and practice, between mind as the end and spirit of action and the body as its organ and means. . . . The advance of physiology and the psychology associated with it have shown the connection of mental activity with that of the nervous system. Too often recognition of connection has stopped short at this point; the older dualism of soul and body has been replaced by that of the brain and the rest of the body. But in fact the nervous system is only a specialized mechanism for keeping all bodily activities working together. (87:336)

He was not content merely to observe the essential unity of man because he thought the dichotomous belief had negative effects:

> It would be impossible to state adequately the evil results which have flowed from this dualism of mind and body, much less to exaggerate them. . . . In part bodily activity becomes an intruder. Having nothing, so it is thought, to do with mental activity, it becomes a distraction, an evil to be contended with. For the pupil has a body, and brings it to school along with the mind. And the body is, of necessity, a wellspring of energy; it has to do something. But its activities, not being utilized in occupation with things which yield significant results, have to be frowned upon. . . . It may be seriously asserted that a chief cause for the remarkable achievements of Greek education was that it was never misled by false notions into an attempted separation of mind and body. (87:141–142)

Dewey's concern that educators understand the importance of the mind-body unity was related to his belief about thought and action:

> No one who has realized the full force of the facts of the connection of knowing with the nervous system and of the nervous system with the readjusting of activity continuously to meet new conditions, will doubt that knowing has to do with reorganizing activity, instead of being something isolated from all activity, complete on its own account. (87:337)

He imposed upon Edward L. Thorndike's basic stimulus-response psychology a concept of mind-body unity that shifted its emphasis from mere empirical stimulus and motor response to *thinking* about both the stimulus and response and placing them into some kind of context or relatedness. "To have an idea of a thing is not just to get certain sensations from it.

It is to be able to respond to the thing in view of its place in an inclusive scheme of action. . . ." (87:30) Thus mind-body unity was essential to thoughtful action which in turn was essential to learning or knowing. "In so far as a physical activity has to be *learned*, it is not merely physical, but is mental, intellectual in quality." (88:68)

This concept of the "whole child" being involved in learning brought a new philosophical respectability to physical education. From Dewey's theory it was reasoned that physical education had a legitimate role in education. The idea developed amongst physical educators, notably Jesse Feiring Williams, that if academic teachers educated the whole child, not just the mind, then the same held true for physical educators. As a direct result emphasis in physical education shifted from caring for the body's health and strength to teaching for the promotion of total educational values.

Dewey also had a direct influence on the formulation of these values. In *My Pedagogic Creed* he said: "I believe that the school is primarily a social institution. Education being a social process . . . in which all those agencies are concentrated that will be most effective in bringing the child to share in the inherited resources of the race, and to use his own powers for social ends." (89:180) If the purpose of physical education were identical with the purpose of education, then Dewey was by extension suggesting new goals for physical education. He dramatized the difference between what he considered to be meaningless physical activity (that is, activity as an end in itself) and an experience in which the emphasis was on the social outcome:

> Suppose that conditions were so arranged that one person automatically caught a ball and then threw it to another person who caught and automatically returned it; and that each so acted without knowing where the ball came from or went to. Clearly, such action would be without point or meaning. It might be physically controlled, but it would not be socially directed. But suppose that each becomes aware of what the other is doing, and becomes interested in the other's action and thereby interested in what he is doing himself as connected with the action of the other. The behavior of each would then be intelligent; and socially intelligent and guided. (87:31)

With these ideas on the social function of education and the inherent role of physical education, the ultimate aim of which was to inculcate students with the social mores of a democratic society.

Dewey's zeal for unification was manifested further in his advocacy of new curricular experiences which combined thought with action. His ideas here did not differ widely from earlier reformers like Froebel, Pestalozzi, and Guts Muths who also believed that the curriculum is best learned by *doing*, rather than by theorizing:

> The knowledge which comes first to persons, and that remains most deeply ingrained, is knowledge of how to do; . . . education, under the influence of a scholastic conception of knowledge which ignores everything but scientifically

formulated facts and truths, fails to recognize that primary or initial subject matter always exists as matters of active doing, involving the use of the body and the handling of material. . . . (87:184)

With this idea he emphasized all sorts of manual training and laboratory experiences in education and devoted an entire chapter to the subject "Play and Work in the Curriculum." In it he noted that,

sometimes, perhaps, plays, games, and constructive occupations are resorted to only for these reasons [making learning easier and management less of a burden], with emphasis upon relief from the tedium and strain of "regular" school work. There is no reason, however, for using them merely as agreeable diversion . . . the grounds for assigning to play and active work a definite place in the curriculum are intellectual and social. . . . (87:194–195)

Another aspect of play's importance was discussed in *Interest and Effort in Education*. (88) One of Dewey's major points was that interest was inextricably necessary to involvement, which in turn was essential to accomplishment. "If we can secure interest in a given set of facts or ideas, we may be perfectly sure that the pupil will direct his energies toward mastering them. . . ." (88:1) He cited play as fundamentally connected to interest because it is *self-activity*, i.e. it requires certain tendencies, habits and powers to be activated, and if carried to a particular result brings self-satisfaction. More than thirty-five years before Johann Huizinga wrote *Homo Ludens* (*Man the Player*), Dewey wrote that "It has been said that man is man only as he plays . . . in the broader sense of whole-hearted identification with what one is doing—in the sense of completeness of interest, it is so true that it should be a truism." (88:80)

Dewey also helped to combat the notion that play was a waste of time by showing that in play, like work, there is meaningful purpose and therefore education can use play to bring about desired ends.

When an activity is its own end in the sense that the action *of the moment* is complete in itself, it is purely physical; it has no meaning . . . play has an end in the sense of a directing idea which gives point to the successive acts. Persons who play are not just doing something (pure physical movement); they are trying to do or effect something. . . . There are definite results which even young children desire, and try to bring to pass. (87:202–203)

Dewey's *direct* influence on physical education was in his concepts of mind-body unity, the value of play, and the use of activity to further the socialization of the child.* But his influence on education has been so pervasive and his writings so numerous and detailed, that he also has had a

---

* Larkin's study which attempted to examine "The Influence of John Dewey on Physical Education," was completed as early as 1936. (202)

strong indirect influence.    The whole climate of American education changed with the advent of Dewey's philosophy.    The growth of pragmatism as an "American philosophy" can in part be attributed to its enduring presence in the school systems of the country.    It will probably be at least another century before the effect of this innovator can be fully analyzed and understood.

# PART V

*European Physical Educators and Institutions*

*GERMAN*

# JOHANN CHRISTOPH FRIEDRICH GUTS MUTHS

## 1759-1839

In 1786, at the age of twenty-seven, Johann Christoph Friedrich Guts Muths assumed responsibilities as an instructor of children enrolled in the Schnepfenthal Educational Institute. He continued teaching there for over fifty years during which time his work as a gymnastics teacher and his many writings on the subject earned him a considerable reputation. Because he was the first physical educator to devote his life to teaching and writing about the subject, some authors have termed him the "grandfather of physical education," reserving the title "father" for Jahn, whose influence on the development of European physical education was also very strong. In this century, American physical education programs and methods have more closely resembled the natural program of Guts Muths than the formal gymnastics of Jahn; thus his contribution has extended far beyond his own time and place.

Guts Muths was born in the ancient Prussian town of Quedlinburg, the son of a tanner. His family possessed a "library" of three great books: a Bible, a geography and the *Acerra Philologica*, a work written in German containing hundreds of selections from the writings of famous Greek and Latin authors. It is possible that he got his first knowledge of the ancient gymnastics from reading these authors. However, his education was not dependent upon these three works for he attended the gymnasium (secondary school) in Quedlinburg and later the University of Halle where he studied theology, mathematics, physics, and modern languages, the usual curriculum of the time.

Compulsory state schools were not then to be found in Prussia, although in 1763 King Frederick had caused the issuance of General Landschule Reglement (general school regulations for the rural and village schools), which set up standards for the establishment of an elementary school system. In the meantime, those who could afford to hired tutors for their children. In this way, Guts Muths became involved in teaching the children of the town physician, a position he held both before and after his years at the University. In preparation he studied Basedow's *Elementarwerk* and the *Methodenbuch*, at that time the only pedagogical training available for a future teacher.

While Guts Muths was still engaged as a tutor for the Ritter family,

FIG. 20.    Guts Muths and Karl Ritter—Memorial in Quedlinburg.

Salzmann opened Schnepfenthal and about a year later, while visiting the school to enroll one of his tutees, Guts Muths decided to become a teacher there.    Life at Schnepfenthal was apparently pleasant for him.    He married a niece of Salzmann's wife and built a small home into a large estate noted for its flowers and fruit.    He spent time in his garden, in woodworking, in hunting and skating, in botany, in painting, in reading and in playing the pianoforte; he raised eight sons and three daughters, two of whom presented him, in his lifetime, with six grandchildren.    All this, of course, was in addition to his work as a teacher and writer.    In June, 1835 when he celebrated his golden anniversary at the Institute, he was still an active teacher.    However, he ceased teaching gymnastics, and in March, 1839 retired completely.    He died in May after a brief illness, having lived, by his own accounts, a full and happy life.    His grave was appropriately placed in the burial ground at Schnepfenthal.

As a young teacher at Schnepfenthal, Guts Muths taught various elementary subjects, particularly geography and French.    Gymnastics had been started in the curriculum by Christian Carl Andre who had set up an outdoor area similar to the Philanthropinum at Dessau.    Soon after arriving at Schnepfenthal Guts Muths took over the teaching of gymnastics; he continued Andre's program, modifying and expanding it as he gained experience.    (Refer to chapter on Schnepfenthal for details.)    For every exercise he conducted Guts Muths kept an accurate record of each student's performance in order to understand his needs and progress.    This kind of individualized instruction disappeared in succeeding physical education and has only begun to reappear recently in the United States.

After a while Guts Muths was able to limit his teaching responsibilities to his favorite subjects: gymnastics from 11 A.M. to 12 NOON daily and geography and technology between 2 P.M. and 4 P.M. After 1802, when a swimming pool was constructed, he became the swimming teacher as well. He was also involved with the daily recreation periods (after the midday dinner and in the evening) and conducted the Sunday afternoon games and excursions. He had a particular love for the outdoors and liked to take long hikes with his students, as well as to exercise in the open air.

Although the large number of people visiting Schnepfenthal to study the program testified to his teaching excellence, it was as a writer that Guts Muths excelled and it is because of his written work that his influence was so profound. It has been said that the series of volumes which he produced formed the first teacher training "school" of physical education. This was true not only in Germany but throughout Europe. Preparing to teach, Guts Muths read Basedow; likewise, others who followed read Guts Muths. The most famous of his works on physical activity was *Gymnastik für die Jugend (Gymnastics for Youth)* which, when published in 1793, was the first modern manual on the subject. Seven hundred pages in length, the book included copperplate illustrations of various exercises and a folding sheet with explanatory drawings of apparatus. Some idea of the wide use and influence of this book can be inferred from the number of times and places in which it was published. The first edition was translated and appeared in an altered and condensed version in Denmark in 1799, in England in 1800, and in the United States in 1802. In the latter two editions the work was incorrectly attributed to Salzmann on the title page. It was also published in Holland, Bavaria, France, Sweden, and Austria, although its authorship was not always acknowledged. Phokian Clias, the Swiss physical educator, apparently used it extensively in writing his *Elements of Gymnastics*, which in turn became the basis of Young's Italian manual. Thus *Gymnastik für die Jugend* was studied on two continents, which even exceeded the extent to which Hieronymous Mercurialis' popular book *De Arte Gymnastica* was used. A second edition, so much changed that it was practically a new work, was published in 1804.

Guts Muths was quite concerned about the physical condition of the people. He observed that:

> Few of our young men or youths possess these qualities [strength, dexterity, firmness, and muscularity of body] united. Many are altogether unexercised, and consequently weak and unhandy: some have considerable suppleness of joint, without even moderate strength of body: others display mere inflexible strength. . . . This is still more true of people of the higher classes, because they are more tenderly brought up, and unused to bodily exertion. They are commonly weak, fearful, and agitated, when they have any unusual occurrence to surmount, any unwonted movement to perform, as to run, to lift, to leap, to climb, or the like. (146:57–58)

He placed part of the blame on education where "everything is calculated for the formation of the *mind*, as if we were altogether *without bodies*." (146:9)  He railed at and satirized customs of dress and diet: "He [the child] is muffled up from head to foot; he reposes on a heated feather bed; his diet consists of the complicated dishes, in which adults indulge themselves; prophylactic and cleansing drugs are employed—as the preservatives of his health." (146:7)  He also criticized the social mores which decreed that "health must not be too florid, as a pair of plump rosy cheeks have a rustic appearance.  Can it be believed, that many parents confine their children within doors, lest the wind and the sun should tan their skins?" (146:12–13)  He deplored recreation that took the form of sedentary amusements: "after serious studies, or other sedentary employments, which by degrees cramp the viscera, we recur to novels, cards, and other similar amusements, invented by folly, which exhaust and debilitate anew the tired nerves and relaxed muscles." (146:77)  Furthermore he claimed the situation was totally *unnatural*.  Frequently citing Rousseau, he urged that nature not be disobeyed or "hindered in her endeavours to improve the body." (146:67)  However it was not up to nature alone to develop the body.  "Nature plants the germs of strength, longevity, courage, and firmness, in *us*, no less than she did in our ancestors. . . . In bestowing on us our faculties, Nature has left the improvement of them by exercise to ourselves, as a preservative against ennui.  *Exercise*, therefore, is not Nature's office, but ours." (146:49)

Thus Guts Muths recommended that education was deficient unless physical education was a part of it.  In fact, he declared that "learning and refinement are to health and bodily perfection what luxuries are to necessaries.  Is not then our education depraved, when it aims at a luxury, and neglects our greatest and most essential want?" (146:viii)  He also justified the inclusion of physical education in schools because of the relationship between the mind and the body.

> No one doubts the great influence of the body on the mind:  the physical treatment of the body, therefore, particularly in childhood and in youth, must tend to determine the character of the man; and indeed affects it more deeply, than is commonly supposed. (146:79)

> If we *harden* the body more, it will acquire more stability, and firmness of nerve; if we *exercise* it, it will become strong and active; in this state it will invigorate the mind, it will render it manly, energetic, indefatigable, firm, and courageous; serenity will be diffused over it; it will be active as Nature; it will never experience the poison of ennui. (146:101–102)

Citing Plato and calling attention to the education of the ancient Greeks, he delineated the purpose of education:  "Let *cultivation* in the whole extent of the word, I mean both with regard to body and mind, be the aim of our education." (146:142)  Therefore, he believed, "Let us then give more force and energy to physical education . . . *harmony between the mind and body* will be the sole and true end of gymnastics." (146:143)

The statements of the need for exercise and the values of gymnastics filled the first part, 184 pages, of *Gymnastik für die Jugend* (originally the first volume). The chapters had some charming titles, including "We are weak, because it never enters into our thoughts, that we might be strong, if we pleased," or "The means, that have hitherto been employed against these consequences of effeminacy, are insufficient." Part One concluded with an interesting "chart" paralleling the qualities of body and mind:

> Health of body—serenity of mind.
> Hardiness—manliness of sentiment.
> Strength and address—presence of mind and courage.
> Activity of body—activity of mind.
> Excellence of form—mental beauty.
> Acuteness of the senses—strength of understanding. (146:184)

Part Two (originally the second volume) dealt with the performance of gymnastic activities. Guts Muths distinguished gymnastics from athletics, commenting that unlike athletes "our youths need not dash out their teeth, fracture their ribs, dislocate their limbs, or strangle one another." (146:185) He said that "*gymnastics are labour in the garb of youthful mirth*. We require of this labour, that it shall promote the circulation, and strengthen the muscles and nerves: accordingly, it must sometimes set the whole body in action, at others particular limbs; and must induce sometimes more exertion, sometimes less, without overtraining." (146:187) He also commented that "a genuine theory of gymnastics should be constructed on physiological principles, and the practice of each exercise be regulated by the physical qualities of each individual. . . ." (146:8) He made a point that was to become an important hallmark of the Guts Muths gymnastics: "Our *gymnasium* is, as far as is practicable, *the open air*." (146:189) When possible, he selected areas naturally suitable for exercising (Fig. 20). Thus observing that "oaks, beech, and other trees, of different ages, grow here close together, and overshadow a pleasant little spot," he marked that area as "appropriate to the exercise of climbing." (146:266)

Guts Muths divided gymnastic exercises into three classes:

> A. *Gymnastic exercises properly so called*, which are intended more for the improvement of the body, than for social diversion.
> B. *Manual labours*.
> C. *Social games for youth*. (146:190)

He systematized body exercises according to kind, and for each generic type he devoted a chapter so detailed that a novice following its instruction could easily learn to perform the exercise. His activities included: leaping, running, jaculation (throwing), wrestling, climbing, balancing, lifting and carrying, drawing, skipping with a rope or hoop, dancing, walking, military exercises, bathing, swimming, reading aloud, declaiming, and exercises of the senses. Guts Muths' style and the nature of his "exercises" can be examined in this sample from his chapter on leaping:

> Lastly we have recourse again to the pole. Its length must be somewhat more than in the high leap, depending upon the distance to be cleared, the depth of the water, and height of the banks. Twelve feet may be a sufficient length. The pole is to be held in the usual manner: the leaper takes a brisk run, sets his pole a little beyond the middle of the brook, and swings himself in an arc of a large circle to the opposite bank. By pressing the hands upon the pole, you may raise the body so high, as to swing nearly over the end of the pole. The more this is done, the greater the elegance of the performance. (146:220–221)

It can be deduced from a study of the material Guts Muths chose to include that his conception of the aspects of a youth's education to which physical education could contribute was nearly as broad as the one held today. He included activities designed to strengthen and develop the body, fundamental movements like jumping and throwing, dancing, body mechanics, aquatics, safety education, and perceptual motor training. It is quite possible that a new translation and some updating of the apparatus would make *Gymnastik für die Jugend* a manual suitable for use by today's teachers.

*Spiele zur Übung und Erholung des Körpers und Geistes (Games for Exercise and Recreation of the Body and Spirit)*, a companion volume to *Gymnastik*, was published in three editions, the first in 1796. It contained detailed descriptions of 105 different games, arranged in groups according to the abilities which they tested or tended to develop. Thus Guts Muths was the first to classify games for their educational functions; such classifications included the power of observation and perceptive insight, alertness, fantasy and imagination, memory, taste and beauty, and intellect and higher levels of judgment. He regarded games as more than a means to bodily development, finding in them a way to develop certain important personality traits. Moolenijzer translated and quoted Guts Muths' comments on the lifelike quality of games:

> On a small scale games imitate in a lively way the numerous and various ways of the course of life, which cannot be reached by any other activity or situation of youth. For nowhere is youth, in its actions, in its entire conduct, so little restricted by adults, nowhere acts it, therefore, more natural, more free, more akin to the course of human life than here. Here is a small insult to endure, a rashness, unfairness, boasting, cheating, disappointment to an expectation, a disagreeable character, a slow bloke, a simpleton, a fop, a superiority of mental and physical strength; here is cause for pain and sorrow as well as for cheerfulness and unhappiness, here is an opportunity for evaluation of courtesy, ability, kindness, etc., in fellow man. (247:92–93)

Moolenijzer also translated Guts Muths' expression of high expectations about what could be accomplished by playing games:

> Games must be . . . exercises which are in some way advantageous to youth. They should more or less move the body and [stimulate] its health, this might be done by running, jumping and so on or by gay laughter and more gentle movements. They should contribute speed, strength and flexibility, to the limbs, harden the body, either accidentally or purposely, against pain and . . . put to lively action some or other [perceptive] sense. They must be entertaining for youth, off and on taxing their expectations, their ambition, their activity, dulling their hyper-sensitivity, test their patience, ensure and challenge their prudence and youthful courage. (247:93–94)

Other works by Guts Muths include a *Small Manual of the Art of Swimming for Self-teaching* in two editions, 1798 and 1833; *Mechanical Avocations for Youths and Men*, again in two editions, 1801 and 1809; *Book of Gymnastics for the Sons of the Fatherland* (1817); and *Catechism of Gymnastics; A Manual for Teachers and Pupils* (1818). The fact that he rewrote many of his books suggests, perhaps, that during his long career as a teacher he was constantly learning new techniques and developing new ideas that he wished to include in his already published works on the subject.

Although the above listed books would be regarded as a more than adequate accomplishment for a lifetime's work, it must be remembered that although Guts Muths taught gymnastics in the morning, he also taught geography in the afternoon. Thus it is not surprising that he wrote numerous books on geography. From his experience of fifty years devoted to active teaching, he edited and published fifty-three volumes of *Bibliothek der Paedagoguschen Litteratur* (*Library of Pedagogical Literature*) between 1800 and 1820. In connection with this enormous task it must be noted that he had access to a library of some seventy thousand volumes in Gotha, besides the good collection at the Schnepfenthal Institute itself.

Expressed throughout Guts Muths' writings and teaching is the belief that youth needs to seek health and strength through gymnastic activity; equally important to Guts Muths was the idea that this is a joyous experience enhanced by the outdoors setting in which it easily takes place. Guts Muths enjoyed the games and exercises he devised and the long vigorous hikes; presumably his boys also loved them. Exercise was never a bitter medicine for one's health but a pleasant activity in which each person was expected to grow in strength and courage. The devoted work of Johann Christoph Friedrich Guts Muths has been recognized by those who are interested in the development of physical education; it is also fitting that in his native town of Quedlinburg a statue of Guts Muths with the boy Karl Ritter, has been erected to commemorate the great contribution he made to the education of Germany's youth (Fig. 20).

# SCHNEPFENTHAL EDUCATIONAL INSTITUTE

Schnepfenthal Educational Institute, modeled along the lines of the Philanthropinum, was another institution designed to put the educational ideas of Rousseau into practice. As at the Philanthropinum,

> all teaching was first intended to create an awareness of the beauties and influence of Nature. Secondly it sought to promote sentiments of happiness and trust between the headmaster, the staff and the pupils. And thirdly it strove to impart a deep feeling of mutual regard among the boys themselves. . . . (288:19–20)

To effect this aim a family-type atmosphere was carefully maintained (a concept also emphasized by Pestalozzi) and the school was located in the country, far from the influences of city life.

The founder of Schnepfenthal was Christian Gotthilf Salzmann (1744–1811), once a village pastor in a country district in Thuringia. In the process of trying to reorganize the schools in his parish, Salzmann became interested in educational theory, particularly that which was expressed in Rousseau's *Émile*. He wrote a treatise called *Concerning the Best Means of Teaching Religion to Children* which was an attempt to reconcile the tenets of Rousseau's philosophy with those of Christianity. This work was censured by orthodox theologians and caused Salzmann to respond with *The Book of the Crab or the Method of Giving an Irrational Education to Children*, which was a satirical work with chapter headings such as: "Means of making oneself detested by children," or "Means of rendering children insensible to the beauties of nature." The book attracted much attention and caused Salzmann to be offered a position at the Philanthropinum where from 1781–1784 he was liturgist and teacher of religion, an experience to which he attributed much of his later success at Schnepfenthal.

When he decided to found a school of his own, Salzmann with the four thousand thaler (approximately four thousand dollars) patronage of Duke Ernest II of Saxe-Gotha, acquired property at Schnepfenthal in Thuringia, about seventy miles southwest of the Prussian town of Quedlinburg, hometown of Guts Muths. In the first eighteen months after the school's opening in 1784, he had nine pupils in addition to his own children, and the numbers steadily increased until he had forty-nine students in 1790, and for the next eighteen years never less than fifty. Salzmann remained as director of the school until his death in 1811, when his son Karl succeeded him in his work.

Life at Schnepfenthal followed a clear pattern.   Mornings were devoted to study of such subjects as French and geography, but by eleven A.M. the gymnastic lesson was given.   In an open space under the oaks shading a nearby hill, the children practiced their running, throwing, and jumping exercises.   An area was established including a jumping ditch, a balance beam and a pair of upright poles.   (Refer to chapter on the Philanthropinum for details of a similar area.)   Christian Carl Andre, the first physical education teacher at Schnepfenthal, instituted a number of varied exercises including marching in time, walking on the balance beam and crossing ditches on the edge of a plank, jumping over a stick placed on the jumping stands, pole vaulting, jumping across a ditch, vaulting, carrying weights with outstretched arms, throwing at a target, foot-races, running and jumping through a long rope swung by two persons, simple free exercises done indoors, skating, coasting, and long walks.   When Guts Muths took over the teaching of gymnastics he introduced additional activities.   For instance, he built a see-saw (a board placed over two poles) for physical education classes.   He also started the practice of having the children go up and down a rope ladder, swing on vertical ropes, climb a mast, hang and travel on the underside of a horizontal beam, balance sticks on the ends of the fingers, do various exercises while standing on one foot, jump over a rope swung close to the ground, throw a wooden discus, wrestle, push against each other, and lift a weight hung on a rod and adjusted (by moving it closer or farther) to the strength of the individual child.   When the weather was bad, practice comparable to modern floor exercises was held indoors in the various movements and positions intended to teach proper carriage of the body.   After the noon meal the children were allowed until two P.M. for recreation which, alternated with musical entertainments, was held again in the evening.   Andre directed games and/or hikes on Sunday afternoons.   Students who showed proficiency in the events were distinguished by wearing a few oak leaves on the hat and sometimes were also rewarded by being allowed to choose the exercises for the following day. After a year, Andre's responsibilities were given to Johann Guts Muths who continued to supervise the school's physical education program for the next fifty years. (207:75)

Besides academic studies and gymnastic exercises, Salzmann believed that some form of manual labor or craft was an important part of a youth's education.   Therefore terraces were laid out upon the sides of a hill near the school and each student had his own patch of flowers, vegetables and fruit to cultivate; pocket money was earned by selling the produce to the Institute.   Another "technological" activity was making things out of pasteboard.   In the school's first year a bookbinder from a neighboring village had given instruction in his trade and in the manufacture of little boxes, pen cases and baskets.   This instruction was eventually continued by one of the regular teachers, who also taught the students to make

FIG. 21.    Plate from *Gymnastics for Youth*.

wooden models of tools and machines used in the various handcrafts. Joseph Röckl, a professor of pedagogy who spent nine days at Schnepfenthal in 1805, published a record of his observations and noted that he saw the students engaged in handling the saw, plane, chisel, and doing paste work.

Röckl also wrote of the frugal diet, the light and simple clothing, the unusually airy rooms for sleeping and study, the regard for personal cleanliness, and the especially active outdoor life.   For besides the games held outdoors, the entire school population occasionally passed a whole day in the open air, hiking to some attractive wooded spot for a picnic lunch. Longer excursions on foot were also taken, though the smaller children were left at home, and a wagon carried the provisions.   There is a record of a four days' trip taken by forty-five people and in one year the students hiked a total of over one hundred miles. (207:76)

This kind of program, in which much of each day was spent in physical training or manual labor and the emphasis was placed upon doing things outdoors, was a revolution in education.   Like Basedow, Salzmann in attempting to apply Rousseau's ideas was conducting a school very different from those to be seen elsewhere in Europe, especially in the northern countries.   Citizens were generally unhappy with school conditions, not only because instruction in the mother-tongue was neglected in favor of Greek and Latin, but because the methods of teaching were severe and unnatural.   Latin and Greek poetry and grammar were drilled into the memories of the children, as were portions of the Scriptures.   A good memory was the most prized trait and in fact, the only one taught for. Schools were dark and dreary and children spent the day at their desks, dressed like little lords, far removed from sunshine or playing fields. The only attention paid to the physical well-being of the students consisted of beating their bodies on the premise that this would encourage more diligent studying. To teach children as if they were really children; to let them learn through their own sense experiences; to allow them to play games; to care that their bodies were well-developed and healthy; to believe that courage, for instance, could be learned through gymnastics; and most of all, to take into account the natural inclinations of the children, were revolutionary ideas.

Salzmann's school, observed as it was by a great number of intellectuals and would-be educators, helped to pave the way for others of its kind and foresaw the reform of the whole German educational system which took place after the defeat by Napoleon at Jena in 1806 and the creation in 1808 of a Bureau of Education. Furthermore, the influence of schools like the Philanthropinum and Schnepfenthal created a climate for the work of later educators such as the Swiss, Pestalozzi. And lastly, although physical education was conducted in different ways during subsequent periods of history, the Schnepfenthal Educational Institute set important precedents regarding its place in the curriculum.

# FRIEDRICH LUDWIG JAHN

## 1778-1852

*Deutsches Volksthum* (*German Nationality*), Jahn's chief literary work, appeared in 1810. Its central thought—the unity of Germany—is reflected by an emotionally expressed passion for the German language, customs and history, by a love for the fatherland, and by a desire to see it bound into one strong nation able to throw off the French conquerors. It can reasonably be said that Jahn's life was devoted to this aim and that the *turnvereine* which he established were meant to be the instruments to forge the spirit and strength necessary to achieve a powerful, united German state.

Friedrich Ludwig Jahn was born in 1778 in Lanz, a small Prussian village between Hamburg and Berlin. His childhood was conventional except that his status as the son of a village pastor somewhat prevented his association with the local peasant children. His interest in history, geography and the German language began with lessons from his father and was supplemented by tales of veterans of the Seven Years' War who lived in the neighborhood. As a child he experienced the atmosphere of freedom in which the peasants lived; most owned their own farms and a spirit of self-reliance and independence permeated the region. At thirteen he entered the gymnasium at Salzwedel and three years later the eighth class at the Gymnasium zum grauen Kloster in Berlin which he left after six months. He spent five years at the University of Halle studying theology, some time at Jena, about a year at the University of Greifswalk in Swedish Pomerania, and months at the University of Göttingen; he completed no degrees, however, and prepared for no profession. Finally he entered a training school for teachers, the Königliche Seminar für gelehrte Schulen and made teaching his profession.

Jahn's peripatetic schooling was due largely to his personality and interests which caused him difficulty with school authorities and led him to study the prescribed program in a desultory fashion. His interest in Prussian and German history and the German language and literature, subjects generally neglected at that time, absorbed an increasing amount of his time. While at Halle he wrote a small pamphlet on *The Promotion of Patriotism in Prussia*; the tract glorified the state and its rulers and was a plea for more attention to the study of Prussian history in the schools and universities in order to develop love for country. At the same time he campaigned against

FIG. 22.   Friedrich Ludwig Jahn.

one of the strongest traditions in German universities, the *Landsmann-schaften*; these were student clubs and associations of fellow-countrymen, such as the Westphalians, or the Pomeranians, which were derived from the approximately three hundred independent national states then within Germany. His opposition to their spirit of provincialism coupled with their dissolute life of drinking and dueling, provoked incessant brawls and the consequent disapproval of the authorities. He continued what today would be called "subversive activities" at Jena and Griefswalk, being thrown out of the latter institution, and went on to Göttingen. In the interim he completed a volume entitled *Contributions to High Germany Synonymy* (1806) embodying material collected in all parts of Germany while he was on walking trips. The book showed his love of the German language as well as his sensitivity to the country and the popular dialects of its people.

While at Göttingen Jahn learned that Frederick-William III of Prussia was finally going to battle Napoleon, whose policies were threatening Prussia's existence. He rushed to join the army but got to Jena in time only to witness the last battle and defeat which cost Prussia nearly half of her territory. He was more successful in participating in the 1813 War of Liberation against Napoleon which two years later culminated in the defeat at Waterloo. In this instance Jahn joined the Free Corps sponsored by the Baron von Lützow, serving as a sergeant for the Black Hunters which included Froebel as another volunteer.

In the meantime Jahn had become a teacher at the Graue Kloster (Gray Cloister), the school which he had briefly attended fifteen years earlier, and also at Plamann's School for Boys, which was run according to methods advocated by Pestalozzi. He taught history, German and mathematics and used the traditional Wednesday and Saturday "half-holidays" for outdoor play with the younger boys. In the spring of 1810, when he began to meet the boys at the Hasenheide, a nearby stretch of wooded land, the *turner* movement was born. Games like "Robber and Traveler," simple exercises such as running, jumping and wrestling, rudimentary apparatus such as a jumping bar made of a rope sandbagged at either end resting on light poles thrust into the sand, and an occasional *turnfahrt* (gymnastic excursion) which combined a walk and a game, characterized the afternoons. Jahn saw to it that the activities were varied and interesting; he interspersed periods of storytelling and conversation between activities during which time he forged a well-disciplined group of boys who loved and respected his leadership. Undoubtedly his storytelling, which included tales from German history, helped the boys achieve a feeling for their homeland which was intensified by the general camaraderie of the games. A badge (Fig. 23) given to participants in later years firmly connected German history and the medieval, knightly tournaments that were a part of it, with the new gymnastic exercises. It bore four numbers: 9, battle in the Teutonic Forest; 919, beginning of the age of chivalry; 1519, end of the tournaments; and 1811, opening of the first *turnplatz*. (25:3) Jahn's purposes definitely included preparing youth for combat against the nation's enemies. He said:

Fig. 23.    *Turner* Badge.

When all men, able to bear arms, have become valiant by warlike exercises, have become ready for fighting by warlike plays, belligerent and watchful by a patriotic spirit, then will a people be able to defend its frontier. "Defenseless" meant "disgraceful" to our ancestors and this maxim should be inscribed on every banner. (25:3)

In the spring of 1811 Jahn and his boys spent their afternoons working at the Hasenheide, enclosing it and constructing apparatus for their exercises. (Refer to chapter on the Hasenheide Turnplatz for a complete description of its physical properties and the activities conducted at it.) The exercises were neither orderly nor organized; each boy invented his own and taught them to the others. Jahn's purpose was essentially to provide an opportunity for vigorous, wholesome activity in the open air and to teach the boys to work together in harmony. It was not until the following winter that Jahn and some of his oldest students began to study the subject of gymnastics, using two excellent German sources: Guts Muths' *Gymnastik für die Jugend*, and Gerhard Ulrich Anton Vieth's *Enzyklopädie der Leibesübungen (Encyclopedia of Bodily Exercises)* which was published in three volumes in 1794, 1795 and 1818.

By the end of the next season (1812) the play area *(turnplatz)* had been moved to a larger and better situated place and over five hundred people attended, including adults who were only allowed to take part on Sunday. Participants and spectators from all classes and ranks were present as the activities continued to grow in popularity. Squad leaders *(vorturner)* had to be trained to deal with the increasing numbers and the need for a critical study of gymnastics and some arrangement of the material became evident. Some of the best *turners* (gymnasts) organized a society to work on the systematic development of activities and purchased equipment for use in an indoor area so that they could work through the winter. By 1816 there were over a thousand *turners* in Berlin and in 1818 at the annual celebration on October 18 marking the anniversary of the Battle of Leipzig, the *turners* and spectators numbered several thousand.

While Jahn was fighting in the War of Liberation the work was continued by his associates, one of whom, Johann Bornemann, published in 1814 *Lehrbuch der von Friedrich Ludwig Jahn unter dem Namen der Turnkunst wiedererweckten Gymnastik (Manual of the Gymnastics Revived by Friedrich Ludwig Jahn Under the Name of Turnkunst)*, which paved the way for Jahn's own book published two years later. A group of older *turners*, originally nine in number, began to meet on Saturdays under the leadership of Hans Ferdinand Massmann in order to organize the work further. They practiced songs, discussed regulations, revised the exercises by series, fixed rules for the games and chose leaders for the squads. When Jahn returned it was the experience of this group that helped to prepare his famous manuscript *Die Deutsche Turnkunst (German Gymnastics)*, which was published in 1816.

The preface to *German Gymnastics* told the history of the Hasenheide Turnplatz and the origin of the word *turnkunst*. Jahn had used *"turnen"* as his root word, rather than gymnastics, because he believed the word to be of German origin whereas gymnastics was from the Greek word *gymnazein* meaning "to exercise naked." From the root he developed a nomenclature that included *turner* (gymnast), *turnverein* (gymnastic society), *turnkunst* (the art of gymnastics), *turnplatz* (place or grounds for gymnastic exercise), *turnfahrt* (gymnastic excursion), *turnfest* (gymnastic festival), and *vorturner* (gymnastics leader). Also included in the preface was a history of gymnastics, especially popular festivals. Part I of the work, "The Gymnastick Exercises," was divided into eighteen sections devoted to walking, running, jumping, vaulting the horse, balancing, exercising on the horizontal and the parallel bars, climbing, throwing, pulling, pushing, lifting, carrying, holding the body outstretched horizontally, wrestling, jumping with the hoop and with the rope, and miscellaneous exercises. In each case both the exercise and the necessary apparatus were described.

Part II dealt with "Gymnastick Games." In Charles Beck's translation the following points, among others, were made:

> The *gymnastick games* form an essential part of gymnasticks, and, therefore, every gymnastick institution should have a large place, without the precincts of the gymnasium, destined for this purpose, and consisting of high-grown wood, thickets, bushes, and bare spaces. . . .
>
> Our object, therefore, will be not so much to describe new plays but to shew what render some superior to others.
>
> In the first place, all games which are played sitting . . . are to be exempted; a good gymnastick play requires motion, in order to attain its end, which is, to render the body active and strong.
>
> In the second place all plays for gain are excluded. . . .
>
> A good gymnastick play should not require too great and extensive preparations;
>
> it should be easy to be understood, and yet founded on a certain rule and principle;
>
> it should not entirely, or to a great extent, depend on chance; it should occupy a sufficiently large number;
>
> .    .    .    .    .    .    .    .    .    .    .    .    .
>
> it should not be uniform and without variety;
>
> it should require active and dextrous players, in order to be played well. . . .
> (38:141–142)

Part III dealt with the construction of an outdoor *turnplatz* and detailed specifications for sufficient equipment to be used by four hundred persons working in squads. Part IV discussed the management of the grounds and exercises, including details about administering a program. Part V contained a bibliography of about 170 titles and two folding plates illustrating a plan of an outdoor *turnplatz* and the various forms of apparatus. *Die Deutsche Turnkunst* was a charming and thoroughly written book intended as a guide for the formation of *turnvereine* all over Germany. Although it was a practical manual, the ideology of German nationalism was conveyed throughout the work with the intention of guiding the spirit as well as the technique of future gymnasts.

It was this same "spirit" that ultimately caused the banning of the *turnvereine* and the closing of all the *turnplätze* then established. In the beginning Jahn received not only popular approval but official support as well. The Prussian government originally provided him with a salary of five hundred thalers (roughly five hundred dollars) which later was increased to eight hundred and then one thousand thalers. A yearly grant of 150 thalers for the support of the Hasenheide Turnplatz was established and timber for building purposes was given free of cost. The Crown Prince visited the Turnplatz and was pleased with it. In 1817 the universities of Jena and Kiel each conferred on Jahn the honorary degree of Doctor of

Philosophy in recognition of his services to the fatherland in time of need, of his stimulating influence on the young, his power as a public speaker, and his efforts in behalf of the German language. Minister von Schuckmann sent copies of *Die Deutsche Turnkunst* to authorities in other areas of Germany for distribution. Visitors came from all over to be trained as teachers of gymnastics. Jahn travelled with a group of *turners* giving demonstrations and making speeches which were very cordially received. He also took an interest in a new organization of general student unions, the *Burschenschaften*, which was founded to correct the abuses of the *Landsmannschaften*, and also to promote the physical and moral vigor of its members. It grew out of a group from the Free Corps in which Jahn had served and had as its major ideal a free and united Germany. Gymnastics quickly became part of their program and representatives from Hasenheide assisted the *Burschenschaften* to develop *turnplätze* and programs.

But concurrent with these developments were some important political events. After the War of Liberation the people were disappointed in their expectation that Germany would not only be freed from the French, but that it would become a united country constitutionally ruled. Instead, the Germanic Confederation of 1815, created at the Congress of Vienna under the leadership of the Austrian Prince Metternich, was a loose confederation of thirty-eight semi-autonomous states. Reactionary decrees were issued with the intent of suppressing any rebellion against the divine authority of the various monarchs. The idea of a strong, united Germany was an anathema to the ruling powers. The *turner* motto which Jahn coined: *"Frisch, froh, stark und frei, ist die Turnerei"* (99:363) meant "Gymnasts are vigorous, happy, strong and free."* The common man drawn into the movement was imbued with that spirit of personal and political freedom. Thus the *turnvereine* which attempted to develop a patriotic spirit and were so popular among the German people, represented a potential political threat which was further strengthened by their close alliance with the *Burschenschaften*. Furthermore, beginning in 1817 Jahn delivered a series of lectures on German nationality in which he criticized customs of dress, speech and manners, thus alienating some of his audience. In addition, a ceremony was conducted by one of Jahn's closest colleagues, Massmann, in which writings hostile to unity and constitutional liberty were symbolically burned; a reactionary writer was assassinated by Karl Ludwig Sand, one of Jahn's *turners* and a member of the Jena *Burschenschaft*. Although he was later exonerated, it was generally assumed that Sand's act merely carried out a decision made by one of Jahn's organizations, and therefore Jahn was arrested and tried for the murder. That year (1819) the Turnplatz remained unopened, ostensibly because the Prussian Ministry was perfecting a union of gymnastics with the whole scheme of instruction in the

---

* Another version of the motto was "*Frisch, frei, fröhlich, fromm, ist des Turners Reichtum,*" meaning "Vigorous, free, cheerful, devout are the gymnast's riches."

schools.  But the Frankfort Diet ratified the Carlsbad Decrees which provided among other things for a commission to search out "the origin and ramification of revolutionary conspiracies and demagogic associations." The *Burschenschaft* was dissolved and in 1829 Frederick-William III decreed that *turnen* should absolutely cease throughout Prussia.

After Jahn's trial, although he was absolved of complicity in the murder and acquitted of a second charge of "repeated irreverent and insolent utterances regarding existing conditions and regulations in the state," he was forbidden to live within a ten-mile radius of Berlin or any city containing a university or higher school for boys.  He continued to receive a pension of one thousand thalers from the government, but he remained under police surveillance even when he moved to Freyburg in Thuringia, about thirty miles southwest of Leipzig.  In 1840 the more liberal Frederick-William IV ascended the Prussian throne and soon afterwards all police restrictions were removed and Jahn was awarded a high German decoration, the Iron Cross.  In 1842, by cabinet order, gymnastics was formally recognized as a necessary and indispensable part of male education.* Although Jahn maintained his interest in the *turnvereine* he never again took an active part in their leadership.  He died and was buried in Freyburg in 1852 and later a *turnhalle* (gymnasium) was built over his grave as a memorial.

Despite the various decrees against it, between the years 1829 and 1840, the movement Jahn started did not cease totally.  It flourished in the German states which permitted *turnen*; even in Berlin, Ernst Eiselen, the assistant who had directed the exercises at the Hasenheide Turnplatz while Jahn was in the Free Corps, was allowed to open a private indoor and outdoor gymnasium in 1828, a special room for girls four years later, and a branch institution in 1836.  Besides his work in the gymnasium, which included the training of teachers, Eiselen published in 1837 the book *Turntafeln* which contained numbered lists of exercises.  With Frederick-William IV on the throne, and the imminence of the French Revolution which caused great excitement in Germany, there was a strong revival of the movement.  The *Deutsche Turnerschaft*, a union of German and Austrian gymnastic societies, was organized in 1868.  By 1915 in Germany there were over eleven thousand societies with over a million members.

Jahn's work was not limited to Germany alone.  *Turnvereine* were established in the United States by the German immigrants (refer to chapter on Normal College of the NAGU).  Starting in 1848 in Cincinnati, more than 150 Societies were formed during the next fifteen years.  The fact that in 1893 four thousand *turners* performed in unison at the Chicago World's Fair was an indication of the popularity of the movement in

---

* In 1894 it became a required subject for secondary school girls (two days per week) and later it was also required for elementary girls. *A Manual for the Physical Training of Girls in Prussian Schools* was published in 1913. (365:228)

America.   Furthermore, German gymnastics spread to the schools of both Germany and the United States where in the former it became the core of the physical education program and in the latter was adopted by some public school systems, primarily in the Midwest.   In 1825 and 1826, some of Jahn's students who had fled to America to escape arrest when the movement fell into political disfavor, opened and directed outdoor gymnasiums similar to the early Jahn *turnplätze*, in Northampton, Cambridge, and Boston, Massachusetts (refer to chapter on the Round Hill School).

*Turnvater* Jahn (Father Jahn) was of singular importance in the development of a gymnastics program which combined physical strength and skill with social discipline for the purposes of furthering national goals.  Germany honored him and the *Turnerschaft* erected monuments in Berlin and Freyburg.  In the memorial *turnhalle* in Freyburg numerous items pertaining to the man and his work were gathered in the Jahn Museum in tribute to a great leader.

# HASENHEIDE TURNPLATZ

The Hasenheide Turnplatz like the grounds at Olympia in Greece and the Campus Martius outside Rome was an area designated for the activities of physical education. At Olympia sports were performed—track, wrestling, boxing; on the Campus Martius next to the temple dedicated to Mars the god of war, the Roman fathers trained their sons in the art of combat; but at the Hasenheide the boys were made strong and skillful in the performance of gymnastic exercises and taught unifying social values through simple childhood songs and games.

The first season at the Hasenheide was purely spontaneous. German schools were accustomed to having Wednesday and Saturday afternoons as "half-holidays," which meant freedom from the usual classes and studying; the teachers, however, were still expected to remain with the children to supervise their activities. In the spring of 1810, Friedrich Ludwig Jahn began to use that time to meet some of the boys at the Hasenheide, a hilly and wooded stretch of land on the southern slope of the Spree valley. They played games, did exercises and used the natural setting in the manner of boys everywhere—such as performing hanging exercises on the limb of an oak. Some of the exercises advocated by Guts Muths were also occasionally practiced. It was a popular activity and the number of boys who came increased weekly.

The next year Jahn planned more carefully. During the early spring Wednesday and Saturday afternoons he and the boys fenced in a rectangular area in an opening in the woods. They built a small hut where clothing could be left and within the enclosure they set up simple apparatus which included a horizontal balance beam, a rope hung from a pole tied across two trees, a jumping ditch, a figure eight track with a wrestling place in one of the circles, and two climbing poles fifteen and twenty feet high. There were also a group of horizontal bars made by tying three tree trunks to a group of pines set in a triangle, a handmade inclined ladder, and two sets of fixed standards for use in high jumping and pole vaulting. When this first Turnplatz (place for doing gymnastic exercises) opened in June there were eighty to one hundred boys, most of whom had paid fourteen groschen (thirty-three cents) to defray the expense of keeping the grounds and apparatus in good condition. Boys of good character who could not afford to pay were given free admission. By the end of that summer about two hundred boys were regularly attending, including students from another school and from a local orphanage.   Before long Jahn realized the desirability of special clothing and appeared one day in long trousers and a short jacket of gray unbleached linen.   The outfit was so inexpensive and durable that it was quickly adopted and soon became the uniform of the *turners*. A particularly important outcome was that the uniform dress helped to eliminate distinctions of rank and class.   Such differences were also diminished by the simple lunches of bread, butter, eggs and water; tobacco, brandy and sweets were forbidden.   During the summer months Tuesday and Friday afternoons were added to the schedule so that the boys could go four times a week to the Turnplatz.   The activities were not well-organized and the boys generally preferred the games and wrestling to working on the apparatus.   However, they did "explore" the apparatus, inventing things to do which were then imitated by the others.   That first season (1811) on the Turnplatz was characterized by an informality that was quite feasible with the relatively small number of boys attending.

The next spring the Turnplatz was moved to a new, better and permanent location which was larger and less exposed to the weather.   Near the

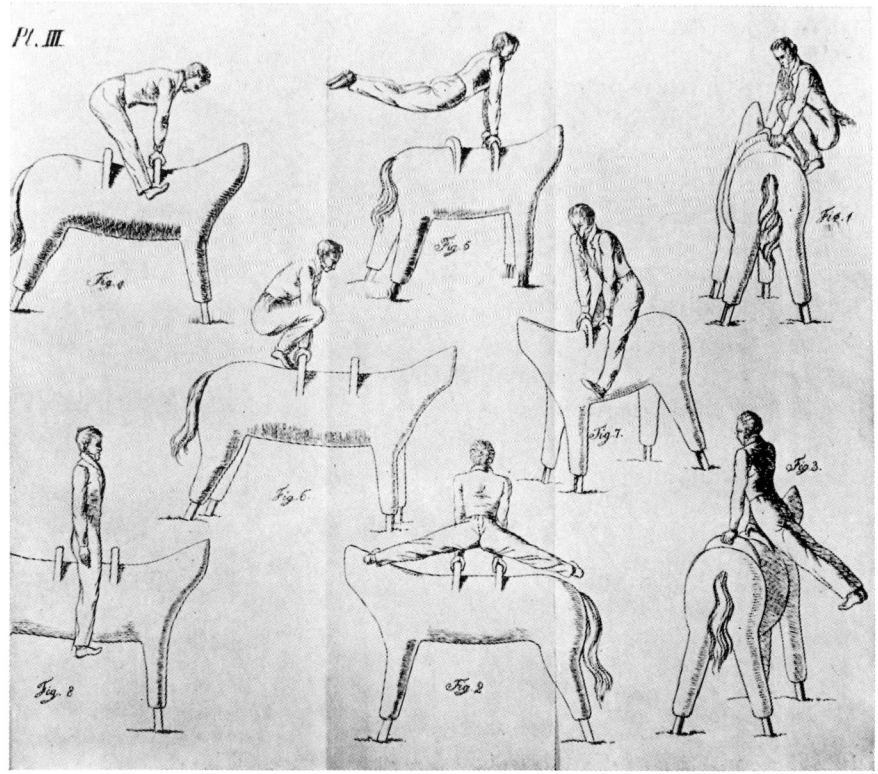

FIG. 24.   Vaulting the Horse.   (From Beck's Translation of
*Die Deutsche Turnkunst.*)

first site, this one lay on a plateau at the head of a slope, protected from the wind on three sides by dense thickets. It was set up in much the same manner as the first except that the hut was located in the center and a meeting or resting place, the Tie, was laid out. In addition to the old apparatus three vaulting bucks or horses without pommels, at heights of three, four and five feet, were constructed out of tree trunks. Near them were the first crude models of parallel bars—three pairs of thin beams about twelve feet long set parallel about two feet apart. About the same height as the bucks, they were originally used only to strengthen the hands and arms for vaulting.

In the preceding winter Jahn had begun to write down and arrange the exercises, but individual inventiveness was not yet formalized out of the program. In particular, the boys competed in inventing new methods for using the parallel bars and the horizontal beam. Three *turners* who had received instruction in vaulting throughout the winter continued to meet for special practices with small groups of skilled students for whom a live horse was brought to the Turnplatz. Interest in the jumping and the games decreased as emphasis shifted to excellence in performance on the apparatus. One activity that still retained its old popularity was the *turnfahrt* which consisted of a long hike, some sort of game or exercise performed at the destination, followed by the return hike.

During the next few years, until 1818, the Turnplatz continued to develop in popularity and organization. The evident physical benefit, the atmosphere of comradeship and harmony permeating the endeavor, the diminished importance of class and social barriers, the patriotic ideas emphasized by Jahn and brought out in the songs and stories that were a part of the activities, all contributed to the growth among the participants of a strongly national feeling of solidarity. *Turnkunst* (the art of gymnastics) was originally developed for the students, but adults who wanted to were allowed to take part on Sundays. Although Jahn guided the enterprise, using strict discipline including punishment with a rope-end, the increased numbers caused him to organize his student assistants into a group of *vorturners* (squad leaders). To these he demonstrated new exercises and they in turn taught their own groups. During the winters some of the best *turners* began to meet to work out new exercises, study written material, plan and organize the exercises (a task which culminated in several publications—refer to chapter on Jahn for details) and train new leaders. While Jahn and most of the *turners* old enough to bear arms were away fighting in the War of Liberation his assistants took over and continued to develop the Turnplatz, designing and constructing new apparatus with the 150 thalers (approximately $150) and free lumber granted them yearly by the government. (207:91–92)

On October 18 and 19, 1814, the first anniversary of the Battle of Leipzig was celebrated at the Turnplatz with huge bonfires, songs by the *turners*, and a great exhibition of competitive exercises.  It was estimated that ten thousand spectators witnessed the event including many persons of distinction and delegates from neighboring towns.

The general pattern for the afternoons at the Turnplatz became formalized:  first, a self-chosen exercise (*kurturnen*) followed by a period of rest; then all participated in the orderly exercises (*turnschule*) by squads grouped according to age.  The *vorturner* for each squad kept records on attendance and proficiency and led their groups using a written set of exercises in tabular form (*turntafeln*) which showed the steps of progression in each group.  There were days, however, wholly given over to games and almost every Saturday night games were played all night long.  After the exercises the boys returned to the city in groups and before they scattered at the Kottbus gate, joined for a final song.  The program was thus conducted with great seriousness and an effort was made to be purely German in speech, custom and dress.  The friendly competition helped to encourage the development of manliness and also to forge unity within and between the groups.  It is understandable that throughout Germany *turnplätze* were modelled along the lines of the Hasenheide and usually under the direction of a charismatic leader like Jahn, motivated by patriotic feelings.  The common incentive was the wave of love for the fatherland which swept over Germany at the time of the War of Liberation.  *Turnen* proved a wonderful vehicle for developing the spirit of mutual concern for Germany sparked by the War. (207:94–95)

Unfortunately, the authorities stood to lose their power in a unified Germany, and in 1819 the Hasenheide Turnplatz was officially closed by the government.  Other *turnplätze*, especially outside of Prussia, were per-

Fig. 25.  Hasenheide Turnplatz.

mitted to remain open and the movement therefore continued to attract followers.   However, as the schools began to adopt the program and incorporate *turnen* into the school day, the *turnplätze* began to become more of a place for adults or university students.   Separate societies for adults (*Männerturnvereine*) were formed.   The exercises as they had been developed were more suitable for older, stronger people than for the young boys for whom the first Turnplatz was constructed, and thus lent to the shift upward in age of participants.

The popularity of *turnen* did not cease with the decrees against it.   When more liberal rulers were in authority the movement regained and surpassed its original strength.   In 1860 the first general German convention of *turners* and a *turnfest* (gymnastic festival) were held at Coburg with more than a thousand adult *turners* representing 139 cities or villages.   The next year was the fiftieth anniversary of the opening of the Hasenheide Turnplatz and the event was celebrated by a second convention and a *turnfest* in Berlin.   This time participants increased to 2812 adult *turners* representing 262 places.

Although the movement rose and fell in succeeding years, responding sensitively to political developments, the effect of Jahn's work begun in the Hasenheide Turnplatz was felt throughout Europe and in the United States.   The development of indoor gymnasiums was an inevitable result of the Hasenheide; the beautiful gymnastic equipment seen in today's gymnasiums had their origin in the hand-hewn branches and crude beams of the Hasenheide; and the belief in the value of gymnastic exercises for the development of a strong individual in a unified group began in 1811 at the Hasenheide Turnplatz.

# ADOLF SPIESS

## 1810-1858

Adolf Spiess helped to create, organize, introduce, train teachers for, and write about a system of German school gymnastics. As Friedrich Jahn has been considered the father of gymnastics, so Spiess has been thought of as the father of school gymnastics. His background eminently suited him for what became his life's work because he was taught and participated in gymnastics from his earliest childhood days.

Spiess was born in 1810 in the small town of Lauterbach, part of the Grand Duchy of Hesse located in southwest Germany. His father, in addition to his pastoral duties in the Evangelical Lutheran Church, opened a private school to prepare youths either for the *gymnasium* or for a mercantile career. Since he had made several trips to Schnepfenthal to observe the methods used there and had become friendly with Guts Muths (whom the young Adolf also met), he chose to incorporate gymnastics into the daily program of his own school. There were exercises and games patterned after those of Guts Muths, supplemented by weekly hikes and dancing lessons during the winter months. Three years after Adolf entered the school at age six, students were introduced to the Jahn gymnastics by a young man from the University of Giessen; parallel bars and a horizontal bar were added to the equipment.

In 1824 some of the boys organized a society to practice gymnastics regularly outside of school hours, meeting in a private *turnplatz* and using Jahn's *Die Deutsche Turnkunst* as a guide. In 1828 when Spiess began to study theology at the University of Giessen he joined the *Waffenverbindung* (the outlawed *Burschenschaft* under a new name); this organization provided him an opportunity to develop skill in fencing as well as to participate in a variety of athletic endeavors including riding, swimming, skating, dancing, gymnastics, and hiking, in all of which he was said to be quite proficient. While still a university student he visited Guts Muths and Jahn, a fact which seems to indicate that even in his early twenties he had an unusually strong interest in gymnastics. He also spent some time in Berlin where he frequented Eiselen's private gymnasium, learning new exercises there.

By 1830 he was giving regular instruction in gymnastics, first to a dozen boys on a garden *turnplatz* and then to nearly one hundred and fifty boys in one of the city parks. Jahn had worked with small groups, each with their own leader, but Spiess modified this traditional method by gathering the entire group to perform together at the start of each session; as they stood or marched simple exercises were performed in rhythm, or running and jumping exercises were conducted under the command of a single leader. He commented: "Class exercise, by keeping a number of pupils in moderate activity, creates a method in gymnastic art which, aside from the drilling of the separate members of the class, has in view the cultivation of power and influence of a great number united in order." (337:4) This had the effect of further formalizing gymnastics into a system. However, within the year the authorities clamped down and prohibited the group to exercise in public.

After receiving his degree in 1832 Spiess returned home and assumed duties as a private tutor; in 1833, however, he left for Burgdorf, Switzerland, his political involvement having caused him to flee Germany to avoid arrest. There he was appointed teacher of gymnastics, singing, writing, and drawing in the new school run by Friedrich Froebel and his assistants, all of whom were very sympathetic to his ideas. An open air gymnasium was laid out according to Jahn's model, and in the castle next to it (where for five years Pestalozzi had conducted his famous school) a place was equipped for winter use. By the spring of 1834 even the youngest of the school's boys received systematic instruction in gymnastics for a two-hour period three times a week. After a short time classes for girls were instituted with specially devised exercises. There were also frequent hikes and every autumn a *turnfest* was held, both of which were considered essential parts of the school training.

In the fifteen years he lived in Switzerland (eleven in Burgdorf and four in Basel) Spiess was in great demand. In addition to his work with Froebel he taught part-time in several schools, including the normal school at Münchenbuchsee where he worked with about one hundred future teachers. In 1848 he moved to Darmstadt, the capital of Hesse, to introduce gymnastics into the schools of that state. He also had to train the teachers and supervise their work, a position which commanded the title: *Oberstudienassessor*. At Darmstadt there was a unique new *turnhaus* (gymnasium) surrounded by a double *turnplatz*, which contained a 100 × 60-foot room which a movable partition could convert into two rooms; this was the first such building in Germany. Teachers from all over Hesse, Germany and Europe came to take training and learn his system and the Spiess method was adopted in more than thirty-five schools outside of Hesse. In 1855 tuberculosis caused Spiess to stop teaching and in 1858 he died in Darmstadt.

By the time of his death physical training had become a part of the German school day. The Jahn *turnplatz*, although primarily used by school boys, had an existence separate from the school, reflecting the concept that

Fig. 26.    Adolf Spiess.

the latter was a place only for "mental training."  Under Hans Massmann who had attempted to organize a statewide system of physical training, cities tried to construct one central *turnplatz*—a vast exercising ground—which resembled a public playground instead of a place for educational endeavor.  Spiess did not originate the idea that the school must be concerned with the whole life of the young including the physical and social aspects.  In fact, the Prussian cabinet had formally recognized gymnastics as a necessary and indispensable part of male education and had designated Jahn's assistant, Hans Ferdinand Massmann to put that idea into practice. When he proved incapable of doing so, Spiess made the attempt and succeeded, largely because of his great experience as both a gymnast and teacher.

First of all, Spiess had attempted to place gymnastics on an equal footing with other areas of study.  *"Each school should so interpolate the instruction of gymnastics in its daily programme as to be of corresponding importance with other branches of study."* (337:7)  To accomplish this it had to conform to good pedagogic principles, the most important of which was that the material be arranged in progressive steps suitable for different grades.

> Gymnastic exercises in our schools should be the means of educating the body in the same measure as the other branches educate the mind, and, like the other branches be taught from the beginning. . . . What has begun with the children of six to ten years of age must, of course, be continued and further developed with children of an older age. (337:3, 7)

Spiess collected, analyzed and classified all of the possible positions and movements of the body and published between 1840 and 1846, four volumes titled:  *Die Lehre der Turnkunst (System of Gymnastics)*.  However, his later and more famous book, *Turnbuch für Schulen* (*Gymnastics Manual for Schools*), was a much more valuable teacher's guide because only the more successful exercises were included, arranged in order of difficulty and categorized according to age and sex. He explained the method to be used for lessons and devised new forms of apparatus on which most of the class could work simultaneously under the supervision of one teacher.

Included in Spiess' analysis and arrangement of the material were some ideas new to German gymnastics. The first volume of *Die Lehre der Turnkunst* described free exercises; these were exercises either with no apparatus or small hand apparatus that could be performed in a limited area. Probably derived from Ling, these were intended to teach body control and graceful posture, performed while the student was standing or walking. Since large numbers of students participated, this caused the need for some system of moving the group as if one individual, which was solved by the development of class exercises in marching (*ordnungsübungen*), the subject for the fourth volume. Marching particularly suited Spiess because he believed that children learning to obey commands were developing a sense of discipline and order which was, he frequently reiterated, one of the primary goals of physical education.

> Tactic exercises [marching] which are always taught in classes, are the best means to accustom the single members of the class to be exact and concise in executing all commands, so as not to spoil the performance of the whole class of which he is but a part. (337:6)

> And since corporal deportment . . . can here be made the object of instruction in single, as well as class exercise, gymnastic art is really made the one branch of instruction in school life which teaches how to practice and display discipline, and which strives to realize (actualize) the spirit of order in form and deed. (337:4)

The other two volumes classified gymnastics into hanging exercises such as on the ladders, ropes and climbing poles, and supporting exercises, including the balance beam, parallel bars and horses. Interest in gymnastics was further motivated by Spiess' development of rhythmical arrangements for the free exercises and the combination of marching, dancing or other rhythmical movements into a fixed series which could be executed with musical accompaniment. This innovation has been continued by gymnastic performers to this day; even at the highest levels of competition free exercises are performed to musical accompaniment, and marchers often keep cadence to the music of a band.

The teacher was not expected to train "a few highly gifted pupils to perform comparatively difficult feats," but rather "he must strive to prove that gymnastic exercises possess educating power, and if possible by gradual advancement to bring each and every pupil in the class to the realization of the fact that gymnastic exercise is necessary to his education. . . ." (337:4) Spiess stated:

The school does not need higher gymnastics, *i.e.*, the pupils need not attempt difficult and dangerous feats.  What the school needs are calisthenic exercises and such other gymnastic exercises that are easily performed by the masses, but at the same time invigorate both body and mind and strengthen them for new labor. (337:2)

To carry out the proper execution of gymnastics classes as a school subject necessitated, according to Spiess, teachers who were educators by profession and who had been specifically prepared in gymnastics, to which end he conducted many school and training seminars.  "It is absolutely necessary that teachers by profession shall instruct the gymnastic classes. . . . We demand of the teacher of gymnastics the same qualifications and abilities that we expect from any other teacher. . . ." (337:7) But he expected that the teacher would learn "to handle and utilize the means which make his profession as educator, besides his other functions, that of disciplinarian." (337:4)  He underscored the point by reproaching those who thought that the gymnasium should be a place of freedom from customary discipline:

We do not belong to that class of men who, from sentimentality, rave over an imaginary life of youth and believe that the strict discipline and order of the school should give way to a so-called freer or looser discipline in the gymnasium. Here, as everywhere else, the pupil must first learn what it is to obey, before he is allowed to do as he pleases. (337:5)

One further aspect of Spiess' work should be given special notice:  he consistently sponsored gymnastics for girls as well as boys.  Although this was not entirely new, Spiess deliberately encouraged programs for girls and even devised special exercises for the "weaker sex."  The free exercises were especially intended for girls and younger boys because they did not demand the strength needed for the heavy apparatus.  In the *Turnbuch*, exercises were specified according to sex as well as age.

He hoped that within each school gymnastics would be a required subject in an equipped gymnasium, both indoor and outdoor.  Elementary classes were to have an hour each day during the school hours, under the supervision of the classroom teachers; high school students, although needing less time, were to have special gymnastics teachers.  Periodic examinations were to be administered at the same time as the general examinations, and *turnfeste* were to be held annually.  Actually these conditions were not fully realized until long after Spiess' death.  Although a Prussian ministerial order of 1844 directed that all higher schools provide indoor and outdoor facilities, instruction was to be given by a regular staff member and was to take place during the traditional Wednesday and Saturday half-holidays, rather than during school time.

In the United States, German pedagogical gymnastics were introduced into schools in New England and the Midwest (where a wave of German immigration had taken place around the middle of the nineteenth century). Several public school systems including Milwaukee, Kansas City, Chicago, Cleveland, and St. Louis, based their curriculums on German gymnastics (refer to pp. 273–274).

Adolf Spiess has always been fondly remembered as the "founder of school gymnastics in Germany and of gymnastics for girls in particular." (207:109)  His system, which was designed for masses of schoolboys and schoolgirls was more rigidly formal than Jahn's *turnen* for small voluntary groups.  It demanded absolute obedience and discipline and had no room for individual innovation or preference because the entire group performed simultaneously, as a unit, and because Spiess sought to insure that *every* part of the body was exercised.  Later German physical educators such as von Schenckendorff dropped some of its aspects such as the marching, but parts of the general gymnastics program remain in use even today, constituting a living memorial to Spiess.

# ROYAL CENTRAL GYMNASTIC INSTITUTE:

## BERLIN

Prior to the founding of the Königliche Zentralturnanstalt (Royal Central Gymnastic Institute) in 1851 in Berlin, there had been several attempts to develop physical education teacher training programs in Germany. Jahn organized a leaders' course in 1815 which was sparsely attended and Eiselen held several privately-organized and financed courses in his own gymnasium between 1832 and 1842. In 1848, under the direction of Hans Massmann who had been called upon to organize a statewide system of physical education in Prussia, the Zentral Bildungsanstalt für Lehrer in den Leibesübungen (Central Training School for Teachers of Gymnastics) was opened in the Eiselen gymnasium. Two 3-month courses were given yearly, primarily to candidates for teaching positions. By 1849 this venture, too, had failed because of lack of interest, the last class having only nine students.

However, in 1847 Hugo Rothstein (1810–1865) had established in Berlin the Central Institute for Gymnastic Instruction in the Army, where he taught the Swedish gymnastics of Per Ling rather than the German gymnastics of Jahn. Rothstein was a lieutenant in the Prussian artillery and a teacher in the artillery school at Berlin. Upon returning from a visit to Sweden he had published an article on "Gymnastics in Sweden and Ling's System of Gymnastics" (1844) which attracted such favorable official attention that he was sent by the government to the Royal Gymnastics Central Institute of Stockholm for a full course. He also spent three months at the Danish Royal Institute of Military Gymnastics in Copenhagen. The next year Hans Massmann published a translation of Ling's writings, *P. H. Ling's Schriften über Leibesübungen*, and Rothstein began work on a series of volumes about the Ling system, *Die Gymnastik, nach dem Systeme des Schwedischen Gymnasiarchen*, which he published at intervals between 1847 and 1859. However rioting, which broke out in Berlin in the spring of 1848, caused the closing of the new Institute in less than a year.

The Ministry of War and the Ministry of Education then combined their efforts and on October 1, 1851, the Royal Central Gymnastic Institute opened in a new building on Scharnhorststrasse with Rothstein as director of instruction. The intent was to train both military and civilian teachers in a single school; two separate divisions were established under the single administrator.   Besides Rothstein, the staff consisted of one military teacher, two military assistants, and two civilian teachers for the courses which were given free of cost for nine months, from the beginning of October to the end of June.

Although the two civilian teachers favored the Jahn-Spiess gymnastics, Rothstein favored the Ling system because it was "scientifically" based and used it in his own teaching.   He actually banned the use of horizontal and parallel bars at the Institute, advancing anatomical and physiological reasons against them, which caused a great commotion from the *turnvereine*.   After petitions, statements and opinions multiplied and the controversy was broadened to include the comparative merits of the two systems, a commission of medical men was appointed to study the issue. On the last day of 1862 the highest medical authority in Prussia, the Royal Scientific Deputation for Medical Affairs, ended the conflict by stating that exercises on the bars were justifiable and not to be rejected; he therefore ordered that the bars were to be used by civilian students.   This action caused Rothstein to resign his directorship, thus ending the Ling influence in Germany.

Actually, the Ling system had been abandoned in the civilian division since 1860 when Carl Euler was appointed its instruction director upon the retirement of the other two civilian teachers.   Under Euler the division grew in numbers of students, and therefore teachers, and also in independence from the military division.   Until 1860 only seventy-five civilians had participated in the nine courses offered, the yearly enrollment ranging between five and eleven; in 1857 the course had been decreased from nine to six months.   Starting in 1863, short special courses were given to elementary school teachers. (267:37)   By 1864 the enrollment had increased sufficiently to need an additional teacher and in 1865 another assistant teacher was hired.   In 1877 the military and civilian sections were permanently separated, the former assuming the title Royal Military Gymnastics Institute, and the latter the Königliche Turnlehrer-Bildungsanstalt (Royal Training School for Gymnastics Teachers).   When the Training School entered its new building on Friedrichstrasse in 1879 it had a director who was the state representative, an instruction director, two regular and three assistant teachers, and a student enrollment of thirty-five men divided into four squads, each under the care of a teacher. (267:38)   In 1866 Euler began to conduct private lessons for women who wanted to teach gymnastics and in 1880 regular state courses for women were added.

Mornings at the school were devoted to instruction and afternoons to the practice of activities.   The curriculum included anatomy, physiology, hygiene, and first aid for a total of five hours a week.   History of physical education (with an emphasis on Jahn) and methods of teaching were studied three hours a week.   Instruction on the apparatus, one hour a week

Fig. 27.    The Prussian Landesturnanstalt.

for two months, was doubled for the last four months.    Fencing too was doubled from three hours a week the first two months to six hours a week for the duration of the course.    Practical activities which reversed the pattern, going from eleven hours during the first two months to nine hours thereafter, included the use of wooden and iron wands, dumbbells, jump ropes, climbing platforms, ladders, Swedish apparatus, horses, parallel bars, springboards, rings, ropes, and the vaulting box.    Pole vaulting, javelin throwing and wrestling were introduced into the curriculum about 1880, but otherwise the course of study remained about the same until 1890 when time allotted for outdoor games and track and field was greatly increased. Also included in the curriculum were three hours of swimming which did not become part of the regular course until 1874, and two hours of practice teaching per week, first with each other and later with school children, bringing the total clock hours of required work for the course of study to approximately 850. (267:39)

In 1879 the building consisted of three gymnasiums, a library and a model physical education equipment room.    When the curriculum expanded in 1890 a nearby playground had to be used, and by 1906 most of the games and track and field events were conducted outdoors.    By 1927 there were about fifteen acres of play space, mostly contained within the circle of a 680-meter track, and a building containing five gymnasiums and all the accoutrements of a modern physical education plant, although the swimming still was conducted at a nearby city pool.    By that time, however, the school had undergone two name changes:    in 1905 to the Landesturnanstalt (State Gymnastics Institute), for by then it was taken over by the Department of Education, and in 1921 to the Preussische Hochschule für Leibesübungen (Prussian Physical Education College), placed under the Ministry of Science, Art and Popular Education. It had also been moved in 1911 to its permanent location in Spandau, a suburb of Berlin.

Its eminence in the field was superseded when, in 1920, the Deutsche Hochschule für Leibesübungen, a *private* institution, opened in Berlin. The rise of the Nazis caused the latter school to close in 1934 but in 1947 it reopened in Cologne as the Deutsche Sporthochschule (German Sports University) and is today a major institution for training physical education teachers in Germany. It should also be noted that beginning as early as 1892 various universities in Germany established courses of study for the university students to prepare to become physical education teachers; summer school playground courses were introduced in 1908 and later required of all physical education teachers seeking to attain state certification.

At the Central Institute no final, all-embracing examination was required of the students although students were graded in their written lessons in the theory classes, and of course on their ability to perform the physical skills. Beginning in 1866 teachers trained outside the Central Institute were required to take an examination under its auspices in order to qualify as physical education teachers. Later, after courses had been established within universities, arrangements could be made to take the examination in any one of a number of cities.

Although the Central Institute's influence receded with the growth of other similar curriculums, it served as Germany's first successful, state-run attempt to provide well-qualified teachers for the physical education program. It is a mark of the respect with which the Prussian state regarded the subject. Although the gymnastics aspect of the program was based on Jahn's and Spiess' work, study was not limited to gymnastics; the new sports and games, particularly track and field activities, were emphasized. Perhaps most significantly, the Institute attempted to train teachers, not just performers. Its curriculum helped physical education to assume a place of importance in the educational system on equal footing with other subjects which required trained teachers. Today in Germany, unlike in many European countries and Great Britain, it is possible to earn a doctorate in physical education at the University of Frankfurt (367), a fact which attests to the academic foundation laid by Germany's early teacher training schools. The spirit of the Royal Central Gymnastic Institute was of a place where both bodily strength and character could be developed, and the teachers who left there brought that idea, drawn originally from the *turners*, to the schools of Germany.

# EMIL THEODOR GUSTAV
# VON SCHENCKENDORFF

## 1837-1915

The movement away from *turnen* and towards ball games and athletics began in the central German city of Brunswick among the teachers and students of the Gymnasium Martino-Katharineum. Konrad Koch, a teacher of classical languages and history, and his colleague Hermann Corvinus, both of whom had been *turners*, influenced the movement by taking students to Saint Leonhardplatz on the outskirts of the city to play a variety of running and ball games such as "Prisoner's Base" and "Kaiserball." Koch's father-in-law, Friedrich Reck, had observed rugby when travelling in Great Britain and at his suggestion this was introduced to the boys by the school's *turnlehrer* (gymnastics teacher), August Hermann. The next year he introduced baseball and the following year, cricket. By 1879 participation in games was required for the lower and middle school classes, and in 1882 for the upper classes, which made the Gymnasium Martino-Katharineum the first German school to give games a place in the curriculum. (207·133–134) Because of Hermann, Koch and Reck, all of whom wrote and lectured on the need for arousing interest in competitive games and exercises, the idea spread rapidly. The Jahn-Spiess gymnastics had become increasingly formal and removed from the outdoor exercises on the early *turnplätze*. In part this was due to the ban on *turnen* which drove it indoors where it could be performed out of sight. Where Spiess had de-emphasized hiking, games and dancing, his followers had virtually eliminated them. The rigidly classical curriculum of the higher German schools (Latin, Greek, mathematics, and religion were the chief subjects) was complemented by an equally rigid gymnastics program of short duration (two hours each week), almost universally conducted indoors. The "new" games and sports were seen as a return to the outdoors as well as a means to develop student initiative.

A judge from Dusseldorf, Emil Hartwich, provided strong leadership to the idea when he founded the organization of a *Zentralverein für Körperpflege in Volk und Schule*, a permanent non-political body devoted to exercise, particularly games, festivals, skating, swimming, and rowing. Attempting to get schools to increase the time allotment for physical education, Hartwich coined the dualistic slogan: "The morning for the soul, the afternoon for the body." (267:31)   His group helped to get playgrounds built in many places, but it came in conflict with the more traditional *turnvereine* and when Hartwich was killed in a duel in 1886, the organization collapsed.   However, pamphlets continued to be disseminated, such as the one by the Prussian Minister of Public Worship and Instruction, Gustav von Gossler, who said that schools must foster play in a systematic way as an expression of youthful life, and for the benefit of body, mind, heart, and soul.

In 1881, Dr. Emil von Schenckendorff, a resident of Görlitz in Prussian Silesia, began to take an interest in the playground movement.   A man very much concerned with public affairs, he had been a member of both the City Council and the Prussian Chamber of Deputies; he had also served the government for ten years in the army and nine in the telegraph service, though poor health had forced him to resign from each.   One of his concerns was the one-sided intellectual education offered in the public schools, which he tried to counteract by organizing the Görlitz Manual Training Society and helping to found the German Central Committee for Manual Training and Home Industry.   He corresponded with Hartwich about the idea of introducing games to the young people of Görlitz and in 1883 added this form of activity to the city's program.   With the help of the director of the city Gymnasium, Gustav Ernst Eitner, and the younger teachers in the school, games were introduced gradually beginning with the lower classes.   Eventually not only all ages of school children but young men and even adults began to take part in the new program.   An annual *spielfeste* (playday) was established which also helped to interest the people.   When the national convention of philologists met in Görlitz in 1889 an exhibition of games was arranged for them, which caused a demand to train teachers capable of introducing them to the school.   Von Schenckendorff secured the necessary approval and arranged for four courses to be given, at which attendance totalled about 120 teachers, mostly from Germany and Austria but one from as far away as Russia. (207:141–142)

The next step taken by von Schenckendorff was to employ Hermann Raydt to determine and tabulate the exact status of the games (or playground) movement in Germany.   Raydt, who was interested in promoting games, had already proposed that the English-style playground be adapted to German school conditions.   With Raydt's information at hand, based on 273 replies to questionnaires, von Schenckendorff invited a number of prominent men, including leaders in the *Turnerschaft* and in the games movement, to meet in Berlin and from this was formed *Der Zentral-Ausschuss zur Förderung der Volks-und Jugendspiele in Deutschland* (the Central Committee for the Advancement of Folk and Child Play in Germany).   Von Schenckendorff was chairman and Raydt, Koch, Eitner, and Hermann were all appointed officers.   Its broad aim was "the embodiment of play in the life of the people. . . ." (200:326)

FIG. 28.  Emil Theodor von Schenckendorff.

In the twenty years between 1891 when the Central Committee was formed and 1911 when von Schenckendorff prepared a review of its activities, the Committee was able to sponsor a variety of open-air activities, including games, hikes, swimming, rowing, skating, skiing, and bobsledding. The Committee disseminated information by publishing magazines, pamphlets, small books, and a yearbook, twelve hundred copies of which were distributed annually by the Royal Prussian Bureau of Education. It sponsored a series of national congresses all over Germany, approached influential persons to secure their aid, and arranged over six hundred courses* which were attended by approximately 20,500 men and women teachers who wanted to prepare to become playground leaders. The Committee also issued and periodically revised a series of small guides containing authoritative descriptions of the most important games and their rules.  By 1912 there were twelve volumes covering sixteen games, plus ten booklets giving advice on matters such as how to introduce games to a community.

The Committee's work was strengthened by the Prussian government's issuance, in 1909, of a new manual of instruction which officially introduced the "new" physical education to the schools.† The apparatus exercises

* These were supplemented, beginning in 1905, by similar courses offered by the Prussian school authorities, who trained about sixty thousand teachers in the first six years.

†America's "new" physical education was introduced by Thomas Wood in a famous article (379) written in 1910. Refer to p. 377–378 for a synopsis of its basic principles.

were limited and the bulk of the program was to be devoted to games and track and field; activities were to take place outdoors whenever possible.

However, von Schenckendorff was aware that although his Committee had widely disseminated information, trained teachers and encouraged programs, the playground movement had replaced obligatory gymnastics in only a few scattered places. Voluntary play-afternoons were widely in evidence, but games had not yet become a standard aspect of the educational curriculum. At universities there was increased interest but facilities were inadequate for games activities. In effect, it could be said that a wide difference existed between governmental decrees and actual local practice. But during the last ten years of the nineteenth century, the number of playgrounds in cities over five thousand almost doubled to 2092. (200:331)

Nevertheless, German schools moved away at varying rates of speed from the mentally intensive, organized exercises of Adolf Spiess towards the English-style sport activities advocated by von Schenckendorff and his Committee. Von Schenckendorff must be considered the foremost contributor to the playground movement for it was due to his unceasing effort that physical education for the youth of Germany was expanded from narrow, disciplined gymnastic exercises to include fun and free-spirited games. He also helped prepare for the foundation of sports clubs, which became popular not only in Germany but throughout Europe.

PART V *(Continued)*

*European Physical Educators and Institutions*

*SWEDISH*

# PER HENRIK LING

## 1776-1839

The founder of Swedish gymnastics, Per Henrik Ling, was as famous for his literary abilities as for his gymnastic system. For the former he was accorded membership in the Swedish Academy (1835), a distinguished body of eighteen scholars; he was given the title "Professor" and was decorated with the Order of the North Star. His collected writings fill three large volumes of more than 2500 pages, of which only 350 are concerned with gymnastics. Throughout his writings a decided nationalistic attitude emanated, expressed for instance, in the subject of his great work on the entire mythology and ancient legendary history of the Scandinavian race, the *Asarne* (the *Aesir* or Northern gods). Originally published in 1816, this work was reissued in a revised and more complete form in 1833, winning for Ling a prize from the Swedish Academy. His most successful dramatic work was *Agne,* a tragedy in five acts, printed in 1812 and presented on the Stockholm stage after his death. He also translated a three-act comedy written in Danish, *Den Misundelige (The Envious Man),* and innumerable poems in four languages: French, German, Danish, and his native Swedish. Among these were *Eylif the Goth* (1814) in which he revealed his desire to revive the old Norse vigor in the new generation, and *Gylfe* (1810, 1812, 1816) which dealt with the loss of Finland to the Russians and expressed some of the Swedish bitterness towards that occurrence.

Ling was born in 1776 in Småland, a southern province of Sweden in which his ancestors had lived for more than seven generations. His father, a minister, died when Ling was only four and his mother, the great granddaughter of a famous Swedish author, died when he was thirteen. He attended the high classical school in Vexiö (where the botanist Linnaeus had studied) and in 1793 enrolled at the University in Lund. After two semesters he seems to have gone to Stockholm and worked as a clerk and private tutor of French and German. From 1799 to 1804 he lived in Copenhagen where he acquired his thorough knowledge of Danish and at the University there came under the influence of the great Danish poet Oehlenschläger and the romantic philosophy of Schelling taught by one of his Norwegian followers. The latter introduced him to the literary heritage of his ancestry—the old Norse mythology, including the great Icelandic *Edda* poems dating from the ninth through the eleventh centu-

Fig. 29.    Per Henrik Ling.

ries A.D., in which are described the Old Scandinavian athletic games. From this experience can be dated Ling's lifelong interest in the ancient Northern sagas. (158:1–2)

While in Copenhagen he also took up fencing, at which he became quite adept. It is said that he suffered pain from arthritis which was alleviated by the exercise, thus inciting his interest in the medical effects of exercise. He also visited Nachtegall's private gymnasium where he probably became acquainted with vaulting the horse. Another of his activities was to enroll voluntarily on the Danish side when Nelson and his English fleet fought a battle in Copenhagen harbor in 1801, although Ling did not actually see action. With much profit from his five-year stay in Denmark, in that the seeds of his career were sown, Ling returned in 1804 to Sweden to become fencing master at the University of Lund. He sent to Denmark for a vaulting horse and introduced it to his fencing students in Lund. During the eight years he remained there both his fencing method and gymnastics became very popular and he was invited to give courses during the summers in the cities of Gothenburg, Malmö and Christianstad. Ling also gave private lessons; he advertised in the Lund paper for three or four boys to live with him and study languages, mathematics and drawing as well as vaulting, swimming and fencing. While at Lund, Ling studied anatomy and physiology and worked out his original systems of bayonet fencing and gymnastics. (207:151–152)

Meanwhile, Sweden's international posture had deteriorated rapidly from the time when it was a great power in northern Europe. Most of its southern and eastern Baltic provinces had been lost to Russia early in the eighteenth century. In 1805 Gustavus IV attempted to stop Napoleon by entering into a coalition with England, Russia and Austria; as a result French troops occupied Swedish Pomerania and in 1807 took Stralsund and Rügen, the last Swedish possessions south of the Baltic. By opening his ports to English ships, the King incurred the enmity of Russia whose soldiers invaded and conquered Finland in 1808, thus depriving Sweden of a territory which had been hers for centuries and which constituted about one third of her empire.  The King was dethroned and replaced by the childless Charles XIII.  In 1810 the Swedish Diet elected a French general, Jean Baptiste Jules Bernadotte to succeed him; he titled himself Crown Prince and ascended the throne in 1818 as Charles XIV John, founding the present Swedish dynasty.  Bernadotte, who was extremely anxious to prepare his country militarily, supported Ling's idea for a physical training institute because he saw it as useful to his military ambitions.

In Denmark Nachtegall had begun to train gymnastic teachers for the army and the schools and Ling believed he could do the same in Sweden. The loss of national territory made the Swedes fiercely determined to ready themselves to meet the enemy and Ling proposed that fencing and gymnastics were suitable means of accomplishing the necessary health, physical strength and character.  In 1813 he was given the position of fencing master in the Royal Military Academy at Karlberg, but more important, his plan to make Stockholm a center for physical training was approved by the government and the King.  In 1814 the Royal Gymnastics Central Institute or Kungl. Gymnastiska Centralinstitutet (RGCI) was opened in an old cannon foundry.

It was at the Central Institute that Ling developed the theory of gymnastics which eventually became known all over the world as the Swedish system.  J. G. Thulin, a principal at the Sydsvenska Gymnastik-Institutet in Lund, in 1931 quoted Ling's own summary of his system:

> Physical exercise must be based on the laws of the human system, and influence not only the body but also the mind.
> The fundamental principles can be briefly comprised in the following four clauses:
> 1. The aim is an all-around harmonious development of the body.
> 2. The attainment of this is sought by means of biologically and physiologically grounded physical exercises of definite form and, as far as possible, of known effect.
> 3. The exercises must have developmental and corrective values, be easily understood and satisfy our demands of beauty.
> 4. The exercises must be carried out with a gradually increasing degree of difficulty and exertion.  (361:625–626)

In its early history the majority of the students at the RGCI were young military officers; this probably influenced the preponderant development of the military aspects, although Ling had organized the system around four principal components:  pedagogical, military, medical, and aesthetic.  In the *General Principles of Gymnastics* he defined them in this way:

> (1) Pedagogical gymnastics, by means of which one learns to bring his body under the control of his own will.  (2) Military gymnastics, in which one seeks by means of an external thing—e.g., a weapon, or by means of his own bodily power—

to subject the will of another person to his own.  (3) Medical gymnastics, by means of which one seeks, either by his own proper posture or with the help of another person and by helpful movement, to diminish or overcome the ailment which has arisen in his body through its abnormal relations.  (4) Aesthetic gymnastics, through which a person endeavors to give bodily expression to his inner being, thoughts, or impressions.  (158:8)

Despite the need for classifications, Ling stated that the divisions have a "mutual interdependence" which he conceived of as a common concern for the attainment of unity:

> Pedagogical gymnastics develop the innate endowments to unity among the parts of the organism.  In military gymnastics unity is sought between the body and the weapon in relation to the expressions of an antagonist.  By means of medical gymnastics one seeks to restore unity between the parts, which has been lost through their abnormal relations; and through aesthetic gymnastics the subject expresses the unity which exists between the mental and bodily being.  (159:543)

These divisions grew out of a *philosophical* belief about human nature, and the relationship of men to themselves and to the external world.  To Ling the powers of the organism existed in three "ground forms":  the dynamic, in which the being strove to liberate itself from matter, and the chemical and mechanical in which being unified with matter.  These corresponded in the organism to the nervous, circulatory and muscular systems, respectively, and *health* was the result of their mutual harmony.  Out of these arose four behavioral potentials:  subjective-active, objective-active, subjective-passive, objective-passive:

> In the first case we imagine one acting by means of his own force in order to maintain and develop it; in the second case his action is directed against some force external to himself; in the third case his organism is in a state of perturbation of some kind, so that he is less able to act than to suffer himself to be acted upon— i.e., he must submit to the mechanical influence of some external agent; in the last case one simply gives expression of his inner being to some outer being.  (159:543)

From this idea about human behavior he developed the four divisions of gymnastics which he thus believed to be in harmony with the laws of the organism.

While it was common in earlier, pre-Cartesian days, for science to be an expression of philosophy, Ling's ideas were disparaged because of their scientific untenability.  This was ironic because Ling himself insisted that gymnastics be scientifically based.  In fact, he defined "theory of gymnastics" as "the doctrine of bodily movements in consonance with the laws discernible in the organism." (159:543)  He also stated that gymnastics should be a "preservative against the katabolism of the organism" and as such must be imbued with physiological and pathological ideas. (183:75)

While at Lund he undertook the study of anatomy and physiology with the intent of following its principles; within the limits of what was then known he was considered a fairly good anatomist. Although he declared that no exercise should be included until its effects were known, misconceptions were formed which led to later rejection of his whole system. For example, Ling stated that "in general, everyone should pay the greatest attention to the development of the chest." (182:271) Based upon the belief that an expanded chest provided more room for the lungs, and thus led to increased metabolism, it was considered of benefit to develop the thorax. Position and movements were prescribed to achieve this end and attempts to determine their effects were made by taking measurements. It was thus "scientifically determined" that the chest was expanded and vital capacity therefore improved as a result of the special positions and exercises. But in later years it has been demonstrated that increased metabolism relates to the extent of *change* in dimension of the thorax, as caused by the contraction and relaxation of the diaphragm, rather than the *static* volume or shape. Therefore the demonstrated chest growth had no positive effect upon respiration and, in fact, the strained positions that were advocated hindered the mobility of the diaphragm resulting in a diminished capacity. One of the more stringent rules of Swedish exercises—that gymnastic movements should help regular breathing and that no exercises were to be chosen which caused constriction of the chest—therefore served no function despite Ling's belief that his measurements demonstrated effect.

Seeking exercises with demonstrable effects Ling rejected much of Jahn's work as being too complicated and questionable. Where Jahn began with the apparatus and tried to devise movements that could be performed upon it, Ling began with a desired result and developed apparatus or exercises to produce it. Over the years he invented the stall bars (still used today in every Swedish gymnasium), the Swedish boom, the Swedish box (vaulting box), the window ladder, and the oblique rope. (385) The apparatus were constructed so that only fundamental and simple movements could be performed upon them and students were expected to use all pieces in one lesson doing one exercise upon each. Thus the emphasis was not on developing ability to do advanced stunts (as with the *turners*), but on getting through the entire series in a continuous manner according to command.

Although he invented apparatus, much of it still used today, his own predilection was for free exercises without even the use of hand apparatus. He set forth their advantages as follow:

1. That more can exercise at one time under a teacher.
2. That such movements can be made in a great variety of places. . . .
3. That the trouble and expense of providing and keeping apparatus in repair are eliminated.
4. That the fact that the entire squad or class must make the exercises at the same moment promotes strength and agility and rapid attainment of bodily control.

5. That the execution of gymnastics at the word of command reenforces the effect of strict military drill.
6. That free movements are more easily adaptable to the bodily peculiarities of individuals.
7. That they are better than machine gymnastics for overcoming awkwardness and stiffness. (159:545)

Ling stressed *positions* as distinguished from movements; an exercise, in effect, consisted of movements from position to position, done on command. The precision of the performance was thus the precision of the body position in each successive position. He divided all movements into trunk, head, arm, and leg movements, and each position specified the exact location of each segment of the body. He made tables of movements, usually containing from ten to twelve movements. For example, the sixth table in his *Reglemente för Gymnastik* comprises twelve movements: 1, leg movement; 2, arm movement; 3, head movement; 4, trunk movement or back move-

FIG. 30.    Swedish Gymnasts Performing at an Exhibition.

ment; 5, leg movement; 6, arm movement; 7, leg movement; 8, arm movement; 9, jumping movement; 10, trunk movement; 11, leg movement; and 12, arm movement. (159:545) The primary consideration was that the chest be in a fully expanded position, a requirement which generally placed the lower back in a strained arched position. As practiced, style rather than movement became the dominant factor. Ling gymnastics began to consist of positions retained for the length of time it took the teacher to observe and correct faults. This meant that an entire class was often held for a long time in the artificial and strained position specified. Even vaulting and jumping were analyzed in that manner by stopping the landing in spring standing position or even holding the vault in the middle of the movement. The more conscientious the teacher, the less beneficial the exercise (in modern terms which stress dynamic strength and flexibility) and the more boring the class. As a result, Swedish gymnastics never became really popular even in Sweden.

However, Ling himself never faced the problem of student disinterest or complaint. He advocated that the children "now and again run about and make a noise for a short time. This keeps the spirit and strengthens vital inner parts of the body." And he also said: "To cut out enjoyment from gymnastics and strive only for solid work without deviation from a set scheme is to kill the spirit of gymnastics." (183:93) As a teacher he carried out his own admonitions, holding classes that were stimulating and successful. One of his students stated that "the father of our gymnastics was surely an excellent *methodmaker*, but one must not think that he let the style smother the spirit. He possessed an exceptional ability to put life into the lesson. . . ." (183:93) Furthermore, most of Ling's own students were military cadets for whom he sought to produce results, not pleasure. They were used to commands and authority and responded well to both. The military aspect of Ling's gymnastics, which was the area to which he gave greatest attention, was suitably developed. In later years, when Ling's son, Hjalmar, attempted to develop the pedagogical division, the exercises turned out to be less suitable for school children.

Ling's writings on physical education were comparatively meager. In 1836 he published a *Manual of Gymnastics* (*Reglemente för Gymnastik*) and a *Manual of Bayonet Fencing* (*Reglemente för Bajonettfäktning*) for use in the army. In 1838 he published a small handbook covering both subjects: *Soldat-Undervisning i Gymnastik och Bajonettfäktning*. The work which sets forth the principles of educational, military, medical, and aesthetic gymnastics, after an opening chapter on the laws of the human organism, the *General Principles of Gymnastics* (*Gymnastikens Allmänna Grunder*), was put together and published a year after his death by Georgii and Liedbeck, two of his successors at the Institute. A small book of less than 250 pages, it was published in the incomplete and fragmentary form in which Ling left it.

As creator of a new system of gymnastics, thereafter known as the Swedish system, Ling earned a firm reputation as an innovator.    His greatest successes were with medical and military gymnastics; aesthetic gymnastics was never really developed and Hjalmar Ling must be credited with the development of pedagogical gymnastics.    His insistence on basing gymnastics on scientific principles may be regarded as his most important and longest lasting contribution to modern physical education.    Ling's personal integrity and patriotic aims imbued Swedish gymnastics with a spirit in keeping with the best traditions of education.

One hundred years after the death of Per Ling, the Swedish government chose to honor him by issuing a commemorative stamp and creating an international gymnastic celebration of Olympic dimensions.    Known as the Lingiad the event took place in Stockholm in 1939, attended by 7,300 participants from thirty-seven countries in all parts of the world.    Since its initiation, the memorial Lingiad has taken place each decade, thus establishing a living memorial to the memory of Per Henrik Ling.    The importance of Swedish gymnastics to American physical education is acknowledged by the honor bestowed on Per Ling by the American Academy of Physical Education which designated him a Fellow in Memoriam.

# ROYAL GYMNASTICS CENTRAL INSTITUTE: STOCKHOLM

The Kungl. Gymnastiska Centralinstitutet i Stockholm (Royal Gymnastics Central Institute of Stockholm or RGCI) was opened in 1814 as a consequence of the ideas and planning of Per Henrik Ling. Ling, a great nationalist whose goal was "a fine and sturdy Youth for the North," (58:3) persuaded the Committee on Education, appointed at that time, that such an institution would aid in building up the physical prowess of his countrymen. Recent military defeats made this an especially attractive idea and on May 5, 1813, just three months after Ling's idea was proposed, the King formally approved the plan; by 1814 the RGCI was opened. An old cannon foundry located in Norrmalm, a northern suburb of Stockholm, was equipped and Ling was appointed the first director. The RGCI continued to operate from that building until 1944 when it was moved to its present location adjoining the Olympic Stadium in Stockholm.

Because Ling believed that gymnastics served an appropriate function in medicine, education and national defense, instruction was given in all three areas; however, military gymnastics received the most attention. Ling continued to teach fencing and gymnastics at the Royal Military Academy at Karlberg and the Artillery School in Marieberg. The new king, Charles XIV (the French General Bernadotte), discerning the military advantage of such instruction, sent army officers to take the course at the Institute. Having taken this training they in turn taught the army rank and file. Some of the soldiers stationed near the city were also sent to the Institute for the practical training it afforded. To fulfill the purposes of the military the instruction was kept to simple levels and was taught with army-style authoritarianism. The aim was to produce well-trained soldiers in an efficient, rapid manner. This preponderance of soldier-students and the corresponding teaching techniques which were developed created a semi-military atmosphere at the Institute and in general pervaded the development of Swedish gymnastics. The large number of military officers who graduated from the Institute simultaneously gave status to gymnastics and prevented it from achieving great popularity with the common man who did not find pleasure in the narrow, unflexible program.

By 1830 the faculty of the Institute had grown to include the director, a head teacher, and two other teachers. Among these was Lars Gabriel Branting who had joined the faculty in 1818, was promoted to head teacher in 1830 and upon Ling's death in 1839 succeeded to the directorship. Branting (1799–1881) had been a weak and sickly child who in the first year of the Institute was sent to Ling for treatment through medical gymnastics. Later he became a student at the Karolinska Mediko-Kirurgiska Institut, Sweden's largest medical college, where he evidenced special skill in anatomy and physiology and also studied chemistry. With this background it was natural for Branting to pay particular attention to the development of medical gymnastics and when he became director this aspect of the school's program received new and thorough attention. Branting can be credited with the idea that medical gymnastics were beneficial not only because they brought about muscular changes, but also because they affected the nerves and blood vessels. His work earned various awards, among them designation as a knight of the North Star and the Prussian Red Eagle, the Danish St. Olaf and Dannebrog, and Commander of the Order of Vasa.

Carl August Georgii (1808–1881), an army lieutenant who was trained at the Karlberg Military Academy, joined the staff around 1829 and became head teacher ten years later. He taught anatomy as well as medical, military and school gymnastics and published treatises on the Ling method of kinesiotherapy and physical education. He also was one of the two editors responsible for publishing Ling's *General Principles of Gymnastics*.

During Branting's directorship, three additional staff members were engaged, including Truls Johan Hartelius (1818–1896) who began to teach at the Institute immediately after graduating from it in 1852. Subsequently he became a qualified physician and made a particular contribution to the development of medical gymnastics by writing textbooks on anatomy, physiology, histology, and hygiene; one of his works on medical gymnastics was translated into three languages. He also edited the *Tidskrift i Gymnastik*, a semi-annual periodical on gymnastics largely written by the teachers at the Institute. In 1848 the first woman, Gustafva Lindskog, was hired and upon her death three years later was succeeded by Ling's daughter Hildur. Both women taught medical gymnastics and also were involved in the physical training of school girls, an activity started by Branting who introduced gymnastics to girls in the large Hillska School just outside of Stockholm. The Institute itself did not offer regular courses for women until 1864 when Colonel Gustav Nyblaeus was director. Nyblaeus was the first in a long series of directors who were military officers. Upon his retirement in 1887 he was succeeded by Captain Lars Mauritz Törngren who was at that time the head teacher in school gymnastics. Törngren (1839–1912) made a number of contributions to the growth of the Institute and the profession including a book on school games, *Fris Lekar* (1879), which was the result of a visit he made to England where he observed the English sports and games program. He also wrote an official manual of gymnastics for the Swedish navy and a manual for use in institutions training teachers for the elementary schools, *Lärobok i Gymnastik för Folksskollärare och Folksskollärarinneseminarier*, published in Stockholm in 1905 and later translated into German. In 1893 he visited the United States and attended the eighth annual meeting of the AAAPE. (207:158–161)

In 1864 the King appointed a Board of Directors for the Institute (previously it had been under the control of the Stockholm Committee on Education). The course was lengthened from one year to two years, each consisting of a six-month semester, and the Institute was officially organized into sections representing military, medical and educational gymnastics with a head and second teacher for each section. Nyblaeus, as well as being director, headed the military gymnastics section, Hartelius the medical, and Hjalmar Ling (refer to chapter on him) the school gymnastics.

By this time the RGCI had established a reputation and people in Europe and America interested in gymnastics, including some eminent physicians, came to observe the Swedish method. Among these was a Prussian officer, Hugo Rothstein, who was sent by his government to take the course. Rothstein later became the first director of the Royal Central Gymnastic Institute in Berlin, which originally adopted the Swedish rather than the Jahn system of gymnastics (refer to chapter on the RGCI in Berlin). Senda Berenson, the head of Smith College's physical education program, was the first American woman to study at the Institute. The Baron Nils Posse, a graduate of the Institute, was invited to bring the Swedish system to the Boston schools, thus extending the influence of the RGCI still further.

In 1900 Fred Leonard, a noted American physical educator and historian of the profession, spent three months studying at the RGCI and in his published description of it he detailed the course of instruction which was followed at that time. (207:165–171) Since 1887 three separate courses were available to male students: (1) the Instructor's Course comprised a year's study, qualifying its graduates to teach only in the elementary or lower secondary schools; (2) the Gymnastic Teacher's Course required a second year of study, enabling graduates to teach gymnastics in any public educational institution in the country; and (3) the Gymnastic Director's Course, during a third year of study, prepared teachers of medical gymnastics. For women both the courses in medical gymnastics and school gymnastics could be completed in two years because they were expected to learn fewer practical exercises. Each of the three one-year courses ended with a public examination and certification for those who passed. The Institute's responsibility, however, continued with a series of public school inspections designed to give help to the new young teachers it graduated.

Entrance requirements included passing an examination that would qualify a student to enter one of the national universities, plus good health

Fig. 31.    Class of Women Students at the Stockholm Central Institute.

and some aptitude for gymnastics.    The entering age limit was thirty years except for physicians who also had the advantage of being able to complete the three-year course in medical gymnastics in less than the required time.    In 1900 there were about sixty men enrolled, most of whom were army or navy officers or non-commissioned officers.    Women students were fewer in number but their enrollment steadily increased.    In the 1960s the Institute's capacity was only about 150 students a year, but many more potential physical educators enrolled in teachers' colleges and training colleges.

The curriculum at the RGCI was a combination of theoretical and practical studies.    During their first year students studied anatomy three times a week throughout the year and physiology twice a week during the second semester.    The theory of school gymnastics and fencing was studied twice a week for an entire year and military gymnastics twice weekly for a half year.    Supplementing the lectures was an hour each day of practical instruction in school gymnastics, another in foil fencing and a third in sabre and bayonet.    There was also daily practice in teaching, an opportunity resulting from the Institute's policy of having three hundred boys from a nearby higher school take lessons there for an hour each morning, and two hundred from a secondary school each afternoon.    The young boys exercised in squads, each under the direction of a first-year student.

Second-year students took turns for a week at a time directing the exercises of six squads combined.    They also practiced teaching by giving individual instruction in fencing to the first-year men.    Besides their teaching experiences, the second-year curriculum included advanced anatomy lessons with dissection; further work in physiology; twice-weekly lectures on kinesiology or the theory of bodily movements; additional study of the theory of school gymnastics; instruction and practice in medical gymnastics, and practical work in the same subjects studied the first year. Swimming was not required either year but proficiency in it was necessary for graduation.

Since the third year was for students interested in medical gymnastics, the lectures dealt with anatomy, physiology and pathology; study of the theory and practice of medical gymnastics was continued, and students assisted in giving treatment to patients who came to the Institute. A portion of the Institute's building was comprised of two clinics, one for free patients and one for paying ones, where medical gymnastics was practiced. However, by Swedish law treatment by means of medical gymnastics was permissible only by physicians or from a prescription by a physician.

The courses for women were substantially the same, only shorter, and their practice teaching took place in private schools outside the Institute. Women did not, however, take courses with their male colleagues.

Despite its increasing enrollment and obviously established position, the RGCI was criticized on two important points. The first was the military nature of the directors, teachers and subsequently the method. Because the Institute was training military men as teachers, the schools of Sweden commonly had military rather than civilian teachers for physical education, a circumstance which had the effect of stunting the growth of Swedish gymnastics. Soldiers tended to obey rather than to question and thus they perpetuated precisely what they were taught, resisting all attempts at change. The second criticism had to do with the scope of the program and the ability of a single institution to combine pedagogical, military and medical gymnastics. In 1922 a Stockholm professor, Patrik Haglund, wrote that "the amalgamation of three different interests which are fundamentally too specialized to be combined to any advantage . . . must strangle each other, and, in fact, have done so." (148:25) He called for a reorganization of the RGCI arguing that:

> The present staff of medical gymnasts at the Institute must be replaced by a staff of doctors trained in the hospitals for all kinds of mechanical and physical therapeutics. A re-constituted army will no longer be satisfied with the *status quo*, and the schools avowedly need gymnastic teachers who will give their time entirely to the school. (148:25)

Two Royal Commissions, in 1910 and 1915, studied the question of the Institute's reorganization and needs and recommended radical changes, which were never accomplished, perhaps because they were so far-reaching. In 1935 another attempt was made to remove the military influence by limiting admission to the Institute to already qualified teachers who wanted to earn a specialization in physical education. Changes took place gradually, and at the present time the Institute prepares only teachers of physical education, in a two-year course which qualifies them to teach in the higher schools.

The Swedish government assumed the financing of the Institute from its inception; regularly enrolled students have never been asked to pay tuition.   As director, Ling was given a salary of five hundred rix-dollars (approximately five hundred dollars), which in 1830 was doubled and before his death raised to two thousand rix-dollars.   In addition an annual allowance of one hundred rix-dollars was set aside for rent and a single grant of four hundred rix-dollars was made for the purchase of necessary equipment.   About a year later the King granted 9800 rix-dollars more to improve the facility and the next year appropriated further funds to hire the first assistant teacher.   In 1863 over 167,000 rix-dollars was granted to remodel and add to the buildings and funds were also appropriated to hire the new teachers needed to reorganize the program.   A large sum (eighty thousand kroner or approximately $15,200) was granted in 1894 to improve facilities and instruction.   Money was also appropriated as needed to hire faculty.

The Royal Gymnastics Central Institute has had an important place in the profession from the time it opened its doors in 1814.   From it emerged not only a method of physical education (Swedish or Ling gymnastics), but generations of teachers for the schools of Sweden and the world at large. Although "pure" Ling gymnastics is a thing of the past, there is hardly a country whose schools do not exhibit traces of it in their programs, and free exercises (now called floor exercises) has become an Olympic event. Physical education in America went through, in the early years of its growth, what has been called "a battle of the systems"; what emerged included vestiges of each system.   The greatest tribute to the RGCI, however, lies in the fact that it endures until this time and that even today students from all over the world attend its courses to study the Swedish method.

# HJALMAR FREDERICK LING

## 1820-1886

Hjalmar Ling was more influential in the international development of Swedish gymnastics than his famous father, Per Ling. The elder Ling's talents were used largely to develop military gymnastics; Lars Branting forwarded the early development of medical gymnastics; and Hjalmar Ling gave form and scope to educational gymnastics. Because of his work, physical education was introduced into the elementary and girls schools as well as into the higher schools.

When the Royal Gymnastics Central Institute was reorganized in 1864, Hjalmar Ling was placed in charge of school gymnastics, a position he held for eighteen years until his retirement in 1882. Although the Institute had been training teachers for fifty years this particular branch of gymnastics had received little attention and physical education in the schools clearly reflected such disregard. The majority of the teachers were military men who did not understand that since the aims of military and educational gymnastics were different, the methods must also be different. In many schools the entire program consisted of heaves (movements to aid respiration by developing the upper part of the chest) and vaulting. In others only free standing work was done and that just from the simplest starting positions, although apparatus was to children by far the most interesting aspect. A large collection of exercises was available, but the ability of the teachers to select those suitable for educational needs was lacking. The RGCI itself collaborated very little with the public schools, and textbooks were practically nonexistent.

Hjalmar Ling's first approach to correcting this situation was to publish a guide to educational gymnastics. The first edition of the *Tabeller i Friskgymnastik* was published in 1866. Ling wrote a total of four editions, the last in 1876; Lars Mauritz Törngren who succeeded Hjalmar as head of school gymnastics edited two more, the last in 1897. This work, together with a *Supplement*, was for many years the only printed guide for Swedish educational gymnastics. To write it Ling assembled the large mass of material developed at the Institute and also devised new forms of apparatus especially adapted to school needs and organized for use with large numbers of students. From this collection he selected the most suitable exercises and classified them in groups according to expected effects. Within each group he arranged the exercises in a progression according to difficulty. Since Ling believed that during each gymnastics lesson the body should be systematically worked, exercises having different effects were put together and placed in a certain order. This was the concept behind the Swedish *table* or *day's order.* Progression was insured by placing the movements in a sequence depending upon their degree of difficulty. Thus graded series of exercises were made available from which the teacher could use those which were appropriate to the age, level of ability and sex of the class.

Besides the day's orders, Ling printed instructions concerning the method of using them. The students were to learn the various positions and practice getting into and holding the starting position. Then the exercises were to be executed by a series of *commands,* a method which the Swedes liked because they believed this enabled greater concentration on the exercises rather than on remembering the order of the exercises. Furthermore, quick response to commands was believed to be an aid to developing discipline, a concept which further reflected the military atmosphere pervading the endeavor. For example, starting from an "erect standing" position, the student might be commanded "Hips—firm! Slightly, trunk backward —bend! Upward—stretch!" (289:63), meaning that his hands would be placed firmly on his hips in the "wing" position and his trunk would then

Fig. 32.    Swedish Gymnastic Exercise.    (From Posse's
*Handbook of School Gymnastics.*)

be arched backward to the "arch" position and forward to the "stoop" position.

Each table was intended to be repeated for a particular period of time, such as every day for a week; each exercise was executed at least three times to each side; and an attempt was made to repeat exercises from table to table to insure continuity.    A day's order was coordinated internally as well as externally to the orders which came before and after.    Hjalmar Ling in his syllabus encouraged "permittable changes" from the day's order— he intended it to serve primarily as a guide and not as a rigid structure. But in practice the day's order was rarely deviated from and for years after Ling's death the tables used for the student's training were similar to those developed by him.

Like his father, Hjalmar was concerned with the relationship of gymnastics to breathing.    He emphasized the necessity of the "expanded chest" to allow full breathing, and described how to achieve it in erect standing position:    "It is done with some appearance of *puffing oneself up with pride. . . .*" (182:272)  Major Oswald Holmberg, a lecturer at the RGCI, quoted Ling as developing the following methodological criteria:

> The conditions for a correct gymnastic *position* are the same as for full breathing, as for one giving greatest beauty and strength in performance.    Every correctly performed gymnastic movement done with full attention and will-power can therefore be regarded as an exercise for the thorax.    A correct position is clearly shown by the carriage and relationship of the head, neck, chest, shoulders and abdomen.    While this applies firstly to *positions* it applies also to *movements*, as the latter are dependent on the former.    Therefore all performers of gymnastics are dependent not only on *degree*, but also on *style*, even as regards vaulting (183:96)

In general, this emphasis on style was regarded by Hjalmar Ling as even more important than the ability to do increasingly difficult tasks. Ling was afraid that the pursuit of great prowess would lead to a one-sided development (technique without precision) of the gymnast's abilities; he also feared that teachers would then tend to favor their better students to the detriment of the majority.    Although he personally advocated some flexibility in this matter, allowing students who had not absolutely perfected the style of an exercise to continue on to a new one (provided they later returned to and perfected the old one), the other teachers of Sweden were not as lenient.    In 1955 Holmberg criticized their practice:

> The result was that pedantic progression led to lack of interest amongst the pupils, who were never allowed to try their strength on more difficult and strenuous tasks, and who found it difficult to appreciate the change caused by a trunk leaning backward taken with hands on hips one week, and the next with arms bent. (183:95)

Ling was not particularly concerned with such criticisms of his method. First of all, he was a theoretician, not a practitioner.    In fact, he was a rather reserved and shy man whose main aim in life was to collect and arrange his father's works. He cautioned teachers to include variety in the tables and to teach with the greatest spirit, saying that "whoever fails to obtain both *form* and *life* with 30–50 children should never have anything to do with gymnastics." "To guard against the danger of pedantry in the teaching of gymnastics there are no 'Antidotes,' any more than there exist any artificial means by which one can fill a human being who is impossible as a teacher, with a stimulating spirit." (183:99)

Although Hjalmar Ling used most of his energies to further school gymnastics he also realized the importance of sports, noting that

> the work for muscle isolation, which is necessary in the beginning to simplify the movements and avoid by-movements, will later be unnecessary or harmful. One will then glide over to applied exercises and more enjoyable *sports* and exercises in open order be less used. (183:100)

Three years after publication of the *Tables* Ling brought out a supplement, the *Tillägg til Tabellerna* (*Supplement to the Syllabus of Tables*), a book which went through four editions, the last in 1894 put out by Törngren. He also published a work on kinesiology or the science of bodily movements, the *Rörelselära* (1866). In addition he helped with the editing and writing of the *Tidskrift i Gymnastik*, the Institute's semi-annual periodical. When he died he left a collection of nearly two thousand drawings of positions and movements used in gymnastics, about a quarter of which were later published in Stockholm.

Hjalmar Ling was well-prepared to carry on his father's work. Born in 1820 in Stockholm he received a secondary school education and in 1842 completed the course at the Institute. He immediately became a teacher

FIG. 33.  Hjalmar Ling.

there, working under Branting and Liedbeck's tutelage in both educational and medical gymnastics. From the physician Liedbeck he increased his knowledge of anatomy and then in 1854 went to Paris and studied both anatomy and experimental physiology. In addition to learning French, he also acquired a knowledge of German on his two trips to Germany, which were made for the purpose of introducing the Swedish method of medical gymnastics. In 1858 he was appointed head teacher under Branting (who was the director from 1839–1862) and took charge of educational gymnastics in 1864. For some years he also was in charge of the physical education in the Nya Elementarskola, one of the city's higher schools for boys. His familiarity with foreign languages enabled him to compile quite a library of gymnastic literature which he left with the Institute. He died in 1886 and was buried near his father at Annelund. (207:161–162)

Although Per Ling is considered the author (or father) of Swedish gymnastics, were it not for the work of his son Hjalmar Ling the system would never have been incorporated into the schools of Sweden or any other of the many countries (e.g. Denmark) which adopted it. If Hjalmar cannot be regarded as the creator, he must be credited for being the organizer and arranger of material which thus became available to large numbers of teachers and school children. The Swedish system of gymnastics should properly be considered the brainchild of both Hjalmar and Per Ling.

PART V *(Continued)*

*European Physical Educators and Institutions*

*DANISH*

# FRANZ NACHTEGALL

## 1777-1847

Franz Nachtegall, the "father" of Danish physical education, is honored chiefly for his work in disseminating gymnastics, particularly in the schools of his country. He did not create a system of his own but instead advocated and taught the gymnastics of Guts Muths. In fact, his whole interest in the subject seems to have been inspired by a reading of *Gymnastik für die Jugend*.

Nachtegall was born in Copenhagen in 1777 and lived there for his entire life. His father, a German immigrant tailor, provided for his son's early education in a private school, which was followed by his entering the University as a theology student. Liking physical activity from boyhood, Nachtegall became proficient at fencing and vaulting during the time he studied at the University. The death of his father forced him to leave before completing his degree, in order to support his mother and himself and to do this, Nachtegall gave private lessons in Latin, geography and history, which involved long hours of work for little pay.

FIG. 34. Franz Nachtegall.

At that time he read Guts Muths' work and inspired by the ideas, Nachtegall first began to teach gymnastics in his own home and then to a club which he organized of university students and young business men. On November 5, 1799 he opened a private outdoor gymnasium in the yard of number 45 Østergade, the first institution for physical training to be opened in modern times.  Although he began with only five young adults, within a year he had twenty-five, and by 1804, 150 children and adults had enrolled.  He also trained six teachers to assist him.  At the same time he was teaching gymnastics in about nine of the city's public and private schools, an opportunity which began with an invitation to give private lessons in a naturalistic school patterned after Basedow's Philanthropinum. (207:181)

His own gymnasium was modelled after Guts Muths' playground in Germany.  It included hanging ladders, rope ladders, masts and poles for climbing, and beams for balancing.  A wooden horse was used for vaulting, and mats were placed to insure a soft landing.  Although mats were probably used ever since vaulting was practiced, the first *report* of their use is by Nachtegall. (385:649)  Per Ling, the creator of Swedish gymnastics, attended the gymnasium while he resided in Copenhagen and was certainly influenced by the Nachtegall-Guts Muths system, although he later avoided the use of apparatus or "machine gymnastics."

By 1804 Nachtegall was lecturing on the history and method of physical training to an audience composed of students from the University and a college for teachers, as well as some military officers; he also gave training in gymnastics to military and naval cadets and non-commissioned officers. He founded the Society for Promoting the Art of Swimming which gave free lessons to charity-school boys, arranged meets and distributed prizes. In the same year, the King appointed him Professor of Gymnastics at the University and Director of the Military Gymnastic Institute (det Militaere Gymnastike Institut) which was newly established by royal decree. The Institute still exists and is the oldest in Europe for training gymnastics instructors.  The original intent of the Institute was to diffuse gymnastic training throughout the army and navy, but only four years later civilians were also admitted to the fifteen- to eighteen-month course to prepare instructors for teachers' colleges and elementary schools.  The Civil Gymnastic Institute thus established was short-lived (1808–1816), although a total of thirty-one students actually completed the course.  National financial difficulties due to military defeats in the Napoleonic Wars, particularly the loss of Norway and Helgoland, were the main reason for the closing of the Civil Institute.

However, the commitment to the gymnastics which Nachtegall had introduced was not lost, especially since Frederick ascended the throne in 1808.  The first edition of Guts Muths' *Gymnastik für die Jugend* was dedicated to the then Prince Frederick whom he expected to "be inclined

to favor a more vigorous sort of education than had hitherto obtained."
(159:542)  The Prince had studied gymnastics with Nachtegall and was
highly influential in his teacher's campaign to bring physical education to
Danish schools.  In 1801 gymnastics was introduced into the first public
school in Copenhagen and in 1809 an ordinance was passed requiring
secondary schools to provide instruction in gymnastics whenever possible.
In 1814 the same requirement was extended to boys in elementary schools,
although it was almost three decades later before a single other European
country made such a regulation.  A daily lesson was to be given outside of
school hours and therefore every school was supposed to have the necessary
apparatus and an outdoor space of 3,200–4,800 square feet.  In order to
insure that teachers would have the requisite ability, in 1818 gymnastics
became a required subject at the Seminarier (teachers colleges).

In 1821 Nachtegall was appointed Gymnastikdirektør with authority
over all civil and military gymnastics in Denmark.  However, despite his
efforts and the government's support with strong legislation, the nation's
programs were poor or non-existent.  The country was still in financial
straits and the purchase of the requisite grounds and apparatus was not
always possible.  There were few teachers trained in the subject; furthermore, the importance of gymnastics in the schools was not generally ceded.
To improve the situation an attempt was made to concentrate on the
Copenhagen county and within a few years all the schools in that area,
both public and private, were giving instruction in gymnastics.

The need to train teachers grew more acute and Nachtegall planned for
forty or fifty children from one of the local public schools to receive instruction at the Military Gymnastic Institute.  A relationship between the
Institute and the public school was established and together they comprised the Normalskole for Gymnastikken, affording opportunity for both
military and civil teachers to conduct classes under supervision.  In 1828
when the Normal School opened, 200 teachers and 160 boys worked together on gymnastics.  In 1836, when during a tour of the Seminarier
Nachtegall discovered generally poor apparatus and teaching methods, he
arranged for the teachers of gymnastics at three of the teachers colleges to
take a summer course at the Normal School.  In this way he not only
caused the creation of the school but frequently had a direct hand in
bringing students to it. (207:183)

In 1838 recognition of the value of physical education for women finally
led to the establishment of an experimental school for girls.  Like the young
boys they received three lessons a week at the Institute.  Although this was
supervised by Nachtegall, their teachers included three army sergeants
and two women, an indication that military and educational aims were
still the same, even for women.  However, the program demonstrated an
obvious need for training women teachers, and in 1939 the Normal School
of Gymnastics for Women (Normalskole for Kvindegymnastik) was estab-

lished.  Women took courses at the Institute in teaching methods and exercises and worked with the young girls in the same manner as their male colleagues.  This ultimately led to the introduction of gymnastics for girls in many of the Copenhagen schools.

A further step in the upgrading of Danish gymnastics was the publication in 1828 of a *Manual of Gymnastics for the Village and Town Schools of Denmark (Laerebog i Gymnastik for Almue-og Borger-Skolerne i Danmark)*, written by Nachtegall and a four-man commission.  At the King's ex pense copies of the *Manual* were distributed to all Danish schools and school authorities and simultaneously an order was issued requiring gymnastics instruction to begin immediately in all schools.  Within ten years almost all Danish elementary schools had complied; however, the large numbers of teachers required for the undertaking virtually insured that the majority were military men.  Since the primary force behind the widespread adoption of this kind of training was the aim of producing strong men, able to fight for Denmark, the military influence was not thought objectionable.  As in Germany and Sweden, gymnastics was appreciated for its military rather than its educational values.

Nachtegall's *Laerebog i Gymnastik til Brug for de laerde Skoler i Danmark (Manual of Gymnastics and Regulations for the Secondary Schools of Denmark)* was published in 1834 on the heels of two regulations intended to insure the teaching of gymnastics in the secondary schools.

When he became sixty-five, Nachtegall resigned as Director of the Institute but for five more years continued as the Gymnastic Director of Denmark, touring the schools and teachers colleges in an unceasing attempt to improve gymnastics instruction.  His successor in both positions was Captain Niels George la Cour, a military officer.  Before long the Normal School branch of the Military Gymnastics Institute ceased to exist and beginning in 1859 non-commissioned officers were ordered to the teachers colleges for three-year tours as gymnastics teachers.  Military gymnastics held absolute sway and the program throughout Denmark dwindled in popularity.

Franz Nachtegall's heritage was largely ignored until the twentieth century when Knud A. Knudsen, a civilian, was appointed state inspector. However, his contribution should not be underestimated.  He did not found a new "system" but he led his country, years before any other, to see the importance of physical training as part of the school program.  He had a reputation as a good teacher, but more important in a historical sense, was his power to organize programs and persuade authorities to fund and introduce them in their schools.  Because of his work Denmark was a leader in physical education and an inspiration to other countries to adopt similar programs.

# NIELS BUKH

## 1880-1950

It took a farm boy, Niels Bukh, to understand the difference between strength and suppleness and translate it into a system of gymnastics. Bukh said: "When I was 35 years old, I asked myself how it could be that after having for 25 years energetically practised a so-called rational gymnastic system, I was stiffer and more inefficient than when I started as a boy." (59:633) The answer to his question led him to develop a new gymnastic system; Danish gymnastics as the world knows it is primarily Bukh's system of *Primitif Gymnastike.** His theory was predicated on the following assumption:

> Even where growth takes place under the best possible conditions, the habits and demands of daily life, first during school-time and later on through the constant repetition of an occupational posture or exclusive use of one part of the body, tend to produce an unequal bodily development, destroying the physique of youth, whose form was, of old, and still should be, the expression of perfect beauty and poise. (58:2)

Bukh was particularly cognizant of this because he witnessed the tendency of agricultural workers (and other manual laborers) to overdevelop one set of muscles while the opposite groups remained underdeveloped; e.g., a strong-armed man who spends weeks tossing hay up and away from him is usually incapable of doing even a single pull-up. Primary gymnastics were intended, therefore, to be *corrective* in nature—to *precede* other gymnastic forms. The objective was "to clear the way of obstacles, to lay the foundations, and build upon the basis of the normal physical condition." (58:12) "Later on . . . when the faults of development are rectified, a transition is made from fundamental to postural or athletic gymnastics . . . demanding the highest degree of muscle sense and co-ordination." (58:9–10) His concept of gymnastics was grand:

> I look upon gymnastics as a noble and rational cultivation of the human body, and consequently as a matter of the greatest importance to every nation which wishes to be healthy and capable. Gymnastics exercises involve the fundamental

---

* The title on the American edition of Bukh's textbook is *Primary Gymnastics;* English language writers often call it Fundamental or Primitive Gymnastics but the latter term has implications differing from Bukh's concept of "primary" or "first."

training of the human body, the object being to remove the acquired deviation from the natural induced by civilisation, and to restore the harmonious, the beautiful, and what was originally sound and efficient. (59:633)

In explaining his theory Bukh noted that its essential principles were in accordance with those stated by Per Ling who enunciated the value of beginning with corrective work. But the Ling system as practiced omitted that fundamental step. In 1884 Swedish gymnastics had been introduced in Denmark by N. H. Rasmussen and its popularity spread rapidly through the schools and rifle clubs (*skytteforeninger*)*. In 1899 when the government published a new *Handbook of Gymnastics* for official school use it was based primarily on the Swedish system. But the corrective work was omitted and "when the necessity for this corrective groundwork was recognized in the course of training the young men and women of Denmark, a Danish type of training was developed." (58:3)

Bukh stated that "the aim of the Danish fundamental or primary gymnastics is to give, first and foremost, a thorough working and toning up of the whole body." (58:3) He believed in the ancient Greek ideal of physical perfection—of perfect beauty and poise—preserved by training in gymnastics or athletics. Inherent in the Greek ideal was the concept of harmonious body development, wherein the physique is upright and symmetrical with strength and power under complete voluntary control and used "in the service of right." In Bukh's lifetime, the devastation of Europe in two world wars must have made especially clear the need to use physical power discriminatingly, in conjunction with moral force. He believed that gymnastics, which involved the achievement of difficult goals, could demand from participants their whole energy and will and thus affect their personality. "The body is moulded and the character developed by the exertion of will and energy necessary to surmount the increasingly difficult obstacles and problems placed across the road leading to the goal." (58:4)

The three main "faults" which primary gymnastics sought to correct were: stiffness, lack of power and awkwardness. Thus the emphasis was placed upon developing mobility, strength and agility which together could effectuate graceful movement. The movements used by athletes often accomplish this, but of course athletes tend to work on the specific movement needed in their sport or event and therefore develop only certain body areas. Furthermore, the need for equipment and space make it difficult for large numbers of people to be aided in their physical development. Bukh utilized the movements of athletics and

---

* Patterned after the English National Rifle Association, these clubs were originally formed (1861) to practice rifle shooting and perform military drills, but gradually gymnastics became the more popular activity. The clubs were common to most villages and served as social centers, usually having facilities which included a gymnasium, lounge and coffee room.

collected them in a suitable form that one may attain, for instance, the great development of strength and the freedom of arm movements of the discus and spear thrower without apparatus; the athlete's need of powerful and agile legs may be acquired without the track, hurdles, or jumping stands; and where it is possible, to produce the Graeco-Roman wrestler's fine supple and powerful physique by training and making the body supple through trunk twistings, bending and stretching, and muscle contraction. (58:7–8)

Exercises were designed and grouped into leg, arm, neck, lateral, abdominal, and dorsal exercises and then further classified as to their effect, i.e., mobility, strength or agility. In every work session all groups and classifications of exercises had to be included in an alternating fashion.

> The work should continue in a general form, with the understanding that there must be a constant change between mobility-, strength-, and agility-producing types of work and alternating use of limbs and trunk, as only through the versatility of the work is the best execution obtained—the alternating change of type and group of work being sufficient rest to prevent fatigue and satisfying the craving of youth for continued movement. (58:13)

The kind of exercises included were similar to those in Swedish gymnastics with the important omission of breathing exercises which Ling considered the anchor of his whole system. Bukh, utilizing the theories of later physiological research which claimed that increased respiratory capacity was the result of increased demand, relied upon *unceasing* effort for fairly long periods of time (averaging forty-five minutes per session) to accomplish increased cardio-respiratory functioning. Circulation was also affected by the style of a Bukh lesson. No matter at what level of difficulty the exercises were performed, "the fundamental readjustive work should be taken in a free, vigorous rhythm, so that pleasure and warmth are derived from the action, as the rate of circulation is increased in all parts of the body." (58:8)

Rhythm was essential to the Danish system. It was here that skill was called for from the gymnastic leader who by the quiet use of proper cueing (naming the next exercise while the class is doing one for which a final signal is then given) was able to modulate the rhythm and keep the class moving as a whole. Bukh was exceptionally adept at doing this as the following description by an observer indicated:

> He conducts a class in somewhat the same manner that a Toscanini would direct an orchestra. The pupils give of their maximum effort, and never once does their interest lag while Bukh has the direction. One wonders while watching them whether they are able to keep up the pace that has been set as they go through the long sweeping trunk movements and the rotations. But just as the limit of effort is about reached the tempo is changed and a slow rhythmical movement takes the place of the deep powerful one. And so as one movement flows into another for a period of fifteen to twenty minutes with never a let-up, the director is always the perfect master of the class. (329:58–60)

Swedish exercises were easier to lead because they involved giving commands; the strain of the held positions was relieved by having the class rest in an "at ease" position. Danish gymnastics relied upon the teacher's skill in choosing and leading the exercises in such a manner that one part of the body rested while the other worked.

In both Ling's and Bukh's systems the teachers were aided by published Day's Orders which presented complete lessons in a progressively difficult series. Bukh's was published in his book *Primary Gymnastics* (58) in which, after a description of exercises in every category plus marching and vaulting, he included twelve sample Tables. The work was basically divided into three groups. In the first the students did free standing exercises using light, general, introductory movements. In the second, heavier and more strenuous work was performed either alone or in pairs, at the stall bars or on the floor. Marching was inserted next, as a suitable break, and was followed by the third group consisting of vaulting and tumbling exercises.

Although Bukh's exercises were varied, one type was particularly characteristic of his system, the more so since it was not deliberately employed by the Swedes or Germans. He stressed *stretching* exercises, particularly along the spinal column and thoracic region where lack of mobility tended to produce postural defects. Good posture during all exercises was also emphasized as a means of increasing mobility which with good muscle control and coordination was expected to produce free and graceful movements.

Bukh's interest in gymnastics began early in life.* He was born on his father's farm in Snejbjerg, five kilometers (about three miles) west of Herning in Jutland. Both his parents were descendants of old farming families. Five years later his father became a high school teacher at Vallekilde, a school possessing a large gymnasium in which Swedish gymnastics were taught. Although Bukh had no particular ability in gymnastics he possessed leadership qualities and by age seventeen was leading his friends in their work. He attended the Vallekilde High School for two winters, the Askov High School, and the Ladelund Agricultural High School where he studied and taught gymnastics as well. After one more course, at Tune Agricultural High School, he took over the management of his father's farm. During his years of farm work he also led gymnastics in the clubs in surrounding districts and his teams frequently won first place in exhibition competitions.

At age twenty-eight he decided to make a career of gymnastics and accordingly enrolled at the State Institute of Gymnastics in Copenhagen for the one-year course. At the same time he attended Teilmann's Institute of Gymnastics where he studied medical gymnastics and massage. Following

---

* All biographical data on Niels Bukh was courteously provided by the Danish Embassy.

Fig. 35.   Niels Bukh.

that experience he enrolled at Vordingborg Teachers' College where he completed teacher training and passed the teacher examination in 1912. The same year he led the Danish Rifle Club's gymnastic team at the Olympic Games in Stockholm. The following year he was the leader of a team of Danish gymnasts on an exhibition tour through Antwerp, Brussels, Paris, and England.

When Bukh was thirty-four his sister and brother-in-law took over the management of the Ollerup Folk High School and Niels Bukh purchased one of the school buildings. There he established a gymnastic leader training school in conjunction with the Folk High School. It was this endeavor which led to the founding of his own independent gymnastic high school and his lifelong devotion to training gymnasts and gymnastic leaders. (Refer to chapter on Ollerup for details.)

The success of Ollerup was in large part the result of Bukh's effectiveness as leader. His ability to command and lead festivals was without peer; his exhibitions were received with acclaim in Denmark and around the world when he traveled with his teams. In 1931, after a tour through Poland, Russia and Japan, the team gave displays in Canada and the United States. Bukh's system had been introduced in America in 1925. Colleges such as Radcliffe, Barnard, Wellesley, Mount Holyoke, Smith, and Goucher began to teach the exercises, and Bouvé and the Central School of Physical Education of New York (now Russell Sage) began to include Bukh gymnastics in their teacher education programs. (3:26)

Niels Bukh was the first and only gymnastic leader ever to be invited to give a demonstration of gymnastics in the Danish Parliament building for members of the government. Many other honors were conferred upon him in the course of his work and travels. Among these were the Danish Knight of Dannebrog, the Danish Silver Cross, the Knight of the Icelandic Falcon, the Commander of the Belgium Leopold II Order, Honor Emblems from the 1912 and 1936 Olympics, the Honorary Cross of the German Eagle 1st Degree, the Commander of the White Rose of Finland, and the Knight of the French Legion of Honor. From colleagues in the United States he received an honorary Doctor of Pedagogy degree from Russell Sage College (1939) and was elected a Fellow of the American Academy of Physical Education (1946). At Ollerup a granite memorial was erected on the Academy grounds, placed there in tribute by the alumni.

Bukh's gymnastics never became as popular around the world as might be expected from the results he achieved. Although *Primary Gymnastics* was translated into eight languages, less gifted teachers seemed unable to duplicate his methods. Certainly it required special training and understanding to administer Danish gymnastics in the required rhythms—and it also took exceptional memory—for the entire sequence had to be performed without a break. Nevertheless, Niels Bukh's contributions were original and the principles which he enunciated were adaptable to other less systematized forms of exercise.

# OLLERUP GYMNASTIC HIGH SCHOOL

Ollerup High School of Gymnastics stands in most beautiful natural surroundings on fertile, idyllic Funen, the island that gave birth to Hans [Christian] Anderson. On its hill the school building is in good style; there are sports ground, gymnasium, swimming hall and open-air swimming pool. In the park and grounds are statues of splendid human bodies.*

The Ollerup Gymnastic High School (Gymnastikhojskolen) was founded by Niels Bukh. After working with a small number of students, beginning in 1914, he formally opened the school with a festival in May, 1920. Ollerup was housed in a large stone building containing living and dining areas, classrooms and a spacious gymnasium. In 1923 a small stadium was built. It was a large athletic field encircled by a cinder track of four hundred meters, and had Greek statues on either side. The stadium's inaugural festival was attended by sixteen thousand spectators including the King. In 1926 Bukh had a modern swimming pool built by his students from the plans of a local architect, with filtering and disinfecting apparatus brought from the United States. It was Denmark's first indoor swimming pool; even today very few Danish schools have pools. At the same time side wings were added to the building, increasing its capacity to 150 students. In 1931, after a profitable world tour, a large (76 × 40 meters) athletic shell and an outdoor swimming pool were added to the facilities. In 1935 an outdoor arena with capacity for fifty thousand spectators was built; and three years later a large new building was added. Improvement of the facilities has continued; each course has room for 180 students and 1,000 people can be accommodated for a festival. Much of the construction work on all the facilities was done by alumni as a contribution to their school. Unhappily, in 1943 the Germans occupied Denmark and took over the school, utilizing it as a refugee center. It was not until 1947 that Niels Bukh was able to complete restoration of the badly damaged facilities and resume classes. When Bukh died three years later his will provided that the Gymnastikhojskolen become an independent institution, administered by a board of directors. It is currently owned and supported by its alumni on a non-profit basis and also subsidized by the Danish State.

The Ollerup School is a folk high school, one of about eighty or ninety such schools attended each year by over seven thousand students usually

---

* Information relating to the founding of Ollerup, its facilities and programs was supplied by the Danish Embassy, Washington, D. C.

FIG. 36.    Ollerup Gymnastic High School.

between the ages of eighteen and twenty-five.    The folk high school movement was the brainchild of Bishop Nicolai F. S. Grundtvig (1783–1872)
who believed that adult education would help to restore the spirit and
confidence of the Danish people.    The territorial losses and financial problems resulting from the Napoleonic Wars were aggravated in 1864 by
Germany's annexation of Schleswig-Holstein—almost two fifths of Danish
territory.    So many Danes were living under foreign rule, forbidden to
speak their own language, that a means was sought to unify and re-
invigorate the Danish culture itself.    Adult high schools were started (in
1851) and in most cases attended by agricultural or domestic workers who
had completed elementary school and immediately become employed.
The folk high schools were residential schools, private enterprises often
carried on for generations by single families, but they were also supported
in part by the state through direct subsidies and grants to needy students
for up to one third of the small fees.    Danish language, literature and
history and mathematics were taught in all of the schools and about a third
of the time was devoted to a particular subject in which the school specialized.

The Ollerup school specialized in the theory, practice and history of
gymnastics and athletics, and in physiology.    Male students usually attended Ollerup for the five-months winter course (November-March when
there was little farm work to do; that course is now co-ed) and women for

three months in the spring.  In 1925–1926 about 150 men and an equal number of women were enrolled; in 1962 there were 175 students.  In Ollerup's first forty years about fifteen thousand teachers were graduated.  In addition to the regular courses offered at Ollerup, special summer sessions were held, often for visiting groups of foreign students who wished to study the Danish methods.*  For example, many Americans went there to study Danish gymnastics under Niels Bukh.  When the courses were completed students returned to their original occupations, culturally enriched, and prepared to lead village clubs in gymnastics, games and dancing.  They were privileged to wear the O.D. pin, standing for *Ollerup Delinsfrere* or leader of gymnastics, and usually conducted free sessions in their village community building (*forsamlingshuset*).  Today almost every village in Denmark has a gymnastics team, most of which perform at the annual national meets. In the foreword to his book, *Primary Gymnastics*, Bukh interpreted the aims of the folk high schools and of Ollerup in particular when he said:

> In times like these, when in so many directions our earlier faith and confidence has turned to doubt and hesitation, it is encouraging to reflect on those forces which continuously strive to benefit our greatest heritage—the sturdy working youth of our country.  Chief among these forces are to be reckoned the voluntary leaders of the gymnastic and rifle clubs—those men and women who have led our country on until, for voluntary gymnastics, it takes the foremost place among nations. . . . They must prepare themselves to take the lead in football and other sports as well as gymnastics, so that the whole of the physical side of youthful education is conducted on the right lines.  The women's club leaders must always remember that true womanliness consists not only of smiling grace and shimmering beauty, but also of energy, goodwill, and capability to undertake strenuous work. (58:v)

The program at Ollerup followed a simple daily routine, beginning each morning with marching exercises and singing Danish songs, an activity which lent to development of national pride.  This was followed by about twenty minutes of exercises using the Bukh system of "primary gymnastics."  The last activity phase consisted of exercises on the stall bars, vaulting over buck, horse or table, and tumbling exercises.  The activity lesson ended with more marching and singing.  It has since become a tradition in all Danish gymnastic clubs that practice sessions and performances begin and end with marching and singing; the Danish flag is prominently displayed at these times.  An excited visitor from England witnessed a class from the viewing gallery above the gymnasium:

---

* International courses are still given each summer for a week or ten days. Instruction is in English and students study either the "Gymnastic Line," or the "Athletics Line."  Information can be obtained from the Gymnastikhojskolen, Ollerup, Denmark.

Suddenly the lower doors opened, and as into an arena, half a hundred men stripped to the waist, just wearing shorts and shoes, and without the slightest pause begin the work that was to last 45 minutes without cessation of movement for one second. . . . Back lyings and trunk fallings, twisting, shoulder stretchings, none too tenderly administered, followed on each other in a continuous stream. . . . Pictures of Dante's Inferno swam before me, the drops of perspiration grew on the floor, and the bodies before us visibly lost their bones and became more and more rubber like. . . . The work grew faster, the floor was covered with long 30 yard strips of soft felt, and running somersaults succeeded each other at such a pace, that one's eye lost one's own man in the maze of whirling figures, and next moment not one of the 100 feet was on the ground as the 50, with a gay shout disappeared with cartwheels and hand-walks to the shower baths inside. (222: 158)

The rest of the day was devoted to academic classes such as were taught in all folk schools, and also special Ollerup subjects like anatomy and physiology. Following dinner the students had a free hour in which to practice their exercises, play games such as football (soccer), or do track and field events. Every night the students gathered again for more singing.

Dorothy Sumption, the author of *Fundamental Danish Gymnastics for Women* (352), took a three-month summer course at the Gymnastikhojskolen and, in a description of some exhibitions she witnessed, gave a clear picture of the spirit behind Bukh's endeavor:

On Saturdays and Sundays Mr. Bukh would take his group of boys out to different parts of the country where they would give demonstrations, the proceeds going toward the swimming pool. The exhibitions were always held out in the open, and hundreds of people from miles around attended. It was an inspiring sight to see the group of students entering the field, led by the standard bearer, a young man of wonderful physique dressed in a white uniform and carrying the Danish flag. They marched with a steady, firm step as they sang with fervor and spirit one of the national hymns. (351:1092)

The Gymnasium at Ollerup was very simply equipped. The main apparatus consisted of Swedish stall bars (an invention of Per Ling) mounted on three sides of the room. No ropes, rings or poles of any kind were suspended from the ceiling. However, there were bucks, horses and benches for vaulting and extra long, thin mats for tumbling. Equally simple was the uniform which consisted of black cotton shorts for the men and a loose cotton garment like a modern tennis dress, for the women; both sexes went barefoot.

As a folk high school, Ollerup filled an appropriate place in the history of a movement unique to Denmark. But the work there also contributed to the international development of physical education. Bukh and his students made various trips to demonstrate the special Danish system of gymnastics, winning converts and influencing programs far beyond the scope of their own country. In 1923 they toured the United States for six

FIG. 37.    Bukh Leading Ollerup Students in an Exhibition.

weeks and as a result many American teachers studied at Ollerup, including a group of about thirty for whom a special six-week course was given in the summer of 1926. Bukh and his gymnasts toured most of the world and gave exhibitions in at least five Olympiads. In 1949 at the second annual Lingiad a group of Ollerup students under Bukh's leadership gave an exhibition that was described by a critic for the Brussels' newspaper *Le Soir:*

> The highest perfection in team-work synchronization was achieved by Niels Bukh's fabulous Danes, the young men who lead a hermit-like existence at the famous Ollerup Institute. We for our part have never seen more beautiful clock-work precision, a more harmonious blend of individual talent within a gymnastic team as a whole. (299:35)

Although Bukh died in 1950, the Gymnastikhojskolen has continued to flourish, bringing an important program to the young adults of Denmark and developing volunteer leaders primarily for the rural areas. They have also continued Bukh's practice of giving exhibitions, the last group having toured the United States in 1966. Thus Ollerup continues its contribution to physical education.

PART V *(Continued)*

*European Physical Educators and Institutions*

*SWISS*

# ÉMILE JAQUES-DALCROZE

## 1865-1950

"The creation in the organism of a rapid and easy means of communication between thought and its means of expression by movements allows the personality free play, giving it character, strength and life to an extraordinary degree." (97:20) With these words, Jaques-Dalcroze claimed for rhythmic gymnastics, or eurythmics as they were known in England and America, sweeping benefits for the whole individual. Although the term rhythmical gymnastics denoted a particular mode of physical drill, its purposes extended far beyond those usually associated with gymnastics, and the nature of the exercises was quite different from either gymnastics or dance.

In part, the uniqueness of eurythmics as an aspect of physical education may be attributed to its origin as a method for improving the power of musical expression, particularly the rhythmic sense, of music students. Dalcroze, who was a writer, composer and Professor of Harmony at the Geneva Conservatoire, was critical of the musicians of his time who, though trained in technical facility, had learned nothing of the self-expression involved in playing music. Furthermore, he observed that his students were unable to deal with simple rhythmic problems. Both of these deficiencies resulted in faulty musical interpretation and anomalies such as opera singers walking and gesticulating without paying any attention to the time. He came to realize that they needed training in the "instinctive transformation of sound movements into bodily movements. . . ." (97:24) To accomplish this he developed a method, the object of which was "to create by the help of rhythm a rapid and regular communication between brain and body. . . ." (97:19) However, the goal of his method was not delimited to such a practical, mechanical end:

> But, as an artist, I wish to add, that the second result of this education ought to be to put the completely developed faculties of the individual at the service of art and to give the latter the most subtle and complete of interpreters—the human body. For the body can become a marvellous instrument of beauty and harmony when it vibrates in tune with artistic imagination and collaborates with creative thought. It is not enough that, thanks to special exercises, students of music should have corrected their faults and be no longer in danger of spoiling their musical interpretations by their lack of physical skill and harmonious move-

ments; it is necessary in addition that the music which lives within them . . . should obtain free and complete development, and that the rhythms which inspire their personality should enter into intimate communion with those which animate the works to be interpreted. (97:21)

The method required great attentiveness and concentration because each arm and leg may have been moved in a different rhythm. The movements of the arm expressed time; the movements of the feet and body expressed note duration. One exercise was described as consisting of "beating various times in canon, that is, one arm beginning one beat later than the other; of beating different times with each arm, perhaps seven to one arm and three with the other; of marching to one rhythm and beating time to another; . . . of marching the counterpoint of a rhythm. . . ." (97:51) Other kinds of exercises known as "plastic expression," were designed to teach the pupils to express the type of music being played. To achieve this an "alphabet" of twenty arm gestures in various combinations was developed and used to express any kind of emotion. These too involved great concentration as the student sought to harmonize completely with the music, listening for every note, every accent, every change of key, and every rhythm. Movement, posture and facial expression were also used to indicate shades of feeling. An observer described a performance employing plastic expression, given at Hellerau, in 1911:

> Two pupils undertook to realize a Prelude of Chopin, their choice falling by chance on the same Prelude. . . . The first girl lay on the ground the whole time, her head on her arm, expressing in gentle movements of head, hands and feet, her idea of the music. At one point near the end, with the rising passion of the music, she raised herself on to her knees; then sank down again to her full length. The second performer stood upright until the very end. At the most intense moment her arms were stretched above her head; at the close of the music she was bowed to the ground, in an attitude expressive of the utmost grief. (97:62–63)

The notion of the movements being a kind of visual notation of the music, beat by beat, is the opposite of the modern dancers' attempt to complement music and dance. In the latter technique the structure of the dance, and its ideas take precedence over the music. The former technique is more akin to ballet, which, in the classical tradition is choreographed as a response to the music. The usefulness of the Dalcroze method for ballet dancers was evident to Diaghilev who, after observing a demonstration, asked Dalcroze for an instructor in rhythm; his dancer, the famous Nijinsky, was greatly influenced by eurythmics. The Diaghilev Ballet and the Russian Academies in Saint Petersburg and Moscow took instruction, and before 1918 eurythmics was incorporated in the official syllabus of the State Choreographic Academies. In later years, though, even at Hellerau the movements became independent of the music. After World War I drums and tom toms were used to heighten the internal rhythm of the performers. As the rhythms of the individual students gradually developed into a collective group rhythm, they took on the added dimensions of a social act, and attempts to individually interpret the music ceased. In Germany, this emphasis on group rhythm (developed also by Bode and Laban) became the keynote of German gymnastics.

Émile Jaques-Dalcroze was born in Vienna in 1865. His father, a Swiss from Saint Croix (hence Dalcroze), and his German mother brought him to Geneva at age eight, where he became a student at the same Conservatory of Music in which he later taught. He continued studying music under Delibes in Paris and Bruckner in Vienna; for a short time he was musical director of a small theatre in Algiers, where he became acquainted with the complex and unique rhythms of Arab music. When he assumed his professorship at the Geneva Conservatoire in 1892 he had already achieved a reputation for his musicianship. In 1905 he gave a public demonstration of his method at a music festival in Solothurn, which was enthusiastically received, and in 1906 he held the first training course for teachers. The

Fig. 38.   Émile Jaques-Dalcroze.

two-week course was given repeatedly over the next three years and in 1909 Dalcroze began granting diplomas to prevent untrained individuals from posing as teachers of his method.   In 1910 the brothers Wolf and Harold Dohrn built for him a College of Music and Rhythm in Hellerau, a suburb of Dresden.   The course there took from one to three years of study and was attended by Europeans of many nationalities, including children of all ages, students of music, art and dancing, and adults seeking to improve their culture and health.*   When the College was completed in 1912 there was accommodation for five hundred students, an indication of the popularity of the Dalcroze method.

Inevitably, Dalcroze concluded that his method had wider applications:

> It is true that I first devised my method as a musician for musicians.  But the further I carried my experiments, the more I noticed that, while a method intended to develop the sense for rhythm, and indeed based on such development, is of great importance in the education of a musician, its chief value lies in the fact that it trains the powers of apperception and of expression in the individual and renders easier the externalization of natural emotions. (97:35)

He began to advocate that lessons in rhythmic gymnastics become a part of the ordinary school day because they "help children in their other lessons, for they develop the powers of observation, of analyzing, of understanding and of memory, thus making them more orderly and precise."   (97:26) He believed that such training would make "pupils more responsive, more elastic and of more character than they otherwise would be.  Therefore, the study of rhythm, as well as education by means of rhythm, ought to be most closely connected with school life."   (97:26–27) He advocated that training begin at age six with half an hour's lesson, three times a week during the regular playtime, decreasing to two lessons a week by age twelve.

The Dalcroze system did not achieve great popularity in the United States, although several of his students taught in America.   Today Dalcroze schools exist in Geneva, London, Paris, New York, and other cities.   Rhythmic gymnastics of the Dalcroze type sometimes found their place in American schools as the following routine by Carl Schrader, then Massachusetts State Supervisor of Physical Education, illustrates.   It was given at a meeting of the State Physical Education Society, Atlantic City, New Jersey, in 1925, and demonstrated clearly the learning progression developed by Dalcroze.

*A*

I.   a.   March with stamping every step.
     b.   March with stamping every four steps, followed by four on tip toes.

.    .    .    .    .    .    .    .    .    .    .    .    .

     f.   March with stamping every three steps, followed by one on tip toes.
     g.   March with stamping every three steps, pause one count.

---

* Everyone began the day at Hellerau with a Swedish gymnastic lesson.

### B

I.  a.  Stamp on the first of two marching steps.
    b.  Clap on the first of two marching steps.
    c.  Stamp and clap on the first of two marching steps.

### F

I.  a.  Starting position of arms is upward.
    b.  In two-four time beat down on one, return upward on two with less forceful movement.
    c.  In three-four time beat down on one, on two separate the arms sideward, on three raise them upward again.
    d.  In four-four time beat down on one; on two cross forearms in front; on three move arms sideward; on four raise them upward again.

### G

I.  a.  Continue marching as in B Ia with F Ib.
    b.  Continue marching as in B IIa with F Ic.

### H

I.  d.  Combine marching as in B IVg with F Ib, F Ic and F Id.
    e.  These combinations also with arm beatings as in G Ij. . . . (327:667–668)

Although Americans prefer games and dancing to eurythmics, it must nevertheless be remembered that the work of the musician Dalcroze helped to establish precedents for the expression gymnastics of Rudolf Bode, the natural dancing of Isadora Duncan, the theories of Rudolph von Laban (who studied and rejected the method), and the work of many important modern dancers such as Hanya Holm and Kurt Joos. Mary Wigman, considered to be the originator of modern dance in Europe, became interested in dance through a demonstration of eurythmics and later studied with Dalcroze. Furthermore, eurythmics, or rhythmic gymnastics, is being taught in schools even today, notably those in England; they were introduced there by students of Madame Martina Bergman-Österberg who included the subject in her teacher training curriculum at Dartford, and by Dalcroze himself who went to England to demonstrate and teach his method. Finally, in an era in which the health and corrective purposes of exercise were foremost, Dalcroze focused attention on the body as an instrument for expression.

# FRANÇOIS DELSARTE

## 1811-1871

"I would rather my father were not known at all . . . than to be known as he is in your country, that is, as a professor of gymnastics." (85:562)   Delsarte's daughter, Mme. Marie Delsarte-Geraldy, giving a lecture in America commented further that she was amused at having dumbbells given to her to use during a lecture "in a gymnasium, as usual." Delsarte's system of gestures designed to accompany oratory was never meant to be a system of gymnastic movements.   Nevertheless, in late 19th-century America it became a very popular form of gymnastics for young ladies in schools and private organizations such as the YWCA.   As taught in America it was expanded far beyond the few simple gestures conceived of by Delsarte to be used by ministers, actors and singers.   The popularity of Delsarte gymnastics in the form in which they were promulgated in the United States, may be attributed to the extravagant claims made by his followers.   For example, speaking to the NEA in 1897, Anna P. Tucker of the School of Expression in Cleveland stated that through a

> knowledge of the Delsarte principles and the power to impart them we are enabled to teach muscular control, power through repose, grace, rhythm, and correct poise. . . . It seems to me the prime result of physical education is to create power, and grace, which is modified power. . . . This result is largely obtainable by the Delsarte method, or ethical physical training.   Delsarte's law of strength at the center, flexibility at the extremities, when properly applied, imparts vigor, sinewiness, and grace. (363:881–882)

His followers also believed that "expression" was natural gymnastics and therefore the highest form of gymnastics.   Emily Bishop, a well-known Delsarte teacher, said that "the final aim of Americanized Delsarte Culture is to lead man back to nature's ways, to make him healthy, free, strong, simple, natural." (9:81)   Public schools in the East (e.g., Boston) and the Midwest, introduced Delsarte gymnastics as a successor to those of Dio Lewis, both being considered light, gentle exercises for women.   In the 1890s Delsartean gymnastics in turn gave way to the more vigorous Swedish or German gymnastics and the very popular aesthetic dancing first introduced by Melvin Ballou Gilbert in 1894 to students at the Harvard

Summer School.  However, even proponents of more vigorous exercise, such as Dudley Allen Sargent, continued the occasional use of Delsarte to cure "muscle-bound" athletes.  In a few schools, such as Rockford and Elmira Colleges, the Delsarte system was used by departments of elocution in conjunction with the physical education department.  And when the values of the various gymnastic systems were debated, Delsarte was usually included in the comparisons.

Delsarte was a performer, teacher, theorizer, and something of a mystic. Born in Solesmes of an impoverished family, he was left to make his own way in Paris from the age of ten.  Dreaming of being a great singer he succeeded in obtaining admission to the Conservatory in 1825 but after a few years ruined his voice by using it improperly.  Becoming a lyric singer at the Opera Comique, from 1829–1834, he was forced to resign when his voice could not stand the strain.  He turned to teaching singing and elocution and as he developed his theories, became famous for recitations, during the first half of which he expounded his ideas, and in the second half demonstrated them with readings and songs.  His lectures were attended by his students and a transient population of followers and critics who turned up at the performances, held at night like plays or concerts.  The following eye-witness commentary published in a contemporary newspaper, about a performance of "Iphigenia's Dream," illustrates those evenings:

> All were held trembling, breathless by that worn and yet sovereign voice.  We were amazed to find ourselves yielding to such a spell; there was no splendor and no theatric illusion.  *Iphigenia* was a teacher in a black frock coat; the orchestra was a piano striking, here and there, an unexpected modulation. . . . And then, when the tale was told, cries of enthusiasm arose, as if *Iphigenia*, in person, had told us of her terrors. (85:292)

The popularity of Delsarte's recitations is evidenced by the fact that he was invited to perform before King Louis Philippe and his family.  He also was given the Hanoverian medal of arts and sciences and the Cross of a Chevalier of the Guelph Order from the King of Hanover who retained Delsarte as his personal instructor.

The theory which Delsarte proposed, claimed to be a science of aesthetics based upon the observation of what is natural in the expression of human emotions and ideas.  Denying artistic expression based upon reason as frequently false and misleading, he sought to base his method on experience—on pantomiming natural expression.  He said that "Gesture is the direct agent of the heart.  It is the fit manifestation of feeling . . . it is the spirit of which speech is merely the letter . . . it is . . . always anterior to speech, which is but a reflected and subordinate expression." (85:466–467)  He noted "How many things, in fact, the shoulder reveals by those slight changes unseen by ignorant persons, and expressing particularly the delicate and exquisite charm of spiritual relations!"* (85:443)  Based on these beliefs he formulated a series of nine "laws" which described specific relationships between gesture and emotion or thought.  The process by which he delineated a law regarding movements of the head is an example of the general nature of his work.  After observing that a mother contemplating her child bent her head toward it, but that a painter admiring his work threw back his head, he drew upon his memory to find several other seemingly contradictory examples.  Then he designated three categories of attitudes: sensuality, tenderness and indifference, and determined that the direction of inclination of the head depended upon which of the three attitudes prevailed.  Sensuality, for example, is "addressed exclusively to the form of its object; it caresses the periphery of it, and, the better to appreciate its totality, moves away from it.  This is what occurs in the retroactive attitude of the head." (85:428)  When he finished describing the three attitudes of the head he declared that "henceforth [he] . . . possessed completely the law of the inclinations of the head, a law which derives from its very complexity the fertility of its applications." (85:429)  From these three basic attitudes or positions, combinations were developed into nine actions, each of which signified a different emotion.  The same kind of formalized gestures or movements was developed for each of the parts of the body.  A diagram (Fig. 39) from a course given by Delsarte's daughter (85:547) illustrates how positions of the arm express a variety of meanings:

Based upon his "laws," Delsarte and his followers developed exercises to educate each part of the body to express an idea or emotion.  The following exercise was taken from the leading American textbook of his method, Genevieve Stebbins' *Delsarte System of Dramatic Expression:*

*Exercise II.—Resigned Appeal to Heaven.*
(a) Right shoulder rises slightly, while head sinks in opposition; (b) upper arm makes rotary movement, which turns eye of elbow out; (c) then forearm unbends; (d) hand expands in tenderness; head has been slowly rising in opposition and is right, oblique, back, when movement ceases. (340:117)

Below the exercises comments were noted in boldface:

**N.B.—The action of head and arm in above movements must be made simultaneously.  Each action flows into the subsequent one.  Always retain a gesture as long as the same thought or emotion is retained, or one remains in the same mood.** (340:118)

---

* In *The Silent Language* written in 1959 (149), the anthropologist Edward T. Hall set forth a highly sophisticated communications model which demonstrated that tone of voice and gesture, as well as a number of other factors such as space relations and time sequence, are vital elements of the communication process. While Hall's emphasis was on cultural significance, his serious study lent fresh credence to the assumptions underlying Delsarte's theories.

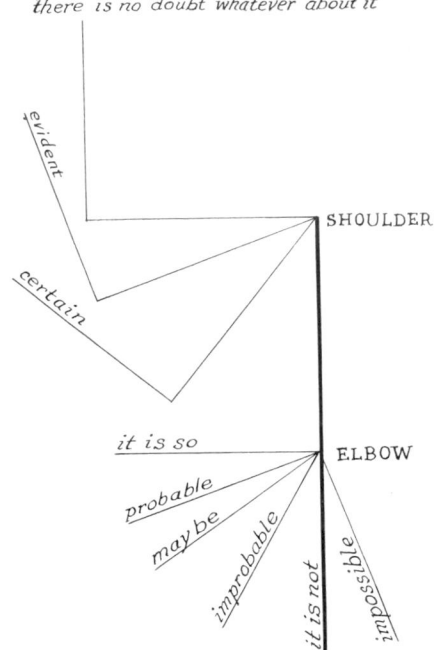

Fig. 39.   The Meaning of Various Arm Positions.

In America, the followers of Delsarte, wishing to emphasize the flexibility which he stipulated as essential, developed a series of "decomposing exercises" which, inasmuch as they involved complete relaxation, or withdrawing of force from the muscles, are akin to modern relaxation exercises. Stebbins said:

> The first great thing to be acquired is flexibility of the joints.   These exercises free the channels of expression, and the current of nervous force can thus rush through them as a stream of water rushes through a channel, unclogged by obstacles.   We name these exercises *decomposing*. (340:11)

Students were expected to practice "decomposing" for many hours a day. Stebbins included twelve exercises for various parts of the body, such as this one for the foot:

*Exercise VII.*
Lifting foot from the ground, agitate it as you do the hand.   You better seat yourself for this exercise.   Be sure the foot falls from the ankle decomposed. (340:13–14)

The movements of Delsarte gymnastics were associated with refinement and culture.   In part, this was probably due to Delsarte's observation that "there is very little harmony or relation between the exquisite joints of a refined nature, the swift and flexible movements of an elegant organism, and the evolutions clumsily executed by torpid limbs, ankylosed, as it were, by labor at once hard and constant." (85:443) He thought inflexibility was vulgar. "Lack of elasticity in a body is disagreeable from the fact that lacking suppleness, it seems as if it must, in falling, be broken, flattened or injured; in a word, must lose something of the integrality of its form." (85:464)  Furthermore, like the Greeks, he admired beauty of form and related it to nobility of function.  Beautiful expression represented ideal beauty.  His statement that "Beauty is based on three conditions:  Clearness, integrity and due proportion" (85:452) served as a guide for the movements; they were to be simple, faithful to the emotion or idea to be expressed, and harmoniously designed.

Besides formulating laws of movement, Delsarte set forth laws of vocal proportion, having to do with voice tone and intensity.  Because of this several colleges in the United States included the study of Delsarte in their elocution classes.

Although some of Delsarte's informal writings were collected and published posthumously (85), he never comprehensively described his system in writing.  Therefore his followers were free to interpret him as they chose. Delsarte was invited and planned to visit America to demonstrate and teach his ideas, but the Franco-Prussian War of 1870 intervened; subsequently his health became poor and he died in July, 1871.  Delsarte gymnastics ceased to be a vogue among physical educators, but dancers became interested in it.  Ted Shawn, one of the most famous of the early modern dancers, wrote a book, *Every Little Movement*, on the Delsarte system.  The system's basis in natural expression appealed to the modern dancers whose natural movements made it significantly different from formalized ballet.  Finally, Delsarte gymnastics, as the antithesis of the Swedish and German systems, provided one more option, one more strand, for the expanding conception of what comprised physical education.

8

# PIERRE DE COUBERTIN

## 1863-1937

Pierre Fredy, Baron of Coubertin, provides an excellent example of how a single dedicated man can exert a far-reaching influence and affect the lives of great numbers of people. Even as a young man in his twenties he seemed to have an extraordinarily clear understanding of the relationship between government, education and sports, and he conceived plans to bolster the one in support of the others, so that ultimately the French nation would emerge united and energetic, prepared to assume a lustrous world role.

Coubertin's feeling for France had many roots. His ancestors had immigrated there from Italy about four hundred years earlier; at the time of Pierre's birth his aristocratic family owned a castle and land in the Havre region. After his early education at the École Saint Ignace, a Jesuit day-school, he attended Saint Cyr, the French military academy. However, despite the narrow, reactionary education which he received at the Jesuit school, he could not envision a career in the military. Resigning from Saint Cyr, he enrolled at the University of Paris where he successfully completed his Bachelor of Art, Bachelor of Science and Bachelor of Law degrees. He also took a post-graduate course in political science at the École des Sciences Politiques. But beyond his family and education, he was sensitively aware of the pathetic condition of French spirit. Coubertin was seven when the Franco-Prussian War began and subsequently brought humiliation to the French people. The formation of the Third Republic in 1870 did not quiet the ongoing conflicts between the aristocracy and the republicans which undermined the unity of France. Despite his own noble background, Coubertin was a strong advocate of the Republican government and supported its democratic policy. Thus his life's work was primarily motivated by a desire to help regenerate the French nation. Although he was somewhat successful, criticism of his ideas finally drove him to leave Paris (ca. 1915) and take up permanent residence in Lausanne, Switzerland. He died and was buried there in 1937, but some months later, in March, 1938, on the 110th anniversary of Greek independence, his heart was buried at the stadium at Olympia.

Coubertin's first interest was in educational reform. Between 1884 and 1888 he made two or three trips a year to England, primarily to study the

F<small>IG</small>. 40.    Baron Pierre de Coubertin.

education offered at the public schools such as Rugby and Eton.    Convinced that the English devotion to sports and its entrenchment in the
schools was a key element in the moral discipline and strength of character
which he thought underlay English power and expansion throughout the
world, he said that "no education, particularly in democratic times,
can be good and complete without the aid of athletics. . . ." (80:53)  He
made unfavorable comparisons between the English youth, manly, self-
willed, and imbued with a kind of fundamental integrity, and the young
Frenchman whom he thought soft, overly refined and prone to vices.
(333:436-437)

By 1887 he was publishing articles in French journals urging educational
reform modelled on the ideas of the great English headmaster Thomas
Arnold.  He said that "the powerful originality of the reforms executed by
the genius of Thomas Arnold . . . was that of building physical courage,
righteousness of character, command of muscular and moral elements.
The intellectual alone is not capable of this; athletics, exalted and coordinated, is." (215:50)  In 1888 he published *L'Éducation en Angleterre*, an
account of school life in England, and a year later *L'Éducation Anglaise en
France*.  After his first trip to America and Canada in 1889 he published
*Universitiés Transatlantiques*.  He also started a monthly magazine, the
*Revue Athlétique*, which was meant to service the athletic interests of
French schools and universities.  Despite his efforts, he was unable to
accomplish many reforms in the French school system.  The Franco-
Prussian War made the need of better physical training apparent;
it led to the formation of gymnastic societies and the enactment of a series
of laws making gymnastics compulsory (1872, 1880, 1887, 1905).  However,
in practice, the official program which was recommended could not be fol-

lowed due to the lack of facilities and equipment, as well as enthusiasm. Nor were French educators ready for "English sports." The Baron related typical French prejudices against them:

> First, athleticism, it was said, was something essentially British and had its place only in British schools. . . . Second, in England, because of that, studies were weak, sports being incompatible with serious study. Thirdly, sports were a pleasure and, therefore, had no moral value except for the leisured classes, in whom they checked the tendency to idleness. (215:73)

Convinced that France was tired from fighting several wars, he commented: "How readily one pardons it for having played dominoes instead of using in active exercises its poor wearied muscles!" (81:697) Against this background, plus the opposition of the gymnastic societies (who sponsored mostly Swedish gymnastics and military drill), and the tendency towards professionalism in the few sports such as rowing that were popular, Coubertin sought to rekindle the spirit of athleticism. In connection with the 1889 Paris Exposition he successfully held the first international congress on physical education, trying to reconcile the various interests into an eclectic system with athletes holding the primary position. He organized in 1891–1892 the *Union des Sociétés Françaises de Sports Athlétiques* (USFSA), a confederation of athletic clubs and societies similar to the AAU. By 1914 there were over six hundred member societies and 500,000 members. He also arranged for the first international contests held in France. In 1892 the first Anglo-French football match was held in Paris; the French defeated the London Rowing Club in a race on the Seine; the French Union (rowers) was recognized by the Henley Regatta Committee, and the French rowing crews were admitted to university contests on the Thames. Discussing this in a lecture at the Sorbonne, in 1892, he said: "Let us export rowing men, runners, fencers. There's the free trade of the future, and the best way to insure peace." (49:93)

It was with that spirit that he set about organizing the modern Olympics. He was not the first to conceive of the idea; an earlier attempt in 1875 had actually resulted in some events taking place in Athens, but they were poorly organized and considered a failure. In 1893 Coubertin made his second visit to America during which he aroused great interest, especially in the colleges, in his plans for the Olympics. In June, 1894 he held a conference in Paris ostensibly to settle the question of amateurism. (49:93) While there, delegates from seventeen nations agreed on the formation of a permanent International Olympic Committee which would have full supervision of the games; it was decided that participating countries would rotate to host each quadrennial celebration, and Greece would host the first games. Paris was chosen for 1900 and the United States for 1904. The new Olympics were to be "modern in character, not alone because of their programs, which substituted bicycle for chariot races, and fencing for the brutalities of pugilism, but because in their origin and regulations they were international and universal . . . ."* (80:39)

The Baron envisioned great accomplishments accruing from the revival of the Olympics. Foremost among these was peace.

> Should the institution prosper, . . . it may be a potent, if indirect, factor in securing universal peace. . . . We shall not have peace until the prejudices which now separate the different races shall have been outlived. To attain this end, what better means than to bring the youth of all countries periodically together for amicable trials of muscular strength and agility? The Olympic games, with the ancients, controlled athletics and promoted peace. It is not visionary to look to them for similar benefactions in the future. (80:53)

One of the concrete ways in which he hoped to bring about international cooperation was through the purification of athletics, his other major objective. Noting that "discord remains supreme from one end of them [sports] to the other," and that "in this deplorable state of things professionalism tends to grow apace," he dreamed of putting "an end to the quarrels of amateurs. . . ." (80:53) He recognized that no country could impose its rules and habits on the others:

> The Swedes will not yield to the Germans, nor the French to the English. Nothing better than the international Olympic games could therefore be devised. Each country will take its turn in organizing them. When they come to meet every four years in these contests, further ennobled by the memories of the past, athletes all over the world will learn to know one another better, to make mutual concessions, and to seek no other reward in the competition than the honor of the victory. (80:53)

Thus he hoped that the need to cooperate and make "mutual concessions" regarding the games would transfer to matters of foreign policy. And the spirit of amateurism would be fostered because it was sufficient recompense to hear the "people cheer the flag of their country in honor of their achievement."† (80:53)

---

* When the 1896 Games were over the Baron was therefore pleased that "the international character of the institution was well-guarded by the results of the contests. America had won nine prizes for athletic sports alone (flat races for 100 and 400 meters; 110-meter hurdle race; high jump; broad jump; pole-vault; hop, step, and jump; putting the shot; throwing the discus), and two prizes for shooting (revolver, 25 and 30 meters). . . ." France and England each won two prizes Greece eight, including the marathon run, Germany five, Australia, Hungary, and and Austria two, and Switzerland and Denmark each took one prize. (80:48)

† In his description of the spectators' joy at the Greek victory in the marathon (1896), he described a woman who unfastened a gold watch set with pearls and presented it to the victor, and an innkeeper who presented the same man with an order good for 365 free meals; Coubertin did not condemn those rewards as professionalism. On the contrary, he noted that the winner showed his sense of honor by refusing a check for ten thousand francs.

The introduction of artistic features in conjunction with the Olympics, such as festivals, music, poetry, and beautiful ceremonies, was another of Coubertin's ideas. Besides being in keeping with the Greek tradition, he believed it epitomized the highest ideals of sport:

> That we may keep athletic sports in the noble and chivalrous character of the past, and that they may continue to play in modern education the splendid part which the Greek Masters assigned to them, *the sports must remain closely associated with the noblest expression of art and literature.* Otherwise, human imperfection tends always to change the Olympia's athlete into a circus gladiator. (49:93)

After launching the Olympics, Coubertin continued to work for the amateur sport movement. Among his other accomplishments in this area were the founding of the Bureau International de Pedagogie Sportive, the central purpose of which was to uplift mankind through participation in nonprofessional sport (215:32), and the founding in Lausanne of the Olympic Library and Museum. He also was responsible for the Union Pedagogie Universelle, an organization dedicated to a new educational plan for French children. He wrote several important books including a *Universal History* and a work on *The Evolution of France Under the Third Republic* (79). He wrote hundreds of articles throughout his lifetime, many in English, a language he learned as an adult; the sum of his written work totalled almost six thousand pages.

Coubertin was evidently a man of great physical vigor. He took part in many sports but was never considered a fine athlete. His dedication to sport in education and the revival of the Olympics with its spirit of nobility and purity was born not of his own love for participation, but from his desire to strengthen and unify France and all of mankind. It was his pride that the Olympics brought together king and commoner in the true democratic sense. It is difficult to evaluate the success of his work. The Olympics grew into a huge international success and sport ultimately became popular in France, although to this day the schools of France pay less attention to it than do those of most European countries. Some critics would judge that the spirit of amateurism was ultimately lost in the commercialism which has more and more enveloped each passing Olympiad. Nevertheless, Coubertin expressed an ideal which is still held sacred throughout the world.

PART V *(Continued)*

*European Physical Educators and Institutions*

*ENGLISH*

# ARCHIBALD MACLAREN

## ca. 1820-1884

Archibald Maclaren's belief in the importance and power of physical training was unshakably strong. Convinced that "mind and body should be viewed as the two well-fitting halves of a perfect whole" (237:34) he advocated that at every age attention must be paid to both. The purpose of physical training for the civilian was not merely the development of strength, a necessity for soldiers, but of health:

> Yes, it is *health* rather than *strength* that is the great requirement of modern men at modern occupations; it is not the power to travel great distances, carry great burdens, lift great weights, or overcome great material obstructions; it is simply that condition of body, and that amount of vital capacity, which shall enable each man in his place to pursue his calling, and work on in his working life, with the greatest amount of comfort to himself and usefulness to his fellowmen. . . . Health is the uniform and regular performance of all the functions of the body, arising from the harmonious action of all its parts. . . . (237:24-25)

His interest in health was probably not unrelated to his study of medicine, which he engaged in for a time. He also studied fencing and gymnastics in Paris, where he went as a sixteen-year-old boy; at approximately the age of thirty he opened his own fencing school in Oriel Lane, Oxford. His experience at Oriel Lane, which was soon expanded into a gymnasium, and at his University Gymnasium, which he opened in 1858, reinforced both his convictions and his reputation in the field of physical training. As a result he was asked to work out a system of physical education for the army. In 1862 he published his first book, *A Military System of Gymnastic Exercises for the Use of Instructors*, and in the "Introduction" described its contents:

> The exercises forming the courses of this system are arranged progressively, commencing with the most simple and initiatory, and terminating with the most arduous and severe; the former being such as will not overtask the powers of the weakest and most inexpert recruits, and the latter such as will test and increase those of the most practised athlete; the effort required for the performance of the exercises thus gradually increasing with the advancing capacity of the learners. The entire range of exercises is performed with apparatus either moveable or fixed; all exercises of mere position or posture have been avoided . . . the exercises are given in such great variety, that while every part of the complex structure of the human body may receive ample and suitable employment, the form of such employment may be varied almost daily. (236:3-4)

215

These words set forth the basic approach to gymnastics used by Maclaren. Although his exercises greatly resembled those of Jahn, in essence he adopted no system and in fact criticized those then popular in Europe. Of Ling's belief that ". . . movement—mere motions . . . could be so systematized that they could be made to embrace the whole muscular system, would be sufficient for the development of the whole bodily powers" (237:78), Maclaren said:

> The error is so deep-seated and so all-pervading, that it lies in a misconception not only of what Exercise is, but of the necessity of administering it with a reference to the condition of the individual. . . . And to argue that a given mode of Exercise is fit for the healthy and strong, because it is found to be beneficial to the ailing and the delicate, is to argue against all rule and precedent.* (237:78–79)

Although he thought the Prussian system excellent for converting the recruit into the trained soldier, he commented that it "aims at giving to a number of men acting in concert, the lifeless, effortless precision of a well-directed machine." (237:80) He termed the French system:

> a system of bodily exercise, but not a system of bodily training; based on, in many respects, erroneous principles of physical culture, yet productive of great benefit, physically and morally, to the soldier: with much that is useless, much that is frivolous, much that is misplaced and misapplied, and much that has no claim whatever to be admitted into any system of bodily exercise, military or civil. . . . (237:88)

Thus he concluded that all systems yet devised were deficient and he based his efforts on his own experience "developed and matured by every means which I could bring to bear upon it by physiological theory or practical test." (237:89)

Maclaren's "tests," like those of Ling, were sometimes based on questionable assumptions. For instance, he relied for his "proof" upon a series of anthropometric measurements which he made on the soldiers sent to train under him.†

> I . . . received the detachment just as it stood, and following my method of periodic measurements, I carefully ascertained and registered the developments of each at the commencement of his course of instruction, and at certain intervals throughout its progress. . . . One of these men had gained five inches in actual girth of chest . . . five inches of additional space for the heart and lungs to work in. . . . (237:73–74)

---

* Compare this to current arguments against the use of Newell Kephart's theories of developing the motor bases of perception as an aid to learning, via special so-called sensory-motor exercises in the physical education program. Physical educators impressed with his results with the slow learner have sometimes simply adopted it for the normal child.

† Maclaren was probably the first physical educator to use such a technique systematically, although Per Ling also employed some form of measurement to show development through exercise.

The assumption was not examined that a greater chest girth, or an "expansion of the osseous framework upon which the muscles are distributed" (237:74), as determined by photographs, did not necessarily lead to improved health or physical conditioning (refer to p. 159).

His second book for the army was *A System of Fencing for the Use of Instructors in the Army*, published in 1864. He claimed to be the first to set down "an intelligible theory of the scientific use of the sword" (236:197), although he acknowledged that other fencing manuals existed. He also wrote *A Series of Exercises for the Regulation Clubs* (1863) for use at "all stations where dumb and bar bells are not supplied." All three army books were published in 1868 in a single volume and together constituted the textbook for physical training of the English soldiers.

In 1861 the government built a gymnasium at Aldershot modelled after Maclaren's Oxford Gymnasium. Two detachments of non-commissioned officers were sent to Maclaren for training and then directed to Aldershot to form a normal school for the preparation of other teachers. The Aldershot gymnasium was the first British teacher training school for physical educators, though it received only soldiers as students. However, many former graduates of its course eventually left the military and took positions as gymnastic instructors in English schools. Thus Maclaren's system became diffused throughout both military and civil institutions. In 1900 the Board of Education recognized Aldershot, and three other institutes or organizations, as suitable bodies to issue certificates of competence.

Despite Maclaren's personal involvement with the army, he also was concerned with educational gymnastics, and clearly separated the two kinds:

> Whereas the purely educational system stops at the first aim, viz. the cultivation of the body only, leaving the after-use of this power to be determined by the individual wants of the possessor, a military system should be two-fold, aiming first at cultivating the body to its highest attainable capacity, and then at teaching the manner in which this physical power may be applied to professional purpose. (237:90)

His theories of educational gymnastics were presented in *A System of Physical Education* (1869), a book which detailed the theoretical and practical aspects of gymnastics in the clearest English language version then published. He viewed exercise as an essential part of education and pleaded the "necessity of providing a regular system of physical education in connection with the purely mental culture of schools, because it is at this period of life, and it is under a school regime that it is most needed, and would most powerfully influence health and strength, present and future." (237:49) He stated: "Exercise alone of all the agents of growth and development [air, food, clothing] can be regarded in an *educational* light — alone is capable of being permanently systematized and administered as a means of progressive bodily culture." (237:4)

Maclaren classified exercise under two headings: recreative and educational. The first included school games and sports which he considered valuable because they molded character as well as bodies, but nevertheless he noted that "not one of them has for *object* the development of the body, or even the giving of it, or to any part of it, health or strength. . . . And in this, as purely recreative exercise, lies their chief value, the forgetfulness of self, the game being all-in-all." (237:36) He went on to demonstrate that in most games the lower limbs and right arm are the primary parts of the body involved, the rest being neglected. Therefore, he recommended educational exercises which could "modify the growth and distribute the resources of the body so that each particular part shall have its legitimate share, and so to increase these resources that each part of the growing frame shall have its wants supplied." (237:39)

By the time Maclaren was writing his books, sports and games had already become an indigenous part of English school life and were spreading to the working classes who were beginning to enjoy reductions in working hours. In nineteenth-century England, sports not only proliferated but became organized under various governing bodies. In the schools, athletics were believed to help form social qualities and thus they held an important place in public school education. Maclaren's pleas for exercise in the schools were therefore unlike those of men like Locke, Mulcaster and Milton, who were trying to get some physical activity into an otherwise "mental" curriculum. His object was a balanced program which included both the recreative games *and* the developmental exercises. Furthermore, he cautioned:

> There is one point which should be borne in mind, namely, that the lesson should *not* be taken from what is called play-time. *Nothing* should be taken from play-time, and nothing should be introduced into play-time but play. The lesson should be taken from actual school-time and should be regarded and reckoned as actual school-work. (237:99)

He dealt with methodology, and stressed the need for progression, variety, and reference to individual capacity, as he did in his work on military gymnastics. He also specified that:

> Each class should consist of not less than ten or more than fifteen learners. It is not desirable to preserve a too formal attitude or discipline during the lesson, while at the same time it will be readily perceived that the due observance of certain rules and regulations is necessary, not only for the sake of preserving propriety, and of securing the good government of the gymnasium, but also for the sake of the advantage to be derived from the careful performance of the exercises, and for the safety of the learner during the practice. (237:111)

This concept of the extent and purpose of discipline is in accord with American physical education which generally views discipline as a means

FIG. 41.    Archibald Maclaren.

to attaining an atmosphere in which learning can take place.  The opposite approach was taken by Spiess (refer to p. 143) who viewed it as an end in itself.

Archibald Maclaren, born around 1820 on the north bank of the Forth in Scotland, died in 1884.  His attempt to ensure the use of apparatus exercises in England was not very successful.  Eventually Swedish gymnastics was introduced into both the schools and the army and ultimately an English system of movement training which became "modern educational gymnastics," took hold in the primary schools.  Sports continued to be the most popular form of exercise.

Maclaren's cogent writings helped to strengthen physical education, and his *System of Physical Education* became an important handbook for teachers of apparatus exercises.  He was one of the first to attempt to demonstrate the effects of exercise by the use of anthropometric measurements and photographs.  Finally, his reputation as a "man of the highest character and with warmth and tenderness underlying reserve of manner" (207:206), helped to add dignity and respect to his profession.

# RUGBY SCHOOL

"What were you sent to Rugby for?"

"Well, I don't know exactly—nobody ever told me. I suppose because all boys are sent to a public school in England."

"But what do you think yourself? What do you want to do here, and to carry away?"

Tom thought a minute. "I want to be A 1 at cricket and foot-ball, and all other games, and to make my hands keep my head against any fellow, lout or gentleman. . . . I want to carry away just as much Latin and Greek as will take me through Oxford respectably." (188:200)

Those words spoken by Tom Brown, hero of the novel *Tom Brown's School Days* (188), give an interesting insight into the relationship between sports and nineteenth-century British public schools (i.e., British private schools). The novel by Thomas Hughes is considered to be a reasonably accurate reflection of life at Rugby and the boys who attended such a school. In effect then, Tom Brown indicated that the top priority in the hierarchy of goals of well-to-do British boys attending public schools, was to be good at sports. Certainly success at sports was an important aspect of social status at Rugby.

This development in nineteenth-century England contrasted markedly with the parallel development of gymnastics on the European continent. It differed in activity, in purpose, and in method of practice. The gymnastic movement's primary goals related to bodily health, perfection of physique, perfection of movements, and development of controlled power to be used in service of the nation. They were to be achieved through strong discipline, uniformity of spirit and action, and long hours of devotion to perfection of the body as instrument, under the authoritarian commands of the "leader" or teacher. The English sports movement's primary goals related to pleasure, personal and group success, group loyalty, and demonstration of courage and manliness. They were to be achieved through strong group spirit and pressure and long hours of informal participation under the guidance of unauthoritarian student leaders. The goals of the gymnastics movement were in a sense achieved as by-products of the sports movement and vice versa.*

---

* When, in the last quarter of the nineteenth century, both movements came to the United States, they were kept separate even within the same institution. Thus sports were originally controlled by the students and reflected the British purposes

**220**

English sports, as they were practiced at Rugby under the headmastership (1828–1842) of the great educator Thomas Arnold, were representative of a school activity common to resident public schools.   By Sydney
Smith's definition given in 1810 in an article in the *Edinburgh Review*, a
public school was an endowed place of education of old standing, attended by
the sons of gentlemen who resided there from age eight or nine to eighteen.
(224:16)   At the beginning of the century there were seven schools which
fitted this definition:   Charterhouse, Eton, Harrow, Rugby, Shrewsbury,
Westminster, and Winchester, all of which were boarding schools.   City
day schools such as St. Paul's and Merchant Taylor's (at both of which
Richard Mulcaster had been headmaster two centuries earlier), while en-
joying great reputations as public schools were not involved in the sports
movement.   Nor were the elementary or grammar schools (which correspond to the public schools of the United States) in which physical education consisted either of military drill or Swedish gymnastics or both
(refer to p. 228).   By 1800 the recreation activities of the British aristocracy
were centered in "sport" meaning hunting, shooting and fishing.   Public
school students practiced these activities, often in a cruel or lawless way,
in keeping with the general tone of public schools in the early part of the
century.   School boys, regarded as naturally evil, had the "devil" beat out
of them through vicious flogging; lying to authority was universal; bullying
was a perennial problem; and with beer the staple beverage, drunkenness
was not uncommon.   Football, when played, was a form of mass fighting.
Living conditions were unhealthy and quite rough.   In the *History of
Rugby School*, the author commented:

> At that period [early 1800s] a great outcry was being made against public
> schools by many, and the whole system was being denounced as incapable of
> improvement.   Public schools were declared to be hotbeds of vice and cruelty.
> And nothing but evil was supposed to come out of them. (308:223)

Yet by 1864 the Clarendon Commission, a group formed to study the public
schools, reported that:

---

and systems, while gymnastics became part of organized physical education classes,
directed by the teacher and reflecting some of the purposes and methods of the
Europeans.   Slowly the two movements became desegregated, blended into single
programs and single institutions; the techniques and the purposes appropriate to
one were applied to the other.   The American sports movement which emerged was
an incongruity which juxtaposed the activities of sport with the essence of gymnastics.   The English passion for sports and the emotional relationship of the group
to its team, coupled with European authoritarianism, perfectionism and belief in
disciplined uniformity, was a corruption of both systems.   Today's sport teams continue to reflect the unlikely merger:   in their rigid, coach-dominated, anti-senti-
mental devotion to power, they are the antithesis of "sport."

> It is not easy to estimate the degree in which the English people are indebted to these schools [the nine public schools it studied] for the qualities on which they pique themselves most—their capacity to govern others and control themselves, their aptitude for combining freedom with order, their public spirit, their vigour and manliness of character, their strong but not slavish respect for public opinion, their love of healthy sports and exercise. (224:49)

The change that took place has been attributed to two main factors: the reforms promulgated at Rugby by the headmaster Thomas Arnold, and the sports movement.

The first master of Rugby School, Edward Rollston, took office in 1574. Between then and the time Thomas Arnold assumed the headmastership in 1828 a body of traditions had grown up as firmly entrenched as English common law. The changes made by Arnold were therefore slow but consistent and, aided by the general forces of change in society then occurring, were ultimately adopted by the entire British public school system. Changes were in accord with his primary goal: to develop Christian moral character. Despite his personal scholarliness and his belief in the virtues of the classics, Arnold's greatest emphasis was on making students virtuous, manly, honorable, Christian gentlemen. He commented: "With regard to reforms at Rugby, give me credit . . . for a most sincere desire to make it a place of Christian education. At the same time my object will be, if possible, to form Christian men. . . ." (28:179) One way in which Arnold accomplished his purposes was by strengthening the system of self-government, ending the customary bullying by giving older boys legal responsibility for supervised governing of the younger ones:

> English boys are living together amongst themselves alone; and for this their habitual living they require a government. It is idle to say that the masters form, or can form, this government. . . . Those to whom the power is committed, are not simply the strongest boys . . . they are those who have risen to the highest form in the school . . . their business is to keep order amongst the boys; to put a stop to improprieties of conduct, especially to prevent that oppression and ill-usage of the weaker boys by the stronger. . . . Meanwhile this governing part of the school, thus invested with great responsibility, treated by the masters with great confidence and consideration, . . . learn to feel a corresponding self-respect for the character of the school, and by the natural effect of their position acquire a manliness of mind and habits and conduct infinitely superior, generally speaking, to those of young men of the same age who have not enjoyed the same advantages. (20:361–362)

Secondly, he forbade the practice of certain activities which were brutal in nature, including riding to hounds, and traditions which caused the boys to strip the town of flowers, fish and small game. The result of many of these changes from activities which had served as diversions for the boys and took up much of their time was increased participation in sports as a kind of replacement activity. This indirect sponsorship of sports participation was probably the reason that Arnold's personal contribution to the growth of sports has been unduly emphasized in the literature. He was not against play and in fact valued its recreational qualities very highly. Just before his arrival at Rugby he wrote to a friend:

> The Rugby prospect I contemplate with a very strong interest: the work I am not afraid of, if I can get my proper exercise; but I want absolute play, like a boy, and neither riding nor walking will make up for my leaping-pole and gallows, and bathing, when the youths used to go with me, and I felt completely for the time a boy as they were. It is this entire relaxation, I think, at intervals . . . that gives me so keen an appetite for my work at other times. . . . (339:95)

However, Arnold's role was little more than to encourage by giving permission and occasionally appearing at matches. Football and cricket were played at Rugby long before his appointment. In fact, the game Rugby was "invented" at the school five years before Arnold arrived. A plaque on the Doctor's Wall at Rugby commemorated the event with the following inscription:

> THIS STONE COMMEMORATES THE EXPLOIT OF WILLIAM WEBB ELLIS WHO WITH FINE DISREGARD FOR THE RULES OF FOOTBALL AS PLAYED IN HIS TIME FIRST TOOK THE BALL IN HIS ARMS AND RAN WITH IT THUS ORIGINATING THE DISTINCTIVE FEATURE OF THE RUGBY GAME. A.D. 1823. (325:31)

Cricket was another favorite game at Rugby. In a revealing discussion between Tom Brown, Arthur and a master, reasons for the popularity of cricket and football were discussed:

> "Come, none of your irony, Brown," answers the master. "I'm beginning to understand the game scientifically. What a noble game it is too.!"
> "Isn't it? But it's more than a game—it's an institution," said Tom.
> "Yes," said Arthur, "the birthright of British boys, old and young, as *habeas corpus* and trial by jury are of British men."
> "The discipline and reliance on one another which it teaches is so valuable, I think," went on the master, "it ought to be such an unselfish game. It merges the individual in the eleven; he doesn't play that he may win, but that his side may."
> "That's very true," said Tom, "and that's why foot-ball and cricket, now one comes to think of it, are so much better games than fives' or hare-and-hounds, or any others where the object is to come in first or to win for one's self, and not that one's side may win." (188:226)

It was this kind of belief on the part of both students and masters, at Rugby and other schools, that led to the encouragement of sport. Its goals were totally in harmony with the goals of the public schools; like the system of self-government it was a valuable tool for developing those character traits deemed desirable by Thomas Arnold and, in fact, British aristocratic society. The Clarendon Commission recognized this in its 1864 report:

The bodily training which gives health and activity to the frame is imparted at English schools, not by gymnastic exercises which are employed for that end on the continent—exercises which are undoubtedly very valuable and which we should be glad to see introduced more widely in England—but by athletic games which, whilst they serve this purpose well, serve other purposes besides. . . . The cricket and football fields . . . are not merely places of exercise or amusement, they help to form some of the most valuable social qualities and manly virtues, and they hold, like the classroom and the boarding house, a distinct and important place in Public School education. (226:177–178)

Rugby school was, of course, famous for Rugby football.  It received an eminent mark of respectability when in 1839, the Dowager Queen Adelaide, widow of William IV (Victoria was then the reigning Queen), visited the school.  While being escorted around the grounds the following scene occurred:

Her Majesty proceeded completely around the Close on the gravel walk, and expressed a desire to see us play foot-ball.  A fearful thing for thin boots, swell trowsers, and a treacherous November soil!  These are thoughts suggested, perhaps, by later years—there was no hesitation *then*.  Only when we had hanged up our waistcoats and coats on the palings by the tump at Little Side, we presented anything but our usual martial appearance arrayed in white trowsers, belts, and velvet caps. . . . Play, however, we did in a way; we can't say it was a very scientific performance.  Her Majesty seemed most impressed when the ball went up with a tremendous punt into the air, or half traversed the Close in a drop. (308:239)

Fig. 42.  Football at Rugby School.

This interest by the Dowager Queen, whose royal ancestors had once banned football, showed how far the association of athletics with the school had come.  At Rugby School a great deal of time was devoted to playing.  The two hours after dinner (between 1:30 and 3:30) were set aside for play on Tuesday, Thursday and Saturday afternoons—the traditional half-holidays.  The time was not devoted to practicing, but rather to playing matches of football, cricket or fives.  Matches were totally in-school affairs; the first "foreign" football game took place on Saturday, November 16, 1867 against a "scratch" team, and throughout the nine-teeth century the majority of games continued to be intramural.  Endless combinations of groups matched each other:  house against house, or form (class) against form were the most common.  Games were also played against various groups of Old Boys (graduates).  Championship or "cock house" matches for a cup were among the most exciting.  Even today intramural matches are played with considerable spirit and excitement al-though the opportunity to win one's school colors in an interschool match has placed greatest value on those games.  The growth of interschool games inevitably led to increasing playing time.  The Clarendon Commission found that at Rugby three hours, three days a week and two hours, two days a week had to be spent on games in order to obtain a place on the cricket eleven (the school team). (224:51–52)

In Thomas Arnold's time control of sports was largely in the hands of the boys, particularly the captains.  In *Tom Brown's School Days* the master described this exalted position:

> "And then the captain of the eleven!" said the master, "what a post is his in our school world!  almost as hard as the Doctor's:  requiring skill and gentleness and firmness, and I know not what other rare qualities." (188:226)

As captain, Tom was responsible for coaching, selecting players, and doing the job of team managers today such as taking responsibility for equipment and facilities.

As sports grew more extensive, Games Committees were formed.  The first mention of one at Rugby was 1853; it consisted of both masters and boys.  (308:323) Ultimately the Games Committee took over the manage-ment of athletic programs, particularly the scheduling of facilities.  At Rugby the first playground was purchased in 1749.  When the Games Committee was organized there was ground sufficient for seventeen games to be played simultaneously.  The advent of the Games Committee also gave a larger role to masters than previously.  Although masters had sometimes volunteered to assist in coaching, eventually they were expected to do so and were hired for that purpose.  However, despite their vastly increased organization today, sports have not completely left the hands of the students who at least share in decision-making.

Compulsory attendance at games was apparently a feature of sports at

Rugby, though like other rules it was enforced primarily by social pressure·
All boys were expected to *want* to attend the Schoolhouse match for instance. The Schoolhouse was the largest house at Rugby and until 1850
customarily was matched against the entire school instead of a single other
house. In a chapter describing the Schoolhouse match, Hughes summarized the attendance situation:

> To-day, however, being the school-house match, none of the school-house
> praepostors stay by the door to watch for truants of their side; there is *carte
> blanche* to the school-house fags to go where they like: "They trust to our honor,"
> as East proudly informs Tom; "they know very well that no school-house boy
> would cut the match. If he did, we'd very soon cut him, I can tell you." (188:74)

Each of the British public schools had its own favorite sports based on
both tradition and locale. Schools with access to waterways naturally took
to rowing, for instance, something Rugby could not do. One of the traditional Rugby activities was the Big Side Runs: one of the runs, the
Crick, was for a distance of fourteen miles. The winner of one Crick run
circa 1840, finished the course in only eighty minutes. (308:270–272)

A custom prevalent in the public schools was "fagging," i.e., the com-
mandeering of younger boys to do tasks for older ones. Arnold believed
fagging to be a vital part of the system and "legalized" its practice for
sixth form boys. One of the chores of a fag was to watch for balls at
cricket or fives, score or umpire at cricket, or stand behind the goals in
football. At the end of the Big Side Runs fags were waiting with coats for
runners to wear home. The bat boy on a baseball team probably resembles
the modern version of fagging at a sport activity.

There were no uniforms for sport at Rugby in Tom Brown's days. He
was amazed to notice that the players in the Schoolhouse match wore white
trousers to show their loyalty. In later years caps and jerseys showing the
house crest and colors were added, and earning the right to wear one's
house and/or school colors became an important part of the award system.
Generally the team captain had the right to decide who had won the colors.
Making the school team entitled one to wear the school blazer, a special
reward.*

The conduct of sports in English public schools has changed from the
days when Thomas Arnold was headmaster. Sports are more diversified,
played on a higher level, more "professional" in their coaching, more geared
to interschool competition, and perhaps fewer students participate. The
movement was widely emulated throughout the country, at first in the
public schools and later through other levels of popular education. The
belief that sports contributed to development of character and leadership
qualities was epitomized by the quotation, probably apocryphal, but attrib-

---

* This is paralleled by the American practice of awarding school letters, sweaters
or blazers to special players or members of the winning teams.

uted to the Duke of Wellington, that "the Battle of Waterloo was won on the playing fields of Eton." That sports could contribute to such an achievement was due completely to the nature of the sports movement. If students learned to lead it was because they were responsible for leading— for organizing, managing, selecting players, coaching, and distributing awards for their games. If students learned sportsmanship it was because they set their own rules in accord with the common good and therefore were willing to adhere to their spirit; those that were not were taught to by the example and pressure of their peers. If students learned selflessness or "team spirit" it was because the reward was to wear the colors of the house and thus reinforce group identification. If students learned courage and fortitude, it was because that was a quality valued by their peer groups; it was expected of them at a time when games were often violent in nature and small boys competed with large ones in contact sports. It is impossible to separate the practice from the result; games are not inherently character building. What was started at Rugby under the administration of a man dedicated to the building of Christian gentlemen, was a system to fulfill that goal. It was through that system that Arnold, Rugby and the English sports movement made their innovative contribution to physical education.

# THE BERGMAN-ÖSTERBERG PHYSICAL TRAINING COLLEGE

In 1888 one of the two teacher training colleges in England that included any kind of physical education classes in their programs was the Whitelands Training College, where Martina Bergman had introduced Swedish gymnastics. As long as military drill (required for boys in the Education Act of 1870) provided the entire content for physical education programs, ex-soldiers were suitable as teachers. However, sentiment increased for substituting gymnastic exercises for drill in the public elementary schools. Swedish gymnastics had been introduced in England in 1838 as a form of medical gymnastics, and as such had chiefly interested doctors and patients in need of therapeutic exercise. It was a doctor, Mathias Roth, who recognized its advantages for healthy people and pressed for the introduction of Swedish gymnastics in elementary schools. Finally, in 1877 the School Board of London equipped eighteen schools with gymnastic apparatus and appointed a Swede, Concordia Löfving as Lady Superintendent of Physical Education. She was assigned to train London schoolteachers. Upon her resignation she was replaced in 1882 by another Swede, Miss Martina Bergman (later Madame Bergman-Österberg, 1849–1915), a recent graduate of Ling's Institute in Stockholm. Under Österberg Swedish exercises slowly became a part of the elementary school programs in London and by 1895 the national Education Department issued an edict making physical education, including Swedish or other suitable exercises, a subject eligible for grant money. In 1900, supervised games, well-established in private schools, also became eligible as an alternative form of exercise.

As the popularity of physical education rather than drill increased, the shortage of qualified teachers was painfully apparent. Only a few school boards were able to train volunteers to be teachers, and students from the teacher training colleges, or the army, knew only military drill; a few schools were able to hire graduates of the Royal Central Institute of Gymnastics at Stockholm. For women the problem had an additional complication. As Madame Österberg said:

> Let us once for all discard man as a physical trainer of women; let us send the drill sergeant right about face to his awkward squad. This work we women do better, as our very success in training depends upon our having felt like women, able to calculate the possibilities of our sex, knowing our weakness and our strength. (224:137–138)

FIG. 43. Martina Bergman-Österberg.

With this aim in mind, and to meet the shortage of qualified physical education teachers, Österberg bought a house in Hampstead, built a gymnasium in the garden, and in 1885 opened a Training College for Teachers. During the course of her service with the London School Board (which terminated in 1888) she had trained 1312 teachers and introduced her system into 276 schools. (224:115) But the identification of gymnastics with public education inevitably also identified it with the poorer classes, and Madame Österberg hoped that in her College she could work to "improve the development of women of the upper and middle classes. (240:288) Her primary interest was the development of mature, responsible, free women—producing physical education teachers was a secondary goal.

Although there were few students to start with (four the first year), due to the rigorous standards and high fees, the Österberg Physical Training College became an institution of influence and importance. In 1895 the campus was moved to Dartford where it still functions today as an important element in the training of women physical education teachers. After Österberg's death in 1915, the College was given to Britain in the form of a trust; it is now a constituent college of the University of London Institute of Education. By 1915 more than five hundred women had graduated. They were middle class students who could afford the fees and desired to enter a profession, most of which were virtually closed to women in England until the post-World War II era, notwithstanding the Sex Disqualification Act of 1919.

Despite her connection with Swedish gymnastics, Österberg equipped her gymnasium (the first fully-equipped one in the country) with German apparatus as well as Swedish equipment; she acquired a games field and secured use of the Hampstead Baths for classes in swimming. Although she taught the traditional Swedish program similar to the one at the Royal Gymnastics Central Institute, she also included German vaulting, tennis, cricket, waltzing, national dances, and American basketball. The latter game was developed by her students into netball, which is still a popular girls' basketball-type game in British countries where it is taught in the last years of primary school.   About 1895, after the College was moved to Dartford, field hockey was introduced and lacrosse was added soon after the turn of the century.   The increased space also allowed for hard tennis courts, a running track and both indoor and outdoor gymnasiums.   In addition to activities, students studied anatomy, animal physiology, chemistry, physics, hygiene, and theory of movement. (240:289–292)

Practice teaching, either in London or at Dartford with local children, was an important curricular adjunct.   But besides teacher training, courses were offered in massage and remedial gymnastics given in a special clinic at the College.   This practice, modelled after the RGCI in Stockholm, continued until 1964, and many of the Dartford graduates chose to enter private practice with their own clinics rather than enter the teaching profession.

Initially the program lasted a year and ended with a display of competence and the awarding of a certificate.   A second-year was soon added and by 1906 Madame Österberg wanted a three-year training course to include the whole range of physical education activities: gymnastics, indoor and outdoor games, dancing, and Dalcroze eurythmics.   This goal was, however, not immediately realized although now there are seven colleges in England for the training of women's physical education teachers, all offering a three-year, specialized course; several of these colleges were founded by Österberg's students or assistants.   The modern course at Dartford includes the study of English and the theory and practice of education, as well as study in the art and science of human movement.

Madame Österberg was a woman of great personal strength and will. While she was much loved by her students, she was also known as a stern disciplinarian—in fact, she was referred to as "Napoleon."   Carelessness, fatigue, lack of effort, and sloppiness, were never tolerated at the College. She was known to remind her students of their unworthiness, reputedly saying: "I have only two years in which to make fine women of you.   Not a moment can be wasted.   Remember, my dears, it does not matter how good you are, you will never be good enough for the profession you have chosen."   (240:294) She used this approach in support of her aim "to send out fine women to do fine work."   (260:7) Her strong will was also evident in the way she reacted to the formation of the Swedish Physical Educationalists, or the Ling Association, now the Physical Education Association. In 1899 several former Österberg students formed the Swedish Physical Educationalists Association with the idea of raising professional standards and publishing a list of women qualified to teach Swedish gymnastics and give massage.   At first, graduates of the Stockholm Central Institute and the Österberg College were the only ones to be admitted as members but other colleges were gradually approved by the Association.   Its promotion of Swedish gymnastics exclusively led Österberg to denounce the group, and further to fight it by forming a rival association, the Bergman-Österberg Union. The Ling Association initiated its own diploma examinations as early as 1901; the Union was instrumental in pressuring the Board of Education to examine students and grant government diplomas, a practice which did not begin, however, until 1932.

The Österberg College was also responsible for developing the gym tunic as a replacement for the blue dress favored at Ling's Institute. The tunic, designed by one of Österberg's students, was eventually worn internationally. In America it is most often seen on field hockey players who adopted both the game and the uniform from England.

The influence of Martina Bergman-Österberg and her Training College was great. She set in motion the training of generations of women physical education teachers for England; she influenced international physical education, especially American, both by personal visits and through her students who were employed by the women's colleges offering physical education programs. Goucher College, for instance, always had an Österberg graduate on its staff between 1897 and 1927. (3:52) Furthermore, her philosophy of a varied physical education program helped to keep the English schools from teaching only Swedish gymnastics, although the Swedish system did become well-entrenched for over forty years. Her insistence upon rigorous standards of conduct, skill and teaching helped to upgrade the profession of physical education as an appropriate school subject. Lastly, her belief in and demonstration of the capacities and potentialities of women, helped to break down the Victorian ignorance and prejudice which prevented the full emancipation of women.

# KARL GAULHOFER—MARGARETE STREICHER*

**1885-1941**                                    **1891-**

The development of the Austrian school of thought started at one of the most difficult but opportune times in Austrian history. The collapse of the Austro-Hungarian empire after World War I was immediate cause for an almost complete disintegration of the economic and social structure which had perpetuated itself under the centuries-long rule of the Hapsburgs. Even before the war, demands for educational reforms had been expressed (66:8), but the change-over from empire to republic exposed in a dramatic manner the pressing needs for implementation of a new, democratic-oriented educational philosophy. In the framework of this renewal which extended to all areas of education, Karl Gaulhofer and Margarete Streicher developed and introduced the concept of *Natürliches Turnen* ("natural" physical education). Although the country was poor and financial support for the new program very slim, and old concepts and convictions could not be abandoned overnight, Gaulhofer and Streicher benefitted greatly from the fact that the time was ripe for a change. Endorsements from physicians, psychologists and educators added validity and support to their method while theory and practical implementation gradually gained popularity with specialists and classroom teachers. Promotion of their theories was further enhanced by a curious combination of the teaching and supervisory responsibilities of Gaulhofer and Streicher which gave them rather extensive control over the physical education curriculums of the public schools as well as over the preparation of physical education teachers.

Karl Gaulhofer was born in the neighborhood of Graz, a town in southern Austria, where he received his secondary and college education. At an early age he joined the ranks of the *turnverein* in which he was active as a performer and a leader. One of Gaulhofer's athletic achievements was a second place in the pentathlon at an international meet in Berlin in 1903. (126:2) His leadership abilities and his teaching qualities were demonstrated early when, while still in high school, he was appointed as assistant to his physical education teacher. (124:196) In 1903 Gaulhofer entered the University of Graz where he majored in physical education and natural science. In 1904, although not yet old enough to be eligible for a teacher's credential, Gaulhofer received special permission to take the state examina-

---

* This chapter was written by Dr. Nicholaas J. Moolenijzer of the University of Missouri—Columbia.

tion for physical education, which he passed successfully. (126:3) In 1908 he obtained his credentials in natural history and mathematics and in 1909 he completed his doctoral studies with a dissertation in botany. (133:1)

Although schooled in the concepts of Jahn and Spiess, Gaulhofer experimented freely during his relatively short teaching career in Brück an der Mur (1907–1914). Familiar with the writings of the early pioneers Guts Muths and Vieth and influenced by the theories of such progressive contemporaries as Eckhart, Schmidt, Bode, and Spitzy, Gaulhofer developed his own program of physical education. (66:48) In contrast to the narrow system of Spiess, Gaulhofer's program included a wide variety of activities and allowed for much individuality in performance. In 1914 the outbreak of World War I interrupted Gaulhofer's teaching career. However, his activities had not gone unnoticed as might be deduced from the fact that in 1919, shortly after his return from the war, he was appointed head of the department of physical education in the Federal Ministry of Education. Entailed in this position was a series of interrelated responsibilities which greatly facilitated the dissemination and application of the modern approach to physical education. Among Gaulhofer's new responsibilities were: the direction of the national physical education program; the supervision of the physical education teacher training institutes; acting as a lecturer and the chairman of the physical education teacher training institute of the University of Vienna; and serving as editor of the physical education section of *Quelle*, the national education journal. (126:4)

Although Gaulhofer and Streicher's philosophy had found wide acceptance and was implemented all over Europe, Gaulhofer was discouraged by the economic and political conditions which seemed to slow down progress in his own country. In addition he was dissatisfied with the burden of his administrative responsibilities which interfered with his desire to be more productive academically. In the hope of remedying this situation he accepted in 1932 an appointment as department chairman at the Academy for Physical Education in Amsterdam, a position he held until his death in 1941.

Although his untimely death was a great loss, it did not prove a calamity for the further development of the Austrian school. From the very beginning cooperation between Gaulhofer and Streicher had been so close that it was not possible to distinguish which part each had contributed to the development of their philosophy. Gaulhofer wrote:

> One look at the two volumes of Natürliches Turnen indicates this with all clearness. We have . . . developed together the entire curriculum. Which part each of us has in it perhaps neither of us can tell with certainty, let alone any outsider. (132:5)

It was natural, therefore, that Streicher assumed most of Gaulhofer's responsibilities, including the editorship of *Quelle* when he left for Holland in 1932, and that she assumed the entire leadership after his death.

Although born in Graz, Margarete Streicher grew up in Vienna.  After completion of her secondary education she enrolled in the University there, majoring in biology.  (125:1)  Due to conditions in her family she was not encouraged to participate in physical activities in her early years.  However, during her first year at the University she was persuaded by a friend to enroll in a course for physical education teachers in which, to her own amazement, she did quite well.  In 1912 she obtained a credential for physical education.  While teaching physical education and natural history at a girls' secondary school in Vienna she continued her studies at the university where she obtained her Ph.D. in natural history in 1916.  Streicher's lack of background in physical education made her unwittingly break with tradition when she experimented with her own forms of exercise during her first years of teaching.  As all of the men teachers and supervisors were away at war she was not hampered in this experimentation and consequently was able to develop her own method.  Later Gaulhofer was to remark:

> Here I am philosophizing for so long how "natural" physical education should be organized and then I find a young teacher in Vienna who has already realized what I have in mind.  With one stroke all uncertainty disappeared and I saw the direction that should be followed for its practical application. (169:11)

In 1918 the quality of Streicher's teaching had been recognized and she was appointed as lecturer at the physical education teacher training institute of the University of Vienna   Appointment as inspector for girls physical education followed in 1924.  In 1920 when she was charged with conducting an in-service course in physical education, Gaulhofer and Streicher combined forces for the first time.  During the next decade they jointly established the philosophy of the Austrian school. (248:3)  It should be emphasized that this partnership was for its time and place an unprecedented occurrence because it was an "equal" partnership.  For the development of the Austrian School, particularly after Gaulhofer's death, this proved highly significant.

During a time when public opinion in Austria believed a woman's place was in the kitchen, Streicher entered into a partnership with one of the most influential leaders of the profession.  An avid feminist, Streicher was very conscious of her "rights" and her "place":

> Before I learned to know Gaulhofer and Nohl [one of Europe's foremost pedagogical philosophers, 1879–1965], I was already of the heretic opinion that women should take their cause in their own hands.
>
> .     .     .     .     .     .     .     .     .     .     .     .     .     .
>
> In this joint effort with Gaulhofer I had absolutely no intention, as my mother used to call it, to play the role of a mason's wife.  That is always having to do the work of secondary importance only . . . after which to disappear as quickly as possible. (345:3)

Fig. 44.   Margarete Streicher

Now and then indirect, half-hearted attempts have been made to assign to Streicher a role of secondary importance.   Commenting on her acceptance as an equal partner in their cooperative efforts Streicher noted:  "Gaulhofer never wanted the so cherished term of 'Mitarbeiterin' [assistant] applied to me because, in his words, it did not properly state the state of affairs." (347:155)   Gaulhofer's statements support this unequivocally.   Reflecting on their work he remarked:  "I will always judge it to be my most beautiful hours when I, together with Dr. Streicher, began to test all our conclusions against our basic principles, and how everywhere in our writings and practical applications we found corroboration. . . ." (124:192)   Although Streicher's emancipated point of view occasionally caused them to disagree, she maintained that it was of utmost importance that both the masculine and feminine concepts of education be represented in the new method to make it educationally sound.   She noted that "it is such that neither male nor female eyes alone sees the world in its true relationship . . . [but] as in a stereoscope the pictures taken from two different positions must melt into one.   Only then the picture is true." (345:3)

Gaulhofer and Streicher tried to disseminate their theories through workshops, in-service training programs and articles. These essays were later published in book form and appeared in several volumes under the title *Natürliches Turnen* I and II; Volumes III–V were published later by Streicher. The material of the workshop programs was published as *Grundzüge des Österreichischen Schulturnens* (*Foundations of Austrian Physical Education*).

Gaulhofer and Streicher held the opinion that the way "to practice physical education with a child cannot be decided by a system. . . . This is, as is any form of education, determined by the nature of the child and the goal of education." (122:8) This means that physical education would therefore need to adapt its program according to the most recent findings of research in related fields. As a consequence Gaulhofer and Streicher did not regard *Natürliches Turnen* as a finished product which limited itself to a rigid system but as a method which they expected to grow and expand. (125:89)

Like Guts Muths, Gaulhofer and Streicher did not mean by the term "natural" a return to primitive conditions but rather they proposed an adaptation of physical activities to the nature of man in all his biological functions. This included emotional, intellectual and social as well as physical characteristics. A dichotomy of mind and body was rejected:

> Physical education in contrast to moral or intellectual education or besides these two does not exist. There is but one, the "Total Education," which includes the entire young individual whose physique, morals and intellect are so closely knit, that one cannot separate that which really belongs together. (121:1)

Consequently it was urged that "physical education . . . should make itself consciously available to harmonious education" (124:8–9) in order to contribute to the physical, mental, aesthetic, and ethical development of the individual. The concept of "natural" was defined further in terms of "how" rather than "what," and emphasis was placed on "becoming" something rather than on "doing" something. (124:147, 81) Implications of the concept of "natural" may be identified briefly as follows: (1) it was an approach, a manner of performance, rather than a system or a group of particular exercises; (2) it was attentive to biological principles (346:26; 122:41); (3) as applied to movement, it connoted a process of moving from one status of balance to another with a minimum expenditure of energy (124:126, 176); (4) it assumed that a natural movement is an integrated mental-physical concept and an expression of a personality which reflects the person's individual style of performance. (125:131)

In sharp contrast to the artificially-designed movement exercises of the other European methods, the Austrian school, in harmony with its axiom "physical education is education of the individual with the body as point of application" (125:60), advocated the development of the natural func-

9

tions of man. "The development of movements needed for every-day life and for the physical labor which so many people must perform is the most important aim of physical exercises; not the acquisition of skills which nobody needs in daily life." (124:76) For this purpose, in *Natürliches Turnen* Gaulhofer and Streicher developed a generic classification of exercises, the so-called "System of Pedagogical Physical Exercises" (349:108) ranked on the basis of educational concepts. In this organization everyday movements, labor movements, and physical play were employed, all classified generically in terms of their function in the life of the individual. Exercises were related to human purposes rather than to mechanical considerations. Noting that man seldom executes individual functions separately but generally groups them into larger purposeful complexes of coordinated action, the Austrian school stressed the utilization of activities which offered many possibilities for function rather than only for narrow, athletic specialization. (349:111; 125:180) Furthermore, the importance of outdoor activities in which nature could be experienced, was stressed as an essential aspect of physical education:

> The essence of physical education is practiced during the regular physical education period; but where in the rest of education the requirement "out of the classroom out into the world" penetrates more and more so here, too, outdoor games, hiking, swimming, skiing, and skating are increasingly recognized as an essential part of physical education without which it cannot attain its goal. We like to take pupils outdoors . . . literally, and through this, hope to help them rediscover the road to nature. (124:13)

Afraid of the "great danger [that] physical education would deteriorate from the high level of educational development to drudgery" (123:3), and that their philosophy might crystallize into a rigid system, Gaulhofer and Streicher resisted requests for a detailed curriculum guide. However, to bridge the transition period they regularly published articles which provided new ideas for practical application of their theories. Ever since the principles of the German *turnen* were introduced, formal "exercise possibility" oriented methods had dominated the physical education scene. *Natürliches Turnen* broke with this tradition and focused attention on the individual, on his nature, and on his right to be educated according to his nature. (247:249)

The concepts utilized by Gaulhofer and Streicher in the development of their method of *Natürliches Turnen* proved quite revolutionary to the physical education practices of their time although they correlated closely with views of education then prevalent. This may explain the acceptance of Gaulhofer and Streicher's system by other European nations, many of which adopted its principles and incorporated its practices into their own programs. In the decade following the introduction of *Natürliches Turnen* many European physical educators attended workshops in Austria; it was during this period that the term "Austrian school" was developed. While translation and substitution of terminology soon helped to make the newly imported concepts indigenous, most modern approaches to European physical education clearly show the marks of Karl Gaulhofer's and Margarete Streicher's influence.

# PART VI

*American Physical Educators and Institutions*

# ROUND HILL SCHOOL

The Round Hill School was an experiment in American education. Founded at Northampton, Massachusetts in 1823, it was one of the few good college preparatory schools in existence, and was the only school predicated on the concept of individualizing instruction. It was further distinguished by its inclusion of physical training, a subject ignored by other schools. Round Hill was modelled after the German gymnasium with overtones of Fellenberg's Hofwyl School (refer to footnote, p. 91).

Like the European schools, Round Hill offered an education in the classics with much attention to excellence in academic performance. The curriculum emphasized languages, particularly modern ones, and Latin, Greek, French, Spanish, German, and Italian were offered although not all in the first year of its founding. In addition, students studied writing, elocution, rhetoric, history, moral philosophy, Roman antiquities, mercantile arithmetic, and higher mathematics. They were also given dancing, riding and gymnastics lessons. (307:437 438) Graduates of Round Hill, like those of the gymnasium, had mastered subject matter equivalent to that offered by American colleges of the time.

From Fellenberg, whose school the founder Joseph Cogswell visited while in Switzerland, was borrowed the idea of the educative and practical values of having students engage in manual labor. Besides requiring the boys to cut their own wood for fires and clean their own rooms, plots were assigned for plant and vegetable gardens; carpentry tools were available for the boys to make kites, bows and arrows and traps. The latter "weapons" were used to hunt birds and squirrels, which, along with potatoes, apples, corn, and chestnuts, were cooked by the boys in Crony Village. The Village consisted of several wooden huts made by the boys; it was a popular retreat until it began to threaten school discipline and was ordered demolished. (37:40–41) As at Hofwyl, masters and students ate together at a single table. In later years, the Round Hill curriculum began to include practical subjects such as bookkeeping, horticulture, statistics, and surveying. (37:57)

Fellenberg's influence was also manifest in Cogswell's behavior as a schoolmaster, seemingly modelled on what he witnessed at Hofwyl:

> More heartfelt joy I never witnessed in my life, . . . because they had the happiness to be placed for their education in a school, the head of which was

rather a father than a master to them. . . . Instructors and pupils walked arm in arm together, played together, ate at the same table, and all without any danger to their reciprocal rights; how delightful it must be to govern, where love is the principle of obedience! (73:87–88)

Cogswell not only abolished the traditional educational tools of reward and punishment (though in fact, some of both occurred), but he personally led the excursions and some of the exercises. He was a man of strenuous physical habits (he claimed to have walked 1700 miles in eleven weeks during a summer in Switzerland), and his letters show an active role in the boys' exercises and outings.

October 26, 1823: . . . For the last fortnight we have had a regular trial of skill in running around our wood, which is a measured distance of half a mile. Five minutes before 8 we let the boys out for their morning exercise, and head them in a race. . . . To-day I run twice round, making a mile, in $6\frac{1}{2}$ minutes, and next week we have ordered a double heat for all the boys. . . . November 28: . . . We take a great deal of exercise. . . . Every Saturday afternoon we walk from twelve to sixteen miles. The day after Thanksgiving I took six of them with me to Hartford. We walked the first twenty-one miles before noon. . . . August 5 [1824]: . . . I took the boys a walk of ten miles through the woods in search of berries and had a good frolic with them. (73:144–146, 154)

Joseph Cogswell and the co-founder, George Bancroft, were interested in establishing a good school of the kind each had observed during European travels. Bancroft was particularly attracted to the Schulpforte, a Prussian school where masters and students lived together in an old monastery. In a letter to Harvard's President John Kirkland, Bancroft described the situation: "I find it quite instructive to observe their institution from time to time; they know how to unite gymnastic exercises, music, and the sciences; and this is the mode of education, which Plato has extolled as the perfection of art." (43:56) Dissatisfied with the state of Harvard, where they were both employed, and filled with ideas gleaned from observing European schools, they agreed to establish a secondary school. Round Hill was selected for its location, "about half a mile from the village of Northampton, on the brow of a beautiful hill, overlooking the Connecticut, and the rich plain through which it flows, and the fine picturesque hills which form its banks. . . ." (73:135–136) In a letter in 1822 Bancroft explained their intentions:

We will together establish a school, the end of which is to be the moral and intellectual maturity of the mind of each boy that we take charge of; and the means are to be first and foremost *instruction in the classics*. We intend going into the country, and we shall choose a pleasant site, where nature in her loveliness may breathe calmness and inspire purity. (37:25)

Round Hill opened on October 1, 1823 with fifteen boarders and ten day students; at its height in 1827 there were 135 students. In the ten years of its existence students came from at least eighteen different states, including many southern ones where education was very poor, and from as far away as Mexico, the West Indies and Brazil. (332:206)  Two three-week vacations were the only holidays provided for in the school year.  Tuition was $300 a year—$125 more than at Harvard College.  This large sum enabled the directors to give individual tutoring.  In 1826 a newspaper account noted there were 112 boys and ten instructors, besides the two directors. (307:438)  Each boy progressed at his own rate, using a textbook suited to his personal competency, reciting individually when he was ready.  In later years, financial problems forced modification of the system to classes, which were kept small (approximately six in each). (37:57)  A school costume was adopted to establish a general uniformity. (37:37)  The day began at six with prayers and ended, for most students, at 9 P.M. In a schedule crowded with classes, study periods, declamation, and dancing lessons, the two hours from 5–7 P.M. were set aside for exercise and recreation. "At this time the classes in gymynastics [sic] have their instruction, when the weather permits." (307:439)

It was because of this instruction in gymnastics that Round Hill is credited with a role in the history of physical education.  From the beginning the founders intended to provide physical training.  In their first prospectus it was stated: "We would also encourage activity of body as the means of promoting firmness of constitution and vigor of mind, and shall appropriate regularly a portion of each day to healthful sports and gymnastic exercises." (207:218)  This position was amplified in a circular issued three years later, in 1826:

> It may be impossible to engraft on any modern nation a system of education corresponding to that which prevailed in ancient Greece.  But something must be done.  Food, sleep and exercise must be regulated . . . temperance and exercise be set . . . to keep watch over health. Games and healthful sports, promoting hilarity and securing a just degree of exercise, are to be encouraged.  Various means of motion are to be devised and applied; and where these are regularly used everything is done to assist nature in strengthening the youthful constitution.  If in addition to regularity in the use of exercise, the kinds of it are so arranged that the several powers of the body may successively be brought into action and gradually led to greater exertions, it will not be long before the physical being assumes a new appearance, and in addition to the acquisition of a control of the body, beneficial results will be visible in general industry, deportment and morals.  The attempt, therefore, to provide the various means for gymnastics exercises merits to be encouraged; . . . the best that are known should be employed.  We are deeply impressed with the necessity of uniting physical with moral education; . . . we may say, that we were the first in the new continent to connect gymnastics with a purely literary establishment. (207:237–238)

That a teacher able to give instruction in gymnastics was secured, seems to have been the result more of chance than planning.  In late 1824, two German political refugees, scholars and former *turners* forced to emigrate

FIG. 45.   Charles Beck.

because of their liberal viewpoints, arrived in the United States.*   Charles Beck, an accomplished classical scholar, ordained and with a doctorate in theology, was recommended for a position at the Round Hill School.   In

---

* Charles Follen (1796–1840), Charles Beck (1798–1866), plus Francis Lieber (1800–1872) who arrived in 1827, introduced German gymnastics to America and thus were responsible for several "firsts" connected with organized physical activity. However, none of them made the teaching of gymnastics their life's work; their connection with it was "extracurricular" and short-lived and each subsequently achieved reputable success in other endeavors.

Charles Follen became the first teacher of the German language at Harvard University and also introduced Jahn gymnastics to the students.   His friend Beck helped him to set up his "gymnasium" by providing advice and drawings of apparatus.   The *Harvard Register* recorded that "one of the unoccupied common halls was fitted up with various gymnastic appliances and other fixtures were erected on the Delta [the college playground]." (161:23)   Thomas Wentworth Higginson described the apparatus as consisting of "high uprights and crossbars, with ladders and swinging ropes, and complications of wood and cordage. . . . Beneath some parts of the apparatus there were pits sunk in the earth. . . ." (207:240)   This "gymnasium" was, in 1826, the first college gymnasium in the United States; Follen in the 1827–28 Harvard catalogue was listed as "Superintendent of the Gymnasium."   He also opened in 1826 an outdoor gymnasium or *turnplatz* in Boston.   Open to the public, the Tremont Gymnasium was also the first of its kind in America and was very popular for a short time.

Within a year Follen resigned and was replaced by Francis Lieber who, in addition to carrying a certificate from Jahn himself, testifying to his excellence as a gymnastics teacher and leader, had a similar endorsement from Major-general Pfuel, the inventor of a new method of teaching swimming and founder of the Prussian Military Swimming Schools.   Lieber not only took directorship of the Tremont Gymnasium but he established in Boston a swimming school, which proved to have more enduring popularity than the *turnplatz* and was also the first of its kind in America.

1825 he became an instructor in Latin and gymnastics, and thus opened the first school gymnasium and conducted the first school gymnastics program in this country; it came to an end with Beck's resignation in 1830. He went on to become University Professor of Latin at Harvard and at one time represented Cambridge in the Massachusetts State Legislature.

The Round Hill property was large—originally about fifty acres with three buildings on it; in addition, Cogswell purchased another thirty-five contiguous acres. (37:44–46)    Thus there was ample room for the *turnplatz* which was laid out on the northwest side of Round Hill, in a space of eight or ten acres bordered on the west side by a brook.   A mast, bars, ladders, and other pieces of apparatus used in German *turnplätze* were placed on the grounds.   George Shattuck, once a Round Hill student, re-called that "the whole school was divided into classes, and each class had an hour three times a week for instruction by Dr. Beck." (161:22)   That the program and layout of the *turnplatz* was on the order of the Jahn rather than the Spiess system is indirectly demonstrated by Beck's trans-

Fig. 46.   Exercising on a Turnplatz.
(From Beck's *Treatise on Gymnasticks*.)

lation of Jahn's *Treatise on Gymnasticks*. Apparently acting in response to numerous requests, Beck rendered an English translation of the work (38) mentioning the Round Hill School in the preface as being the first school to introduce gymnastic exercises. Obviously he was referring to the kind of exercises and gymnastic games which he had translated. Bassett, in a definitive article on Round Hill claimed that "neither rain, cold, nor snow interfered with outdoor exercise" (37:48), but a newspaper account of 1826 stated otherwise. (307:439) It is likely that the boys had some continuous program of supervised physical activity, substituting in the winter ice skating and sledding for the gymnastics classes. There were also riding, dancing* and swimming classes, the latter conducted by Beck on the Mill River. Shattuck's recollection that "baseball, hockey and foot-ball were the games. I remember playing in a match game . . ." (161:22), indicates that there was some form of organized sport. The daily run and frequent long hikes rounded out the bulk of the physical training program.

Unfortunately the Round Hill experiment came to an end in 1834. Although Cogswell overextended himself through land purchases which caused financial difficulties, the chief cause of the school's demise probably lay in its variance with the American system. Graduates of Round Hill were too well-prepared for the colleges of that era. Ready to enter the junior or senior year, they nevertheless had to pay tuition for all four years under the system the universities were then enforcing. Thus the excellence of the Round Hill education not only could not be used to full advantage but actually caused families a financial disadvantage. The number of students declined, forcing the school to close. Some twenty years passed before George Shattuck, finding no school for his sons that compared with his alma mater, founded the St. Paul's School in Concord, New Hampshire on the Round Hill idea. Others followed suit, in some measure ensuring the perpetuation of Cogswell's and Bancroft's educational theories.

The practice of including instruction in physical education became common in American schools both private and public. The pattern of combining intellectual and physical education and the belief in the importance of physical activity and its contribution to the health and character development of students were concepts enacted at Round Hill. Metzner attributed the endowment of a gymnastic field and apparatus at Yale (1826), the New Haven Gymnasium (1826), and the Amherst College *turnplatz* (1828) to Beck and Follen. (244:405) Other colleges such as Brown and Williams followed suit. A number of schools, such as the Livingston County High School in Genesee, New York, the Mount Hope Literary and Scientific Institution in Maryland, the Mount Pleasant Classical Institution, and the Amherst Academy in Massachusetts, and several others, set up outdoor gymnasiums and included gymnastics in their programs. These

---

* Along with drawing and music, dancing was considered to be a necessary accomplishment of a gentleman.

were deliberate attempts to emulate the Round Hill School's philosophy and practice. However, their enthusiasm for gymnastics was short-lived.* In general, private boys' schools patterned their activities after the English system of sports. Public schools, in later years, preferred Dio Lewis' light gymnastics, Swedish gymnastics or Sargent's eclectic system. Where German gymnastics was introduced, it was chiefly due to the influence and work of the North American Gymnastic Union. Nevertheless, as the site of the first school gymnasium, employer of the first gymnastics teacher, and the introduction of German gymnastics in America, Round Hill School was of unusual significance in the history of physical education.

* This evidence of the influence of Round Hill School is the result of research by John Hyde of the University of Massachusetts. It is included in his master's degree thesis on the Round Hill School.

# CATHARINE ESTHER BEECHER

## 1800-1878

It may seem contradictory that Catharine Beecher, one of the most outstanding leaders in furthering the cause of education for women, should be regarded as an anti-suffragette and a conservative in the feminist movement. Yet her stated beliefs about the potential contribution of women and the importance of educating them to fulfill a role in society, were in oblique opposition to the aggressive demands of the women's rights leaders for equal educational opportunity, the vote, and personal freedom to work, travel and live. The activities of Isabelle Beecher Hooker, a well-known suffragette who addressed the Committee on the Judiciary of the United States Senate on the franchise for women and thus violated the social convention that women do not speak before a group of men, caused her sister Catharine to comment: "My soul is cast down at the ignorance and mistaken zeal of my poor sister, Bell and her co-agitators. Can you not lend a pen to show what a mercy it is to women *to have a head* to take the thousand responsibilities of family, and how much *moral* power is gained by taking a subordinate place?" (344:132) While not opposing the right to vote, she nevertheless stressed that women's proper roles were as mothers and teachers: "What is the profession of a *Woman?* Is is not to form immortal minds, and to watch, to nurse, and to rear the bodily system, . . . upon the order and regulation of which, the health and well-being of the mind so greatly depends?" (129:147) Although not exactly a revolutionary concept, neither was it a common practice to prepare women formally for such responsibilities. In the 1830s when Catharine Beecher began her crusade, the ideal of womanhood being promulgated in the East, especially at exclusive women's schools, was of refined elegance coupled with intellectual learnings similar to the male counterparts. Beecher protested that women had poor health because their days were spent indoors, studying books, music and art, and that they learned nothing about keeping a home and bringing up children. She said: "Is it asked, 'how can young ladies paint, play the piano, and study, when their hands and dresses must be unfitted by such drudgery?' The woman who asks this question, has yet to learn that a pure and delicate skin is better secured by healthful exercise, than by any other method. . . ." (41:55) The customary tight clothing was also considered objectionable because corsets did the work of muscles, causing the latter to grow weak from disuse, and the lungs were impeded

FIG. 47.   Catharine Beecher.

from inflating fully and easily.   She compared Americans with women of
other countries and noted that "walking and riding and gardening, in the
open air, are practised by the women of other lands, to a far greater extent,
than by American females." (41:44)   And she somewhat acidly observed
that "so little idea have most ladies, in the wealthier classes, of what is a
proper amount of exercise, that, if they should succeed in walking a mile
or so, at a moderate pace, three or four times a week, they would call it
taking a great deal of exercise." (41:45)   Practicing what she preached,
she claimed to exercise two hours a day, usually riding horseback before
breakfast. (344:112, 116)

Beecher was born in East Hampton, Long Island but from the age of ten
she lived in Litchfield, Connecticut.   When she was still quite young her
mother and her aunt, Mary Foote Hubbard who was "the poetry of [her]
childhood" (344:73), died, and when she was twenty-two, her fiancé
Alexander Metcalf Fisher drowned in a shipwreck.   Sensitized by these
deaths, she turned her energies toward "doing good."   Her decision and
ability to take an active role in society was relatively natural considering
the remarkable family from which she came.   Her father Lyman Beecher,
and brothers Henry Ward, Edward and Thomas became renowned
preachers; her sister Isabelle became famous as a suffragette; another sister,
Harriet Beecher Stowe, was a leading abolitionist and the author of *Uncle
Tom's Cabin*.

Beecher found that "generally speaking, there seems to be no very
extensive sphere of usefulness for a single woman but that which can be
found in the limits of a school-room. . . ." (344:103)   Accordingly, she
directed her energies toward education and founded the Hartford Sem-

inary (1824) and the Western Female Institute in Cincinnati (1837). She became interested in teacher training, convinced that normal schools for women would at once provide for their attaining a respectable occupation and would serve the needs of thousands of children particularly in the newly settled West, for whom no trained teachers were available. To this end she founded the American Women's Educational Association (1852) the stated purpose of which was:

> To aid in securing to American women a liberal education, honorable position and remunerative employment in their appropriate profession by means of endowed institutions on the college plan of organization; these institutions to include all that is gained by normal schools, and also to train women to be healthful, intelligent, and successful wives, mothers and house-keepers. (344:127)

The Association's efforts caused schools to be started in Milwaukee, Wisconsin and Dubuque, Iowa; both educated women and trained teachers.

Besides her work with the schools, Catharine Beecher was a prolific writer. Her book *Treatise on Domestic Economy*, and the later editions written with her sister Harriet Beecher Stowe, *The American Woman's Home*, her work on *Physiology and Calisthenics for Schools and Families*, and articles in popular magazines such as *Harper's New Monthly Magazine* were all "best sellers" of their time. They provided the young housewife with explicit directions on everything from the construction of houses to lessons on physiology to aid in the care of the sick; she set forth rules for setting the table, washing the clothes and the maintenance of health and family unity. Underlying her philosophy of education was a vision of the mother as the core of the family, which marked a relatively new perspective of the importance of both mothers and families. Anchored in this philosophy was the concomitant belief that women need to know and practice health habits and means of exercising and see that their children do the same. This idea was based on the understanding that "there is such an intimate connection between the body and mind, that the health of one, cannot be preserved, without proper care of the other." (41:195)

In matters of physical health she stressed the need for exercise. In her *Educational Reminiscences and Suggestions* she described how she acquired this point of view:

> An English lady of fine person and manner came to us [at the Hartford Seminary] as a teacher of what then had no name, but now would be called *Calisthenics*. She gave a large number of the exercises that are in my work on *Physiology and Calisthenics*, published by the Harpers, and narrated how she had cured deformities in others by her methods. The whole school took lessons of her, and I added others; and though the results were not conspicuous, they convinced me that far more might be done in this direction than was ever imagined. . . . From this came the system of Calisthenics which I invented, which spread all over the country, and which Dio Lewis, courteously giving me due credit, modified and made additions to, some of which I deem not improvements but objectionable, for reasons stated elsewhere. (83:66)

The Beecher system of calisthenics was introduced in schools wherever she taught. Basically, it was a system of light exercises, sometimes performed with light weights, "arranged on *scientific principles*, with the design of exercising all the muscles, and of exercising them *equably* and *harmoniously*. It embraces most of what is to be found in the French and English works that exhibit the system of *Ling*. . . ." (40:iv) In the name calisthenics, from "the two Greek words *kalos*, signifying *beautiful*, and *sthenos*, signifying *strength*" (40:iv), was incorporated its purpose. Besides the attainment of a beautiful and strong body, calisthenics was to serve "as a mode of curing distortions, particularly all tendencies to curvature of the spine; while at the same time, it tends to promote grace of movement, and easy manners." (41:56) Beecher distinguished calisthenics from gymnastics by specifying that the latter was ordinarily more strenuous and required apparatus and a special exercise room. She also took care to "exclude all those severe exercises that involve danger, either from *excess* or from *accidents*." (40:iv) These were not deemed suitable for females, though Beecher stated that her system "contains all that either sex needs for the perfect *development* of the body." (40:iv)

Included in her books were instructions to teachers:

> The method should be to go over the first fifty exercises, performing each movement only *once*, so as to learn the method. The next time all should be performed *twice* each, and done moderately. Then let one be added each day to the number, till the whole is completed as directed in the book. Each day let the quickness and force be increased, till they are done as forcibly and quickly as possible, except those that are directed to be slow movements, and these are to be done with all the *force* possible. (39:9)

FIG. 48.   Illustration from Beecher's *Calisthenics*.

Mindful that "exercise is so much more healthful and invigorating, when the mind is interested, than when it is not" (41:130), she wove great variety into her system and had the exercises performed to music "to serve as an amusement. . . ." (41:56) On this principle she also endorsed games and sports as fine forms of exercise: "Long and formal walks, merely for exercise, though they do some good, in securing fresh air and some exercise of the muscles, would be of triple benefit, if changed to amusing sports. . . ." (41:131) In fact, she believed games an important adjunct to family unity:

> Another resource for family diversion, is to be found in the various games played by children, and in which the joining of older members of the family is always a great advantage to both parties. . . . There has been a tendency to asceticism, on this subject, which needs to be removed. . . . But jokes, laughter, and sports, when used in such a degree as tends only to promote health, social feelings, and happiness, are neither vain, foolish, nor "not convenient." It is the excess of these things, and not the moderate use of them, which Scripture forbids. The prevailing temper of the mind, should be cheerful, yet serious; but there are times, when relaxation and laughter are proper for all. There is nothing better for this end, than that parents and older persons should join in the sports of childhood. (41:253–254)

She was also aware that by playing with children, adults "will learn . . . to understand the feelings and interest of childhood; while at the same time, they secure a degree of confidence and affection which can not be gained so easily in any other way." (83:89) Having suffered a nervous breakdown from overwork, despite her disciplined regime of two hours a day of exercise, eight hours of sleep and proper meals, she came to the conclusion that beyond this "an hour or two every day in which you will have nothing to do but rest and amuse yourselves" (344:116), was important for everybody.

However, Catharine Beecher did not stray as far from the Calvinist tradition in which she was nurtured as those words might imply. She claimed that through recreation "the body is strengthened, the mind is invigorated, and all our duties are more cheerfully and successfully performed." (41:244) She stressed that "the only legitimate object of amusements, is to promote health, and prepare for more serious duties. . . ." (41:245) She detailed criteria for forbidding recreations:

> No amusements, which inflict needless pain, should ever be allowed . . . all sports, which involve suffering to animals, should be utterly forbidden. Hunting and fishing, for mere sport can never be justified . . . we should seek no recreations, which endanger life, or interfere with important duties. . . . Avoid those amusements, which experience has shown to be so exciting, and connected with so many temptations. . . . It is on this ground, that horse-racing and circus-racing are excluded. Not because there is anything positively wrong, in having men and horses run, and perform feats of agility, or in persons looking on for the diversion; but because experience has shown so many evils connected with these recreations. . . . So with theatres. . . . So, also, with those exciting games of chance, which are employed in gambling. (41:244–245)

She also placed dancing in the category of forbidden amusements.  In the early years at the Hartford Seminary she permitted dancing, charging fees for the extra lessons; she came to believe, however, that it should be "objected to, on the same ground as horse-racing, card-playing, and theatrical entertainments; that we are to look at amusements as they *are*, and not as they *might* be." (41:246)  Acknowledging that open-air dancing might be healthy, she painted a picture of dancing as typically done in a room filled with young people in tight dresses, undergoing unnatural physical exertion for several hours, during which time

> the blood is . . . less perfectly oxygenized than health requires; the pores of the skin are excited by heat and exercise; the stomach is loaded with indigestible articles, and the quiet, needful to digestion, withheld; the diversion is protracted beyond the usual hour for repose; and then, when the skin is made the most highly susceptible to damps and miasms, the company pass from a warm room to the cold night-air.  It is probable, that no single amusement can be pointed out, combining so many injurious particulars, as this. . . . (41:246–247)

Dancing also exerted an evil influence on the personality, for "those, who enter the path to which this diversion leads, acquire a relish and desire for high excitement, which make the more steady and quiet pursuits and enjoyments of home, comparatively tasteless." (41:248)  She urged people to do calisthenics instead of dancing because all the benefits said to accrue to the latter, e.g. ease, the grace of manners, graceful movement, and a pleasing carriage, could be accomplished by the former.

Beecher proposed a plan for the education of women that emphasized physical and domestic education.  She specified that an hour's confinement studying should be followed by sports in the open air, at least for a half hour per day; an hour a week should be devoted to studying lessons in health; and one person should be given the official duty of supervising health and physical education in a school.  In the schools for which she was responsible, these directions were faithfully carried out.

Catharine Beecher's ideas were not greatly admired in her lifetime. Many schools adopted her ladylike gymnastics for a period and then ceased to use them; they did achieve popularity under the salesmanship of Dio Lewis, whose own system was in large part derived from Beecher's. Her concept of the woman and her domestic responsibilities conflicted with the feminine ideal of the period, and was not widely accepted;* however, her practical suggestions on domestic matters were found useful.  Her behavior and thinking symbolize the contradictory attitudes of the whole period in regard to physical education.  Convinced of the validity of the *mens sana in corpore sano* concept, she advocated steps to insure health,

---

* The famous Seneca Falls Convention on Woman's Rights occurred in 1848, during the prime of Beecher's drive to underplay intellectual achievements and stress woman's role as the keeper of the home.

and even recognized the usefulness of sports and games for mental health. Although she found pleasure in sports, the puritan in her insured that she deny pleasure for its own sake; she banned any activities such as cards, horseracing and dancing that did not make a direct contribution to the health of the individual. In America she was one of the first forceful figures to campaign for the inclusion of some form of systematized, regular physical education program, under the direction of a specifically designated instructor, in schools for children. Her direct influence on physical education cannot be calculated, but her role as an innovator seems historically secure.

# DIOCLESIAN LEWIS

## 1823-1888

Dio Lewis holds a unique place in the history of physical education. Belonging to the tradition of Galen and Mercurialis rather than of the educators, he shared his predecessors' concern with the observed poor physical condition of people, and like them he believed in exercise as preventive medicine. Most of his ideas were not new, although they were "different" to the Americans of his time. His exercises were not unique (despite his claims to the contrary) but they were largely unknown to the audiences he addressed.

In the ante-bellum period when Lewis first began working, physical activity was largely ignored by the populace. German gymnastics was practiced by German immigrants and their descendants; George Windship (1834–1876) achieved some popularity with heavy gymnastics (primarily weight lifting) through demonstrations and in his private gymnasium in Boston; Catharine Beecher had vigorously campaigned for the inclusion of calisthenics in schools, but only a few female seminaries still followed her injunction; since the 1820s, with the arrival of Follen and Beck (refer to chapter on Round Hill), many colleges and some private organizations had erected gymnasiums or *turnplätze* where some form of apparatus work was practiced in an irregular manner; sport activities such as rowing, track and field, and baseball, while gaining momentum, had by no means reached a large segment of the population. Furthermore, the feminine ideal still favored the pale, vapid woman who suffered from headaches and was not allowed to "overdo." Hearty vigorous activity was considered somewhat vulgar and even walking was snubbed by the gentry. Lewis, in a tone of troubled amusement, commented that despite the beautiful Common and Public Garden in Boston, "not one fashionable lady in ten ever steps inside of the Common. It is not the *style*." (211a:230) Both men in their work and children in their natural proclivity for action, were believed to have all the exercise they needed.

Lewis publicly argued against these conceptions. He stated that "the imperfect growth, pale faces, distorted forms and painful nervousness of the American People" (210:9) were evidence of the need for systematic exercise. He believed that "in the present condition of the young in this country from one-quarter to one-third of the school hours should be given to physical training." (211a:219)   He claimed that exercises could be used both for prevention and cure of tuberculosis, an idea based on the notion that "in every case of consumption certain groups of . . . muscles are defective.   Restoration of the lost symmetry calls for those exercises which will develop the defective groups." (211a:247)   While not objecting to recreational activities or even military drill, per se, he pointed out that participation in them would not develop the body's weak parts, e.g. the arms, shoulders and chest:

> Whatever artificial muscular training is employed, should be specially adapted to the development of the upper half of the body.
> Need I say that the military drill fails to bring into varied and vigorous play the chest and shoulders? . . . In all but the cultivation of uprightness, the military drill is singularly deficient in the requisites of a system of muscle training, adapted to a weak-chested people. . . .
> Dancing, to say nothing of its almost inevitably mischievous concomitants, brings into play chiefly that part of the body which is already in comparative vigor. . . .
> Horse-back exercise is admirable, . . . but may it not be much indulged, while the chest and shoulders are left drooping and weak? . . .
> Skating is graceful and exhilarating, but . . . is it not true that the chest muscles are so little moved, that the finest skating may be done with the arms folded? (210:12–13)

Although others, particularly educators, were beginning to express similar beliefs in the importance of physical education, it was a combination of the "New Gymnastics" and the personality of its promulgator which made implementation possible.   Lewis was an energetic and forceful personality, totally convinced of the rightness of his causes, though he relied on logic, intuition and personal experience rather than scientific evidence to support his theses.

Born near Auburn, New York, he left school at age twelve and worked in factories until he was fifteen.   For the next few years he taught in district schools and also spent three years apprenticed to a doctor.   However, his career in medicine took place under skeptical circumstances since both the A.M. and M.D. degrees claimed on the title pages of his books were honorary, the A.M. awarded in 1864 by Amherst College, and the M.D. by the Homoeopathic Hospital College of Cleveland, Ohio in 1849.   He did enter the Harvard College Medical Department in 1845 but failed to complete the course.   Besides advocating homeopathy, a somewhat suspect medical science, he was interested in phrenology and published journals on both subjects.   Ardently against alcohol, he belonged to the society of The Sons of Temperance, which to his displeasure refused to ban tobacco or include women in their midst.   His wife, Helen Cecelia Clarke, became consumptive (three of her sisters died from it) and his successful attempt to cure her probably lay behind Lewis' interest in exercise and its potential for aiding health by strengthening the upper body (arms, chest, lungs).

Fɪɢ. 49.   Dio Lewis.

His position on two important issues of his day—slavery and women's rights—was decidedly liberal.  As a dedicated abolitionist he fought vigorously against slavery and had the courage to enroll a black student (ca. 1867) at his school in Lexington. (92·113)  As an advocate of women's rights he believed in coeducation, even in the gymnasium, and the classes in his Normal Institute included men and women in about equal numbers. The fee was, however, lowered for women.  "Ladies will be charged twenty-five per cent less than the above prices, and that reduction is made because of the unjust disparity of compensation which everywhere obtains between male and female labor." (211b:cover)  He continually railed against the restrictiveness and weight of women's clothes, "the corset and the long, heavy skirts, from which, I am sure, without being able to demonstrate it, that ninety per cent of the so-called female weaknesses come. . . ." (92:90) He also recognized the ability of women to do gymnastics well.  "In every one of the thirteen classes of graduates [from the Normal Institute] the best gymnast was a woman.  In each class there were from two to six women superior to any of the men." (92:90)

It may have been his interest in the health of women that led him to develop the "new gymnastics."  As Higginson stated in his now famous *Atlantic Monthly* article, "Dr. Windship had done all that was needed in apostleship of severe exercises, and there was wanting some man with a milder hobby, perfectly safe for a lady to drive." (178:300)  Lewis said, "My object is to present a new system of Gymnastics.  Novel in philosophy, and practical details, its distinguishing peculiarity is a complete adaptation, alike to the strongest man, the feeblest woman, and the frailest child." (210:9)   He acknowledged, though, that "its beautiful games, graceful attitudes, and striking tableaux, possess a peculiar fascination for girls." (210:5)

In contrast to German or "heavy" gymnastics, large and fixed apparatus was not employed.   "Dispensing with the cumbrous apparatus of the ordinary gymnasium, its implements are all calculated not only to impart strength of muscle, but to give flexibility, agility and grace of movement. . . . Each and every piece is held in the hand, so that any hall or other room may be used for the exercises." (210:9)   This was an advantage which aided the rapid adoption of the new gymnastics in schools.   Gymnasiums were non-existent and the cost of apparatus deterred its purchase.   However Lewis' calisthenics could be performed in the schoolroom, with great convenience and no expense.   The extensive sale of *The New Gymnastics for Men, Women and Children* (210) causing ten editions to be published from 1862–1868, and the *Atlantic Monthly* (208, 209) and *American Journal of Education* articles by Lewis, describing his system, indicate that people were also finding it an adaptable method for use in the privacy of their homes.   *Weak Lungs and How to Make Them Strong* (211a) was another of his popular books.

Lewis deliberately attempted to make gymnastics palatable.   All exercises were done to music to make them more interesting and because "five times as much muscle can be coaxed out, under this delightful stimulus, as without it." (210:14)   He also devised games and relays done with bean bags and Indian clubs*, thus introducing mild forms of competition.   He claimed that "the exercises . . . when performed by a class, are found to possess a charm superior to that of dancing and other social amusements, while the interest increases with the skill of the performers." (210:5)

Contrasting heavy and light gymnastics, Lewis clarified the purposes of the latter:

> The only question which remains is that which lies between all heavy and light gymnastics, viz:   whether strength or flexibility is to be preferred. . . . Men, women and children should be strong, but it should be the strength of grace, flexibility, agility and endurance; it should not be the strength of a great lifter. . . . The principal object of all physical training is an elastic, vigorous condition of the nervous system. . . . (210:61–63)

He was also remarkably modern in stressing the importance of cardio-vascular conditioning:

> But what I desire to urge more particularly in this connection, is the importance, the great physiological advantages, of just those exercises in which the lungs and heart are brought into active play. . . . A man may stand still and lift

---

* These were exactly like those still found today in textbooks of activities for the elementary grades.

kegs of nails and heavy dumb bells until his shoulders and arms are Sampsonian, he will contribute far less to his health and longevity, than by a daily run of a mile or two.

Speaking in a general way, those exercises in which the lungs and heart are made to go at a vigorous pace, are to be ranked among the most useful. (210:66)

The program of the new gymnastics consisted of free exercises (e.g. circular arm movements or hopping in place), gymnastic games (e.g. pin running, a relay in which the runners transfer Indian clubs from one place to another), and exercises with light hand apparatus (e.g. wooden rings about six inches in diameter, wands, Indian clubs, two-pound wooden dumbbells, and six- to ten-inch square bean bags). One of Lewis' inventions was a "gymnastic crown," an iron crown weighing from three to ten pounds, padded and ornamented. It was meant to be worn for five to fifteen minutes, morning and evening, while walking, squatting, climbing stairs, etc. The expected results were an erect spine and an elastic gait. (210:99–100) He also invented a book holder so that students would be able to sit erect at their desks as they studied. A favorite gadget for persons with weak lungs was the spirometer, a device which, when blown into, was meant to force the air into every part of the lungs. (211a:259–260)

The most important criterion for the exercise room was that it be well-

FIG. 50.   Illustration from *The New Gymnastics*.

ventilated.    Indeed, Lewis stressed this point for all living quarters. Since most exercises were to be performed with the feet in a stable position, heels together, toes turned out approximately at a 50° angle, Lewis recommended painting foot patterns on the floor about fifty-five inches apart. This saved explanations as to where and how people were to stand.    Costume for exercise was designed by Lewis to insure freedom of movement around the waist and shoulders (Fig. 51).

In 1860 Lewis had an opportunity to bring the new gymnastics to the attention of leading educators from all over the country, gathered in Boston to attend the annual convention of the American Institute of Instruction. His successful lectures to them, coupled with a demonstration to a committee at the public gymnasium he had opened on Essex Street, helped to disseminate the new gymnastics and thereafter schools all over the country began to try the system.    A resolution affirmed "that the members of this Institute have . . . witnessed with great pleasure and interest the exercise in gymnastics, under the direction of Dr. Lewis, and that we believe it eminently worthy of general introduction into all our schools, and into general use." (206:47–48)

To train teachers for the new gymnastics, the Normal Institute for

FIG. 51.    Illustration from *The New Gymnastics*.

Physical Education was incorporated in 1861 and located in Boston, the first school of this nature in the United States.  Several distinguished gentlemen served on its Board of Directors, including the president of Harvard College, Cornelius C. Felton and the governor, John A. Andrew. The program was ten weeks long and "tickets for the course" cost seventy-five dollars plus a five-dollar matriculation fee and a ten-dollar diploma fee. Instruction was given in anatomy, physiology, hygiene, and gymnastics:

> Each will be drilled by Dr. Lewis in person, with such care, that he or she cannot fail to become a competent teacher of gymnastics.  And each will have two drills a day. . . . All will be made familiar with at least two hundred different exercises, . . . and will be allowed, every one in turn, to lead a small class, in order to learn more perfectly the arts of leadership. . . . (211b:5)

Students were also taught the principles of the " 'Swedish Movement-cure'; a department of the Institution, devoted to the treatment of curvature of the spine, paralysis and other chronic maladies. . . ." (211b:4)  Prospective students were assured of employment:

> The demand for teachers has risen to fever heat.  Were five thousand teachers, male and female, prepared to enter upon the good work they would find no difficulty in effecting pleasant and most profitable engagements.  There is not a village of five hundred inhabitants, in the Free States, in which it would be difficult to open a class of ladies and gentlemen that would pay, for two hours in the evening, at least three times as much as is generally received for the six hours of rather unhealthy labor in the public schools. (211b:6)

There is some discrepancy as to the number of actual graduates, Lewis claiming about 250 people and his biographer 421. (207:263) In either case, it was a substantial number for those Civil War years.  The Institute closed in 1868.

From 1864–1868 Lewis also conducted a girls' school at Lexington, Massachusetts (the last year was at Spy Pond because the Lexington building burned down).  For a time, Catharine Beecher was a member of the faculty.  He deliberately sought girls with poor physical conditioning and attempted to restore their health through a regimen of two half hours a day of gymnastic exercises, dancing three evenings a week, bowling, long walks, and a lot of sleep.  He used anthropometric measurements to demonstrate his success in improving the health of the students, a technique employed by professional physical educators for the next half century.

For at least two decades, Lewis' gymnastics were the primary, if not the only, physical education available in public schools.  The presence of Indian Clubs and wands in the equipment closets of schools even today, testifies to their use until most recent years.  Hartwell commented on his influence:

The doctrines and methods of the Lewis gymnastics, which were novelties and seemed original to most of his followers and imitators, spread rapidly over the whole country, and, if we may credit certain eulogists of the system, even into "Europe, Asia, and Africa." His skill in securing the aid and backing of educationists and notabilities contributed materially toward making Dio Lewis the most conspicuous luminary, for a time, in the American gymnastical firmament, but failed to make him a fixed star. (159:556)

Lewis was a controversial figure in the history of physical education. He was damned by many as a charlatan, presumably because of his unscientific procedures and his exaggerated and unsupported claims. On the other hand, men of eminence such as Harvard's Felton, and D. B. Hagar, President of the American Institute of Instruction, enthusiastically commended him. Through his *Gymnastic Monthly and Journal of Physical Culture*, the Normal Institute, his Lexington School, countless classes, lectures, and demonstrations, and numerous publications, he succeeded in popularizing gymnastics more than any other man of his era.

# NORMAL COLLEGE OF THE
# NORTH AMERICAN GYMNASTIC UNION

In 1866 when the Normal School of the North American Gymnastic Union offered its first course in New York City,* only one other institution in America existed for the purpose of training gymnastics teachers: the Boston Normal Institute for Physical Education, established by Dio Lewis in 1861. Normal College was first conceived in 1856, just six years after the first convention of *turner* societies had resulted in the formation of a *turnerbund* in America. The Bund was the union of six *turner* societies organized from political refugees who immigrated to this country during the suppression of the democratic revolutionary movement in Germany in 1848–1849. The *Turnzeitung*, established as the official organ of the Bund during its second convention in 1851, reported that by November, 1851, twenty-two societies had been organized in the United States with a total membership of 1,672. Physical training was conducted without professional teachers as under Jahn himself. Increasing numbers made evident the need for trained leaders who could help *turnvereine* fulfill their goal of providing gymnastics for everybody (i.e., German-Americans of all ages and abilities). Accordingly, the Pittsburgh convention in 1856 adopted the following resolution: "A school shall be set up at the place where the National Executive Committee is located for the complete physical and mental development of Turn teachers." (350:51)

However, the Turnerbund was internally split over political issues. From the beginning it was, like its counterpart in Germany, a politically-oriented organization which manifested a belief in freedom and free-thinking. In fact, interest in gymnastics became secondary to the critical social issues of the day. In 1855 the convention platform expressed the majority position against slavery: "The *turners* are opposed to slavery, and regard this institution as unworthy of a republic and not in accord with the principles of freedom." (244:98) The southern societies opposed this, which, together with other organizational disputes, divided the Bund into two parties; they were not reunited until 1859. At the same time,

---

* There is some evidence that in Rochester, New York in 1861, a course was started which was forced to close before completion due to the onset of the Civil War. This aborted attempt, if it occurred, would thus have been the very first of its kind in America. Rinsch's history of the Normal College (303) was published on its hundredth anniversary in 1966 and thus assumed the 1866 date as the formal beginning.

sporadic attacks, both verbal and physical, were made on *turner* groups by members of the American (Know-nothing) Party and other nativistic groups who resented the presence of foreign elements, especially unassimilated ones who continued, as the *turners* did, to speak their mother tongue and keep aloof from society. As late as 1870 the Executive Committee had to clarify their Americanism. They issued a statement which, in part, read:

> The *Turners* of America have nothing in common with the *Turners* of the old fatherland (Germany), except the system of health and physical education. Of our endeavors for reform in political, religious and social fields, of the struggle against corruption and slavery in all forms, the *Turners* of Germany know nothing, although this has been the object and inspiration of our *Turner-bund*. (207:312)

When the Civil War began the only building in Baltimore that continued to fly the Union Jack instead of changing to the state flag of Maryland (used as the rebel standard), was the Turner Hall. As a result the building and two others connected with German presses, were completely destroyed by rebels. (244:100–101) Thus, even though the 1856 resolution was strengthened by the 1860 convention's acceptance of a plan to establish a seminary, the organization struggling with its political problems and declining in membership lacked the financial resources to carry it out. Subsequently more than half the *turners* joined the Union forces during the Civil War, depleting the membership and enabling the Turnerbund to maintain only a nominal existence.

After the Civil War, reorganization took place and the name was changed to the North American Gymnastic Union (which became the American Gymnastic Union in 1919). It was agreed that physical training rather than politics would be the first object of the *turnvereine*. (207:298–299) Interest in a normal school was renewed and in 1866 a new plan for it was approved. The curriculum for the one-year course included: the history and aims of *turnen*, anatomy, first aid, aesthetic dancing, theory of physical education systems, terminology, and the practice of gymnastics with emphasis on teaching methods. Classes were held in the evening to allow participants to work during the day. Only members of *turnvereine* were eligible to enroll and a per capita tax of ten cents a year was levied on all *turners* to support the operation. Nineteen students from various parts of the country enrolled under five faculty members; nine men took the final examination and five were awarded diplomas. (350:51)

Two more courses were given in New York (1869, 1872) and one in Chicago (1871), each of six months duration. In the latter course, fencing, physiology and hygiene were added to the curriculum. Of the forty students originally enrolled, seven received first class diplomas, four second class, and three *vorturner* certificates. (350:51) The NAGU, dissatisfied with the results, passed a resolution in 1874 at the Rochester convention:

Be it recommended that the N.A.G.U. institute one more attempt at forming a normal school of gymnastics, but that this attempt be undertaken in the West,* provided that the next convention may determine whether or not the Normal School shall continue after this ensuing year. (55:167)

The Normal School then moved to Milwaukee where it functioned under the leadership of George Brosius from 1875–1888. During that time the course varied from four to ten months duration; about 129 participated and 103 diplomas were awarded.

Students were no longer allowed to work and attend school; admission to the Normal School was contingent on passing a preliminary examination, being a member of a *turnverein* for at least one year, being able to speak and write either English or German fluently, and pledging to devote the knowledge and skill acquired to the advancement of the movement for at least three years. (384:58–59)  From 1889 to 1891 the Normal School was located in Indianapolis, but it returned to Milwaukee and a new gymnasium building adjacent to the National German-American Teachers' Seminary and the German and English Academy. The three schools were able to utilize the teaching and facilities of each other while maintaining separate identities.

With the new physical plant, the scope of courses was increased and a one-year course for students who held an American high school diploma, or could pass equivalent examinations, was offered.† Students were examined quarterly with the intent of revealing where extra work was needed. The closing examinations lasted four days and were held in the presence of a commission empowered by the Executive Committee of the Bund to qualify those who received diplomas as first or second grade teachers. (9:182–183)  In addition to the courses previously listed, the curriculum by 1895 included: English and German language and literature, history of civilization, pedagogy, vocal music, dietetics, orthopedic gymnastics, massage, anthropometry, fencing, swimming, wrestling, boxing, and principles of the NAGU. (55:220)  Practice teaching was done when the students from the Academy and Seminary came to the gymnasium for their classes. According to Brosius (55:220–221), 1495 hours of instruction were devoted to physical work and 646 (about thirty percent of the total) to mental work. Only a fraction of the physical study (forty-eight hours) was spent learning swimming, boxing or wrestling, although fencing received suitable instruction time. Study of the English language consumed the bulk of the "mental work" time (119 hours) with German and physiology running a close second (106 hours apiece). Only five hours were devoted to ortho-

---

* This refers to the Midwest, where the movement was strongest.

† The three courses between 1895–1899 were of two years duration. Then the School closed until 1902 when it opened under the directorship of George Wittich and returned to one-year courses.

pedics and anthropometry, because "the faculty aims to educate teachers of physical culture and not amateur physicians." (76:268)

In 1907 the Executive Committee of the NAGU adopted resolutions to the effect that

> after August 31, 1907, the Normal School of Gymnastics be conducted in the city of Indianapolis under the name of "The Normal College of the North American Gymnastic Union"; that one-year, two-year, and four-year college courses be offered prospective teachers of physical training who, prior to matriculation, completed the four-year course of an approved American high school, or who pass equivalent entrance examinations in high school subjects, including at least three years of high school English; and that in addition to physical training and practice in teaching the work of each college year includes courses in letters and science equivalent to one year's work as counted by universities toward the baccalaureate degree. (244:655)

The College, incorporated under Indiana laws, was empowered to confer academic titles and degrees. A B.S.G. (Bachelor of Science in Gymnastics) was awarded for a four-year course, and an M.S.G. was awarded to Normal College graduates upon completion of one additional year's study and an accepted thesis. Graduates of other institutions were required to study two years, and write a thesis, to earn the M.S.G. In 1910 Normal College was given a class A accreditation, which meant that its graduates were exempted from examination for teaching positions in the public schools. It was formally opened on September 23, 1907, under the directorship of Carl J. Kroh and two years later, of Emil Rath who for the next twenty-five years led the Normal College and made it a respected institution in American education. In 1923 the course was lengthened to three years and in 1932 to four, under the terms of a new affiliation with Indiana University. The College announced:

> The affiliation offers a unique advantage to students of the Normal College since under this plan it will be possible for the student to obtain by a combined four-year course in both schools the degrees of both institutions. It will also enable students to obtain a licence to teach physiology and health education and an elective third subject in addition to physical education. (2:161)

In 1941, a merger was completed creating the Normal College of the American Gymnastic Union of Indiana University. Students attended the College at Indianapolis for two years and then moved to the Bloomington campus for their last two years where they earned a Bachelor of Science degree in Physical Education.

The direction the school took in the twentieth century reflected the change of leadership, the progress of the times and the rising influence of the American Association for the Advancement of Physical Education. Henry Hartung, a graduate of the Normal School and a physician, writing in 1903, observed:

True to the maxim of our renowned Turnvater Jahn, that gymnastics must be practiced in accordance with the spirit of the age and in conformity with the conditions of climate, country and race, the system as practiced by the American Turnerbund is not identical with that of the Turners of Europe, nor does it present the same features to-day that it did at the time of its infancy, a little over fifty years ago. (156:273)

He pointed out the popularity achieved by the Turnerbund among native Americans; the organization, once strictly German and German-speaking, by then had enrolled in its schools "thousands of children, young men and women of other than German parentage." (156:273) Graduates were required to be able to teach in English. Over five thousand women were active members, a vast increase since 1878 when Miss Laura Gerlach was the first female graduate of the Normal School. However, as late as 1904 "the proposal that women be admitted to membership in the societies of the Turnerbund on equal terms with men was voted down by a small majority." (259:219) Collectively, *turner* property had a substantial value of about $2,682,000 including halls, club rooms, regular day schools, Sunday schools, reading rooms, libraries aggregating about seventy thousand volumes, and well-equipped gymnasiums. The Union had swelled to 250 societies, enrolling 35,757 *turners*, including "actives" (regular participants between eighteen and forty years of age), "juniors" (youths between fourteen and eighteen years) and *Altersriegen* (old men over forty who still participated). The day school classes which children attended after school, twice a week for one or two hours had over thirty thousand children, a sixth of whom were of non-German parentage. (156:247–277)

*Turner* activities had increased in scope:

The Gymnastic Union has imitated to some extent the custom of the ancient Greeks, with whom the practice of gymnastics was not limited to the work in the palaestrum; running, leaping, wrestling, . . . etc., but whose gymnasiums were also meeting places for scholars and citizens, young and old, for the purpose of discussing questions of the day,—philosophy, poetry and affairs of state. (156: 275)

Copying the Olympic idea, *turnfeste* were held every four years in a large city; wreaths of laurel or oak leaves were awarded not only for physical feats but also for essays, speeches, recitations, singing, and other musical productions. (156:275) The actual physical work had also undergone a great change:

I may state that our system of training includes all those wholesome and invigorating manly sports and games, which we consider indispensable to an all-around development of body, mind and character, especially for our young men, as: Boxing, fencing, wrestling, swimming, rowing and all the other manifold forms of field work and ball games. . . . (156:278)

10

FIG. 52.    Display at a German Turnfest.

Heinrich Metzner claimed:

> Play ever was an integral part of *Turnen*, of gymnastics.  Guts Muths' as well as Jahn's gymnastics, were conducted in the open.  The activity upon these grounds were mainly games and what is now grouped under the name of track and field work. . . . As early as the late sixties boys and girls in Cincinnati enjoyed the giant slide and swings in the large playground or garden, as it was then called, back of the old Turner Hall. . . . (244:611–612)

But entering into organized sport activities, especially team sports, was a new venture for the *turners*.  At the school, it was noted in 1909 that "the game of soccer foot ball and a new adaptation of basket ball . . . has proven a great pastime. . . . The German games of 'fist ball' and 'Barlaufen' have also proven attractive games. . . . The freshmen are gradually developing into formidable wrestlers." (265:76–77)  In describing the 1915 curriculum it was stated that:

> The women have been working on the jumps, low hurdles, hurlball, basketball, far-throw, shot-put, kicking the football, and the 100-yards dash; the men on the low and high hurdles, javelin throw, hurlball, broad and high jumps, and sprints. Hockey for women and soccer for men are also being taken up. (265:861)

In 1917 school teams were organized for soccer, football and baseball, the athletic and track and field periods were increased and swimming received more attention.  In addition, scout craft was added to the course of study, with a Boy Scout executive delivering the lectures and leading the practical work. (264:339)  In 1918 it was boasted that the basketball team had won every game.  Girls' bicycle and hiking clubs were formed.  Track and swimming meets were held "to give the Seniors, especially, opportunities to win points to wear their emblems before graduating." (262:92–93)  In less than twenty years, the Normal College curriculum had considerably broadened its scope.  In part this reflected the changing composition of the *turner* population which was increasingly more Americanized.  But the primary cause was probably connected to the proselytizing aim of the movement.

Speaking to the 1912 graduating class, Faust pointed out that "the Turnerbund has aimed throughout its history to introduce gymnastic training into the public school system of the country." (99:364)  "The Turner Convention of 1880 agreed that it could not conceive of a more beautiful gift to the American people than to work to introduce physical education in the public schools." (350:52)  However, their work was not well-known outside of the Turnerbund.  Edward Mussey Hartwell, visiting school and college gymnasiums from Maine to Tennessee, in 1883–84, heard no mention of *turner* work and, in fact, was unaware of its existence.  In 1886, responding to an invitation engineered by Hartwell, the *turners* sent delegates to the second meeting of the AAAPE; three papers and a gymnastic exhibition were given and the active support of twenty-three thousand *turners* was offered to the delegates, marking the beginning of the campaign to acquaint America with the values of German gymnastics as practiced by the *turners*.  This campaign included inviting delegations from the AAAPE to visit the national *turnfeste*, demonstrations and exhibitions at the Chicago World's Fair (1893), publication of a monthly magazine, *Mind and Body*, in English (from 1894 on), publication of a *Textbook of German-American Gymnastics*, edited by William A. Stecher (Boston: Lea & Shepard, 1896).  In 1895 a six-week summer school was held at the Normal College, using many of its regular faculty.  The summer school, which became an annual affair, was the only one in the Midwest; in order to interest teachers from the public schools in its courses which were similar to the regular curriculum, the program was conducted entirely in English. It was meant primarily as an opportunity to study German gymnastics but other systems were represented and compared.  Most important was the Turnerbund's attempt to effect the adoption of German gymnastics by various public school systems.

As early as 1860 in Cincinnati, and 1870 in Cleveland, *turners* tried to introduce gymnastics in the schools, and as late as 1898, Hartwell was forced to comment that "these and similar schemes proved illusory and impracticable.  Even to-day we must admit that no important city or town in the United States has succeeded in maintaining for fifteen consecutive years a genuine and adequate system of school gymnastics." (159:557)  In 1885 fewer than ten secondary schools possessed a gymnasium in which it was possible to do apparatus work.  Beginning in 1885 in Cincinnati, Kansas City, Omaha, and Lacrosse, Wisconsin, alumni of the Normal

College introduced physical education into the public schools, during the eighties and nineties. Chicago, Denver, Cleveland, Indianapolis, San Francisco, Pittsburgh, Spokane, and Terre Haute were among the fifty-two cities in which the *turners* succeeded in starting school gymnastic systems. (350:52–53) In 1915, Metzner reported that practically all the cities to which Hartwell referred then conducted free exercises in their schools, had installed gymnasiums or playrooms, and equipped schoolyards as open-air gymnasiums or playgrounds. Elementary schools were beginning to build gymnasiums, showers and even swimming pools. An average of fifteen minutes a day in primary and elementary grades, and 2 forty-five minute periods a week in high schools was the general rule. Work was generally required from primary grades through the first two years of high school. Using a questionnaire survey, the *turners* concluded they were reaching a school population of over two million with over 350 teachers, most of whom were graduates of the Normal College. Graduates also helped staff the gymnasiums being built in the YMCAs, which along with the private athletic clubs and the Turnerbund, provided the chief sources of non-school physical training in the United States.

It was this connection with public schools and with the mainstream of the growing physical education movement that probably instigated the change in the Normal College curriculum. In order to survive and meet the competition of eclectic systems its base was broadened. From the time American-style Indian clubs were brought into its gymnasiums, the curriculum had departed from Jahn. Without de-emphasizing heavy apparatus, the NAGU managed to encompass other activities within the framework of its goals as stated by its platform:

> The North American Gymnastic Union is a league of gymnastic societies of the United States of America, organized for the purpose of bringing up men and women strong in body, mind and morals, and of promoting the dissemination of liberal and progressive ideas. . . . We recognize in the harmonious education of body and mind one of the most important prerequisites for establishing, preserving and perfecting a true democracy. (156:274)

Speaking to the second convention of the AAAPE, C. G. Rathmann commented: "The influence of the Turnerbund is chiefly due to its favorite offspring, the N.A. Gymnastic Seminary. . . ." (4:22) This influence was considerable. They were the earliest group to press for physical education in the public schools. Prior to achieving that goal (and afterwards), they provided comprehensive programs of gymnastics for thousands of children and adults. As an organization they were a model of the interrelationship of physical activity and socio-political behavior. They developed workable techniques on the various apparatus, graded and progressive, that are popular even today. Had the Bund lost its parochial character at an earlier date, its influence on the early growth of physical education in this country would have been still more pronounced.  Nevertheless, it may be said that the Turnerbund, Greek in its conception, German in its authoritarian organization, and American in many of its activities, was an important aspect of physical education in the United States.  The Normal College was essential to this contribution.

# EDWARD HITCHCOCK

## 1828-1911

Edward Hitchcock was elected the first president of the Association for the Advancement of Physical Education. When the leading members of the profession thus honored him at their initial meeting in 1885, they were recognizing his role as the founder of college physical education programs. From 1861 when he was appointed Professor of Hygiene and Physical Education at Amherst College in Massachusetts, until Dudley Allen Sargent's appointment at Harvard in 1879, Hitchcock was the only college professor in the country to fill such a position.* In the absence of a recognized profession, the pioneer program structured by Hitchcock served as a conceptual model and beginning point for others which followed. In it lay the seeds of practices which were emulated for many years—some still in use today.

The impetus for the inception of a program at Amherst came from its progressive president, William Augustus Stearns. President Stearns was so

Fig. 53.   Edward Hitchcock.

---

* In other college gymnasiums, such as Harvard and Yale, supervision was by unqualified personnel—military drill masters, professional boxers or even janitors. Sargent had directed the Bowdoin and Yale gymnasiums, but both experiences preceded his qualification as an M.D. In 1885 a survey of 26 principal school and college gymnasiums in the United States showed that in only 6 institutions the director was a member of the faculty. (161:64–65)

concerned over the less than adequate health of college students, that he devoted a part of his inaugural address (1854) to the situation, recommending that "I would seriously consider the expediency of introducing regular drills in gymnastic and calisthenic exercises. . . ." (245:29)  Through his efforts a gymnasium was constructed and the trustees agreed to hire a man of stature to head the new department.  The first appointment went to John W. Hooker, M.D., but within a year he was forced to resign due to poor health; Edward Hitchcock succeeded him.

In accordance with a vote of the trustees that he "take a general oversight of the health of the students . . ." (161:31), Hitchcock developed the Amherst plan of physical education.  In an 1878 report he reiterated the school's philosophy:

> This department was not created, nor has it been developed, for the purpose of extraordinary attention to the muscular system.  Its sole object has been to keep the bodily health up to the normal standard, so that the mind may accomplish the most work, and to preserve the bodily powers in full activity for both the daily duties of college and the promised labor of a long life. . . . (207:277)

As Professor of Hygiene and Physical Education he cared for the health of Amherst students in three ways:  by functioning as the medical officer of the college, by giving instruction in hygiene which attempted to influence attitudes and practices, and by planning and supervising a systematic program of exercises and recreation.  Except for Hooker, Hitchcock was probably the first doctor-physical educator in the world—that is, the first to unite medicine and school physical education in one man and one program.  Since at that time one of the prime justifications for including a subject such as physical education in a college curriculum was its potential for improving the health of a student, the "marriage" was a fortuitous one.*

Hitchcock, in his role as college physician, was expected to attend to sick students.  As part of his concern for student health, he also lobbied for better sanitary facilities.  In 1866 he asked for proper bathing facilities: "I *think* it would conduce very much to the personal health and cleanliness *of* the students, if a suitable bathing room could be arranged *in* the basement story of our chapel where hot water could be secured for most of the year." (369:87)  In 1877 he requested that the trustees provide "earth closets" for each dormitory and enclose the college privies in a shed during the winter months, noting that "the exposure to which a man is subject when attending to the call of nature between the months of November and April

---

* After the turn of the century, physical education began to be thought of as an educational endeavor and physical directors began to pursue degrees in education rather than medicine.  Even so, the medical function persisted; today some physical educators (particularly in public schools) are expected to teach health classes, staff school "clinics," give rudimentary physical examinations, conduct vision and hearing tests, and prescribe special exercises to correct orthopedic deviations.

is something serious, and must act adversely to the health in more than one way." (369:88)   Such were the responsibilities of a physical educator!

Beginning in 1865 he gave a series of lectures to every freshman class on subjects such as hygiene, food and digestion, care of the muscles, breathing and vocal organs and fresh air, skin, brain and mind, eyes, reproductive organs, tobacco, alcohol, and sex. Hitchcock thought tobacco and alcohol evil and believed that a strenuous gymnastic program could cure certain sexual habits such as masturbation.   His approach to these and other "vices" related to his profoundly moral outlook concerning man and his body.   The motto on the Barrett Gymnasium, was expressive of his viewpoint.   It read, in part: "Strive to realize the conditions of the possession of this wondrous structure.   Think what it may become,—the Temple of the Holy Spirit!" (369:266)   The viewpoint that religious connotations accrued to keeping one's body healthy, although derived from earlier positions, made its *formal* appearance on the American college physical education scene at Amherst College.

In conjunction with establishing the department, the trustees voted on the basic structure of the program:

> That all the students shall be required to attend on its exercises for half an hour, designated for the purpose, at least four days in the week. . . . That while it may not be expedient to mark the gradation of attainment, as in the intellectual branches, yet regularity, attention, and docility should be carefully noted, so as to have their proper weight in the deportment column of the student's general position. . . . That some time should be allowed out of study hours for those volunteer exercises, of whatever kind, to be under the supervision of the gymnasium instructor. (161:31)

The required class exercises, as designed by Hitchcock, were very similar to those recommended by Dio Lewis under the heading of "the new gymnastics."   He described them in a paper read at a meeting of the American Public Health Association in 1877:

> The required exercise of each man and class is best known as that of light gymnastics, or those bodily exercises performed by a class with one or two pieces of apparatus in the hands, each movement timed to music, and all simultaneous and uniform.   And the only apparatus successfully used at Amherst is the pair of wooden dumb-bells, weighing less than a pound apiece. . . . Each class has its own "exercise" or series of bodily movements with the bells, and these are so managed as to give free, lively, graceful, and vigorous work to the whole muscular system during the time of the exercise.   In addition to the bell exercise, marching by the file and flank is considerably practiced, and during the cold months running, or "double-quick" movements. . . . This exercise varies from fifteen to twenty minutes. . . . The remainder of the half hour is occupied in voluntary exercise.   Some use the heavy apparatus—about one in eight—or take a longer run; others dance, use clubs, sing, pull rope, toss in the blanket, turn somersaults, and occupy themselves in any proper manner to secure exercise, sport, or recreation. (369:78–79)

In conjunction with the exercise program, Hitchcock developed two procedures which were quickly adopted by the profession and are still in use today. One was his requirement that students wear uniforms to participate and the other was the use of a class leader or captain. The captains were elected by their peers and trained by Hitchcock to lead drills and otherwise handle the class in its movements. Some of his captains such as Edward Mussey Hartwell and Watson L. Savage later became noted physical educators.

The only non-gymnastic type of facility available in the old gymnasium was the bowling alleys which were heavily used for recreational purposes. The Pratt Gymnasium, built in 1884, also had rooms for billiards, boxing and baseball practice. By 1891 when the Pratt Field was dedicated, outdoor facilities included space for football, baseball, track, cricket, lacrosse, and tennis. In later years a swimming pool, skating rink and squash courts were also added to the College. But it was not until after 1900 that sports instruction was given in the regular classes.

Addressing the AAAPE in 1895, Hitchcock compared the role of gymnastics and athletics in college programs:

> While the required indoor exercise, regular, methodical, and prescribed, has been and must continue to be, fundamental, and a necessary requirement for the great mass of students, the very success of it has led on to better and more vigorous work for a large proportion of our students. . . . But this is not the natural or ideal form of exercise. Men like animals want air, sunlight, . . . and a contact with mother earth. . . .
> Hence in the last few years have grown up the athletic sports which demand the field, the air, varied temperatures, and the sunshine, and the test of strength, skill, and sport between man and man. . . . And they have come in to stay. (12:197–198)

Hitchcock was not averse to athletics for recreation or intramural type competition, and he developed the practice of excusing competing athletes from regular physical education classes, a procedure which later became standard in most schools. In his 1881 report to the trustees he stated:

> In athletic sports, rowing, base and foot ball, and college games generally, this department has ever given encouraging though not inciting words. . . . With the example of the oldest and largest colleges, and with the comity, rivalry and good fellowship so largely existing, it is but natural that our college should desire to compare its muscle and wind with those in similar positions. . . .
> In our home athletic sports we have taken a deeper interest. . . . And the preparation and participation in these contests, this department has ever regarded as a full equivalent for the required gymnasium exercises. . . . (161:35)

However, like most of the other leading physical educators, he disapproved of the practices associated with intercollegiate sports which, in any case, did not come under the jurisdiction of his department.*    Of football, he said:

> The superb game is degraded.    Its victories are made occasions, by others than the players, for the indulgence of appetite, the undue display of college pride. Too much is made of victory.    The game is not made solely a means for good bodily training and development, or for amusement and diversion; but everything is subordinated to the hope of beating the other team. (12:199)

Despite the wide acceptance of the conceptions and procedures of that first college program, Hitchcock's most popular innovation was anthropometry.    He holds the distinction of being the first American to employ anthropometric measurements in conjunction with physical education. Archibald Maclaren's use of them (refer to p. 216) probably preceded Hitchcock's and may possibly have influenced him since the latter visited London in 1860.    More likely, both men received their inspiration and instruction from Sir Francis Galton, a well-known British anthropologist interested in the subject.    Hitchcock's uses of anthropometry centered around the search for the average, or ideal college student.    In his words:

> The Department of Physical Education in Amherst College has been looking after an anthropometric college standard for about twenty-five years.    To this end thousands of student measurements have been made and tabulated, and progress published from time to time as a supplement to Gymnastic Exhibition Programs. . . . We want to learn what are the Physical Data of the Typical or Ideal College Student, and to do this we know of no better way than to observe every student whom we can lay our hands upon, and secure all the measures which show the proportions of the "Average" or the "Mean" student.    And from this standpoint we must, by labor and study, find out how much proper cultivation and healthy work can better this present average condition: find out how much and how fast we can *further develop the present student average body*. (8:40)

Over the years other measurements were added to the original series of eight: "The first beginnings of this scheme were the eight items of age, weight, height, chest girth, arm girth, forearm girth, lung capacity and pull up, which . . . were taken from every student from 1861 to about 1880. . . ." (245:30)

Seeking a single factor which could serve as a standard for the average man, Hitchcock settled upon height as the best indicator for determining normal body proportions.    He therefore prepared an "Average Anthropo-

---

* At that time, college students organized their own sport activities, including intercollegiate matches, and club-type organizations.    Towards the end of the century, when it became apparent that adult regulation was needed, boards including faculty, alumni and trustees were organized to take control of intercollegiate athletics.    When the University of Chicago, in 1891, appointed Amos Alonzo Stagg, their football coach, to the faculty and made him responsible for both physical education and athletics, it was the first time that the two aspects of the program were coordinated in one department, under the leadership of one man with faculty status.

metric Table" in which the average height of 67.9 inches governed the distribution of the other measurements, except certain measures of strength. "The Table is so arranged that it may be used to record the measurements of any young man, affording him a ready comparison of himself with the normal or average young man as represented by the printed columns of figures." (7:6)  His comment, "that they are prepared as exactly as possible from the directions recommended for procuring anthropometric data by this Association in 1886" (7:6), indicates that despite his innovativeness in this area, Hitchcock was willing to change his procedure for the sake of standardization.  He adopted the standards agreed on by a committee of the AAAPE consisting of himself, William G. Anderson and Dudley Allen Sargent whose procedures at Harvard formed the nucleus of the report. (4:640; 5:34)

When Hitchcock took the position at Amherst College he was unprepared for such a task.  Although he held the A.B. (1849) and M.A. (1852) from Amherst College, and an M.D. (1853) from Harvard, and had studied comparative anatomy in Paris and London for three months in 1860, he had no preparation for, or apparent interest in, physical education.  His employment may in part have been due to the influence of his father, a past president of Amherst College, at that time serving as Professor of Geology. Between 1850 and the time he joined the faculty at Amherst (except for the years he was studying), Hitchcock taught natural history, anatomy and physiology at Williston Seminary in Easthampton, a school he himself had attended.  However, once at Amherst he managed to master the essentials of light gymnastics and when the opportunity arose, became involved in the profession of physical education.  He served as president of the AAAPE from 1885 to 1887 and was a charter member and first president (1897) of the Society of College Gymnasium Directors (now the National College Physical Education Association for Men).  With his father he published a book titled *Elementary Anatomy and Physiology, for Colleges, Academies, and Other Schools* (New York: Ivison, Phinney and Co., 1860).  He also published *A Manual of the Gymnastic Exercises as Practised by the Junior Class in Amherst College* (1884) and ten editions of *A Syllabus of the Health Lectures in Amherst College*.  He wrote numerous articles, most of them on the subjects of anthropometry or his program at Amherst.

The profession honored Hitchcock by awarding him honorary membership in the American Physical Education Association (1905), holding a reception and dinner commemorating his forty years of service in the cause of physical training (1901), and making him a Fellow in Memoriam of the American Academy of Physical Education (1944), an honor accorded to only eight other physical educators.  He was the recipient of an honorary M.A. degree from Springfield College (1907) and an honorary LL.D. from Amherst College in 1899.  Soon after his death, the College also memorialized him by naming its new outdoor facilities the Hitchcock Memorial

Field.   He was honored in numerous other ways by loving cups, dedications and certificates, all testifying to his leadership.   Edward Hitchcock was an unusual man.   Generations of Amherst students affectionately regarded "Old Doc" as their teacher, doctor and counselor.   Perhaps his greatest contribution was to the lives he touched with his warmth, generosity and caring.

# DUDLEY ALLEN SARGENT

## 1849-1924

Dudley Allen Sargent was one of the most pervasive influences in the history of American physical education. In his 1885 report on *Physical Training in American Colleges*, Hartwell listed forty-eight institutions that "have been wholly or partially furnished with Dr. Sargent's apparatus since 1879." (161:56) Included were colleges, Young Men's Christian Associations, private schools, theological seminaries, athletic clubs, and an insane asylum. Sixteen of those institutions also used his system of measurements and methodology. (161:56–57) In 1889 Sargent claimed that his style of apparatus "has been put into three hundred and fifty or more institutions, representing a total membership of over one hundred thousand." (282:65) However, Sargent's apparatus was rarely used by the public schools. (43:80) Boykin reported only one public school of 165 surveyed using the Sargent system. (52:580 593) He directed physical education programs, primarily in colleges, for fifty years, during forty of which he also conducted teacher training programs at the Sargent Normal School and Harvard Summer School for more than five thousand individuals. More than fifty thousand physical examinations were made in his department at Harvard, and the resultant records have in themselves been a contribution to research in anthropology as well as health and physical education. His major papers and addresses total more than forty titles in addition to his books.

His service in professional organizations was equally extensive, including election as vice-president (1885–1889) and president for five years (1890–1891; 1892–1894; 1899–1901) of the American Association for the Advancement of Physical Education, president (1899) of the Society of Directors of Physical Education in Colleges, and for many years, president of the Health Education League, a group which published a Health Education Series of about thirty pamphlets. He was awarded honorary membership in the American Physical Education Association and made a Fellow in Memoriam of the American Academy of Physical Education. These details of his career serve only to demonstrate the prodigious quantity of Sargent's work—the influence of his ideas was still more significant and enduring.

Sargent began his career in physical education as a professional acrobat.

FIG. 54.    Dudley Allen Sargent.

His performing took place in and around his hometown of Belfast, Maine, where he gave public gymnastic exhibitions with a troupe of friends he called Sargent's Combination, and later with a traveling circus. In order to earn money for college, he took the position of Director of Gymnastics at Bowdoin College, receiving five dollars a week for teaching heavy gymnastics, boxing and wrestling. He continued this work from 1869 to 1875 (teaching at Yale also in the last two years), when he graduated from Bowdoin with his Bachelor of Arts degree. Sargent regarded the securing of compulsory attendance at gymnastics classes one of his significant accomplishments at Bowdoin.* Having definitely decided on a career in physical education, he enrolled as a student in the Yale Medical School, the only course of study apparently appropriate to his future work. From 1875 to 1878, he earned his M.D. degree at Yale, again supporting himself by working as Director of the Gymnasium. Failing to receive a desired appointment in a college, the new doctor opened a private gymnasium in New York City which he called the Hygienic Institute and School of Physical Culture. He conducted classes for men and women for both medical treatment and developmental purposes, held development classes for boys and girls under sixteen years of age, gave a training course for teachers, and devised special treatments for invalids. He advertised that "the entire system pursued in this institution is founded upon a medical and an educational basis. . . . If all of the requirements are complied with, I guarantee to produce most favorable results." (315:14) In June he closed the school and left New York to deliver lectures on physical training at the Chautauqua Assembly in August. It was during the summer of 1879 that

---

* In 1894 that college conferred on him an honorary Doctor of Science degree.

Sargent was offered the position of Director of the Gymnasium and Assistant Professor of Physical Training at Harvard. (312) He retained the position until his retirement in 1919, although after 1889 his faculty rank was not renewed; his title thereafter was simply Director of the Hemenway Gymnasium.

Sargent's work at the Hemenway Gymnasium served as a model which was widely emulated throughout the profession. The situation he found at Harvard was similar to that of other colleges: athletes competing in rowing, baseball or football were almost the only individuals using the gymnasium—and they were also the most physically developed students on campus. The great mass of students, particularly the weakest, had no exercise or physical training. Sargent concluded that "of the whole number of students not more than ten per cent give any attention whatever to physical exercise, and that less than six per cent take it systematically as a means of culture and development." (317:108) He chose to focus on the students most needing physical training: "Let us give less attention to the exploitation of the strong, and more attention to the instruction of the weak." (313:585) "The great aim of the gymnasium is to improve the physical condition of the mass of our students, and to give them as much health, strength and stamina as possible, to enable them to perform the duties that await them after leaving college." (282:68) To accomplish this aim, Sargent evolved a comprehensive system of individualized exercise programs. The motivation to work in such a program came, he believed, not through competition but the desire to improve one's physical condition based upon one's knowledge of it. "The opportunity to help men physically is when they begin to attend to their bodily condition, wishing to remedy its defects. . . ." (312:174) Throughout his writings the importance of self-motivation was emphasized; for instance, the dedication page of *Health, Strength and Power* (314) carried the single sentence: *"The chief essential of physical training is voluntary movement."*

The program at Hemenway Gymnasium began with a complete physical examination, and the role of such examinations as the keystone of all physical education instruction was frequently stressed by Sargent in his speeches. His description of the examination shows that it entailed numerous measurements:

> The examinations were as thorough as we could make them. First, each man filled out a history blank. . . . All this information was necessary in order to interpret his condition and decide upon a future course. Following this historical outline, came various strength tests of the muscular force of the different parts of the body as measured by dynamometers, and tests to show the lung capacity. The next step was measurements [anthropometrics]. Every dimension of the body, apparently significant or insignificant, was given. The heart and lungs were examined carefully before and after exercising. . . . Finally we made a careful record of the condition of the skin, of the spine, of the muscles, and of any other point which the tapemeasure failed to indicate. (312:174)

As significant as the examination was the use to which it was put:

> From this data, we prescribed an order of appropriate exercises, specifying the amount of work and the adjustment of the apparatus used. These directions, written on a card, included, besides a prescription of exercise, suggestions for diet, sleep, bathing, and clothing. None of the cards were [sic] printed formulae, but each one was made out according to the needs of the individual.
>
> . . . . . . . . . . . . . . . . . .
>
> At the end of every order of exercise, I prescribed gentle running, unless the man's condition would not allow it. This little spurt is the best conclusion of exercising; for it starts the perspiration, opens the pores, and makes the bath which follows more beneficial. The process of cleansing the skin after exercise . . . is almost as valuable as the exercise itself. (312:174–175)

The examinations were repeated six months later and the prescription adjusted according to the recorded changes. Three "before and after" photographs were also taken for *visual* comparison. Examinations, photographs, and individual exercise programs were the keys to Sargent's campaign to interest Harvard students in their physical condition. Unlike the various systems then prevalent—German, Swedish, or Dio Lewis'—Sargent's system never required the men to exercise in a group, all doing the same thing regardless of physiques or physical needs. The systems of the Swedes and Lewis stressed exercising *all* parts of the body; Sargent stressed exercising in relation to need.

In conjunction with such a system it was necessary to have apparatus which "can be adjusted to the strength of the strong and the weakness of the weak." (282:72) In each of the gymnasiums in which Sargent had worked, he found old apparatus modelled after the German *turnplätze*. He was highly critical of both the usefulness and the condition of the equipment:

> The material is selected without regard to fitness and is put together with little knowledge of its object or design. Hanging ropes are made of hemp and are stiffly tarred to make them durable. This object is effective, for they are never used twice by the same person. The parallel bars are broad at the base and narrow at the top, so as to render the grip insecure; and they are generally made of some splintering material, in order to remind the performer which way he is going. . . . The rungs on the horizontal ladder are . . . left rough . . . while in the vertical ladders they are smoothly polished. Both are carefully avoided, for in the first case every swing forward raises a blister, and in the second case every step upward is attended with positive danger. The sand bag weighs seventy-five pounds and is covered with the heaviest kind of canvas. One solid blow removes the skin from every knuckle. . . . The mattresses weigh four hundred pounds each and are filled with excelsior or corn husks, which from constant rolling have become matted together in lumps. . . . The weights . . . start from a trough filled with sawdust and dirt. Every movement is accompanied by a cloud of dust and a deafening rattle and bang.
>
> This is a fair representation of college gymnasiums throughout the country. (317:112–114)

Sargent claimed that 90% of the population could not derive benefit from the heavy apparatus. He was also critical of dumbbells, Indian clubs and the other paraphernalia of light gymnastics; he believed they were suitable only for very elementary work and the achievement of suppleness, but not sufficiently demanding to develop the muscles. Accordingly he invented a series of developing apparatus which were adjustable and therefore adaptable, and could be used in a variety of ways; less than thirty minutes were needed to learn all the customary movements. They were limited, however, in the extent to which they could cause the development of skilled movements and cardiovascular endurance, and they were rather boring to use. The most important machine in his scheme was a system of chest weights and pulleys. In 1855 Captain James Chiosso had developed a similar device, but Sargent modified and perfected the idea. His apparatus included chest-expanders and developers, quarter-circles, leg-machines, finger-machines, high pulleys, inclined planes, travelling parallels, and hydraulic rowing machines. In all, there were more than eighty developing machines in the gymnasium. Students could work out for an hour, going from machine to machine, adjusting each to suit his own limits of strength and endurance. Sargent never patented his devices, wishing them to be used as widely as possible, but commercial concerns did, and for a number of years he was involved in litigation and conflict concerning their usage and developing rights. They were installed in hundreds of gymnasiums but Sargent himself received no financial profit from his inventions.

The developing machines and exercises were not the only uses to which the Hemenway Gymnasium was put. There were boxing, rowing and fencing rooms, a baseball cage, bowling alleys, a running track, and the heavy

FIG. 55.   Harvard University, Hemenway Gymnasium, 1885.

apparatus associated with German gymnastics. Sargent advocated the various sports, advanced gymnastics, and dancing as a complement to the developing exercises, not only for college men, but for school children as well. He argued that the conception of physical education must be broadened:

> Not only must the ordinary round of light and heavy gymnastics be taught to all of our school children as a matter of daily routine, but they must be taught and encouraged to practice the greatest variety of youthful sports and game. Walking, running, jumping, skating, swimming, diving, rowing, canoeing, bicycling, dancing, fencing, and the various forms of ball playing, are essential parts of a boy's neuro-muscular education. . . . In learning and practicing these different sports there is a training and a culture which comes to the boy which he cannot get in any other way. This experience becomes a part of his psycho-physical organism. (313:583–584)

It should be noted that this speech was given in 1910, by which time such activities were advocated by many physical educators. Sargent was not a leader in advocating games for children, nor was he an enemy of sports, as his diatribes against athletics have implied. He understood that "many of the highest moral qualities, such as courage, fortitude, forbearance, generosity, magnanimity, and nobility of character, may be cultivated on the athletic field . . ." (313:581) but he also believed certain evils accrued to emphasis on participation in intercollegiate sports. He named them as:

> A tendency to specialize in single sports, and narrow the field of physical education; too much time, money and attention given to the development of the major sports like football and baseball, and too little to the development of the minor sports. . . . The high standard of all the popular sports puts them beyond the qualifying efficiency of the average student. All of our sports are pursued too much as ends in themselves rather than as means to ends—and those ends the general improvement and harmonious perfecting of the human organism. (313:581)

Sargent was particularly unhappy with the management of college athletics and served as secretary to the Harvard Faculty Committee which drew up rules regulating intercollegiate contests. He said that "we should so conduct our school sports and exercises as to emphasize their educational and cultural value, and put less stress on the competitive element. . . . Unregulated competition in sports tends not to their preservation but to their destruction." (313:582)

Always skeptical of the practices associated with athletics, some of which he deemed harmful to the health of students, he devised a strength test which could be used as supplementary evidence to qualify students to enter athletics contests. After 1890 these tests were required of all Harvard athletes. Tests of the back, legs, right and left forearms, upper arms (triceps and biceps), chest, and lung strength or capacity, were administered using dynamometers, a manometer, parallel and horizontal bars, and a spirometer. Total strength was computed as follows:

> The number of kilos lifted with the back and legs straight, and the number of kilos lifted with the legs bent, added to the strength of the grip of the right and left hand, expiratory power as tested by the manometer, and one-tenth of the weight in kilos multiplied by the number of times that the person can raise his weight by dipping between the parallel bars and pulling his weight up to his chin on the horizontal bar as previously described. One-twentieth of the lung capacity may be substituted for the lung-strength or expiratory test, but both tests may not be used in computing the total. (324:219)

Candidates for the crew and football teams, for example, were expected to score at least seven hundred points; baseball, track and field performers and intramural football team members needed only six hundred points, and with a standard of five hundred points, lacrosse, cricket and tennis players could be the weakest.* This test, with different computations, later became the basis of Frederick Rand Rogers' strength test for his Physical Fitness Index.

Another generalized measurement devised by Sargent was "the physical test of a man," still known and used as the Sargent Jump Test. Recognizing the limitations of body and strength measurements in indicating potential power, he structured a test using the constant forces of height and weight while applying power to overcome gravity. In essence he devised a system of measuring the precise height a person could jump; using the formula $\text{Index} = \dfrac{\text{Weight} \times \text{Jump}}{\text{Height or Stature}}$, he recorded an index of the effort made. He stated that "the test as a whole may be considered as a momentary try-out of one's strength, speed, energy and dexterity combined, which, in my opinion, furnishes a fair physical test of a man, and solves in a simple way his unknown equation as determined potentially by his height and weight." (319:134) Even today some coaches regard this test as a quick method of getting an estimate of an athlete's potential power.

Measurements taken on the athletes and students in classes were carefully collected so that physical training systems could be better developed and evaluated, and norms for given ages computed. Plotting a student's measurements on a printed chart vividly portrayed his deviation from the norm and could later be used to ascertain the precise physical growth and

---

* Application of this test extended beyond qualifying athletes. At a meeting of the physical directors of fifteen colleges and universities in 1897, it was agreed to adopt the test as an intercollegiate strength test. Given under specified conditions at home institutions, the records of each school's fifty strongest men were published each year and the individual with the highest total score was considered the champion strong man of all the colleges. The school with the fifty strongest men held the strength trophy for the next year. One year Columbia University scored highest with 59,489.4 points, an average of 1157.2 points a man. (317:294)

gain in strength and endurance made during the course of gymnasium work. Furthermore, data were obtained from which students could be compared with those of later years, or with other population groups. Sargent was also able to make comparisons between the physiques and strength of athletes, scholarship students, average students, and those on stipend. These uses made anthropometric measurements seem one of the most important contributions physical educators were making to the scientific world, and Sargent was one of the foremost measurers. In 1893 he published charts showing various segments of the American community, and life-size statues of the "average" man and woman student were constructed for exhibition at the Chicago World's Fair. Sargent's measurement procedures as well as his charts were widely used in colleges and YMCAs throughout the country.

Another of Sargent's interests was in the physical education of women. He argued that society needed women with stamina:*

> If then we recognize the production of a superior physical type to be one of the high aims of a people an aim made significant by our campaign for "better badies [sic]" and by our international athletic contests, we must realize that the physical nature of girls, as well as of boys, should be carefully trained and developed. (316:830)

Therefore he proposed that "there should be in girls' sports and exercises something which calls out the heroic attributes of their nature, as well as the picturesque; something that makes them courageous and daring, as well as skillful, strong, and enduring." (316:830–831) Educators, biologists and women themselves had not appreciated the potential capacity of the female:

> Women themselves had been slow to realize this tremendous power and had constantly overestimated their weaknesses, so that it needed many years of encouragement and of feeling their way through the stages of musical calisthenics and bean-bag drills to convince them that they would not fall to pieces in more violent exercise. (316:831)

Besides approving of basketball, soccer and hockey for women, he also advocated aesthetic dancing (he thought the latter beneficial for men too). He did not approve of ballet dancing but stated:

> The modern gymnasium dancing complies more completely with the requirements of good exercise, because the arms, trunk and legs are brought more generally into action. While the exercises for the feet and calves are not so intense or concentrated as those of the ballet girls, the range and extent of movement in the gymnasium

---

* This same idea led the society of ancient Sparta to give full physical training to young women. Until the later half of the nineteenth century, it was the only society that had seriously attempted to carry out such a program.

dancing is greater.  Not only are the chest, shoulders, and back muscles considerably developed by the free use of the arms, but so many of the muscles of the lower back, abdomen, and thighs are used that great respiratory power is required to sustain the extended action—hence the chest walls are expanded by the effort. (323:219)

Sargent had little interest in dancing as an art form; he saw it primarily as a means to exercise and attain grace, suppleness and good posture.  He did avow the emotional effect, likening the experience to the exhilaration experienced by baseball players making a home run, or a gymnastics performer accomplishing a difficult feat.

He had opportunity to put his ideas about women into practice in his Sanatory Gymnasium which he opened in 1881 so that girls of the Harvard Annex, as Radcliffe was then called, could have a place to exercise.  In the same building he conducted his Normal School, primarily training women physical education teachers.

From the beginning Sargent fought for the recognition of physical education as an academic endeavor; he argued that it should be required and given credit in the same manner as academic subjects.  He also believed that gymnasium directors should be given rank as part of the faculty. Harvard eventually required physical education for freshmen (1919) but has never granted credit, nor did Sargent have faculty rank for the greater part of his career.  Nevertheless, he helped to secure academic recognition for physical education in other institutions by demonstrating the value of his work.

Dudley Allen Sargent was one of the pioneers of American physical education.  He was a performer and a teacher, a scientist and an artist, a thinker and a writer.  In the time of "the battle of the systems," he claimed none of his own, but the Sargent program at Harvard came close to filling what Sargent described as America's need:

> What America most needs is the happy combination which the European nations are trying to effect:  the strength-giving qualities of the German gymnasium, the active and energetic properties of the English sports, the grace and suppleness acquired from the French calisthenics, and the beautful poise and mechanical precision of the Swedish free movements, all regulated, systematized, and adapted to our peculiar needs and institutions. (282:76)

The goal Sargent enunciated, to strive for "the improvement of the individual man in structure and in function" (317:296), represented the ideal of the whole profession.  His emphasis on health and fitness for everybody, rather than on strength or skill for the few, must be regarded as the hallmark of the early physical education programs in the United States. Sargent's share in developing both the goal and the program to pursue it marks him as one of the most important American innovators.

# THE SARGENT SCHOOL FOR
PHYSICAL EDUCATION

The Sargent Normal School was a direct outgrowth of Sargent's exemplary work at Harvard's Hemenway Gymnasium. The demand rose for his apparatus and for teachers to give instruction in their use and in Sargent's general methodology. Furthermore, the Harvard Annex (consisting of Harvard's women students and now called Radcliffe College) invited him to administer a program for the women. To meet both requests Sargent opened the Sanatory Gymnasium on the corner of Palmer and Brattle streets in Cambridge, Massachusetts in 1881; there he gave instruction to the Annex students, the women and children of Cambridge and vicinity, and men and women training to be teachers of physical education. The Normal School still survives today as Boston University Sargent College of Allied Health Professions.*

In 1881 six women accepted Sargent's offer of a free course, "if they would devote themselves for one year to the study and practice of physical training with the view of becoming teachers." (312:197) Apparently the demand for teachers was so great that five of them left within the first two months to take positions. The sixth, Mrs. Mary E. W. Jones, therefore became the first graduate, completing the course in 1882.

The one-year course was lengthened to two in 1891,† to three in 1903, and then to four in 1929 when it became part of Boston University. From 1912, in addition to the regular thirty-two-week school season, students were required to attend two September and two June sessions every three years at the new camp in Peterboro, New Hampshire. This replaced the previous requirement that students enroll in the five-week Harvard Sum-

___

* The Normal School of Physical Training (1894) became the Sargent School for Physical Education (1904), the Sargent School of Physical Education of Boston University School of Education (1929), Boston University Sargent School (1932), Boston University Sargent College (1935), and Boston University Sargent College of Allied Health Professions (1966). The name changes reflected its change in status from an independent, privately-owned school to a segment of a large university. All of the early single-purpose normal schools of physical training which survive today have established similar collegiate affiliations. After Sargent's death the school was given to the University by his family who nevertheless continued their involvement in the school's affairs.

† Although it is generally believed that the two-year curriculum began in 1893, statements by Sargent in his *Autobiography* verify the 1891 date. Wacker's research (368:49, 52, 53) supports the dates given above.

mer School course conducted by Sargent. The tuition (after the first year) remained at one hundred dollars a year until 1902 when it became $125 for first and second year students; in 1904 it jumped to $150. (368:56) The tuition hike was probably necessitated by the construction of a new gymnasium.

From 1883 the Sanatory Gymnasium had been located in a renovated carriage house on Church Street in Cambridge. Although not an elegant facility, Sargent saw value in its accessibility for working people and in the atmosphere provided by the example of manual laborers.* However, the chief advantage of the location was the low rental in that industrial area. In 1904 the new Everett Street gymnasium was opened on the old track and ball ground of Harvard University, not far from the Hemenway Gymnasium. This remained the home of the Sargent School until 1958 when it was moved to Boston to be on the main campus of Boston University. The *APEA Review* carried a description of the new facility:

> It is peculiarly fitting that Dr. D. A. Sargent should commemorate his twenty-fifth year of the service at Harvard by building what undoubtedly will be the largest and most completely equipped private Normal School gymnasium in the world. . . .
> The building is 80 feet long by 50 feet wide and five stories high, with a total floor space of about 20,000 square feet. It will contain a swimming tank in the basement together with adequate lockers and bathing facilities, two gymnasiums with complete and separate equipment one above the other, a running track, handball courts, lecture rooms, library, laboratory, assembly hall and a sun parlor on the roof. (95:151–152)

Later the purchase of the acreage in New Hampshire with its lake and spacious fields, provided ample place to conduct all the curricular activities of the school.

The curriculum required of the Normal Course students circa 1900 was fairly typical of the two-year course requirements during that decade. Consistent with the emphasis on the scientific basis of physical education, the theory courses were almost all in the natural and health sciences. They included anatomy, physiology, biology, zoology, chemistry, and physics in the first year, as well as relation of body and mind, physiology of exercise, applied anatomy, conservation of energy, animal mechanics, mental hygiene from the physical basis, anthropometry and the laws of form and proportion, vital statistics, semeiology (in relation to Delsarte), physical diagnosis, natural heritage, hygiene of occupations and schools, the effects

---

* Concerned with the effects of factory and industrial work on women, he held a "working girl's clinic" two evenings a week trying to correct the effects of cramped positions and lack of exercise. It provided a clear illustration to Sargent students of the positive effects of corrective exercises. His interest in manual labor also led him to develop a whole series of exercises which simulated the movements of such work, e.g., pitching hay, mowing and throwing a lasso.

of variations in exercise, food, sleep, bathing, clothing, and climate. They also studied the science and art of teaching and analyzed sports, games and educational exercises. The textbooks for these weighty courses were *Gray's Anatomy*, *The Human Body* by Martin, and *Elements of Natural Philosophy* by Avery. (322) When the course was increased to three years, histology, mechano-therapy, medical sociology, and the construction and organization of gymnasiums were added to the theory courses. Around 1902 a course in the history of education was included in the curriculum, indicating the new awareness of physical education as an educational subject. Reflecting a contemporary professional trend, a course for playground teachers was added in 1908–1909. In later years curricular changes tended to be in the direction of the social sciences and education; courses in psychology were particularly emphasized.

Matching the theory courses was a long list of practical subjects mostly relating to exercises of various kinds. In the first year these included: exercises with the developing apparatus for the physical development of the *teacher*, massage, free movements, calisthenics, light gymnastics (dumbbells, wands, Indian clubs), chest weights, balance swing and boards, class exercises, voice training (Delsarte), and introductory exercises on heavy apparatus. In addition, students learned mechanical work required in a gymnasium, such as practical carpentry, and splicing, serving and knotting ropes. In the second year more time was spent on light gymnastics as class exercises, and heavy gymnastics; in addition, marching, athletic sports, emergency treatment (first aid), application of developing appliances for weaknesses, adaptation of exercises to individual needs, and practice in working with dynamometers, and dividing and organizing classes were included. (322) Aesthetic dancing, field hockey and ice hockey were all added to the curriculum prior to 1904. Practice teaching began in 1907. In 1909 seven graded classes in a model school were available twice a week for practice teaching and seniors spent four days a week doing clinical work in a children's hospital.

It was not, however, until the Peterboro camp was purchased, that a full complement of sport activities could be developed. Besides camping and the study of subjects now grouped into the category of outdoor education, large fields, tennis courts, and a pond encouraged greater attention to sports. In 1969, the return to emphasis on health with a subsequent de-emphasis on sports education ended this phase of Sargent College and the camp was closed.

Admission requirements included a high school education, but many students actually came after earning a college degree. At the end of each subject students took examinations. If they passed in all of the major subjects they received, upon graduation, a full certificate, "indicating the time spent at the school, the work done, and the nature of the service that each teacher is capable of performing." (161:59) Those unable to obtain

FIG. 56.   A Class of Sargent Girls Performing an Indian Club Routine.

full certificates received letters detailing precisely which subjects they had passed and what their capabilities were. It became the practice for Sargent to record on the diplomas of the most proficient the words: "With honors in theory," "With honors in practice," or "With honors in theory and practice." (366:419)

The curriculum in its detail and scope was not vastly different from other similar normal schools of its time. Whatever the activity emphasis, most physical educators believed in the efficacy of the science background— the detailed and thorough study of the body with attention paid to correctable weaknesses particularly of an orthopedic nature, and to preventive medicine through exercise and good health habits. Recreation and education, if spoken of, were related to mental health and the concept of *mens sana in corpore sano*. The aims of the Sargent School reflected the goals of other contemporary normal schools:

> The objects of this school are to drill pupils in the theory and practice of physical training and to prepare them to teach in this much neglected branch of education; to furnish a course of carefully prescribed exercises, under personal supervision, to those who are in poor health and in need of special treatment; to provide a system of recreative and developing exercises for those who wish to build up their physique and keep themselves in vigorous condition; and to furnish a series of aesthetic movements as a means of attaining poise, grace and suppleness. (322)

What differentiated the Sargent School from the others then existent was its large student body. In the first ten years the school grew to about thirty girls in attendance.* In 1904, 261 had graduated from the full course and about seventy had attended for one year. A 1920 survey of twenty-eight colleges, YMCA schools, and private institutions giving normal courses in physical education showed that Sargent had graduated nearly a third of the total number (3,008 of 9,656). The next highest number was only 885 from Springfield College. At that time the enrollment at Sargent was 470, almost twice the 242 of its next largest competitor, the Savage School (43:87), and advertisements claimed it to be "the largest normal school for physical education in the world." The peak enrollment was in 1923–24 when the catalogue listed 533 students. The total effect was to make what was taught at Sargent common practice in institutions throughout the country. Of the graduates who achieved professional reputations, perhaps Elizabeth Burchenal and Delphine Hanna were the best known.

When Sargent died in 1924 the school was an important and powerful influence on American physical education. Five years later his family gave

---

* Between 1904 and 1914 the school was coeducational, but very few men actually enrolled. (44:112) From 1956 men were again admitted to the school but not to the physical education curriculum. They generally study either physical or occupational therapy.

the school to Boston University under the auspices of which its curriculum slowly evolved and expanded.   In the late fifties physical education became the minority curriculum, as more students were enrolled in the physical therapy program which had begun in 1931.   Therapeutic recreation, occupational therapy and a graduate degree in physical therapy were added to the College in 1961, 1962 and 1965, respectively.   Since the profession of physical education today emphasizes sports and dance rather than health, the College is no longer a strong influence in physical education.   But with its health orientation it continues its contribution to the health professions—a direction which Sargent would have approved.

# HARVARD SUMMER SCHOOL OF
# PHYSICAL EDUCATION

The Harvard Summer School of Physical Education was probably the most important source of professional training in the United States during the early part of the twentieth century. In a profession where degrees were not yet a requisite, this was sometimes the only preparation to teach that attending students received. It was a place to study, exchange ideas with other professionals and introduce new activities. Aesthetic dancing and field hockey, for example, got their start in this country at the Summer School.

The large number of men and women who attended, eighty percent of whom were teachers, suggests its popularity and pervasive influence. In the first three summers, 1887–1889, there were 161 students.* Sargent described the group's diverse composition:

> The most of them were teachers in physical exercises at colleges and secondary schools in different parts of the country. Among the list were several physicians, thirty-two college graduates, army officers, school superintendents and principals, and many teachers and professors in other branches, who attended for their own improvement or in the interest of the institutions which they represented. (282:68)

Enrollment figures rose rapidly; the high point before the turn of the century was 124 in 1897. The largest number ever attending in one summer was 351 in 1924; even in the last year, 1932, there were ninety-nine students. In the forty-six summers of the School's existence a total of 7,680 enrolled, representing 5,086 individuals (some attended more than one summer). They came from all forty-eight states and sixteen foreign countries including faraway places such as Japan, China and Turkey. (366: 426, 431) In 1918, Sargent noted that the 3,052 individuals who had attended represented "1,082 institutions, of which 53 are in foreign countries; it includes 232 colleges, 245 secondary schools, 65 normal schools, and 326 public schools, 11 normal schools of physical education, 72 YMCA gymnasiums, 30 athletic clubs, 27 state institutions, and 4 vocal training schools." (312:212)

The importance of the venture was not apparent to the Harvard authori-

---

* A member of the first class who later achieved nationwide fame was Booker T. Washington.

ties who, with the exception of President Eliot, were not pleased at having such an "un-academic" endeavor on their campus. They also objected to coeducational gymnastics and were dubious of the necessarily abbreviated clothes in which students exercised. Although they granted permission for the use of Hemenway Gymnasium, the entire program was left in Sargent's hands. The courses were listed in the regular Harvard Summer School bulletins but its only real connection with the University was financial. No entrance requirements were stipulated for the Summer School, a policy congruent with the school's purpose:

> The object of the school was to arouse an interest in the general subject, show its relation to education, and in a short time prepare as many people as possible to teach physical training. We tried to open the door, show the extent and richness of the field, and point out the opportunities by suggestions and demonstrations for the brighter minds to grasp. (312:210)

To accomplish its goals, only two courses were conducted in each of the first summers. The theory course consisted of lectures in the sciences considered basic to physical education: anatomy, physiology, hygiene, anthropometry, and applied anatomy, and also lectures on the various gymnastic systems, including their history and philosophy. The practical course included calisthenics, free exercises, tumbling, fancy steps, and work with dumbbells, wands, Indian clubs, bars, vaulting horses, and rings. Students who found the content too extensive for one summer came the next and repeated the course. However, as normal schools began to graduate some trained physical educators, the need for more advanced work became evident. Accordingly, in 1899 a second summer was added to the full course. Lectures on first aid, physical diagnosis, physiology of exercise, the treatment of spinal curvature, and testing for normal vision and hearing were added to the theory courses. The practical program included all the activities then popular in physical education; elementary and advanced classes were given in school exercises, free movements, heavy (German) gymnastics, light gymnastics, Swedish gymnastics, fencing, military drill, aesthetic dancing, and games. Men also had the option of taking a course in gymnastics especially adapted for YMCAs. (366:413) In 1902, in response to the urging of President Eliot, one of Sargent's consistent supporters, the program was extended to four summers with the belief that it would strengthen the profession by raising the standard of academic preparation. Students who were already graduates of normal schools of physical education usually completed the course in less time. The theory course remained essentially the same, the addition of histology and methods of teaching being the most enduring changes. However, the practical course was greatly expanded. In fact, it would have been difficult to match its comprehensive program anywhere else. Early in 1900 sports were added to the curriculum. Men learned boxing and wrestling and the women field hockey and tennis; men and women took track and soccer. In 1908 American school dances (Gilbert), rhythmical gymnastics (Dalcroze method), and school plays and games were advertised as "special features." Notably missing in those years were courses in basketball and folk dancing, both of which gained in popularity in other teacher training programs. Since the students usually taught the same activities during the school year, they became quite proficient by the end of four summers of activity work. The most advanced students took part in yearly exhibitions held during the final week of the course. Between twelve- and fourteen-hundred spectators generally attended and Sargent regarded this as valuable means of educating the public about physical education.

A student taking both the theory and practice courses (some took only one) had a very complete daily schedule. Although in the earliest years all work was completed by 1 P.M., the school day was soon lengthened from 9 A.M. to 6 P.M. and later it began at 8 A.M. Of course students were not required to take all activities offered: for a tuition fee of twenty-five dollars each for the theory and activity courses, they were permitted to take as much work as they wished. Requirements for earning a certificate varied as the Summer School was expanded from one to four sessions. The first year only students with a previous medical degree were able to earn full certificates; this prerequisite was dropped thereafter. From 1905 a student earned his certificate by passing three theory and four practical courses in each of four summers, plus two coaching courses. Although examination and grades were given in each class, no final comprehensive examination was given, as was common practice at other normal schools.

The Harvard Certificate was a coveted reward, well-respected by the profession and by college presidents, school superintendents and principals responsible for hiring faculty. The total number of certificates issued between 1902 and 1932 was 698. In 1922, after Sargent had resigned, arrangements were made with Harvard's Graduate School of Education for physical education students who had graduated from approved colleges to earn a master's degree in education. Working within a specified credit structure they were able to complete the degree in four summers; in addition they had to write a thesis. In all, 152 students became degree candidates and fifty-one degrees were actually conferred by Harvard. (366)

The faculty of the Summer School was possibly the most expert assembled anywhere at that time. In every curricular area Sargent was able to call on eminent people in the profession, many of whom had themselves attended a summer session. Among the most prominent were R. Tait McKenzie, Fred E. Leonard, James Huff McCurdy, and Edward M. Hartwell.

The Harvard Medical School faculty provided an endless source of expert instructors and during the time of the Master of Education program lecturers were also drawn from the Graduate School of Education. The activities were taught by specialists in their fields: Hartvig Nissen taught Swedish gymnastics, Melvin Ballou Gilbert originated and taught aesthetic dancing, Constance Applebee introduced field hockey to this country, Emil Rath of the North American Gymnastic Union presented German gymnastics, and George Meylan, then Medical Director of the Boston YMCA, taught Association gymnastics. In addition, some of the best qualified gymnasts served as student assistants in return for remission of tuition and the prestige of serving on the staff. This ensured expert instruction and a low student-teacher ratio. In the first year there were about a dozen lecturers, instructors and assistants for the fifty-seven students; in 1914 the ratio was 48 to 230. (312:212) The diversity of backgrounds and talents of the teaching faculty greatly contributed to the liveliness of the program, its flexibility and varied subject matter. In a time when many claims were being set forth regarding the appropriate content of physical education, teachers throughout the country were having an opportunity to experience the best that each system could offer.

The closing of the Harvard Summer School of Physical Education brought an end to an important chapter in the growth of the profession in the United States. When Sargent retired in 1919 he was succeeded in the directorship by men of eminence who upheld the high standards established from the beginning. The program was not discontinued because of any lapse in quality nor because of any objection by the Harvard authorities. In part it fell victim to new regulations requiring twice as many courses for a Master's degree at Harvard; a student would have had to study eight summers to complete his degree in education in physical education. Non-degree work was no longer as popular as in the past due to state legislation requiring at least a bachelor's degree for teacher certification. This forced potential teachers into full-time teacher training programs for a four-year period and made the work of the Summer School somewhat redundant. With graduate work impractical, and basic work pre-empted by four-year institutions, there was little choice but to discontinue the program.

Clarence B. Van Wyck, whose research and publication on the Harvard Summer School provides a comprehensive and sympathetic record for the generations who were not privileged to attend it, incisively summed up its contribution:

> When we attempt to measure the extent of the influence which this School exerted upon the development of physical education in America, the important factors to keep in mind are, not the number of years of its life, but rather the particular period of history within which those years were lived—not the size of its annual registrations, but rather the geographical distribution represented by that registration—not the total number of individuals enrolled in the student body, but the positions which those individuals held in colleges, secondary schools, public schools, normal schools, and miscellaneous organizations. (366:426)

# GEORGE W. FITZ*

## 1860-1934

> This is no time for sentiment, for blind following of leaders or the blinder application of cut-and-dried rules. It is no time for political methods, for the bribery of school and college offices to introduce a special form of gymnastics by offers of free instruction, or even of gymnasia. It is a time for loyal, conscientious work and study, and for the re-examination of the foundations of the theory and practice of physical training. (104:339)

With these words George W. Fitz, in his address as President of the Department of Physical Education of the National Education Association, reproached his colleagues. At the time when the "battle of the systems" was raging, he noted that the various claims, counter-claims and accusations were harming the more important cause of establishing physical training in the schools. "As a result of this diversity of claim, school officers and superintendents are beginning to hesitate about the introduction of physical training, overwhelmed by the necessity for a careful consideration and just valuation of the various systems. . . ." (104:338) He assessed the problem with the same succinctness with which he had addressed the Seventh Convention of the AAAPE in 1892:

> We hear much about the theory of physical training and the theory of different systems. What right have we to theories? Physiology has not reached the point where they can say deductively that this should be so and that otherwise. . . . To claim any system to be based upon physiological grounds, then, is not justifiable. . . . As physiologists, we should study the conditions under which the exercises are done, and the results of these exercises upon the system. What we need is scientific work, not the assumption that certain laws require certain exercises. . . . What we want is the clear scientific study of the physiology; the exercise, whether presented in one form or another. Let us see just what each exercise does for the human body, and just what portion of the body it affects and how much in justice we shall be able to say what exercises are best, and what are not so good. . . .
>
> I, too, see the dawn of the day. . . . It will come when we have the equal study of physiology and physical training. . . . (9:203-204)

Fitz's point was well-taken. Though the various systems, particularly the Swedish, claimed to be scientific, in reality little was done to establish

---

* Credit for recognizing the importance of Fitz's contribution and bringing it to the attention of today's historians, belongs to Drs. Walter Kroll and Guy Lewis of the University of Massachusetts.

the validity of their claims. The constant anthropometric measuring lent an atmosphere of scientific credulity to programs, but for the most part the measurements gathered dust on shelves. At best they served to show an individual change in his external physical dimensions and probably served, therefore, as a motivating factor; but they contributed little to the cause of establishing the validity of any aspects or kind of program.

George Fitz probably did more than anybody else to mitigate this situation. In his time he was one of the foremost investigators in the field, and his speeches indicate that he worked hard to get the profession to recognize research's importance. He earned his M.D. in 1891 from Harvard University and while a student probably was influenced by Dudley Allen Sargent, then Director of the Hemenway Gymnasium, to become involved in physical education as an active member of the profession. From 1895–1901 he was corresponding secretary of the AAAPE. It was at his suggestion that the *American Physical Education Review* was started and he served as its edi-

Fig. 57. George Wells Fitz.

11

tor from the first volume in 1896 through the eleventh volume in 1906, with the exception of the years 1901–1903. He was one of the founders and secretary of the American Society for Research in Physical Education. He was a prolific writer and speaker: beginning with the seventh annual conference of the AAAPE, the *Proceedings* record his papers and contributions to discussions; reports of his research were published in professional, medical and scientific journals. He was an inventor, creating many devices for facilitating research and measurement. He was a teacher at the Sargent Normal School and Harvard University. Finally, he founded, organized and ran the first physical education research laboratory in this country. In 1906 his last article appeared in the *APEA Review*, and in an editorial relating to his resignation as editor, his "lack of sympathy with the present conduct of the Association" was noted. (105:36) At that point he seems to have dropped out of the profession, which may partially account for the otherwise inexplicable fact that historians have totally ignored his existence and contributions. He later practiced medicine in Peconic, Long Island, New York where he was living at the time of his death in 1934.

It is his career at Harvard that was of greatest significance to physical education. As a student he might have served as an assistant to Sargent, for in 1888 he designed and made the first multiple camera and automatic labeling device for use in photographing students in the Hemenway Gymnasium. (108) The camera was used by Sargent, who took photographs as part of his physical examination of each student. Sometime before graduation, probably in 1890, Fitz became a teacher of anatomy and physiology at the Sargent School and the Harvard Summer School. By 1892 he was Instructor in Physiology and Hygiene at Harvard University and in 1894 he was promoted to an assistant professor. Like Sargent he continued to teach in both schools. As a faculty member with rank he was actively involved in, if not the instigator of, Harvard's new degree program and laboratory.*

In 1892 the Physiological Laboratory was established as part of the Lawrence Scientific School, a unit of Harvard University. The founding of the laboratory complemented the establishment, in 1891, of the nation's first degree program in physical education, a Bachelor of Science in Anatomy, Physiology, and Physical Training. The purpose of the degree program, as stated in the 1894–1895 catalogue, was "to afford a training for those who expect to take charge of gymnasiums as well as for those who wish to obtain a general education preparatory to the study of medicine."

---

* It is difficult to determine whether the credit for originating and organizing the program should go to Sargent or Fitz. Since the latter had just completed his medical degree when the program began, and since Sargent's name was listed first on the catalogue statement (165), this author tends to think that Sargent was responsible for the degree program in his capacity as Director. However, it was Fitz who usually spoke for the program in any published mention of it while only once in his writings did Sargent ever allude to it in any way.

(165:40)   The course of study was fairly stable over the years.   In 1894 it included English, French or German, and a long list of science courses ranging from those concerning the human body to botany, geology and meteorology; one year of the four was taken at the Medical School.   In addition there were several courses relating specifically to physical training, e.g. anthropometry, applied anatomy, physiology of exercise, remedial exercises, and the history of physical education.   Gymnastics and athletics were taught throughout the four years and students had the opportunity to teach physical exercises, presumably to the general undergraduate population.   Until 1897, attendance at the Harvard Summer School of Physical Education was required.   The faculty involved in the professional classes throughout the program included Sargent, Fitz and James Gray Lathrop, an Instructor in Athletics.   In 1897–1898 the practical work was reduced to one year and by 1899 the program was completely pre-medical.   The first degree was received by James Francis Jones in 1893 and eight others received their B.S. degrees throughout the years it was offered.*

The degree program bore the unmistakable stamp of Fitz's beliefs.   In 1893 he wrote an article for the *Harvard Graduates' Magazine* which explained his convictions and his purposes for establishing the physiology laboratory:

Harvard's establishment of a laboratory for the experimental study of the physiology of exercise . . . is a distinct advance in the history of physical education, for though hitherto there has been much actual instruction in gymnasium and athletic work, and in measuring and prescribing exercise for students, little has been done in the physiological and psychological effects of exercise. . . .

Those engaged in the work have been too busy with the practical side, or too little versed in exact physiological methods, to give much time and thought to the less tangible aspect of exercise. . . . In the absence of exact physiological knowledge, various more or less reasonable and far-reaching hypotheses have been assumed, and elaborate theories and systems of training based thereon. . . . Indeed, physiology seems to have little to do with the development of any system of physical education.

.    .    .    .    .    .    .    .    .    .    .    .    .    .    .    .

What is the real need? . . . What are the tests we can apply? . . . What is it the awkward boys lacks, and how may he be trained into grace? . . . Why is one boy

---

* This may explain Sargent's reluctance to discuss the program in his writings. In 1894 he proudly announced: "Perhaps the most important step that has yet been effected toward preparing young men for such positions of public service is that recently taken by Harvard University in establishing a four year's course at the Lawrence Scientific School in anatomy, physiology, and physical training." (317:1140)   After that he seems to have ignored it in his writings and speeches. He may have considered this first real venture into academia a failure, used as he was to large numbers of students enrolling in his other normal classes.   The University may have objected to employing Fitz with so few students over all those years, which would have intensified Sargent's failure at attempting to sustain a degree program.

a better catcher behind the bat, or able to hit the ball surer in tennis and base-ball? . . . What will give the best muscular development . . . ?

.    .    .    .    .    .    .    .    .    .    .    .    .    .    .    .    .

These problems are exceedingly complicated and difficult of solution . . . yet many of the problems may be solved. . . . To that end, and for instruction in physiology and hygiene, the Physiological Laboratory was established in the Lawrence Scientific School. . . . A comfortable, well-lighted room and $1,000 were given as a foundation. . . . The apparatus is essentially a product of the laboratory, for it is not only made here, but is also specially devised for its work. . . . (109)

The laboratory and an attendant emphasis upon research, was an integral part of the course of study. Students were advised to study experimental physics rather than the "text-book alternative." According to the 1896 catalogue, the Physiology of Exercise course was "intended to introduce the student to the fundamental problems of Physical Training, and to give him training in the use of apparatus for investigation and in the methods of such work." "The object of the experimental work is to make clear the hygiene of muscle, the conditions under which it acts, the relation of its action to the body as a whole; its effect on blood supply and general hygienic conditions, as well as the effects of various exercises upon muscle growth and general health." (165:7, 3) Each advanced student was required to complete some line of original research and report his results in a thesis. Thus the emphasis on physiological research, Fitz's special concern, was the hallmark of the Harvard program.

In keeping with one of the important goals of early physical education programs, the correction of postural defects through remedial exercises, Fitz invented two devices to insure more accurate recording of the examinations: first, the multiple camera and automatic labeling device which took three or four photographs of the same individual from different aspects on the same plate; this aided in the making of a photometric record of deformities. (108) Second, the scoliometer, made of transparent celluloid, which measured spinal curvatures and other asymmetries of the body and provided a graphic record. (110) Fitz also made a footprint instrument for measuring the degree of flat-footedness; a location reaction apparatus, which measured reaction time and accuracy; a device to measure the quickness and speed of thrust in sparring; a modified air gun to test sense of direction; and a ruler-like gadget to test ability to estimate size or distance. (12:98–104) For all of these inventions he devised appropriate tests and used them for studies on Harvard students and patients at the Boston Children's Hospital. Possibly his most famous invention (it earned him notice in the *New York Times* on May 20, 1934) was the micromanipulator for pure culture and microchemical work which aided in the process of rapid selection of unicellular organisms for pure culture, and also permitted rapid chemical analysis of particles. (106) At the first meeting of the American Society for Research in Physical Education in 1904, four of the nineteen papers were by Fitz (according to the preliminary program), including a description of a combined level and armed protractor for body measurements, a new pantograph for body tracing, and a level measurer. (103:61) In later years his studies seemed to be of a more physiological nature, including one on muscular cramp (1926) and one on the physiological cost of insufficient clothing (1914). In 1908 he published a book entitled *Principles of Physiology and Hygiene* (New York:Holt).

Fitz also found time to publish articles relating to the "Hygiene of Instruction in Elementary Schools" (1898), "Play as a Factor in Development" (1897), and "The Physical Examination of School Children" (1901), all of which appeared in the *American Physical Education Review*. In the first two articles he defined physical training as including gymnastics, athletics, manual training, and play and games. But he definitely endorsed the latter as the most important aspect.

> In the spontaneous play of the child with unrestricted opportunities we find again the conditions of use for all the tissues fully satisfied. . . . The whole body is brought to the highest perfection of structure and function. . . . The child is habituated to make rapid judgements in the presence of ever-changing relations. . . . In the game of tag, for instance, he is forced at each instance to watch his fellows, to run, stop, turn and dodge immediately. . . . In this way he gains that perfect control of his body which serves him throughout life. . . . We must not be misled by the fact that they [the mental effects] are subconscious, into thinking that they are not of value, and that the processes by which they are gained are not educational processes.
>
> We thus see that the play develops the individual into the perfect physical adult. It also develops to the highest degree the subconscious and conscious centres concerned in taking care of the body. (107:213)

George W. Fitz was a remarkable man. It is difficult to understand how he could have been so long unrecognized by the profession. Unfortunately his advice was not taken: physical education continued to propound theories without adequate research to support their validity. Even today there is more theory than the facts warrant, though present-day laboratories and researchers are being more seriously supported than heretofore. The establishment and direction of the experimental physiological research laboratory, and the emphasis on doing research in an undergraduate physical education major program, rank as most important contributions to the profession.

# BOSTON NORMAL SCHOOL OF GYMNASTICS

"The establishment by Mrs. Hemenway of the Boston Normal School of Gymnastics, which already has no equal in this country as regards the genuine and thorough character of its training, is an event of capital importance in the history of physical training in America." (362:54) This was the opinion of Edward Mussey Hartwell, spoken when he was Director of Physical Training in Boston. He testified to the special significance of the school which had been founded just two years earlier in 1889. At that time few schools were attempting to train physical education teachers* and unlike the others, the chief purpose of the Boston Normal School of Gymnastics (BNSG), at least at its inception, was to train teachers in the Swedish gymnastics system.

The origin of this emphasis is explained by events leading to the school's founding. Mary Hemenway and Amy Morris Homans had for some years worked together on philanthropic endeavors. Some of Mrs. Hemenway's wealth and energy had been put into establishing sewing and cooking classes in the Boston public schools. With Miss Homans, whom she first engaged as her executive secretary in 1877, she started a normal school for training teachers of cooking. It developed into the Boston Normal School of Household Arts and was transferred after her death to the State Normal School at Framingham. Already interested in domestic training, she was stimulated to thinking about physical culture by a commonplace incident:

> She was struck by the ease with which a strong nurse lifted and handled a heavy child. She reflected how few mothers of her acquaintance were able to do this; and next she was led to consider what advantage would come to the human race, and especially to city populations, if some well considered system of bodily training could be made a part of our general education. This was one of the reasons which led to the establishment of the Boston Normal School of Gymnastics, in which she spent many thousands for the instruction of the teachers in the public schools, until at length the Board of Education adopted the system for the children of Boston. (362:42-43)

---

* The others were: Normal College of the North American Gymnastic Union (1866), Sargent Normal School of Physical Education (1881), Brooklyn Normal School of Physical Education (1886), and the Physical Training Department of the International YMCA Training School in Springfield (now Springfield College) (1887). There were also two summer schools: Harvard Summer School of Physical Education (1887) and Chautauqua Summer School of Physical Education (1888).

At this time Baron Nils Posse was in Boston attempting to build a practice in Swedish medical gymnastics. Through the suggestion of a friend, Mrs. Hemenway engaged him in 1888 to demonstrate the Swedish system to volunteer teachers in a series of lessons. A second, two-year course, also free, was begun in the fall of 1888 with twenty-eight selected teachers.

In November 1889, Mrs. Hemenway, assisted by Miss Homans, instigated a "Conference in the Interest of Physical Training," hoping to bring Swedish gymnastics to the attention of the public. Attended by about two thousand people and presided over by the United States Commissioner of Education, William T. Harris, it was a landmark event in the history of physical education. During the conference the various "systems" were explained by leading exponents and compared as to their validity and uses. As an outgrowth of this conference and the demonstration of Posse (who spoke for the Swedish system at the Conference), the Boston School Committee, on June 24, 1890, ordered that "the Ling or Swedish system of educational gymnastics be introduced into all the public schools of this city." (207:332) Implementation of this act made apparent the shortage of trained teachers, despite the large number that had enrolled in the volunteer courses.

In the fall of 1889 the Boston Normal School of Gymnastics formally opened, offering a two-year course to prospective teachers of physical training:

> Its object is to supply the best opportunities in America for men and women who desire to prepare themselves to conduct gymnasia, or to direct physical training, according to the most approved modern methods. To this end thorough and scientific instruction is provided, not only in the Ling, or Swedish, system of gymnastics, but also in those general principles of physiology, psychology, and the hygiene of the human body, upon which sound physical training must always depend. . . . The Swedish system of pedagogical gymnastics is especially valuable because it is a work of physiological and hygienic engineering. (50:5–6)

All students in good health with the equivalent of a high school education were admitted but were considered to be on probation for one month. Tuition was $150 a year, a sum not sufficient to cover the cost of instruction. The catalogue stated that "the school is largely a contribution to the higher physical education of America."* (50:5) In a room on Park Street Baron Posse, the only teacher, conducted classes consisting of a daily gymnastic lesson and instruction in methods of teaching, the students practicing on each other; applied anatomy and physiology were also taught. In January, 1890 Posse resigned and Claes J. Enebuske, another graduate of the Gymnastics Central Institute, took his place, and retained the position until 1898.

---

* Another such contribution made ten years earlier, was the gift of a new gymnasium to Harvard College by Mrs. Hemenway's only son Augustus.

The next fall the BNSG was moved to a larger facility in the Paine Memorial Hall on Appleton Street where it remained until 1897 when it was moved to the building of the Massachusetts Charitable Mechanic Association on Huntington Avenue. Besides a thoroughly equipped gymnasium and a lecture hall, there was a library of about one thousand volumes, plus hundreds of photographs relating to physical training and pedagogy. There was also a complete set of anthropometric instruments and the Demeny machines for tracing the form of the thorax and studying the respiratory mechanism, the latter in keeping with Swedish gymnastics' emphasis on developing lung capacity. (50:16)

Theory courses were expanded at this time as shown by an 1893 catalogue description. The juniors took three hundred hours of science classes including physics, chemistry, biology, comparative anatomy and embryology, descriptive and topographical anatomy, applied anatomy, and physiology. In addition they studied first aid (emergency), anthropometry, and the theory of gymnastics. Seniors spent 170 hours on science courses, including pathology, physiology, hygiene, and histology. They also received fifteen hours of lectures in sanitary science (personal and public hygiene), seventy-eight in psychology and pedagogy, and fifty hours in the theory of gymnastics and the art of teaching. They studied applied anthropometry and spent eighty-five hours, a considerable amount of time, learning the technicalities of medical gymnastics. An equal amount of time was spent practice teaching in a nearby elementary school.

Activity classes for both years included a daily drill in pedagogical gym-

FIG. 58.   Gymnasium of the Boston Normal School of Gymnastics.

nastics.   The juniors also received a review and instruction in teaching gymnastics, and once a week they were given instruction in gymnastic games, social dancing and deportment.   The seniors' daily drill was supplemented by twice-weekly instruction in fencing.   (50:9)   Late in 1893, about a year after the first basketball rules were published, a male student was dispatched to Springfield to spend a day gathering information about the game.   Interest in sports was not lacking, but only swimming and illustrated lectures on athletics became a part of the curriculum (1897–1898) while Enebuske was principal of instruction.   In 1901–1902 courses were added in track and field, tennis, basketball, canoeing, and field hockey. The outdoor activities took place two or three afternoons a week at the Riverside Recreation Grounds, about ten miles west of Boston.   The theoretical curriculum remained fairly stable, but after the move to Wellesley time for sport activities was considerably increased; basketball and lacrosse were included in the program and instruction was given in teaching and refereeing sports. (334:620–623)

The faculty necessary to teach such a curriculum was secured by employing illustrious experts from nearby institutions on a part-time basis, and by holding a number of the science courses at the Massachusetts Institute of Technology, where faculty, lecture rooms and laboratories were made available to the school.   Thus the 1893 catalogue impressively listed five holders of the Ph.D. and three of the M.D.; of the other six faculty, three were graduates of the BNSG who assisted with specialized phases of physical training.   Among those listed were Josiah Royce, a famous professor of philosophy at Harvard, and H. P. Bowditch, Dean of the Harvard Medical School.   Melvin Ballou Gilbert, credited with developing and introducing aesthetic dancing (refer to p. 364), served at a later time as did Constance Applebee, responsible for the introduction of field hockey to the United States, and Ethel Perrin, a graduate of the school who achieved a great reputation as Supervisor of Physical Education in the Detroit schools. William Skarstrom, an 1895 graduate of the BNSG and holder of an M.D. from Harvard, joined the faculty in 1912 and remained until his retirement. He had previously been a part-time instructor (1899–1903) at the BNSG and the Massachusetts Institute of Technology and had also taught at Teachers College, Columbia University.   He achieved the academic status of professor and professor emeritus.   Through his work as the principal teacher of Swedish gymnastics, and his book *Gymnastic Teaching*, he introduced the first departures from traditional Ling gymnastics to be accepted by enthusiasts of the system.   As a teacher, writer and member of the profession, Skarstrom's contribution was well-recognized and through him the BNSG maintained its reputation for effective training of teachers of Swedish gymnastics.

From the school's founding until 1918 when she retired, Amy Morris Homans (1848–1933) served as Professor of Physical Education and was the school's director and guiding spirit.  Although she was untrained in physical education, she became one of the early leaders of the profession.  The American Physical Education Association recognized her leadership by conferring upon her the first Honor Award, issued in 1931.  She was also a charter member of the American Academy of Physical Education, founder and honorary member of the Eastern Association of Directors of Physical Education for College Women* (now the Eastern Association for Physical Education of College Women), and recipient of two honorary degrees: an M.A. from Bates College in 1909, and a Doctor of Pedagogy degree, awarded in 1930 by Russell Sage College.†  In 1967 her contributions were honored by the National Association of Physical Education for College Women, which established an annual Amy Morris Homans lecture, to be given each year at the national convention of the AAHPER.

Despite her leadership in the profession at large, her greatest contribution was to the students whose professional education she directed.  Her personality was legend:

> In conversation or talks to groups she was always interesting and direct, easily held the attention and often swayed opinion, clarified misunderstandings . . . and stimulated ambition to strive for the things she considered essential for the general good and for the individual's best interests. . . . She was scornful of a narrow-minded attitude, of pettiness, cheap and tawdry things, ostentation; she frowned on unseemly, boisterous, or undignified behavior.  She stressed the importance of self-respect, self-control, and dignity; of good taste, grooming, and manners of well-bred people.  In all these matters she set her students a good example.  She never hesitated in calling their attention to remissness in any one or more of these matters—for which many of her graduates are everlastingly grateful. (334:626)

Miss Homans carried through her program of teaching students to behave with proper dignity and to speak with a well-modulated voice, by individual conferences and occasional lectures in classes.  She aspired that each girl graduate not only as a trained physical educator, but as a lady of fine character.

One of the achievements of her career was the successful transfer of the BNSG to Wellesley College, where in 1909 it became the Department of Hygiene and Physical Education of Wellesley College.  Under the terms of Mary Hemenway's will the school was endowed to carry on for fifteen years

---

* In the spring of 1910 Homans invited the Directors of Physical Training and the Presidents of Athletic Associations of New England colleges for women to a meeting at Wellesley College.  After meeting annually for five years, in 1915 this group formally organized themselves as the Association of Directors of Physical Education for Women.  From this organization, ultimately, came the National Association of Physical Education for College Women.

† The Central School of Hygiene and Physical Education in New York City, which she helped establish and for which she served as Advisory Director, became a department of physical education at Russell Sage College in 1929.

(from her death in 1894) with Miss Homans as director, after which it was expected to become part of an institution of higher learning or find some other means of financial support.   Miss Homans chose Wellesley and a suitable building was erected to be used by the department and the college. Mary Hemenway Hall contained a large gymnasium (100' × 70') with a spectators' gallery, dressing room facilities, a room for corrective work, a multi-purpose room, a library, three lecture rooms, three laboratories, and offices.   The responsibilities of the department were enlarged to include the scheduling and teaching of the required courses (to which the Academic Council gave credit), as well as the preparation of teachers.

Incoming students were required to take the Wellesley College entrance examinations; they also were expected to be without disease and to have a keen sense of rhythm.   They had the alternative of taking five years of work and graduating with a degree from Wellesley with a major in gymnastic work, or studying three years and receiving a BNSG degree.   In 1917, as a result of Miss Homan's efforts, the department became one of the first in the country to offer a graduate program for students with a Bachelor's degree in physical education.   In 1923 when she was an emeritus professor, the first three graduates received their Master of Arts degrees. As a graduate department it achieved great eminence for a long period of time but unfortunately was forced to close in 1954 when the academic policy of Wellesley College no longer supported a professional graduate department on campus.   Endowments were maintained for several years thereafter.   The Amy Morris Homans Fellowship gave financial aid to women for research and study.   A collection of rare books from the great library which was amassed continues to be used by the profession in its now location at the University of North Carolina in Greensboro.

The BNSG was a popular institution; in its first twenty years the average enrollment was sixty-six.   At its peak in 1908 the student body numbered eighty-three. (359:9)   More than six hundred students were graduated from the BNSG and the department, including nine men during the time it was coeducational (before the transfer to Wellesley).   Among these were some of America's most famous women physical educators, including Ethel Perrin, Senda Berenson, Lillian Drew, Blanche Trilling, Mabel Lee, and Mary Channing Coleman.   They took positions as teachers and directors in colleges, schools, YWCAs, and as specialists in medical gymnastics; Miss S. J. Jacobs, for example, was appointed Director of Physical Training in the Los Angeles Public Schools in 1895, and her classmate Miss Alma Greene was hired to spend a year in Europe giving two children gymnastic training. (278:86)   Through its well-prepared graduates the Boston Normal School of Gymnastics was an important influence on the practice of American physical education.

# NILS POSSE

## 1862-1895

Baron Nils Posse, more than anyone else, was responsible for introducing Swedish gymnastics to America. Major V. G. Balcke, professor at the Royal Gymnastics Central Institute of Stockholm, Sweden, summed up his accomplishments in a memorial article:

> He has, in a certain sense, there [the United States] been the path-breaker for Swedish gymnastics, as he was commissioned to organize an institute for the education of teachers of gymnastics—"The Normal School of Gymnastics"—in Boston [BNSG]. Later he opened his own widely known and highly esteemed institute of the same kind, "The Posse Gymnasium." He was Commissioner for the Swedish Tourist Association, etc., and other Swedish sporting organizations at the World's Fair, in Chicago, and arranged there in a meritorious manner the Tourist, Sporting, and Gymnastic Department, which, as is well known, in a certain degree gave character to the Swedish exhibit. He has also worked for the spreading of Swedish gymnastics in America through public lectures and a wide-spread activity as a writer; besides, he organized in Boston a Swedish Gymnastic Club, which on several occasions in an efficient manner has demonstrated our excellent system of gymnastics. (191:231)

These were notable accomplishments for a life that ended with heart failure after only thirty-three years.

The Baron had the proper background and training for his work. His father, a Swedish nobleman and army major, was at one time head of the Royal Army Staff College at Marieberg, possibly during the time when Per Ling instructed the officers there in gymnastics and fencing. After high school Nils completed the fifteen-month course at the Royal Military School at Karlberg, the place where Ling got his start as a fencing-master and taught from 1813–1825. His connection with Ling became more direct when he attended the two-year course at his Central Institute of Gymnastics, though the founder was by then long dead. Prior to that experience Posse spent five years in the army earning the rank of second lieutenant. When he graduated from the RCGI at age twenty-five, he left for America, intending to make a career of medical gymnastics. Within the first three years he published a pamphlet in English on *Medical Gymnastics* (Boston, 1887) which, according to Posse, was the work which led Mary Hemenway to him. (289:7)

Fig. 59. Baron Nils Posse.

Mary Hemenway and the Baron provided each other with entrances into American physical education, though neither had any previous connection with it. Relying on his knowledge, and guided by her own philanthropic spirit, Mrs. Hemenway and Posse approached the Boston School Committee and secured permission to furnish free training to volunteer teachers. With Baron Posse as teacher, by 1890 more than two hundred teachers, masters and submasters had received training in the Swedish system. From that time Posse's career as a trainer of teachers of Swedish gymnastics was established and continued until his death in 1895.

In 1889 Posse was simultaneously giving classes to the Boston public school teachers, instructing the first students at the BNSG, giving public lectures, and arguing the values of Swedish gymnastics before the School Committee. In January, 1890 he resigned from the BNSG and a month later opened his own gymnasium and school on Irvington Street. He later stated that "since severing his connection with the Boston Normal School of Gymnastics, the author has been enabled to propagate the system on a larger scale from a school of his own. . . ." (289:9) In the last six years of his life, ninety-six women and six men graduated from the Posse Gymnasium. (207:379) After his death his wife, Baroness Rose Posse, assumed the directorship, retaining it until 1915 when it was turned over to another famous gymnast, Hartvig Nissen,* under whom it continued as the Posse-

---

* Nissen, a Norwegian, founded a Swedish Health Institute in Washington, D.C., had taught Swedish gymnastics at Washington's Franklin School as early as 1883, and at Johns Hopkins in 1887. From 1891–1900 he was assistant director and then director of physical training in the Boston public schools. He also taught Swedish gymnastics at the Harvard Summer School and the Sargent School.

Nissen School. The Posse-Nissen School, before it closed in 1942, had broadened its curriculum to include all subjects then a part of American physical education. At that time it merged with the Bouvé-Boston School of Physical Education; eighteen students made the transfer along with the Posse Institute's (as it was then called) records and materials. (368:197)

The Posse Gymnasium had three departments: pedagogical for the training of teachers; educational for the physical education of men, women and children; and medico-gymnastic for the treatment of diseases, and for training medical gymnasts (masseurs). The two-year course included both teacher-training and medical gymnastics; a third-year, post-graduate course was also offered. The curriculum was modelled after that of the Royal Gymnastic Central Institute in Stockholm. A high school diploma was a prerequisite for entry; the student also had to pass an examination in anatomy, physiology, kinesiology, and practical gymnastics to be admitted to the senior year. The medico-gymnastic department was successful in securing recognition for its area of work. Five hospitals in Boston established massage clinics, with graduates of the Posse Gymnasium as operators, and senior students were able to practice their skills in three of those hospitals. Some idea of the school's program and outreach can be gleaned from the following 1895 news note:

> The graduating exercises of the class of '94 took place in the gymnasium, on the evening of May 17th. The regular work was illustrated, including fencing. The last thing on the program was a game of Basket Ball. . . . There were twenty-four members in the normal class and fourteen post-graduates. The audience was the largest ever seen in the gymnasium except on the occasion of the first graduation (in June, 1890) when over 1,000 persons were in attendance. (266:68)

The foremost apologist for Swedish gymnastics in America, the Baron commented that he was once accused of "being so liberal that Sweden was too small to hold me." (9:165) In part, this probably stemmed from his belief that all gymnastic systems had common elements because men were physically the same the world over:

> Since body is the basis of human nature . . . it seems reasonable to assume that the education of the body must follow laws quite as definite as those relating to the mind and that all physical training must be based upon the laws of Nature and not upon any arbitrary or artificial consideration. The principles of gymnastics must of necessity be the same the world over, and the so-called systems must become very similar to each other, if they are built on the same leading laws. (290:169)

He looked forward, therefore, to the time when the battle of the systems would be over:

> Physical education has reached a new era: one where the word "system" with its diverse prefixes of nationality will disappear and where the teacher will cease

to feel the handicap of restricting superscriptions. Science and arts are cosmopolitan not national, so the science of gymnastics and the art of applying it must belong to the world at large, even though it happens that its foremost investigators must claim one section of the earth as their native land. (290:169)

However, as the last sentence infers, there was no doubt in Posse's mind that the Swedish system was the *only* truly scientific or rational system and ultimately would prevail over all others. He generously stated that "it is true that scientists from everywhere have added material to the general knowledge of the subject of gymnastics," but "the quantity and quality of their contributions are disappearingly small, when compared to the achievements of the Swedes, and certainly their systems of gymnastics are often and unmistakably at variance with the laws of Nature." (290:170)

The boast that the Swedish system was the only truly scientific system was not based upon research, but on the idea that "science is organized common sense" (290:170), and that the Swedish system was rationally organized. According to Posse, it used only movements that would effect development or needed corrections and used exercises that did not violate any laws of physiology, physics or psychology. Apparatus was employed only when it could produce better results, never for its own sake. Movements were accordingly classified as to effect, e.g. arch-flexions and respiratory, rather than by apparatus, e.g. wand drills and the horizontal bar. All the exercises advocated were placed in order according to the laws of progresssion. Because of this, modifications of the system or a combined American system drawing the best from each, was a mistaken notion: "to gather a few ideas from Swedish gymnastics, a few from the German, a few from some other source, and shake them up together may be systematic, but it is not rational and certainly cannot be any improvement upon these ideas which have been arranged in scientific sequence, the evolution of decades of research." (290:170)

Posse's excuse for allowing the use of dumbbells, Indian clubs, and chest weights, which were not then in popular use in Sweden and did not, therefore, belong to the system, was that they were a popular Americanism. As long as they had the desired effect they could be considered part of rational gymnastics, and be shown to demonstrate the *spirit* of Ling whose only law was the law of effect. Thus he rejected doctrinaire traditionalism and adhered to the spirit of scientific gymnastics. It was probably this flexibility which permitted Swedish gymnastics to survive in America in competition with the more popular German apparatus.

Besides the Posse Normal School, the Baron's greatest contributions to American physical education lay in his papers, both spoken and written. At the famous "Conference in the Interest of Physical Training" held in Boston in 1889, his paper on "The Chief Characteristics of the Swedish System of Gymnastics" (282) was the first and one of the most important documents issued on the subject in this country. His books, *The Swedish*

*System of Educational Gymnastics* (1890), *The Special Kinesiology of Educational Gymnastics* (1894), and the *Handbook of School-Gymnastics* (1891), all published in Boston by Lee and Shepard, the *Posse Gymnasium Journal* which always contained articles by him, as well as articles written in various other journals, together constituted a complete delineation of the Swedish system and a guide to its use. The *Handbook*, for example, contained one hundred progressive tables of exercises which a teacher could use in schools.

Thus in his eight years in the United States, the Baron Nils Posse helped establish Swedish educational gymnastics in the United States and publicized the benefits and workings of the Swedish systems of school and medical gymnastics; he established a normal school where he trained more than a hundred teachers and masseurs who in turn spread the work throughout the country. With his "liberal attitude" he paved the way for Swedish gymnastics to be utilized in the United States.

# EDWARD MUSSEY HARTWELL

## 1850-1922

Edward Mussey Hartwell should be considered one of the fore-fathers of physical education in the United States for his contribution toward defining and explicating the profession. He accomplished this primarily by surveying physical education in both the historical and con-temporary contexts, and presenting to the country a comprehensive picture which could be used as a basis for making decisions and forging new pro-grams.

To such a task Hartwell brought an unusual insight and openminded sensitivity, bolstered by a considerable formal education. The son of a one-time Harvard College Latin tutor and lawyer, with a long New England ancestry, Edward was brought up in Littleton, Massachusetts near Boston. He graduated from the Boston Latin School and went to Amherst College where he earned his A.B. in 1873 and his M.A. in 1876.* While at Amherst he was obviously acquainted with and influenced by Edward Hitchcock. He rowed on the crew and in his junior year was captain of his class in the gymnasium, having in those days a participant's enthusiasm for sports and fitness activities. He earned a Ph.D. in animal physiology at Johns Hopkins University (1881), and an M.D. from the Miami Medical College in Cincinnati, Ohio (1882). His first jobs were in high schools: one year in Orange, New Jersey and three at the Boston Latin School (1874–1877). Among his duties at the latter institution was the conduct of light gym-nastic exercises on the order of the Amherst College plan. As a student at Johns Hopkins he was a fellow in biology, and in 1882 he accepted the position there of Instructor in Physical Culture. He equipped the gym-nasium, newly opened in 1883, with Sargent's developing apparatus and introduced the Sargent method of individual, rather than class, instruction. After two years he became Associate in Physical Training and Director of the Gymnasium, a position he resigned in 1890 to become Director of Physical Training for the Boston Public Schools. In 1897 he became secre-tary of the Department of Municipal Statistics in Boston and thus ended his work in physical education, although he continued to be active in the profession until the end of the century.

He served as president of the AAAPE from 1891–1892, and from 1895-

---

* He also received an honorary LL.D. from Amherst in 1898.

1899, and as first chairman of the section on History and Bibliography of Physical Education of the AAAPE, voted into existence at the seventh annual meeting in 1892. In the preparation of his reports he travelled widely, first through the eastern part of the United States (from Maine to Tennessee in the summer of 1884), and then in 1885 to Europe where he studied about hygiene and gymnastics in England, Frankfurt, Berlin, and Vienna. He also witnessed in Dresden the Sixth General Gymnastic Festival of the German Turnerschaft. It was in Germany that he first learned of the existence of the North American Turnerbund. In 1889 he again spent four months in Europe, this time concentrating on the medical

Fig. 60.   Edward Mussey Hartwell.

application of exercise, studying chiefly at the Royal Gymnastics Central Institute in Stockholm.*  On his third visit to Europe the following summer he gathered materials on school gymnastics and play, thus rounding out his knowledge of what was happening in physical education in Europe.

The first result of his observations was a report for the United States Bureau of Education which was published as a Circular of Information of the Bureau of Education, No. 5—1885 and titled *Physical Training in American Colleges and Universities* (161).  The purpose and content of the report are best illustrated by the introductory letter from John Eaton, Commissioner of the Bureau of Education, at whose request it was written:

> Beyond the instruction in hygiene the main attempts to conserve health in the public schools have consisted in introducing German gymnastics, or in paying a more careful attention to the laws of heating and lighting and the supply of pure air and water.  Sometimes the introduction of manual labor has been looked upon as the sure prevention of all disease; athletic sports have been tried; and recently more careful attention has been given to the whole subject, especially in connection with our colleges.  The Ling system of gymnastics is received with increasing favor.  More and more believe that the best physical training will not aim to make either acrobats or athletes, but to promote health of body and mind.  The efforts of Prof. Edward Hitchcock at Amherst College and of Dr. D. A. Sargent of Harvard have been attended with most beneficial results, and serve greatly to increase the care of the health of college students.
>
> The number of gymnasia of merit has greatly increased.  Calls for a report upon this new development in physical training have been urgent and frequent. I have therefore employed E. M. Hartwell, M.D., Ph.D., to collect the information accessible and prepare a report upon the subject. (161)

With this charge Hartwell surveyed existing programs and prepared a comprehensive report which included:  information on the "ideals of manly excellence"; the historical development of gymnastics in America from its introduction through the "new gymnastics"; the program at Amherst College which was an early prototype; information on the gymnasium buildings constructed in this country, including descriptions and plans of the principal ones; a section on Dudley Allen Sargent's methods and apparatus; details about military drill as a part of physical training; information on "athletic sports" in the United States, details of the Yale system of athletics, and discussion of the problems of professionalism; a section on physical education in women's colleges; and one on instruction in hygiene which also included a chart of forty-six of the principal colleges and universities in the country.  The latter gave details of their programs in hygiene, both practical and theoretical, including information on, among other things, the number of lectures given, the style of drill adopted, and the author of the textbook used.  A section on physical training in Germany and

---

* Apparently he read Swedish, for in 1893 he translated Kleen's *Handbook of Massage* from Swedish to English.  This makes his later citations of Ling's theories especially credible.

the North American Turnerbund was appended when Hartwell learned of German gymnastics during his European trip.* The report constitutes an important historical document giving details on the status of physical training in 1885 that are otherwise not available. In its time it must have served as an impetus to developing new programs and provided guidelines for designing and equipping gymnasiums. Considering the very limited professional literature then available, most of which dealt with directions for exercising or details on how to play sports and games, such information must have been extremely useful.

Hartwell's other survey was published as a chapter "On Physical Training," in the 1897–1898 *Report of the Commissioner of Education* (159). The emphasis was on the history of physical education—particularly its European antecedents. It treated physical education in the United States historically, tracing its development until the time of the report, including a short section on gymnastics in city schools. This report really established the historical context of physical education and brought together, perhaps for the first time,† details of what Hartwell called "the most representative and typical forms of physical training. . . . (1) the Grecian, (2) the mediaeval or knightly, (3) the British, (4) the German; and (5) the Ling or Swedish." (159:514)  The information gathered in Europe provided a starting point for most of the endeavors since produced by historians of the profession. Fred Eugene Leonard, author of America's first published book on *The History of Physical Education*, dedicated it: "To the memory of Dr. Edward Mussey Hartwell who first in America blazed the trail which I have tried to follow."

Prior to the publication of that document, Hartwell expressed his belief in the importance of such a study. Speaking at the first meeting of the Section on the History and Bibliography of Physical Education, at the eighth annual AAAPE meeting, he said:

> One of the principal obstacles to the advancement of physical education in America, it seems to me, is to be found in the general ignorance of the teachings of science as to the nature and effects of such training and in the prevalent indifference to the plain teachings of experience as to the best that has been done towards making physical education a genuine and efficient department of instruction. . . . If we fail to apprehend and to enforce upon our followers the lessons in strategy to be derived from a study of the precepts and campaigns of those who have displayed generalship in our cause, and content ourselves with mere drill and tactics, any efforts that our Association may put forth for the advancement of physical education will resemble a series of guerilla raids, rather than the prose-

---

* On the basis of this information, he succeeded in introducing German gymnastics into the mainstream of physical education by inviting its representatives to attend and present papers at the second AAAPE meeting.

† As far as this author can ascertain, Hartwell's chapter was the first systematic attempt in any language to present details of the history of modern physical education.

cution of a campaign in legitimate warfare. . . . What seems to be most needed at the present time, is a handbook printed in English, to serve both as an elementary text-book in the history of physical education and a guide to its more important literature. (163:128–129)

He went on to recommend that a skeleton bibliography be compiled and that an "Annual Bibliography of Current Publications on Physical Training" be published, a practice continued throughout the publishing history of the *American Physical Education Review* (1896–1929).

Hartwell himself made frequent use of historical examples to make his point. When the subject of physical training in the army was the theme of a speech by the Surgeon General of the United States Army, at the sixth annual AAAPE meeting, Hartwell was quick to detail the experiences of France, England and Germany in that regard. He recommended that "there should be a professor having this matter in charge on the academic board at West Point. If the physical training of the army is to proceed in a well ordered way, *taking account of the experience of other nations in this respect*, an army gymnastic department will, it seems to me, be found necessary." (8:78, italics added) He turned his presidential address on "The Conditions and Prospects of Physical Education in the United States," given at the seventh annual meeting, into a historical review of "the course of events within the field of physical education during the first period of our existence." (9:14) Hartwell bolstered his speeches on athletics vs. gymnastics, given in various forms to different groups, with historical observations about the results of such programs on the nations which chose them. For example, his opening address to the Conference in the Interest of Physical Training (Boston, 1889), on "The Nature of Physical Training, and the Best Means of Securing Its Ends" (282:5–22), attempted to set direction and unify the competing points of view then vying for supremacy in American physical education. Hartwell discussed the historical unity of the field: "The plays of the kindergarten, the athletic sports to which British and American youth are so devoted, and the systematic gymnastics of the Swedes and Germans have all developed from one germ, from healthful play. . . ." (282:19)

Hartwell did not endorse athletics as the proper core of physical education, despite his statement that "in the athletic sports of young men we see the highest and fullest expression of the play instinct." (282:19) In a statement that is probably representative of the perceptions of most of the professionals of his day, he enunciated his support for gymnastics over athletics in a physical education program:

> The essential difference between athletics and gymnastics is one of aim. The aim of athletics, unless of the illegitimate professional sort, is pleasurable activity for the sake of recreation; that of gymnastics is discipline or training for pleasure, health, and skill. We have but to compare the aims, methods, and results of each, and to call to mind the characteristics of the nations which have affected

athletics on the one hand and gymnastics on the other, to perceive that gymnastics are more highly developed, and present more features of educational value. Gymnastics, as compared with athletics, are more comprehensive in their aims, more formal, elaborate, and systematic in their methods, and are productive of more solid and considerable results. . . . Gymnastics have been most popular and general among the most highly trained nations, such as the Greeks of old and the Germans of to-day. The most athletic, and, at the same time, one of the most ill-trained of modern nations, is the British. (282:19–20)

Hartwell argued logically for the place of physical education within education:

The aim of any and all human training is to educe faculty, to develop power. As the means of developing power, certain actions are selected, taught, and practised as exercises; and power when developed takes the form of some action or exercise due to muscular contractions. Viewed thus, muscular exercise is at once a means and an end of mental, and moral, as well as of physical training; since without bodily actions we have no means of giving expression to mental power, artistic feeling, or spiritual insight. (282:5)

He believed that one of the bars to physical education for recognition by the academic world was that "they do not recognize the fact that physical training has a substantive existence and being, has a history as an organized branch of education in the leading countries of Europe." (11:83)

The contribution of Edward Mussey Hartwell, the first American physical education historian, should be viewed in two lights: he clearly demonstrated the need for understanding the historical as well as contemporary circumstances of the field and for the usage of such understanding as a basis for making decisions; he was the first to gather, organize and present data in a scholarly way on the history of European physical education and the growth and development of the subject in the United States. He was honored for his work by being made a Fellow in Memoriam of the American Academy of Physical Education.

# DELPHINE HANNA

## 1854-1941

The name of Delphine Hanna is associated with many of the best-known figures in physical education in this country. In her zest for knowledge about physical activity she took courses from Dio Lewis, Baron Nils Posse and Dudley Allen Sargent. During her tenure as Director of the women's gymnasium at Oberlin College she taught and guided such illustrious people as Thomas Wood, Luther Halsey Gulick, Fred Eugene Leonard, Jesse Feiring Williams, Jay Bryan Nash, and Gertrude Moulton (one of her successors at Oberlin). Were one to trace their students, and their students' students, a family tree of famous physical educators could be constructed, with Hanna in reigning position.

She was one of the best educated women physical educators of her time, having graduated in 1874 from the Brockport State Normal School at Brockport, New York, the Sargent Normal School with the full certificate for one year's work (1885), the University of Michigan (1890) with an M.D., and Cornell University (1901) with a Bachelor of Arts degree. Her Master of Arts degree was honorary, having been presented by Oberlin College in 1901. She also spent many summers in school beginning in 1884 with a summer course offered by Dio Lewis. The next year, having completed her work at the Sargent School, she remained in Boston to study under Dr. Bradford at a newly developed orthopedic center; she learned to diagnose and treat lateral spine curvature and also found time during the evenings to attend the Currie School of Expression where she learned the Delsarte principles of poise and balance. In 1887 she attended the first session of the Harvard Summer School of Physical Education, and in the summer of 1893 she took Baron Posse's course in Swedish gymnastics which was given in conjunction with the World's Fair.

When not in school as a student she was there as a faculty member. For the first ten years after graduating from Brockport she taught in grade schools in Monroe County, New York, Ottawa, and Kansas and the Fairport School in New York. In 1885 she was appointed Instructor in Physical Culture at Oberlin College; from 1887 to 1903 she was Director of Physical Training, Women's Department, and in 1903 was appointed to a full professorship, the first ever awarded a woman in physical education. Upon retirement in 1920 she was designated Emeritus Professor of Physical Education.

FIG. 61.    Delphine Hanna.

Her first interest in physical training had been sparked by observations of her elementary school children who seemed to lack the desired robust health.    Her work with Sargent further served to strengthen her orientation to physical education as a means to health and probably influenced her subsequent study of orthopedics and medicine.    In fact, her early program at Oberlin, with its physical examinations, anthropometric measurements, close attention to individuals, and the purchase of a campsite for special activities, strongly resembled Sargent's program at the Hemenway gymnasium, and much of the apparatus she acquired at Oberlin was of his design, including pulley weights and mechanical bars, vertical ladders, and floor racks. (217:110)    In keeping with this influence, she believed it was the responsibility of the gymnasium teacher to use gymnastic exercises and massage to treat postural deformities, particularly lateral curvature of the spine, or scoliosis:

> There are various reasons why lateral curvature should be treated by the gymnasium teacher.  At present physical education is carried on largely in connection with our schools.  The initial stage of lateral curvature—that reached by preventative measures—corresponds to the time spent in elementary education. The stage of development requiring remedial measures, corresponds to the time spent in secondary or higher education.  The number of cases presented to the gymnasium teacher is much larger than that presented to the orthopedic surgeon. (11:118)

In that same speech which was presented at the ninth annual meeting of the American Association for the Advancement of Physical Education (the

AAAPE), she observed that "Orthopedic surgeons recommend gymnastics for all stages of lateral curvature. The facilities for such treatment are usually much better in the gymnasium than they are in the doctor's office or at home, and the exercises are, as a rule, more regularly taken." (11:118) She prescribed teaching "correct methods of walking, standing and sitting," and "individual instruction . . . until the teacher is sure that they are making efforts in the right direction." (11:120–121) In an article detailing gymnastic lessons she described what amounted to a body mechanics orientation:

> These lessons have been arranged with special reference to establishing the poise that is best adapted to the routine movements of everyday life such as walking, standing, going up and down stairs and the like. . . . These lessons should make some connection between the way a pupil carries herself in the gymnasium and the way she carries herself at home and on the street. (151:515)

She believed that regular gymnastic drills were valuable for treatment, especially in the initial stages when students were in elementary school. However, she was also convinced of the efficacy of gymnastics at the college level where, with anthropometric measurements and subjective reporting, she demonstrated that the health of college women could be improved. Her published data on one hundred women in September, 1899 showed that after about four months work, for four half-hours a week, "forty-eight report their general health the same as on entering, forty-three report a decided improvement, the health of nine is not so good. . . ." (153:279–280)

It was for the scope of her work at Oberlin, rather than her ideas, that Delphine Hanna achieved a reputation as one of the most outstanding women in the field. She had applied to Oberlin for a position because it was known for its liberal, experimental approach to education—it had been the first college in the English speaking world to admit women and blacks from the time it opened in 1833, and in 1841 it awarded the first A.B. degrees to three women for completion of a program identical to that of male graduates. Such a college was delighted to have Hanna but could not afford to employ her. She began her career there receiving only three hundred dollars for the year to cover living expenses, and an equal sum contributed by a friend for equipping her gymnasium which was equally impoverished. Hanna described it in a 1929 letter to alumnae:

> It consisted of what is now the exercise room in the brick part of the building. It had five dressing places, partitioned off from the north end of the room with dirty red curtains in front of them. On top was piled a camping outfit. . . . In one corner was a pile of oats; on the walls were various crude drawings. These I had removed and the room thoroughly cleaned. (53:647–648)

From these beginnings she established a program; her slim budget was used to have the necessary apparatus constructed according to her direction.

She began by examining 125 women and grouping them into classes. Besides the students, she had a class for faculty women, one for grade school children, and one for men. The purpose of the latter class was to train men to instruct other men students for whom no program or teacher were provided. Thomas Wood, Luther Gulick and Fred Leonard got their starts in physical education as a result of being members of that early class. Wood later wrote that "my own view of the importance, possibilities and future of physical education as a vital branch of education was largely opened up and illuminated by her instruction." (217:110)

She also gave private lessons to train girls who wanted to be physical educators, but this one-year program was not listed in the college catalogue and graduates received a certificate from Hanna, not a degree. However, by 1892 she succeeded in having her Normal Course in Physical Training catalogued and extended to two years. A circular announced its purposes:

> For some years past instruction has been given, to a limited number, in the theory and practice of Physical Training. It is now proposed to extend the course and throw it open to all suitable applicants. The aim of the course is— To prepare competent directors and teachers of physical training in colleges, academies, Young Women's Christian Associations, and public schools. Applicants must be graduates of a good high school or have had an equivalent amount of instruction. . . . Tuition for first year, $50. Tuition for second year, $100. Certificates will be given to all who satisfactorily complete the course. All privileges open to regular college students are granted to students in this department. (263:166)

The course of study was similar to that offered by other normal schools at the time (refer to chapter on Sargent School, or Boston Normal School of Gymnastics). It was heavily scientific in its theory work and included prescribed work for individual improvement and daily drills in class exercises, as well as instruction in the arrangement of floor work and the management of classes. Students had an opportunity to practice teach in the college and in local public schools. Hanna was assisted by Fred Leonard, who by then was Acting Professor of Physiology and Director of the Men's Gymnasium; other faculty from the college taught various classes. (263:166) Although normal courses in physical education were by no means commonly found in regular colleges (only Harvard and Stanford had announced programs at that time), an editorial in the newest professional publication, *Physical Education*, unhappily noted that it was only a two-year course:

> If we were connected with an academic institution, we certainly would feel that the course under our general supervision must be the equal in point of time required and of scholarship demanded to that of other schools in the country. . . . We trust that the course at Oberlin . . . may be extended so as to be equal to the other Normal courses on Physical Training and a degree given for the course as it is at Harvard. (263:165–166)

The editors also questioned why the course was for women only, given the coeducational nature of the college. Between 1892 and 1900, thirty-five women earned certificates. Finally, in 1900, after many attempts, a four-year course leading to a Bachelor of Arts degree was established. It was the only one of the four degree courses then available in the United States which was administered by a woman.*

In addition to her growing teacher-training course, Dr. Hanna conducted a program which extended to every student in the college. Besides the gymnasium work she stressed outdoor activity and was particularly concerned that each student should excel in at least one sport playable after college. Swimming, tennis, skating, bicycling, and hiking were among those offered. Her statement on the advantages of skating was typical of her general beliefs: "It is a good physical exercise as it increases lung power, establishes poise and develops easy, graceful movements." (150:56) She favored competitive athletics for women, and organized the Gymnasium and Field Association (1904) to carry on some form of intramural program. Skating was one of its first events because of its suitability for women, and Hanna did comment that she was "strong in the belief that the Women's Athletic Association should differ very widely from those of the Men's Association." (150:56) In a letter to *Mind and Body* she recounted her decision to hold a skating contest:

> One of the privileges of the newly organized Gymnasium and Field Association is the use of the covered skating rink. This created a need of an event and a skating contest was instituted. . . . It promises to be popular; and its advantages are that in preparing for it it attracts a number of girls out of doors when outdoor sports are few; it makes independent skaters of girls who have always depended on a partner. . . . Then, too, it makes an attractive enthusiastic audience of college men and women, each class anxious to have its representatives win. All this forms a gay setting for the eight graceful girls who have already won the championship in their class contest and are now ready to contest for the inter-class championship. (150:56)

Hanna's anthropometric measurements earned her the most fame in the profession. By 1893 she had prepared a chart based upon examination of 1600 women (Fig. 62). It included six measures of height (sitting, to the knee, navel, sternum, etc.), twenty-six measures of girth (ninth rib, thigh, calf, instep, elbow, etc.), two of depth (the chest and abdomen), six of breadth (neck, hips, nipples, etc.), seven of length (shoulder to elbow, stretch of arms, etc.), five of strength (back, chest, forearm, etc.), and capacity of lungs. In 1895 a second chart was made which showed the effects of fifty hours of exercise on five hundred college women over an eight-month period. The chart was modernized in 1915. An examiner could record an individual's measurements on the chart and graphically see

---

* The other courses were offered at Stanford, University of California, and the University of Nebraska. Harvard's course was by then entirely pre-medical.

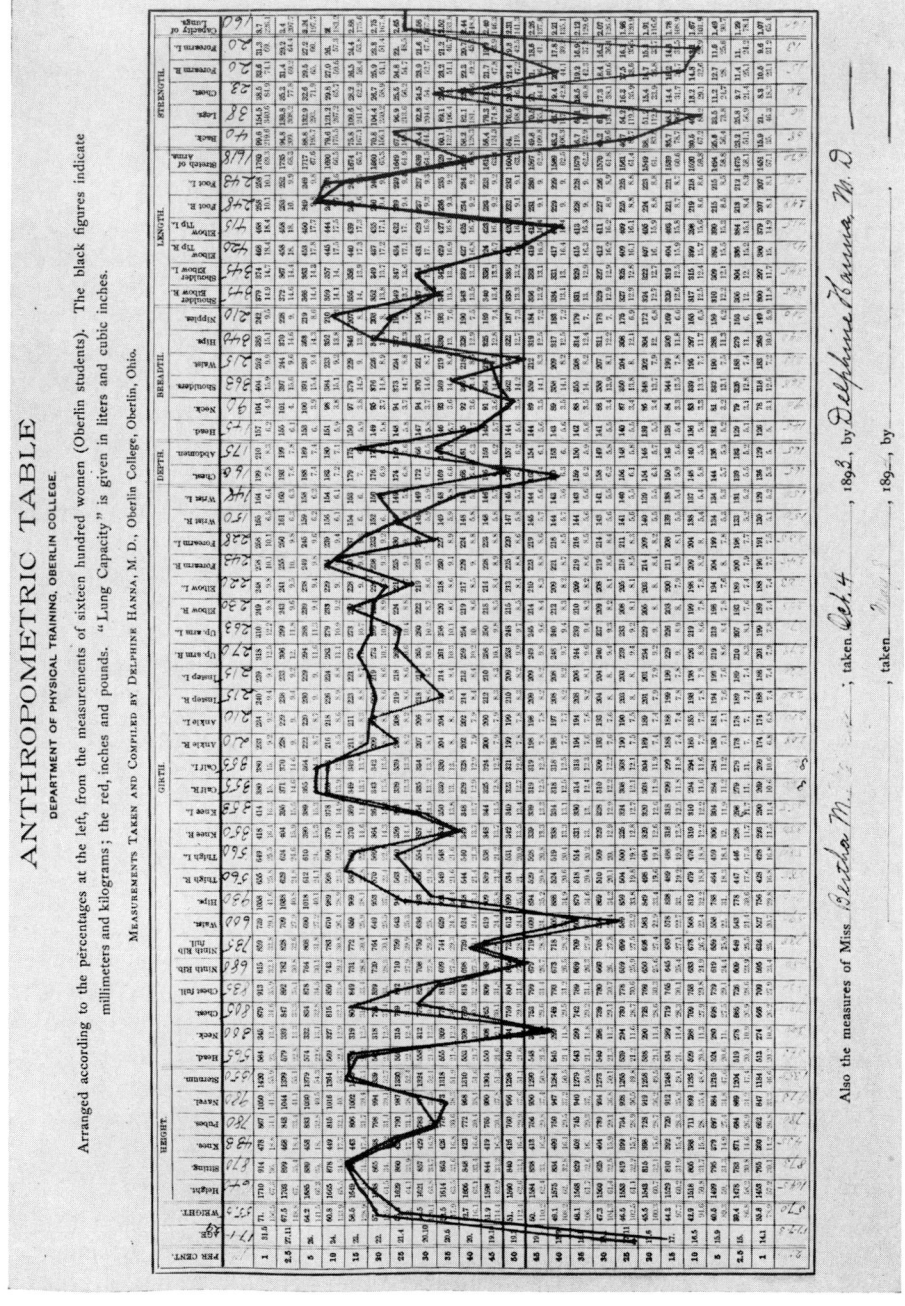

FIG. 62.   Sample of an Anthropometric Table.

precisely in what percent of the sixteen hundred she fell for each measurement.  These charts were widely distributed and used by other colleges employing the individual examination and anthropometric technique for prescribing exercises.  Until Hanna's work norms were not readily available for women, though Sargent and Hitchcock had excellent ones for men.

Hanna was not a writer.  She wrote no books and published few accounts in professional journals, but she was an active, participating member in professional organizations.  One of her best known researches was the survey she published in 1903 on the "Present Status of Physical Training in Normal Schools" (152), in which she presented in chart form pertinent information on the founding, length of course, entrance requirements, and graduates of all the programs then in existence.  She was in the first group of Honor Award recipients in 1931, each of the forty-eight being named as Fellows of the American Physical Education Association.  In 1925 she was selected by her alma mater, the University of Michigan, for membership in the Michigan Hall of Fame.  For a woman to pioneer a new general education program and a new degree program in a private college, before the turn of the century, was a noteworthy accomplishment.  When in 1936 Minnie Lynn, an eminent Oberlin graduate, communicated with Delphine Hanna in reference to a thesis she was preparing on her professional career, Hanna wrote: "I do not want my biography written, for if my work was worthy it is still in progress." (217:51)  The generations of students spawned in her tradition at Oberlin would testify that it is.

# WILLIAM GILBERT ANDERSON

## 1860-1947

In response to invitations from WILLIAM G. ANDERSON, M.D., of the Adelphi Academy, about sixty representatives of various educational institutions and friends of Physical Culture assembled at Adelphi Academy, Brooklyn, N.Y., Nov. 27, 1885, at 10 o'clock. (21:3)

Thus the first paragraph of the record of the first meeting of the Association for the Advancement of Physical Education* indicated the role William Gilbert Anderson had in its formation.

Many years later, in an article in the *Journal of Health and Physical Education*, Anderson discussed his reasons for calling the meeting. He had visited every gymnasium near New York City and inquired about the system of instruction used; he discovered that each individual taught his own. "Feeling that I got little from these visits and interviews and strongly impressed that every man was for himself, the Turners excepted, and that there was neither agreement nor cooperation among the so-called 'Americans,' I wondered if we could not come together and discuss carefully the situation." (15:4) Anderson then secured the support of a number of influential men, such as Charles Pratt, head of Standard Oil and President of the Adelphi Academy Board of Directors, Dr. Albert C. Perkins, Principal of Adelphi, Dr. Andrew D. White, President of Cornell University, and the Reverends E. P. Thwing and T. DeWitt Talmage of Brooklyn:

> With these influential names I wrote to Dr. Edward Hitchcock of Amherst College. He was most enthusiastic and at once joined us.
> Now I felt that I could go to Dr. Dudley A. Sargent of Harvard who was the most influential or powerful man in physical education in this country. The Doctor was not over-ardent, but said he would give the matter consideration. He attended the gathering and put back of it his strength and ability. He should receive the credit due him for he was a tower of strength.
> I was now ready to issue the invitation. . . . (15:61)

---

* A year later the organization was retitled the American Association for the Advancement of Physical Education (AAAPE); in 1903 it became the American Physical Education Association (APEA); in 1937 the APEA and the Department of School Health and Physical Education of the National Education Association, merged, creating the American Association for Health and Physical Education (AAHPE); in 1938 it became the American Association for Health, Physical Education, and Recreation (AAHPER), its present name.

Fig. 63.   William G. Anderson.

The meeting was a success.  Forty-nine people became members, representing various groups interested in physical education.  The two Edward
Hitchcocks (father and son), Sargent, J. W. Seaver, and Miss Helen C.
Putnam came from the most famous colleges:   Amherst, Cornell, Harvard,
Yale, and Vassar, respectively.  Also attending were Robert J. Roberts of
the Boston YMCA and George Goldie of the New York Athletic Club, both
well-known figures in those types of institutions.  William Blaikie, author
of *How to Get Strong and How to Stay So,* and Dio Lewis, who authored
*The New Gymnastics,* were famous writers present.  A hospital, gymnasium
company, and many private schools and academies were also well-repre-
sented.   In all, six women attended, one of whom, Miss Putnam from
Vassar, was elected a vice-president.  The most significant absentees were
the *turners,* a strange omission on Anderson's part because as a boy he had
worked with *turners* in Quincy, Illinois, and therefore knew of their organization.

The most important action taken at that first meeting was the appointment of a committee on permanent organization "to consider the advisability of forming an Association, and if such be regarded feasible, to report a plan of operations." (21:5) By the afternoon, "Rev. D. Thwing reported in behalf of the Committee that a Permanent Organization seemed desirable. . . ." (21:6) A nine-member council was elected, including Anderson in the position of secretary, and given authority to draft a constitution before the next meeting. A committee on statistics and measurements was appointed, consisting of Anderson, Hitchcock and Sargent. The final action was an agreement to meet again next November in the same place.

The purposes of the organization were not stated until the second meeting when they were set forth in the first constitution:

### Article II.—Objects

The objects of the Association shall be to disseminate knowledge concerning physical education, to improve the methods, and by meetings of the members to bring those interested in the subject into closer relation to each other. (4:2)

The AAHPER was not the only organization founded by Anderson. As an undergraduate at the University of Wisconsin, he organized a quartet, an orchestra, an Athletic Association, and started gymnastic classes for co-eds which culminated in an exhibition held in the spring of 1878. At the same time he was playing the flute, piano and banjo, in addition to being president of the Glee Club. His youth had been equally active. Born in St. Joseph, Michigan, the son of a Congregational clergyman, he was brought up in Quincy, Illinois where the circus had its winter quarters. He was so agile as a tumbler and on the horizontal bar that P. T. Barnum's circus offered him a job as a performer. (231:494) He graduated from Roxbury Latin School in Boston, studied two years at the University of Wisconsin, received his M.D. from Western Reserve in 1883, started practice in Ohio, and in 1884 accepted a position as Instructor in Hygiene and Minor Surgery at Northwest Medical College, Toledo, Ohio. In the fall of 1885 he became Director of Physical Training at Adelphi Academy in Brooklyn, New York. Apparently one position was not enough for a man of Anderson's tremendous energies, despite his acknowledgement that "in the Adelphi Academy, where I teach, there are nearly one thousand pupils of both sexes, the majority of whom take exercise daily (obligatory)." (282:55) In 1886 he organized the Brooklyn Normal School for Physical Training (which used the facilities and students of Adelphi) and founded the Chautauqua Summer School of Physical Education, where he served as a teacher, principal and dean until 1904. From 1892 until his retirement in 1932, Anderson was Associate Director and then Director of the Yale University Gymnasium. He reorganized the Brooklyn Normal School in

New Haven as the Anderson Normal School of Gymnastics (1892),* continuing to function there as president and teacher.  He organized and/or taught in many other summer schools including Yale and the Universities of Utah, Montana and Southern California.  (56:126)  He was appointed Director of Physical Training in the public schools of the State of Connecticut.  He also added degree work to his activities, earning Master of Arts (1903) and Master of Science (1909) degrees from Yale and a doctorate in public health from Harvard in 1916.  In 1897 another letter from him provided the impetus for organizing the Society of College Gymnasium Directors which still functions today as the National College Physical Education Association for Men.  He served as fourth president of that group.

As a physical educator Anderson espoused many forms of gymnastics and dancing.  At the first meeting of the AAPE, he described the Adelphi daily drill:

> Fifty per cent of my success is due to the pianist.  Wands, bar bells and sword exercise with wooden rods are used.  Reports to parents are given.  Our anthropometric tables are printed in the September *Adelphian*.  We stimulate a noble ambition and point, for example, to the conspicuous beauty of well-developed biceps, when one is seen in a bathing dress.  (21:6)

Although he began his career teaching light gymnastics, unlike Hitchcock who continued the same kind of exercises for the forty years he taught at Amherst, Anderson changed as he learned new activities; he used elements of all the popular systems.  For instance, speaking to the AAAPE six years later, he stated.

> It is narrow to say that the Delsarte system combines all that should be taught; or that the German system is complete and answers all the requirements, and that above these two stands the Swedish system of gymnastics, which cannot be approached by anything else because it is so complete.  We believe in the Delsarte, German, and Swedish systems.  We try to get the best from each of these. . . .  (9:200)

In connection with this eclectic position he used the term "American system," a phrase which continued to appear in the literature for many years, though everyone agreed that there really was no American system, as such.  The term seemed to provide justification for modifying and combining the various systems, to the dismay of the purist devotees of each.  At the 1889 Conference which centered on the "battle of the systems" Anderson said:

---

* The leadership of the school passed to Ernst Hermann Arnold in 1903.  It became the New Haven Normal School of Gymnastics (1901), then Arnold College for Hygiene and Physical Education (1924), and since 1953 is the Arnold College Division of the University of Bridgeport.  From its beginning in 1886 to the time of affiliation with the University, 2251 students were graduated.  (368:107)

12

The so-called American system is as scientific as that of Ling. Why should it not be? We begin where he stopped; we have his experience. I have much respect for the German and Swedish systems; I have had experience in both: but, taken as they are, they will not suit the American people. We have ideas of our own; and it is not often that methods of other countries will suit us, unless they are modified. (282:54)

However, when in 1896 Anderson's book *Method of Teaching Gymnastics* was published, it was critically reviewed by Hartwell who said: "It is in a sense eclectic, and yet it does not furnish a well-reasoned basis for anything that could properly be termed an American system of gymnastics." (157: 193)

He was always in favor of using music with gymnastic work. "We use and advocate music, and I am a believer in instrumental and vocal accompaniment to gymnastic work, as it aids and interests." (9:201) He introduced dancing to Adelphi—both folk and stage, which almost caused a scandal. (231:498)

At his own normal schools Anderson had the opportunity to train teachers in accord with those beliefs. The 1893–1894 catalogue of his New Haven school listed under "practical" instruction courses in American, Swedish and Delsarte gymnastics, military evolutions, voice training, athletics, and games for the first year. In the second year, students learned a variety of gymnastic forms: advanced light and heavy, artistic, aesthetic, Swedish, and German, in addition to fencing, athletics, games, and public school teaching. (14:5)

The Chautauqua Summer School, second only to the Harvard Summer School in its influence on teacher training, had a similar variety of work, but there students were permitted to choose any or all of the systems to study, rather than tasting each one. Anderson was one of the first physical educators to speak of "specialization"; he recognized that each student could not become an expert or even well-versed in all gymnastic forms:*

It requires a life study for a man or a woman, to thoroughly understand and teach medical gymnastics. It requires just as much time to properly comprehend and teach educational gymnastics. . . . We try to persuade our teachers to select one grade of work and make a speciality of that. It is well for the gymnastic teacher to "Know everything about something, and something about everything." (9:199)

---

* Within the profession the battle of the generalist vs. the specialist goes on. Undergraduate preparation across the country almost universally requires that a student prepare to teach K-12, teams sports, individual sports, aquatics, gymnastics, movement education, games, folk dance, square dance, modern dance, and corrective exercises, in addition to personal hygiene, community health and first aid. Often they are also expected to learn the principles of community recreation, civil defense and outdoor education, in case they may be asked to conduct programs in those areas.

Recognizing this point he staffed his schools with large numbers of teachers, all specialists in their own areas. In New Haven, Jakob Bolin, a well-known exponent of it taught Swedish gymnastics, Ernst Hermann Arnold, graduate of the Normal College of the NAGU, taught German gymnastics, and a student of Genevieve Stebbins, American Delsarte expert, taught Delsarte.

Anderson extended the theory of specialization to public school teaching. Speaking to the Boston Conference in 1889, at the time when Mary Hemenway and Amy Morris Homans were trying to train hundreds of Boston public school teachers to lead a few minutes of Swedish gymnastics in the classroom (refer to p. 309), he said:

> I hardly think it will be a success if pupils are obliged to exercise in the space between the desks, while the regular teacher leads them. . . . I do not believe the regular teacher can or will spare the time to learn the science of physical training, that she may teach gymnastics to her pupils. . . . The instructor of gymnastics, being a specialist, can do better work than the regular teacher, who would be compelled to learn two professions if she were to supervise the work and teach it as it should be taught. (282:55)

The battle for specialized teachers in the elementary schools is still going on today; in most states the classroom teacher instructs in physical education.

As well as being a teacher and organizer, Anderson was a researcher. Like Fitz, he believed that many questions concerning the best practices to follow when teaching could be resolved if more research were done. He was able to use the facilities of the Yale Psychological Laboratory and recommended that "with the opportunities offered by the psychological laboratories connected with our leading colleges, we shall be able to approximate the truth by means of tests, experiments and delicate instruments." (11:40) Some of his own research included a study on reaction time and one on the effect of certain exercises upon the pulse rate. While at Adelphi he did a study involving comparative measurement which sought to compare the effects of calisthenic drill, military drill, or both. (19)

He was also a writer, publishing several volumes relating to the practice and teaching of gymnastics including: *Gymnastic Nomenclature* (1896), *Light Gymnastics* (1898), *Methods of Teaching Gymnastics* (1896), and *Anderson's Physical Education* (1897). He published several articles, mostly in the *APEA Review*.*

Many honors were conferred on Anderson: honorary membership in the American Physical Education Association (1929), an Honor Award Fellow in 1931 with the first group so honored, the Gulick Award (1945), an honorary master's degree from Springfield College (1925), and creation of an award in his name—the Anderson Award—given each year by the

---

* A complete list of his writings is contained in Harold Ray's biography of Anderson. (298:189–195)

AAHPER to a person who exemplifies his philosophy of devoted service to the profession.  Since 1955, seven years after the award was established, it has been given to persons outside of physical education who have contributed significantly to the areas in the AAHPER.

William G. Anderson made a solid contribution to the field of physical education through his work at Yale University, the Anderson Normal School of Gymnastics, the Chautauqua School of Physical Education, and through his publications. Large numbers of people came under his influence and disseminated his ideas throughout the profession.  But his greatest innovation was the call to organize, which resulted in the founding of America's professional physical education organization.

# ROBERT TAIT McKENZIE

## 1867-1938

The search for the ideal man, through the use of anthropometric measurements, culminated in the sculpture of the ideal athlete by R. Tait McKenzie. According to McKenzie:

> The search for a physical ideal was undertaken by the Society of Directors of Physical Education in Colleges, who, in 1902, commissioned the modeling of a statuette embodying the average measurements and proportions of the pick of the student body, selected by taking the best fifty men in the all-around strength test [refer to p. 289] for a period of eight years. These 400 sets of measurements were used to determine the proportions of the *typical college athlete*, who is represented as placing in his right hand the spring dynamometer with which he is about to test his grasping muscles. This youth may be said to embody the proportions and girths of the physically ideal American student of twenty-two. With a height of 5 feet 9 inches he carries a weight of 159 pounds. The girth of his neck, knee, and calf are the same, with the upper arm of 1½ inches less. The girth of his thigh is ½ inch less than that of his head. His expanded chest is 40 inches, the girth of his waist 10 inches less, his hip girth almost the same as his unexpanded chest, while the breadth of his waist barely exceeds the length of his foot, and the stretch of his arms measures 2 inches more than his height. (229:269)

Whereas Sargent sought to ascertain the average measurements of a man in order to prescribe exercise for the ordinary student, McKenzie was interested in aesthetic values. He was fascinated by the beauty of youth and by the renaissance of amateur athletic competition occurring with the revival of the Olympics. His sculptures, among the most famous ever made of athletes, are reminiscent of classical Greek statues in their harmony of body proportion. He acknowledged that "We lean heavily on the fifth and fourth-century Greek ideals for our art . . . and never more so than in our interpretation of the youthful figure in action or at rest." (228:43) "Sculpture is the medium peculiarly suited to portray athletic action. . . . The modern athlete has already made his own contribution to the possibilities for sculpture that should be celebrated and not overlooked or forgotten." (228:41, 43) He had in mind the various new skills and positions not known in ancient times, such as the pole vault, throwing the hammer, new techniques of discus throwing, and the crouching start in running.

FIG. 64.   The Joy of Effort.

The crouching start was first used in 1888 by a Yale runner. McKenzie, believing it gave "a beautiful and graceful combination of lines and mass for the sculpture" (228:43), chose it as the subject of his first figure in the round.   From charts of anthropometric measurements he established his own "canons" of proportions from which he designed "Sprinter" in 1902.* The first bronze cast of "Sprinter" was presented to Theodore Roosevelt who, as President, kept it on his desk in the White House. (207:468) "Sprinter" was given by the students of McGill to the Canadian Intercollegiate Union, a track and field group, where it is awarded annually as the R. Tait McKenzie Trophy.

McKenzie's interest in beautiful athletes sent him to the Rome, Amsterdam, Stockholm, and Paris Olympic Games.   For the Stockholm Olympics in 1912 he designed "The Joy of Effort" (Fig. 64), entering it in the Fine Arts Competition.   For the frieze, showing three runners leaping over a hurdle, McKenzie received the King's Medal from Gustav of Sweden.

* Photographs of the works described here may be found in the article "The Athlete in Sculpture." (228)

The four-foot medallion was set into a wall in the Olympic Stadium in Stockholm. Since that time "Joy" has been adopted for use on medals, seals and certificates by many organizations. In 1967, the AAHPER celebrated the hundredth anniversary of McKenzie's birth, by striking replicas of it and making them available as paperweights. Another work of his associated with the Olympics was the "Olympic Shield of Athletes," the only shield depicting athletes ever made by a sculptor. The shield, five feet in diameter, won the Olympic Art Award at the 1932 Games in Los Angeles.

To physical educators, McKenzie's most widely known work is the official seal of the AAHPER. Designed only a year before his death, the seal consisted of profiles of a typical American college man and woman. The male profile was a product of his long years of studying the faces of athletes; McKenzie was less familiar with women's faces, however. Consequently, he solicited photographs of girls whose faces were representative from a large number of women's colleges and from the study of these he completed the design.

"Competitor" in 1906 was his first work in which average measurements were not used. It was a statue of a young runner in a moment of repose, as he bends to tie his track shoe. McKenzie was a master at isolating the significant moment of an event and eternalizing the instant in a statue. Among the best of these, "Javelin Cast" showed the moment of equilibrium after a delivery, and communicated the athlete's sense of fulfillment. "Flying Sphere," a companion piece to "Javelin Cast," represented the athlete's final moment after releasing the discus, before his body relaxes the tension. "Relay" caught the moment when the baton is passed, from the view of the third man whose face reflected his intense involvement in the situation; the moment before the starting pistol is fired was the pose for "Plunger"; "Invictus" portrayed a boxer, down on one knee, about to get up before he is counted out. Climaxing this series was the sculpture of a group of rugby players, the halfback with the ball breaking out of the scrum; he titled it "Onslaught." In his lifetime McKenzie sculpted 233 pieces in the form of statues, friezes, sketches, plaques, and medals. Many were not of athletes, for his artistic work spanned the broad range of his interests and occupations. Thus there were figures of a boy scout, children in a playground, war memorials, and the famous masks which actually launched him on his sculpting career.

The four masks (Fig. 65) were created to illustrate a lecture and a paper he was writing to describe the dangerous limits of overexhaustion in sport. These masks were acclaimed by the Society of American Anatomists in 1899. Observing that in a race the "great effort is mirrored on the runner's face with unfailing accuracy" (230:190), McKenzie portrayed the face in violent "Effort": "The general impression of this face is repulsive. There is hatred, menace, and rage in it, and yet throughout there is a feeling of

distress that goes, a little way at least, toward softening its hardness."
(230:196) In his mask of the face of "Breathlessness," "the raised upper
lid adds to the look of sorrow and pain, while the down-drawn mouth
angle, the tongue closely pressed against the teeth, the sunken cheek, and
the open mouth, all go to increase the exhausted, haggard look so characteristic of this state. . . ." (229:24) On the face of "Fatigue" "the general
expression is one of vacancy," and in "Exhaustion" "the head is thrown
backward and the chin thrust forward in the endeavor to balance the head
without muscular effort." (229:26) The four masks not only brilliantly
illustrated his points about exhaustion but also revealed the insight of his
powers of observation. In their fidelity to life, rather than idealized beauty,
McKenzie's works departed from the Greek tradition. While he obviously
was mindful of aesthetic principles, unlike the Greeks he refused to sacrifice

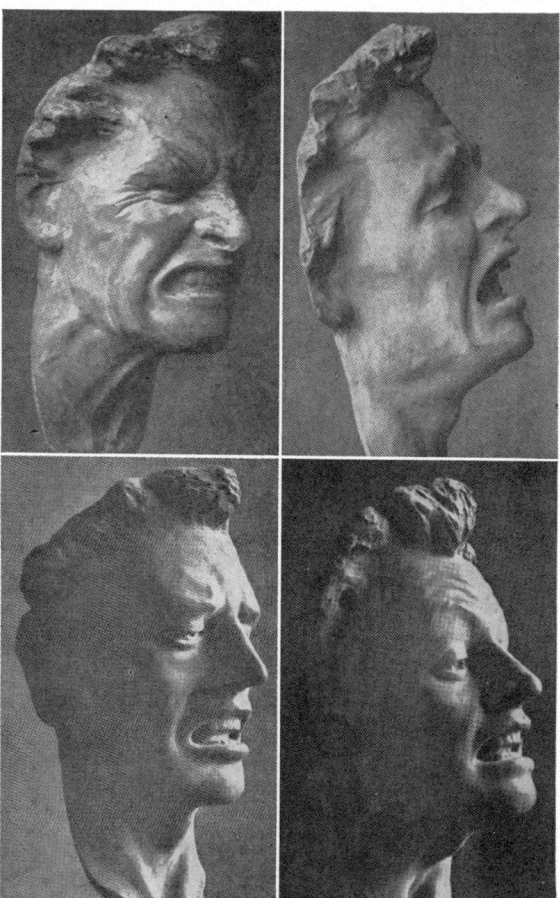

Fig. 65.    Masks of the Runner:    Effort (top left), Breathlessness (top right),
Fatigue (bottom left), Exhaustion (bottom right).

FIG. 66.    R. Tait McKenzie.

fidelity to reality for the sake of art.    The reason for this may lie in the
nature of his working life.

An artist by avocation, McKenzie was first of all a physician and physical
educator.    His view of the human body was rooted in the reality of bone
and muscle, and his knowledge of the great demands on the body during
performance was in part a memory of his own experiences.    Born in
Almonte, Ontario, Canada,* he was an enthusiastic skater, skier and
tobogganist.    While a student at McGill University he elected football,
swimming, fencing, gymnastics (he earned the Wicksteed Medal in 1889 as
the University champion), and track (as Canadian Intercollegiate champion, he established a high jump record which stood for years).    He
received his A.B. in 1889 and his M.D. in 1892 from the University
Medical College.    Before graduation he became the instructor of the
gymnasium (1891), whereupon he submitted a report showing the need for
supervision of student health and recommended that a medical and physical
examination be given each incoming student as the basis for prescribing
medical attention and exercise choices.    The recommendations adopted, in
1896 McKenzie was appointed Medical Director of Physical Education, the
first person in Canada to hold such a position.    From 1895–1904 he was

* Also the birthplace of James Naismith (1861–1939), the originator, in 1891, of
the game of basketball, while he was on the faculty of what is now Springfield College. He preceded McKenzie as instructor in the gymnasium at McGill University.

lecturer in anatomy, and he developed an active medical practice as a specialist in orthopedic surgery. He was also House Physician to the Governor General of Canada. He enhanced his training in physical education by attending the Harvard Summer School; he received his diploma in 1901 and taught anatomy while still finding time to study. Sargent's influence on his thinking is evidenced in the program he founded at the University of Pennsylvania where he was appointed Professor on the Medical Faculty and Director of Physical Education in 1904, and Professor of Physical Therapy in 1907, the first professorship of the latter kind in any American medical school.

Hallmarks of his program were the physical examination and the physical education class required of all students twice a week for four years, with credit and penalties. McKenzie described his beliefs concerning college physical education in a lecture to the American Association for the Advancement of Science:

> The average man may be taken in classes which should begin by exercises of discipline, marching and setting-up movements to word of command. They [sic] should then be examined to find their ability to perform certain exercises of skill, and classified according to their proficiency. A course of graded exercises should follow, closing with a re-examination. (234:483)

Along with other physical educators of his time he distinguished between physical training and athletics:

> In physical training the object is to bring the standard of health up to its highest level, and all excessive strain or exhaustion is avoided while all the activities are exercised.
> In athletic training the object is to bring the human machine to its highest point of efficiency to perform a definite feat, and everything that is useless or detrimental is sacrificed. . . . The object is not primarily health but superlative ability. . . . (234:483)

His cognizance of the responsibility of physical educators to control the direction of athletics was acute and positive. His presidential address to the Society of Directors was a plea for them to rise to the challenge:

> For what occult reasons were gathered together the sages and philosophers of Greece, the traders of Cyprus, and the hardy colonists from beyond the Euxine seas? What was, after all, the lode-stone that drew the Norman chivalry and the Saxon yeomanry in an impenetrable throng against the lists at Ashby-de-la-Zouche? What but the desire to see, and the appreciation of deeds of daring, the display of courage and that dogged endurance that will not admit of defeat, the love of physical contest and the admiration of skill and address that makes the spectator lift his foot with the jumper, or press forward with the ball player, living over again in his own person and imagination the action of the contestant, exulting with the victor and sharing his depression with the vanquished?

What prohibitory legislation can hope to cope with this instinct so deeply rooted in the nature of all virile conquering races? . . .

This great surging tide of emotion . . . cannot be dammed; it must be directed, and it is we, as directors of physical education, to whom, as leaders in the work, is given the task of turning this great power for good or evil in the right direction that it may be used, not for the debauching but rather for the uplifting of the whole nation. . . . (227:77)

In 1931 McKenzie retired and became Research Professor of Physical Education having advised President Gates on the formulation of a long-range plan for physical education at the University.   Known as the Gates plan, one of its chief provisions was for a Department of Physical Education composed of Divisions of Student Health, Physical Instruction, and Inter-collegiate Athletics, all under a single dean and budget. (232:25)  Although the University of Pennsylvania was not the first institution to combine these areas, the provisions of the Gates plan "to give sports back to the students" carried special influence when they were adopted in 1931.   The comprehensive department served as an administrative model for many colleges and universities which hoped it would provide the mechanism for controlling and making more educative, intercollegiate sports.

Early in World War I (1915) McKenzie offered his services to the War Office in London and was sent, along with other new recruits, to the classes in physical training at Aldershot (refer to p. 217).   When it was discovered that he was the author of the class textbook, *Exercise in Education and Medicine* (229), he was given a commission as Major and sent on a tour of the training camps and hospitals. He organized the first of the Home Command training depots at Heaton Park where in the first four months he returned twelve thousand men to the front lines.   Working with men who were unable to stand the intensive training of a regular recruit, and with battlefield casualties, he modified the regular exercises and developed special ones for convalescents.   As the casualties mounted the sixteen training camps became rehabilitation centers; McKenzie devoted himself to devising new treatments and apparatus to restore the wounded bodies to normal condition.   He used gymnastics "to reëducate control, alertness, accuracy, speed, and strength in men who have lost them through neglect, injury, or the enforced idleness of hospital life." (233:92)  He also included other physical activities in his retraining or therapy program, stipulating that "the time taken by these tables [exercises] should not occupy more than half of the hour set apart for exercise.   The second half should be taken up with games and recreation in which discipline does not play a prominent part." (233:99)

When the United States entered the war he was appointed inspector of convalescent hospitals and used his experience and apparatus at Walter Reed Hospital with great success.   Throughout the war he devoted himself to rehabilitation work in the United States and Canada.   Recognizing the importance of physical training to the war effort, he urged the members of the APEA to serve as advisors and instructors in organizing a central staff for the training of recruits:

> This is one place in which the work of the physical educator can be made to help his country. . . . The work of the school and the playground must be kept up as never before and the physical training of the boys and girls carried out with increased efficiency by those who are unable to do the more technical military work. (235:527–528)

McKenzie's professional work extended to writing. He published more than a hundred articles in medical, education and art journals, edited a series of textbooks for Lea & Febiger publishers, contributed chapters on physical therapy to several medical books, and wrote two books of his own: *The Treatment of Convalescent Soldiers by Physical Means* and *Reclaiming the Maimed* (233). In the field of physical education he wrote a classic work, *Exercise in Education and Medicine* (229).

He was president of the APEA for four terms, 1912–1915, and president of the Society of Directors of Physical Education in Colleges in 1901, 1904 and 1909. He was a charter member of the American Academy of Physical Education (Fellow #2) and served as its first president from 1930 to 1938, the year of his death. He was also president of the Academy of Physical Medicine.

Many honors were accorded R. Tait McKenzie. His art works were exhibited at the Royal Academy in London, the Canada Royal Museum in Ottawa, the Metropolitan Museum of Art in New York, and many have a place on college campuses. A memorial lecture sponsored by the American Academy of Physical Education is given in his name every year at the national convention of the AAHPER. The February, 1944 issue of the *Journal of Health and Physical Education* was devoted entirely to him and the cover of each issue that year bears a photo of one of his works. "Column of Youth," a sculpture which portrays a typical American boy and girl, was purchased by the AAHPER for exhibit in the National Education Association building in Washington, where it can still be seen. He was awarded honorary degrees by Springfield College (M.P.E., 1913), McGill University (LL.D., 1921), University of Pennsylvania (A.E.D., 1928), and St. Andrews University, Scotland (LL.D., 1938). He was made a Fellow of the College of Physicians, the APEA, and given honorary life membership in the Society of Directors. His summer home, the Mill of Kintail, near his birthplace at Almonte, is now a museum containing the originals of many of his art works including his "Olympic Shield." In connection with the celebration of his birth centennial, "The Man of Kintail," a movie on his life was made. His work as a sculptor was examined by Christopher Hussey in a book entitled *Tait McKenzie A Sculptor of Youth* (189b) and his work as a physical educator was described in a dissertation by Adelaide Meador Huntor

(189a).  Since 1968 the AAHPER has given an R. Tait McKenzie Award in recognition of professional contributions.

It is hard to capture the unusual spirit of this innovator whose knowledge, culture and breadth of work earned much respect, not only for himself, but for the profession he served.  His work in physical education and physical therapy and his enduring artistic accomplishments made R. Tait McKenzie one of the most notable leaders of the profession.

# LUTHER HALSEY GULICK

## 1865-1918

The Luther H. Gulick Award for distinguished service in physical education is the highest honor afforded to members by the Association. The award was first bestowed by the Physical Education Society of New York City, as a means of memorializing Gulick's contribution to physical education. (24:98)

*Palman Qui Meruit Ferat* (To Him Who Merits It, The Palm), the inscription on the award medal, was an appropriate remembrance of Gulick who posthumously received the first award in 1923. It was created from a fund of fifty dollars donated by Gulick to stimulate research; for want of an applicant the money collected interest and was used to strike the Gulick medal which was designed by R. Tait McKenzie.

Luther Halsey Gulick accomplished a great deal in his short life. In a speech given soon after his death, Sargent summed up his career:

> He was not a visionary or unpractical schemer as some thought, but he saw visions even as a youth of nineteen of greater possibilities for physical education in America than any other man whom I have met. This accounts for his wide interest later in every phase of the subject as testified by his helpful connection with the American Physical Education Association, the Y.M.C.A. movement, the Public School Athletic League, the Athletic Research Society, the School Hygiene Association, the Amateur Athletic Union, the Playground Association of America, the Camp Fire Girls' movement and many other organizations for the promotion of physical development and human welfare. (68:419)

In each of the groups with which he was associated, Gulick held positions of authority or leadership. He was secretary of the AAAPE in 1892–93, president from 1903–1907, and editor of the *APEA Review* from 1901–1903. According to Sargent: "It was largely through the influence of Dr. Gulick that all of the association business and political controversies were finally taken out of the public meetings and put into the meetings of the council as at the present time." (68:419)

In 1904 or 1905 Gulick organized the Academy of Physical Education, an informal group "organized to bring together those who were doing original scientific work in the field of physical training, and to aid in the promotion of such work." (135:342) The group had eleven Fellows,*

---

* Wilbur P. Bowen, C. Ward Crampton, Luther H. Gulick, Clark W. Hetherington, Fred E. Leonard, James Huff McCurdy, R. Tait McKenzie, George L. Meylan, Paul C. Phillips, Dudley A. Sargent, and Thomas A. Storey.

although others occasionally attended, and after the first few meetings, it held week-long sessions annually on Sebago Lake in Maine. One of the unique features of the Academy was its emphasis on substantive issues, particularly research. At the meetings a topic was agreed upon for each Fellow to pursue during the next year. A special Certificate of Merit was devised and presented to "persons contributing original studies of value. . . . The object is simply to promote original research, and to offer to all who are doing such work an opportunity for recognition by those who have been connected the most prominently with the advancement of original investigation and physical training." (135:342, 344) All Fellows of the Association signed each certificate. Gulick's Academy had no relation to the American Academy of Physical Education founded in 1930 and still functioning today. However, he was made a Fellow in Memoriam of the latter group.

His work with the International YMCA movement was of particular importance because he was the first Secretary (head) of the Physical Department of the International Committee of the YMCA of North America and he retained that position from 1887 to 1902. At the same time he was appointed an instructor in the newly formed Department of Physical Training in the YMCA Training School in Springfield, Massachusetts (now Springfield College).* In 1889 when Robert J. Roberts, the most well-known and influential teacher of gymnastics in the Association, resigned the leadership of the department, Gulick became the superintendent, and remained in that capacity until 1900. The curriculum in the Training School and in the summer school established in connection with it, was similar to other normal schools of the time. In 1891 the school began to offer a graduate diploma in physical education for work beyond the regular two-year course; thus it was the first graduate course in physical education in the United States (though the first graduate *degree* program was at Teachers College, Columbia University—refer to p. 386). Four courses were offered: physiological psychology, history and philosophy of physical education, anthropometry, and literature of physical education; a thesis of at least three thousand words was required. Only three men completed the work for this diploma between 1891 and 1900. In 1903 the Massachusetts legislature authorized conferring B.P.E. and M.P.E. degrees, a practice not effected until 1906. (384:99) In 1908 the undergraduate curriculum was extended to three years.

Gulick's parents and grandparents were missionaries; he was born in Honolulu and lived with his missionary parents in Spain, Italy and Japan, as well. Thus he was strongly aware of the ethical principles of Christianity and was imbued with the significance of the spiritual aspect of man's life.

---

* By 1887 there were 168 reported gymnasiums and fifty paid directors of physical work in YMCAs in America. (207:315) The apparent need for supervision and adequately trained leadership led to the formation of the two departments.

Talking to the AAAPE about the purpose of physical education in YMCAs, he emphasized the unity of the spiritual and physical in man: "Our endeavor is for true symmetry, not merely symmetry of body, symmetry of mind, symmetry of soul, but a symmetry of these symmetries, a symmetry of body with mind with soul." (8:44) Originally the YMCAs had used physical work as "bait" to draw young working men into their programs so they could be given spiritual and moral guidance. Gulick established a new conception—a role for physical education as valuable in itself:

> Each nature [physical and spiritual] is an essential part of the man himself. Thus we believe that physical education is important not merely because it is necessary in order to perfect intellectual and spiritual manhood, but because the physical is in itself a part of the essential "ego." (8:43)

Based upon this philosophy he designed the "triangle," now the symbol of the YMCA. The inverted triangle represents the supremacy of the spirit when upheld and supported by the body and mind. In an article written for *The Triangle*, a publication he started (which in 1892 became *Physical Education*), Gulick cited Deuteronomy 6:5, "And thou shalt love the Lord thy God with all thine heart, and with all thy soul, and with all thy might," to explain the central meaning of the triangle. (90:36)

This philosophy was also responsible for changing the character and training of the Physical Directors of YMCAs. Prior to Gulick's time the majority were professional gymnasts, athletes, ex-sparrers, ex-circus performers, or men who had attended a gymnasium for a few months. Gulick stressed that "the putting of physical education on the plane of which I have just been speaking has altered this condition of things and has rendered it necessary that the physical director shall be an earnest Christian man with a broad general education, as well as a definite theoretical and practical training in physical education." (8:44–45) It was this philosophy and emphasis which pervaded the YMCA Training School and Gulick's Association work.

Another important contribution to the YMCA program was his founding of the Association Athletic League, formally adopted in 1895 with Gulick as secretary of the governing committee. The purpose of this League was "to throw emphasis upon those conditions which produce amateur as contrasted with professional sport." (137:43) One activity which the League promoted was a pentathlon composed of the hundred-yard dash, the twelve-pound hammer throw, the running high jump, pole vaulting, and the mile run. Gulick said of it:

> The idea involved in the pentathlon is all around development. . . . It was intended that the pentathlon should be used, not only in local and district as well as state meets, but that it might form the basis for an international contest. The following are the ends at which the pentathlon must aim:—

1st. The events must be those which taken all together will test a man all-round; not merely the different parts of his body, but the same parts in different ways.

. . . . . . . . . . . . .

Our object in adopting such as standard of competition for the associations is not that they shall limit themselves to these five merely, in practice and in local contests, but that they shall afford a basis for inter-association competitions. . . . (140:26–28)

The League also sponsored team games such as basketball, which had been designed for the Association by James Naismith, working, according to some evidence, from an idea of Gulick. Urging that "we must waken to the realization of the fact that Christian character is to be displayed and cultivated in sport" (137:46), Gulick had a Clean Sport Roll adopted, which included the following among nine points:

1. The rules of games are to be regarded as mutual agreements, the spirit or letter of which one should no sooner try to evade or break than one would any other agreement between gentlemen. The stealing of advantage in sport is to be regarded as stealing of any other kind.

. . . . . . . . . . . . .

3. No action is to be done, nor course of conduct is to be pursued which would seem ungentlemanly or dishonorable if known to one's opponents or the public.

. . . . . . . . . . . . .

5. Advantages which the laxity of the officials may allow in regard to the inter-pretation and enforcement of the rules are not to be taken. (90:55)

An earlier edition of the Roll also recommended that "kicking on the floor at officers and players be absolutely stopped " (137·46) The League was not always successful in enforcing the type of behavior desired, but it generally played an important role in fostering the development of clean amateur athletics during a time when malpractice in college athletics was of great concern to physical educators.

Gulick's work with the public schools began with his appointment in 1903 as the first Director of Physical Training in the public schools of New York City, a position he held until 1908. He was already in New York, having been Principal of Pratt High School since 1900, and he re-mained there when he later became involved full time with playground work. Fundamental to the program he established were two beliefs. First, "the object of school gymnastics is to combat the effects of long sitting at school desks." (142:51) And second, gymnastics "must not be regarded as discharging all of the obligations that rest upon physical education." (138:61) For the former point he put into effect a daily "two-minute setting-up drill" although he recognized it was not adequate. In conjunction with the latter he encouraged athletics and dance activities which he organized during after-school hours.

He was convinced that play was an important aspect of education and

Fig. 67.    Luther Halsey Gulick.

defined it as an attitude—"what we do when we are free to do what we will.    It is the spontaneous expression of the inner desire." (141:267) Like John Dewey and Friedrich Froebel, he understood that playing was crucial to learning.    "An interest pursued from choice has much more educational value, both in the extent and permanency of knowledge gained, than has any subject to which the child is driven." (141:177–178)    As early as 1904 Gulick stressed the importance of play as a part of physical education:

> Play is far more important for the child's development than formal school educational gymnastics during those years.    Through these plays, bodily skill as well as vigor of heart and lungs is gained and the muscles are called upon for constant and varied activity.    It is true that they do not seem to have the logical development that can be found in systematic gymnastics, but I believe that this is only a seeming lack. If one considers the plays and games of boys and girls during an entire year, he will find a progressive and most complicated and elaborate scheme. . . . If one looks at the range of sports covered in this methodically haphazard fashion for a year, it will at once be evident that the curriculum of sport is a rather complete one. (142:45)

He also approved of the more highly organized sports:

> Approximately at puberty, interest culminates in the great Anglo-Saxon sports of baseball, cricket, hockey, shinney, basket ball, and the like.    These great games are played in teams in which the individual is subordinated to the whole. . . . They represent the extreme form of muscular exercise. . . . It is my opinion that these extreme forms of exercise are related to the final toughening of the individual for the achievements of life. (142:46–47)

Despite his belief in the importance of play, he did not advocate it within the curriculum, primarily because the physical education period was too brief to go beyond systematic gymnastic exercises. Therefore, to meet the needs of the average boy, he initiated the Public School Athletic League, the first of its kind, launching it in 1903 with a meet held in Madison Square Garden. Although the League was separate from the Board of Education, both financially and structurally, it was staffed with volunteer teachers. One of the League's earliest activities was the Athletic Badge Test. Medals designed by R. Tait McKenzie were awarded in three classes for competition in the standing broad jump, chinning, running high jump, and 60-, 100-, and 220-yard dashes. The League also sponsored baseball, track and field meets, and marksmanship competitions. Instruction in the Badge activities eventually became a part of the regular school program. In 1908 Gulick stated: "During recent years a system of athletic sports has been developed which now includes the majority of all boys in the grammar grades of the public school system. This is our system of 'class athletics'." (143:378)

Gulick stated that inasmuch as running, striking and throwing were the basic skills of all sports, and were the basic skills necessary to man in early societies, "boyhood and manhood have thus for ages long been tested and produced by athletic sports. Athletic sports are thus, to some extent at least, a measure of manhood." (136:159) Since women did not depend upon these skills for survival, "athletics have never been either a test or a large factor in the survival of women, that is, athletics do not test womanliness as they test manliness." (136:159) With this in mind he prevented women from engaging in interschool competition, although he allowed a Girls' Branch of the PSAL to be organized in 1905 (refer to p. 366). Its main activity was the sponsorship of folk dancing, which Gulick regarded as the equivalent of athletics in that it "awakened the enthusiasm of both the teachers and the pupils, so that more life should be thrown into the work," but was better "adapted to the feminine physiological, psychological, social or aesthetic needs." (143:378)

Folk dancing was one of the greatest innovations Gulick made in the curriculum. He believed that:

> Dancing has from the earliest times been a considerable factor in the physical life of many persons, and its evolutionary and sociologic significance should not be overlooked. The pleasurable features of the exercise and the associated influence of music are no mean factors in its physiologic and hygienic effects. (142:63)

His enthusiasm was so great that in 1905, when as President of the AAAPE he was responsible for the convention, he selected "Dancing" as the theme. Appearing for the first time on the program, several papers and demonstrations were given; Gulick devoted his presidential address to "Rhythm and

Education" (145). The resultant effort to place folk dancing in the schools was popularly received. However, in New York City it was only taught at first during after-school hours as a reward for those meeting certain standards of scholarship, attendance and behavior. Gulick was careful to approve only those dances which were clearly beneficial, but nevertheless noted that dancing "fails in that respect which we regard as the first requirement of school gymnastics—namely the correction of that faulty posture which is so frequently induced by the school desk. . . . We recognize folk dancing as a most useful adjunct of physical training, not its principal part." (143:381)  In general, he used both dancing and athletics to enliven interest in the formal gymnastics program, the one serving as incentive to work hard in the other, by being used as a reward activity. He also chose Gilbert and folk dancing as the subject of classes at the New York University Summer School which he directed from its inception in 1905 to 1909. And in 1910 he published *The Healthful Art of Dancing* (139), a compendium of addresses he had made upon the subject.

Gulick's interest in play led him to found the Playground Association of America (later the National Recreation Association); he served as President from its organization in 1906 to 1910. After he resigned as director in the public schools he became chairman of the Playground Extension Committee of the Russell Sage Foundation. From these two offices he was able to provide assistance in the organization of playgrounds, athletics and folk dancing, and to publicize and promote playground work. Remarkably foresighted, he guided the Playground Association to expand the concept of play to one of public recreation and he urged that leaders work with municipal officials to secure support for recreation:

> The recreation problem ranks in importance with the labor and education problems. . . . The choices we make with reference to our leisure are fundamental for morality. In the city, people have small opportunity to make this choice under wholesome conditions. . . .
> The attitude usually taken by the state with reference to public recreation is one of restriction only. We do little toward providing forms of play for social life. . . .
>
> .    .    .    .    .    .    .    .    .    .    .    .    .
>
> We have enormous resources belonging to the state which might be used for recreation and play. Our public school property is well equipped for many kinds of recreation. To use our present public buildings and parks and other city property involves not primarily the expenditure of money, but the conversion of public opinion and the establishment of social customs. (141:120–123)

Although he was able to accomplish most of his purposes with reference to playgrounds for children, his recommendations for adult recreation were too far ahead of his time to be enacted immediately. Furthermore, his committee at the Russell Sage Foundation had become the Department of Child Hygiene with three divisions: health, education and recreation, and

Gulick was working primarily in the health division.  In 1913 he resigned from the Foundation to devote himself more fully to the Camp Fire Girls.

The Camp Fire Girls was the joint product of Dr. and Mrs. Gulick.  The name itself was representative of the values it stood for:  "fire" standing for home, "camp" for solidarity, and "camp fire" for the outdoors.  (90:118)  The organization was interwoven with the summer camp run by the Gulicks on Lake Sebago in Maine.  The name of the camp, Wohelo (from the first letters of "work," "health" and "love"), was given to the Camp Fire movement and Wohelo camps sprung up across the country.  Each Camp Fire Girl chose an Indian name representative of herself, and Gulick's name "Timanous" meaning "guiding spirit" became well-known throughout the movement.  He remained President of the Camp Fire Girls and editor of its publication, *Wohelo*, until 1918 when he took leave to work for the YMCA in connection with the war.  Since he died in the summer of 1918, it was his last great commitment.

It is difficult to summarize the contributions of Gulick, so extensive and diverse as they were.  In addition to all his work he was a prolific writer, publishing nine books, editing the *Gulick Hygiene Series*, writing sixteen handbooks and pamphlets, and 220 articles in journals and proceedings of meetings.*  The book most respected by his colleagues was *The Efficient Life* (1907).  *Medical Inspection of Schools* (with Leonard P. Ayres, 1908) was influential in causing school inspections in many cities.  *Physical Education by Muscular Exercise* (1904) was a comprehensive statement of Gulick's philosophy of physical education which grew out of his lectures to Training School students on the "Philosophy of Exercise"; its concepts are as fresh today as when they were written.  *A Philosophy of Play* (posthumously, 1920) was probably his most significant book in relation to the profession of physical education.  It established with great clarity the importance of play—especially its value as an educative force—and helped to begin the play movement in physical education.

Besides the organizations already named, Gulick founded the Public School Physical Education Society, a group which later affiliated with the American Physical Education Association.  He was the guiding spirit behind the founding of the American Folk Dance Society.  In some official capacity he was connected with the early organization of the Amateur Athletic Union.  And the American School Hygiene Association and the Boy Scouts of America were both organizations which he assisted in founding.

His achievements were the more brilliant because he was not a formally well-educated man.  Although enrolled for a time at Oberlin, rooming with Thomas Wood and coming under the influence of Delphine Hanna, he had severe headaches which caused him to withdraw from college.  Having been inspired by Dr. Hanna and by William Blaikie's book *How to Get*

* A complete and documented list of all of Gulick's writing may be found in Dorgan. (90:155–167)

*Strong and How to Stay So* (47), he left in 1885 and went to the Sargent Normal School, where he studied for six months. Following a short stint as Director of the Gymnasium in the YMCA at Jackson, Michigan, he enrolled in the New York University Medical College and received his M.D. in 1889. That degree represented the only systematic education that Gulick ever had. His Master of Physical Education (M.P.E.) degree, conferred upon him in 1907 by the International YMCA Training School, was honorary.

Luther Halsey Gulick was a special kind of innovator. He was able to translate his creative vision into organized plans of action. Thus his desire to see the good minds of the leaders of the AAAPE used in considering issues rather than business details led to change in the format of meetings and the founding of the first Academy of Physical Education. His belief in the interrelationship of sport and ethical values, and the necessity for leaders who exemplified the ideal in man, led to the development of a program at the YMCA Training School, and the Association Athletic League, where these values could be emphasized; it revolutionized the physical program of the YMCA movement. His view of physical education as encompassing purposes beyond the basic one of health and good posture, led him to form the Public School Athletic League and to institute competition and folk dancing into the school curriculums. His far-sighted view of play as an educative medium, and his insight into the need for adults to plan their leisure wisely so as to insure recreative rest, not only caused the establishment of the Playground Association of America, but directed it toward working for planned public recreation programs. His love for the outdoors, together with his belief and interest in creating opportunities for children to have learning experiences together, out of the school situation, inspired his dedication to the Camp Fire Girls organization.

# JESSIE HUBBELL BANCROFT

## 1867-1952

It was as a pioneering proselytizer that Jessie Bancroft's innovative ability was manifested. During the course of her career she indefatigably brought physical education—the new profession—to the public, school administrators, teachers, business men, and anyone she could reach through articles, speeches and demonstrations. Her career began as an itinerant physical educator, traveling from town to town lecturing in churches, at women's club meetings, before audiences in private homes, and occasionally to classes in private schools. Her preparation for this was meager:

> My own first experience with systematic exercise was in the early 1880's, when Mrs. Jenness-Miller of New York attracted much attention as a dress-reformer, though exercise, diet, and other points of personal hygiene were equally important with sensible dress in the lecture and parlor classes that she and her assistants conducted through the country. The exercises taught were admirable as hygiene, many of them recumbent, and all emphasizing good carriage or posture. I joined one of these classes, and being much interested in the subject took private lessons also, to learn the teacher's viewpoint. (30:666)

Some years later, securing advice from Sargent, about whom she read in a newspaper, she studied a term (1888) at the Minneapolis School of Physical Education, run by Sargent graduates. Next (1889) came a course in kindergartening at the Winona State Normal School (located in her home town of Winona, Minnesota), at which time she also had opportunity to study the Delsarte system. She said of it: "No exercises have more directly or effectively cultivated grace, and their aesthetic quality lured many women into healthful exercise of this and other types." (30:667) After these experiences, plus conducting a successful summer school teaching various types of exercises, she decided to become a lecturer and form parlor classes, since she knew it was impossible to find regular school employment. At that time *turners* were beginning to introduce physical education in the form of German gymnastics into the public schools of the Midwest (refer to p. 273). Boards of Education were not yet ready to make jobs available for physical education teachers and many of the *turners*, such as Carl Betz in Kansas City in 1885, first worked for nothing.

After spending the summer of 1891 studying at the Harvard Summer

School, Bancroft arranged to spend the next season in New York City. Having discovered that physical education there was no further advanced than in the Midwest she felt secure enough to tackle the big city. In searching for employment she visited every one of the eighty private schools for girls around the city, finding only *one* that "had any special provision or instructor for this subject." (30:671) A part-time position she secured at Hunter College led to the appointment (1893) which really launched her into the profession, the Directorship of Physical Training in the Brooklyn public schools. It was a job of great magnitude, for at that time Brooklyn was the fourth largest industrial city in the United States, and there were more than ten thousand children in the schools.

Bancroft's description of the things she accomplished during the first ten years is indicative of what she thought physical education was and also of the role that circumstances forced physical educators to play in any large public school system:

> I devoted each year to the development of one new phase in addition to carrying routine. The items themselves indicate how undeveloped was the field. Having secured a corps of assistants, I introduced games to replace the "whispering recess"; established methods of testing sight and hearing and organized a method of assigning seats according to those powers; made measurements of thousands of children in different racial groups, stripped for the study of contours. Among the many results of this latter research was the revision of tables for the adjustment of school furniture, so that little Italian legs were not dangling in the air, or tall German or Old-stock American backs rounded over desks too low. . . . Applying principles from the new school of industrial, or efficiency, engineering, I worked out more definite methods whereby teachers could estimate the attainment and progress of their pupils in posture, the so-called "Triple-Test" which soon spread throughout the country. (30:675)

She justified the diversity of her concerns by pointing out that "gymnastics would not be needed were there not conditions incident to the school life that are prejudicial to the physical development of the child." (34:281) It was obvious to her that correcting the fit of the furniture would do more to improve the posture of the child than fifteen minutes of exercise each day.

To help teachers evaluate posture she developed the Triple-Test for Posture. It was widely used in the public schools because it was easy to administer quickly to students in a classroom, where most physical education was then conducted. It consisted of a standing test to judge posture in profile, a marching test to determine maintenance of good posture over a five-minute period, and an exercise test to discover which postural muscles needed strengthening.

Bancroft's concern for posture was one of the central facets of her philosophy. After writing *The Posture of Children* in 1913 she founded, in 1914, the American Posture League and served as president from its beginning until 1922. During that period she collected worldwide data on types of

FIG. 68. Jessie H. Bancroft.

foot structure among barefoot, sandaled and shoe-wearing people; she took measurements of several items of height in racial types of adults, for use in designing subway car seats; she took shoulder and chest measurements of men and boys to correct sizes used by the clothing industry; and she took pelvic and scapulae measurements of children and adults for seat modeling. It was a most practical use of anthropometric measurements.

The system Bancroft established to bring physical education to the children of Brooklyn was experimental but served as a model for other large cities. The assistant principals who functioned as department heads met with Bancroft or one of her assistants, received instruction in the exercises for the next week or two, and taught them to the teachers who in turn taught them to the children. Although the students got them third hand, Bancroft was satisfied that the system worked well:

> Those supervisiors met at first once a week for their instructions. They were thoroughly drilled on every movement to be taken; it was explained to them; it was seen that they could do it themselves; they were told how to teach their teachers; what faults to look for with the teachers and with the children. Being daily on the ground to see what the teachers were doing and to correct mistakes, it has surprised me to see how very quickly these people, who have never had gymnastic training, have come to see and appreciate both good work and errors. . . . (12:181)

Because of this system Bancroft believed it necessary to prepare graded courses of instruction consisting of a series of exercises for each school year. The class teachers could be trained to conduct the exercises, but "to expect that class teacher to understand the technicalities of the subject sufficiently to make an intelligent selection of work is ... too much to expect of her." (34:282)   Therefore, Bancroft published two books: *Free Hand Gymnastics* (1895) and *Light Apparatus Gymnastics* (1897), which contained a graded system of physical exercises for schools.   These books were published in several editions, the former one translated into Spanish in 1915.   Her instructions were precise and comprehensive including matters of procedure, as shown by this quote from *School Gymnastics Free Hand,* a publication containing the two works cited above:

> **Each lesson** is to be used one week, that of the previous week being entirely dropped.   When the continuance of an exercise is deemed necessary for physiological reasons, it is included in the new lesson.   No effort should be made to have the children keep in mind any exercises not so indicated.   The object is physical exercise, not memory work.
>
> In conducting the lesson, the order in which the exercises are arranged should be strictly adhered to. (32:25–26)

Bancroft instructed that the exercise periods, generally fifteen minutes broken into two or three periods a day, should not interfere with the recess period where games should be conducted.   She contended that both were necessary for a balanced scheme of physical education.

When Brooklyn lost its status as an independent city and became one of the boroughs of Greater New York, the physical training department was brought under a central administration with Luther Gulick appointed as the head (refer to p. 351).   Bancroft, in 1903, became Assistant Director of Physical Training in the New York City Schools, a post she held for twenty-five years until her retirement.   In her first two years in that position she spoke at more than five hundred meetings, interpreting physical education to teachers and school administrators.   Perhaps it was association with Gulick that led her to redirect the weight she placed on the value of games in a physical education program.   The change in her thinking came in stages, which in a way paralleled the growth of the profession.   First she began to consider the educational values of gymnastics.   By 1910, in direct contradiction to her earlier statements she said:   "Gymnastics are fundamentally and preëminently an intellectual form of exercise. . . . If his gymnastic work be allowed to become automatic, the higher qualities fade from it. . . . The gymnastic lesson should appeal to the mind as well as the body." (33:237–238)   Without forsaking her postural objective, she began to talk of the development of "motor power," or "motor character."   Whereas games had been included chiefly for their recreative value, now motor character could be developed through "the restraint of movements in obedience to rules in games." (33:237)   She added:   "One may not leave this subject of the educational use of physical training without touching on the moral and ethical training inherent in many of its forms, if rightly understood and used.   Nowhere is this stronger than in games, athletics or otherwise." (33:239) She cited Karl Groos (author of *The Play of Animals* and *The Play of Man*, two important early studies on play) and William James to show the relation between play and development. She spoke of "the lack of opportunity for natural play for children and young people . . . who have only the crowded city streets to play in. . . ." (29:17–18)

Subsequently, Jessie Bancroft wrote the most comprehensive and scholarly book on games then published in English. Like the gymnastic books, *Games for the Playground, Home, School, and Gymnasium* (1909) was meant for teachers and therefore included detailed instructions on the teaching of games and the general conduct of recess periods. She gave advice on presenting games, floor formation, choosing sides, and choosing games: "The choice of games to be played should be left to a vote or to the suggestion of the players. The teacher's function in this regard is to suggest, not to dictate." (29:29) Although repeated in dozens of books since, the ideas have never been superseded; most of them still remain the best advice a young teacher can get on the subject. Sections on the nature and origin of games were the first effort by a physical educator in this country to place games in historic and cultural perspective. She attempted to secure games of foreign origin, and interviewed for this purpose immigrants living in the city. She tried to anticipate unusual or diverse conditions for which games might be utilized:

> An especial effort has been made to secure games for particular conditions. Among these may be mentioned very strenuous games for older boys or men; games for the schoolroom; games for large numbers; new gymnasium games and those which make use of natural material such as stones, pebbles, shells, trees. . . . (29:3)

But most important was her system of classifying games according to age groups, the first attempt to prepare a graded course of study on games:

> The grading of games, as for elementary or high school, constitutes a graded course based on experimental study of children's interests. This grading of the games for schools is made, not with the slightest belief or intention that the use of a game should be confined to any particular grade or age of pupils. . . . The games have usually been noted for the earliest grade in which they have been found, on the average, of sufficient interest to be well played, with the intention that they be used thereafter in any grade where they prove interesting. (29:16)

Because of this graded system it became possible to introduce games into the curriculum. It lent credence to the argument that games related to development; it helped to establish the idea of "scientifically" choosing games based on both physiological and social development, and thus could be considered on a par with "scientific" gymnastics. Useful as the book was and is, its role in engendering respectability for games in school was its most important effect.

In addition to her work in posture, especially her connection of anthropometric measurements to the manufacture of school desks, clothing, shoes, and subway seats, and her innovative use of games in the physical education program, Jessie Bancroft could claim many "firsts" in her career. She was the first woman to direct the physical education program of a large city school system, the first woman to publish a considerable body of professional literature,* the first woman to become a member of the American Academy of Physical Education (Fellow #8), and the first woman to receive the Gulick Award (1924). She was made a Fellow of the American Association for the Advancement of Science, and a Fellow of the APEA with the first group so acclaimed in 1931, received an Honorary Diploma from the Sargent Normal School and an honorary M.P.E. from Springfield College.

In a time when her professional colleagues were largely men forging theories and programs appropriate to colleges, Jessie Bancroft, a woman with no college degree or medical degree, armed with a belief in the worth of her subject, an extra amount of spunk, and the willingness, open-mindedness, and capacity to learn, pioneered a physical education program in the public schools.

---

* In addition to works already mentioned, she published *Recess Games* (1895), *Handbook*, Girl's Branch Public School Athletic League (1906), *Handbook of Athletic Games* (1916), and numerous articles including one on "Physical Training" and one on "Games" in the *Encyclopedia Americana*.

# ELIZABETH BURCHENAL

## 1876-1959

If one single person could be credited with the development of folk dancing in America as a school and recreational activity, it would be Elizabeth Burchenal. She was founder of the American Folk-Dance Society and president from its beginning in 1916 until 1929 when it was incorporated as the Division of Folk Dance and Music in the Folk Arts Center in New York City. She was Executive Chairman of the Folk Arts Center, an organization she created and directed from 1929 until her death thirty years later, during which time she assembled an Archive of American Folk Dance. She was the first chairman of the Committee on Folk Dancing of the Playground Association of America. Nationally, she served as Chairman of the National Committee on Folk Arts of the United States, a member representing the United States on the International Commission on Folk Art and Folklore, and the official delegate from the United States to the Fine Arts Section meetings of the League of Nations and UNESCO (United Nations Educational, Scientific, and Cultural Organization). But she was not only an organizer; traveling around the world collecting folk arts materials at their source, she published books of folk dances from around the world, including musical arrangements, and performance directions. Some of these were: *Folk Dances and Singing Games* (1909), *Folk Dances of Denmark* (1915), *Folk Dances of Finland* (1915), *Folk Dances of Germany* (1938), *Folk Dances from Old Homelands* (1922), *Dances of the People* (1938), and *American Country Dances* (1918). All of these books were published by G. Schirmer, Inc., a publisher well-known in the music world. She did her research by traveling to some isolated community in America or a foreign country, living there until neighbors began to receive her socially; from them she learned the intricacies of their dances. Besides the many summers abroad, she spent 1933–1934 in Germany on a research fellowship given by the Oberlander Trust of the Carl Schurz Memorial Foundation. (71:206)

Her work in folk dance was a part of her life as a physical educator. Born in Richmond, Indiana, her mother was a musician and her father, a judge, especially interested in folklore. The family entertained many foreign visitors and Burchenal's interest in folk art can be traced back to experiences she had in this period. (71:196) After earning her A.B. in

FIG. 69.    Elizabeth Burchenal.

English at Earlham College, located in her home town, she enrolled at the Sargent Normal School and earned her diploma in 1898.   Greatly interested in dance she then attended the Gilbert Normal School of Dancing and gained from that experience a belief that dancing could be an important part of a physical education curriculum.*   In 1903 she was appointed an instructor at Columbia University, and living in New York she was exposed to folk dancing through the large immigrant population then flooding the city.   The following description, given in an article in *Woman Citizen*, was typical of Burchenal's experiences:

It was a lucky day for fast-vanishing dance traditions when some of Elizabeth Burchenal's friends invited her to go with them to a most unusual party.   The

* Melvin Ballou Gilbert (1847–1910), a dance teacher from Portland, Maine, developed "aesthetic dancing" to meet Sargent's complaint that dancing did not involve or develop the arms and trunk. (328)   From 1894 when he became associated with the Harvard Summer School, his work spread throughout the country and was generally included in normal school curriculums.   From 1895 he taught at the Sargent School but maintained his own normal school during the summers. His work stressed elegance of form and beautiful movements, hence the title "aesthetic dancing."   For women it offered an opportunity to excel in movement that performers on apparatus enjoyed.   For fuller explication of his work, refer to Gilbert's article on "Classic Dancing." (128)

music was strange, but merry, and the dancing was stranger and merrier still. The guests were mostly baggy men and shawled women only recently come from the other side. They swung and stamped and clapped and she clapped and stamped and swung, taking away with her a new idea of fun. (71:198)

It was during this period that she began the original research in folk dancing and music that became a lifetime's work. Her classes at Teachers College and the Horace Mann School brought her to the attention of Luther Gulick, then Director of Physical Training in the New York City Public Schools. In 1906 he persuaded her to become Executive Secretary of the new Girls' Branch of the Public School Athletic League (PSAL) with responsibility for teaching athletics and folk dancing to teachers in the schools. Because of the work of Burchenal, bolstered by the encouraging support of Gulick, folk dancing became part of the physical education program of a large school system for the first time.

The values of folk dancing as an appropriate part of school physical education were apparent when it was compared to an active game:

> The folk dances that lend themselves best to a recreation and health drive are those which may be classed in the same category with active games most desirable for the same purpose, i.e., those in which large groups take part, which are easy to learn and pass on to others, and which provide vigorous action, forgetfulness of self, keen interest and pleasure, team work and the social element. (65:228)

In addition, folk dancing had important educational values related to the knowledge of another art form and of the customs and traditions of people. Studying other cultures was already an important part of the school curriculum and physical education, via folk dancing, contributed to this aspect of a child's education:

> Folk-dancing has great and worthy purposes to serve: it is a pure and fundamental art-form and as such should be preserved and treasured by us as a factor in the development of art in this country.
>
> The folk-dancing of a people expresses their spirit and character as no words could, and in such a vivid, human and universally comprehensible way that it has an educative value for the general public, whose knowledge of the newer Americans is woefully meager and whose horizon would be broadened by the cultural advantages acquired through contact with people of other countries. I believe most heartily that folk-dancing can be of assistance in what Rabindranath Tagore has called the "World mission America has to perform in welcoming all peoples and making them one." (62:x)

Although Burchenal functioned in the school system, her work was primarily with the adult teachers, and her writings on folk dance indicated her belief that it was a valuable activity for people of all ages and both sexes.

To Burchenal folk was unlike other dance forms:

Real Folk Dancing is the simple, happy, unsophisticated, *social* (in the true sense of the word) dancing of peasants which has sprung just as naturally from the hearts of the people in response to the human need for self-expression, play and social intercourse as wild flowers spring from the soil.

It is quite definitely a thing apart from other kinds of dancing and serves a different purpose if used in its original form and spirit. (63:404)

Most interesting and important was her interpretation of the social recreation aspect of folk dancing:

The spirit and attitude of mind is of simple pleasure and interest in the doing of the dance itself, and enjoyment of the social intercourse and "team play" amongst the group or "set," of people involved in the dance.

In the countries from which they come folk dances *are* the *traditional rural community recreation of the people*, and contain the very essence of *social group play*. They are easy to do being simple and unstudied with stimulating, happy rhythm—they have an amusing game element—they call for the participation of the entire crowd (grandparents, mothers and fathers, young people and children!)—they provide happy relaxation, pleasant physical activity, forgetfulness of self and sociability. (63:404)

When that viewpoint is considered, the use of folk dancing as the principal activity of the Girls' Branch of the PSAL was understandable. Girls like boys needed to participate in some athletic activities, but it was not then believed that competition was good for the female sex. Folk dancing with its "team play," "game elements" and activity demands was the perfect answer. Thus through folk dancing Elizabeth Burchenal found herself one of the pioneers of girls' "athletics."

She held many positions in relation to that role. As Executive Secretary of the Girls' Branch of PSAL from 1906–1916, she was editor of its official *Handbook of Girls' Athletics*. In 1909 she was appointed Inspector of Athletics for the Department of Education in New York City. In 1917 she was made first chairman of the newly formed Committee on Women's Athletics of the APEA.* In that position she represented the Association at the historic first meeting of the Women's Division of the National Amateur Athletic Federation, held April 6–7, 1923 in the National Museum, Washington, D. C. under the auspices of Mrs. Herbert Hoover, then president of the Girl Scouts.

In these various roles Burchenal helped to frame the early policies on

---

* An outgrowth of the Women's Basketball Rules Committee (1899) and the National Women's Basketball Committee (1905), it became the Section on Women's Athletics (1927), the National Section on Women's Athletics (1932), the National Section for Girls and Women's Sports (1953), and the Division for Girls' and Women's Sports (1957). The title changes reflected the status of women's sports as it grew in importance from a committee to a section to the division it now is. They also indicated the change in conception from competition for women only, to include girls. The change in terminology from "athletics" to "sports" reflected new cultural understandings.

athletics for girls and women.   In a report she prepared in 1919 for the New York State Military Training Commission, for which she was assistant state inspector (1916–1918), she set forth policies based upon her experiences with the Girls' Branch:

(a) Athletics for girls should be developed *only* on the bases of play, wholesome pleasure, health, and character building—"Sport for sport's sake."
(b) Athletics should be for *all* the girls (Extensive Athletics).   Any form of athletics is a failure which does not include, and is not suitable for and interesting to, *at least* 80 per cent of all girls.
(c) Eliminate all the disadvantages and mistakes of boys' athletics . . . .
(d) Athletics carried on *within* the school (intramural, interclass athletics) and no interschool competition.
(e) Athletics events and games in which *teams* (not individual girls) compete.
(f) Athletics chosen and practiced with *regard to their suitability for girls* and not *merely in imitation of boys' athletics.*
(g) Girls' athletics directed by competent women instructors and leaders. (60:273)

An examination of policies and guidelines released by various girls' and women's sports groups in the AAHPER shows a consistent belief in approximately the same ideas from then until the early 1960s.

Burchenal was honored for her contributions.   She was made a Fellow of the APEA in 1931 with the first group of Honor Awardees, was a charter member and Fellow (#28) of the American Academy of Physical Education, received an honorary D.Sc. degree from Boston University (1943), and in 1950 was given the profession's highest honor, the Gulick Award.

The work of Elizabeth Burchenal extended well beyond the profession of physical education, for in promoting folk dancing as one of its activities she helped develop and preserve a new art form through which she brought to the American people increased awareness and understanding of the rich cultural heritage upon which nations are built.

# ETHEL PERRIN

## 1871-1962

The hallmark of Ethel Perrin's character was her willingness to be educated. Open to new ideas, responsive to her own experiences, creative and pragmatic in her approach to problems, and possessor of a sense of humor which enabled her not to take herself too seriously, she was able to emerge from her nineteenth-century training to become a leader of twentieth-century physical education. For a full appreciation of the progress of Ethel Perrin's development, which Jay B. Nash said "parallels the strategic years of advancement in the field of physcial education, health, and recreation" (251:405), her witty article "Confessions of a Once Strict Formalist" (273) must be read.

Born in Wellesley, Massachusetts, she attended a private boarding school, the Howard Collegiate Institute in West Bridgewater, Massachusetts, and upon her graduation in 1890, the Boston Normal School of Gymnastics. After the standard two years there as a student she remained for fourteen more on the faculty. She then substituted for the director at Smith College for a year and was engaged in a similar role the following year at the University of Michigan. When she was appointed to direct the physical training program at the Central High School in Detroit, Michigan in 1908, and to be Supervisor of Physical Culture in the Detroit Public Schools, beginning in 1909, a complete reversal of her life situation took place:

> I had never been interviewed in my life and had never even seen, much less spoken to a Superintendent of Schools. . . . I had no knowledge of public high schools having been to a private school only, and no particular interest in them. . . . I had no knowledge of elementary schools in general or in Detroit. I had never supervised anything nor anybody, nor had I taken a course or read a book on supervision. School principals, teachers, and school children were unknown quantities. (273:534–535)

Furthermore, life in New England was much more formal than in the Midwest.

> Professional formality surrounded me and this included not only formal and stereotyped teaching but all matters of behavior and of dress. . . . I shall never forget my astonishment when a freshman [at the University of Michigan] looked

368

me over and said "What a pretty dress you have on." A personal remark from a student to a member of the faculty was a new one to me, but I liked the friendliness of it. (273:534)

The program at the BNSG "was founded and grounded in the Swedish system of gymnastics and no other system or mixture of systems could be mentioned in the same breath. . . . It was wonderful to be cocksure that we alone were on the right track. It gave us a great sense of responsibility and we felt it was our mission to spread pure Swedish gymnastics from Maine to California." (273:533) Yet she developed a full program of sports and games in Detroit and in 1924 wrote:

> The last underlying principle in the democracy of recreation for which I would urge your championship today is this—that in our early physical education we bear in mind the public facilities for adult recreation and prepare our children to utilize these facilities. . . . Pupils should be encouraged to play and to learn new games for their immediate joy. Tennis, golf, swimming and ice skating have a sporting appeal that is not particularly adult; they are equally fascinating games for children. (276:266)

The greatest change for Perrin was in moving from the authoritarian behavior required of the Swedish gymnastics system to the democratic behavior appropriate to the American play movement:

FIG. 70.   Ethel Perrin.

In the Boston Normal School of Gymnastics there was but one way of doing things and we did as we were told, whether we liked it or not, because someone else knew what was best for us. I had always followed this regime willingly because I believed that the one in authority always was right. . . . (273:534)

Yet by 1924 she warned:

The play leader is often the Czar of the grounds; and the . . . play hour smacks of paternalism. . . . I want to see children given as much opportunity as possible to construct their own outdoor play equipment. . . . Let children work out their games too. . . . When this is done, playgrounds will look less like puppet shows than they sometimes do now, play will be freer and easier, and the play-leader will become less of the overlord and more of a fellow playmate. (276:242–246)

She changed in other ways too, learning to see the virtues of co-education, sensible costumes for girls which allowed freedom of movement, interschool sports for boys *and* girls, informality in classes, and assistants from all over the country who could bring new ideas and activities to programs.

In 1909 when Perrin was appointed supervisor, her department in Detroit consisted of three men and three women teachers plus herself; in 1923 when she resigned it had grown to 350 teachers and fifteen supervisors. Until the corps of trained teachers was developed, Perrin depended upon the classroom teachers to carry out her program. In 1914 she explained that the teachers were given "a carefully described plan to follow, a visit once in five weeks from a supervisor, and general meetings for new instructions once a term, to help them on their way." (275:505) At that time they were only allowed ten minutes daily for the regular plan of work, with two three-minute open-window periods for games, all of which took place in the classroom or hall. However, in 1918 the Detroit schools adopted the 6–3–3 plan (as opposed to the old 8–4 plan without the junior high school), and the Platoon System in the elementary schools which filled the playgrounds, pools and gymnasiums with students every period of the day. The changes necessitated three to six special teachers in each building and they were directly responsible for the sudden spectacular growth of the physical education department.* Perrin also succeeded in arranging for each child to have sixty minutes of daily physical activity in school time and plenty of after-school, organized athletics. The department assumed responsibility for health education and forty teachers were assigned exclusively to this phase of the program.

The Detroit program included extra-curricular athletics for boys and girls of both the intramural and intermural types. Under Perrin's supervision were created a decathlon contest for boys and a pentathlon contest

---

* Even today special teachers for physical education in elementary schools are not the rule throughout the country. Although Detroit has maintained this practice, other large schools systems such as New York City, Los Angeles and Pittsburgh still use the classroom teacher.

for girls which were carried out on an interschool basis at the Belle Isle Field Day.  Conducted each year on the island which is easily accessible to the city, it became a big extravaganza for the whole city.  Boys and girls competed in races, distance throws and other field activities in a situation reminiscent of the finest examples of sport competition.

One of Ethel Perrin's most important contributions was her work with athletics—particularly girls' sports.  She was one of the few leaders who approved of competition for girls and she developed a full program in the Detroit schools.  Although the Play Day approach was emphasized as being in keeping with the spirit of sport, other types of competition also took place.  Intramural competition, using a system of collective scoring, was held in the form of stunt tests for the fifth and sixth grade girls; games tournaments including zig zag ball, post ball, and combination pass ball and stunt speed series, open to any girl in the school; and volleyball, field ball and hit pin base-ball. (272:660)  She believed that "athletics for girls are an important part of any program of physical education planned to fit present day conditions of living" (277:22).  At a time when most women physical educators agreed with the public that competition, per se, was bad for girls, Perrin said that "everyone agrees that competition is the big test of self-control, honesty, cooperation and all the other qualities listed to make a good citizen, and yet some would deprive a girl of this natural opportunity for behavioristic development." (272:659)  To those who argued for intraschool rather than interschool competition, she rejoined:

> Some people feel that by eliminating all inter games and making them all intra —the curse is taken away, but just as much hysteria can be manufactured from *intra* as from *inter*, and I can imagine some nervous individual getting upset if allowed only to compete against herself. (272:658)

.   .   .   .   .   .   .   .   .   .   .   .   .   .   .   .

> There is some discussion at present of the value of interschool competitive games for girls.  This is not because girls from one school should not play games with girls from another school, but because such games, in many places, have been poorly conducted. (277:22)

The strongest point generally advanced by the opponents of competition for girls and women was the inherent weakness of the feminine physique and the possibility of harming the reproductive organs.  On that subject Perrin commented:

> So far as I can learn, these extremely conservative people who fear for the future of our race because of possible impairment of the reproductive organs of an athletic woman, have little or no data by which to point the way, and they have to resort largely to the personal opinion of the physician.* (272:658)

---

* Assertions that Perrin regarded with skepticism have in recent years been shown to be unlikely.  Positive data on the capacity of women to compete in almost all forms of athletics without incurring physiological harm have been presented by researchers.

On the positive side, Perrin enumerated what she considered to be the aims and justifications of competitive athletics for women:

1. To encourage participation in healthful athletic activities on the part of all girls in all intermediate and high schools.
2. To develop desirable social and moral qualities . . . by promoting intramural and a limited number of inter-school meets and tournaments.
3. To stimulate in every girl an interest in athletic activity which shall function throughout life. (272:660)

She also noted that it was not the program's aim to encourage the development of stars or championship teams, but rather to provide opportunity for widespread participation.

Perrin's work in this area was not limited to the Detroit Public Schools. When the Women's Amateur Athletic Federation (WAAF) was created in 1923 as a result of a Conference on Athletics and Physical Recreation for Girls and Women called by Mrs. Herbert Hoover,* Ethel Perrin was appointed to its Executive Committee. She served on it for over ten years, several of which were in the capacity of chairman. From that position she was able to work with other leaders to establish national principles for the conduct of girls' and women's athletics.

When Perrin resigned from her Detroit position it was to assume the new responsibility of being Assistant (and later Associate) Director of Health Education for the American Child Health Association, a position she retired from in 1936. In this work she attempted to help physical education make its contribution to health education and vice versa. Convinced that "health is inextricably tied up with all aims and objectives of physical education" (274:15), she organized health clubs in the Detroit schools. However, she took the controversial position that the physical educator could not assume total responsibility for health: "To become a part of a functioning school health program, physical education will first realize that it is only a part and by no means the whole story." (71:140) Like Thomas Wood (refer to p. 379) she advocated that health be a twenty-four hour objective, entailing the cooperative endeavors of school, home and community, and that within the school it should be a "far-reaching program rather than a subject in the curriculum, a supervision of individual health development rather than a mere teaching of hygiene. . . ." (71:139) In the citation for her Gulick Award, Jay B. Nash commented, "her visits throughout the country, her many articles, and her charming personality were in no small measure responsible for the growth of health consciousness during the period after World War I." (251:448)

---

* The history of this important group was detailed by Agnes Wayman in an article: "Women's Division of the National Amateur Athletic Federation." *Journal of Health and Physical Education*, III (March, 1932), 3–7, 53–54. In 1941, after almost two decades of trying to coordinate its work with the Women's Athletic Section of the APEA, the two groups merged (refer to footnote, p. 366).

The work of Ethel Perrin was an excellent example of innovative leadership. The Detroit program was considered one of the most outstanding in the country. Under Perrin's leadership new schools were built with gymnasiums and swimming pools, special physical education teachers were hired for every level of instruction, activity periods were increased to one hour each day, children were given a rich program of activities in an informal atmosphere, and well-conducted competition for boys and girls was encouraged to take place. Perrin's work was admired and imitated throughout the country.

She was a national figure, active in professional organizations including the APEA of which she was the vice-president from 1920–1923, President of the Midwest Society of Physical Education in 1917–1918, a member of the Board of Directors of the American Posture League, a member of the Executive Committee of the Department of School Health and Physical Education of the NEA, and a member of the Board of Directors and the Executive Committee of the NAAF. She was in the first group of Honor Awardees, being made a Fellow of the APEA in 1931, and she was the second woman to receive the Gulick Award when she was so honored in 1946.

# THOMAS DENISON WOOD

## 1865-1951

It was Luther Halsey Gulick, roommate of Thomas D. Wood at Oberlin College, who put into writing a description of one of the important moments in time for both of them:

> One Sunday afternoon we took a long walk out into the woods, and sitting beside a rail fence . . . we looked forward to the future of physical training. . . . And it seems at the present time as if the greater part of the work we have each of us been able to do since then has been but the following out of the lines which we discussed that afternoon. That day, that hour, was a turning point for both of us. . . . (144:25)

Born in Sycamore, Illinois, Wood earned his bachelor's degree at Oberlin College where, like Gulick, he came under the influence of Delphine Hanna. They were in her first class to train men students for leadership roles in Oberlin's program. In his last two years there Wood was in charge of the gymnasium work for men. Convinced that he wanted a career in physical education, he completed A.M. and M.D. degrees at Columbia University (1891), during which time he also worked in YMCAs in New York City and Summit, New Jersey. In 1891 he took his first professional position at the new Stanford University.

Under the leadership of David Starr Jordan, Stanford's first president, Wood was part of the small group which organized the new university. From the beginning he had unqualified support for a sound physical education program, as the first *Register for 1891–92* testifies:

> For the physical training of the students there are two buildings. . . . They are being well equipped with the apparatus and appliances intended for the development and training of students. . . .
> Excellent facilities for athletics have been provided. . . .
> All the work in physical training is under the supervision of the medical director [Wood] who is the professor of hygiene and physical training. (338)

Three courses were offered on an elective basis from that first year. One was a lecture course in Hygiene. The second was in Physical Training which met three exercise periods a week and carried the stipulation: "Credit will be given for systematic prescribed work in physical training as

Fig. 71.   Thomas Denison Wood.

for laboratory and shop work, three hours of exercise to be equivalent to one hour's work of recitation. . . ."*   The third course, in Physical Training and Hygiene, was "intended for those who expect to teach these subjects." It consisted of courses in Hygiene, Theory of Physical Training and Practice in Physical Training and met two lecture and five exercise hours per week throughout the year. (338)

The actual degree program was apparently not effected until the following year, when the *Register for 1892–93* announced that: "The following courses . . . are designed for candidates for the degree of A.B. in Physical Training and Hygiene. . . ."†

The prescribed courses included Personal, Advanced and School Hygiene,

---

* This was probably the first university in the United States to give physical education the same standing as other subject matter by virtue of awarding it academic credit.

† Since Harvard actually began its degree program in 1891 (refer to p. 304) it claims the honor of being the first.   Furthermore, Harvard graduated its first physical educator four years before Stanford—1893 cf. 1897.

General and Applied Anatomy and Physiology, Animal Physiology, Physical Education (emphasizing the study of the history of physical training and of the various systems), Physical Training (which consisted almost completely of work in gymnastics of various types), and Special Courses. The latter course was research-oriented, providing that "special investigations in the laboratory and gymnasium are taken up by advanced students. . . . This work includes investigations into the physiology of special exercises. . . ." (338)

By the next year the *Register for 1893–94* announced a Summer School of Hygiene and Physical Training to be held at Pacific Grove, California. Thus in three years on his first job, Wood was able to inaugurate a general program for credit, a degree program for teaching majors, and a summer school for teachers, all within a university setting. It was unprecedented; even Sargent at Harvard had not achieved such support and academic standing. In part it must have been the result of Wood's educational philosophy which was well-developed and creative at that early stage of the profession and his career. None of his colleagues had ever stated in such clear and certain terms the role of physical education in education, as Wood did when addressing the AAAPE in 1893:

> What is physical education? . . . Many people answer: "The training and development of the physical"; and they consider that the aim and end may be found in anthropometric apparatus, physical measurements, athletic contests and exhibitions, with graphic representations of measurements and of averages.
>
> Now these things are very well in their places, but if our science is to be worthy of the best efforts of men and women, and of the respect and recognition of the educational world, physical education must have an aim as broad as education itself, and as noble and inspiring as human life. The great thought in physical education is not the education of the physical nature, but the relation of physical training to complete education, and then the effort to make the physical contribute its full share to the life of the individual, in environment, training, and culture. (10:9)

Perhaps it was because of this belief that Wood was able to break away from the traditional curriculum of gymnastic exercises, broadening it to include sport activities in general program classes. A student in that early program, Thomas A. Storey (the first Director of Physical Education in New York State), recalled its content:

> These physical exercise programs were formal, informal, social, and attractive. It was an outdoor program as well as an indoor program. Apparatus work, handball, basketball, cross-country, and track and field work were among the activities included. I have never seen more student interest shown anywhere than I saw, year after year, in the organized class work for credit at Stanford University. (343:784)

By 1910, writing for the *Ninth Yearbook of the National Society for the Study of Education*, Wood had formulated the philosophical cornerstone of what came to be known as "the new Physical Education." It marked a turning point in the profession—a shift in emphasis from the goals of health to the goals of education:

> If necessary . . . health qualities must constitute the main goal in this field, but it is most desirable that physical education should occupy itself with a program of activities for the young which would secure these physical aspects of health without fail, as by-products, as it were, while the pupil is being guided in the doing of things which will result in the acquirement of mental, moral and social benefits. Health, then, in the narrower sense, becomes an essential means or condition in physical education to the accomplishment of certain exceedingly valuable results in the general education of the child. (379:80–81)

The new philosophy demanded a new curriculum, and its basis was sports, games and dance, conducted in a manner reflecting the natural instincts of man. Natural physical education harked back to Rousseau, Guts Muths and Gaulhofer-Streicher; its connotations were related to both nature and the evolutionary heritage of man.* Wood said:

> The subject matter of physical education is found in play, games, dancing, swimming, outdoor sports, athletics, and gymnastics (reconstructed to satisfy educational needs). . . .
> This proposed program looks to the process of human evolution for general guidance. . . . Primitive men . . . developed physical and moral powers through play in childhood and by doing very real things in hunting and fishing, in agriculture, in war . . . in supplying human needs. . . . Children and young people must do things today, not necessarily identified in type and purpose with those of primitive life, but in the same general spirit and manner, if the method is to be effective and the results satisfactory. (379:84–85)

From this theoretical basis Wood outlined ten conditions "necessary for rational exercise in physical education if the best results are to be obtained." They formed the basis of the new physical education:

>   I. The activities of physical education should be carried on out of doors, whenever this may be made possible. The gymnasium . . . should never interfere with possible use of nature's infinitely better playroom out of doors.
>  II. The exercises should be natural in type, satisfying by their execution the play instinct and the fundamental powers and faculties as they develop, with due regard to the ancestral habits of activity and to the future practical needs of the individual. . . .
> Formal gymnastics, free-hand movements, for the most part, and much of the apparatus work of the gymnasium, belong to the category of artificial "stunts," mechanical movements lacking the purpose, mental content, and objective which are essential to sensible educational performances. . . .
> . . . Progress in physical education must be away from all formal, artificial kinds of movement. . . .
> III. In physical education . . . the pupils in practice should either: (a) express

* It was only fifty-one years since Darwin's theory of evolution had been enunciated in 1859 and eminent psychologists had interpreted Darwin by connecting man's primitive ancestry and so-called instinctive behavior in contemporary man.

an idea, feeling, or emotion . . . e.g., in dancing . . . or (b) there should be some definite objective aim or effect to be attained as the result of the muscular effort performed, as in maintenance of squad formation in marching, hitting a ball, throwing a ball into a basket, swimming to a given point. . . .

IV.   The activities in physical education should be correlated whenever feasible with the subjects and activities with which the child is occupied elsewhere in the school or outside . . . employ dances and games which have definite relation to the subjects in hand and give the child a most valuable opportunity to express himself more completely in relation to the interest which occupies his attention.

VII.   . . . Evolutions in marching, and sometimes dancing, necessitate precise uniformity in movement. . . . In general, however, it is most desirable that mechanical uniformity should not be demanded, but that, with the observance of certain general principles of action, the pupil should be left free to express individuality in action. . . .

VIII.   Physical education should be supervised and directed with reference to the beneficial, social, and moral results which may be gained by the right performance, in play, games, and athletics, of the large fundamental types of human action. . . .

IX.   In the fifth or sixth elementary . . . grades . . . boys and girls should have the more vigorous games and exercises in separate classes, and from that time onward in their physical education the forms of exercise should be adapted to sex differences as well as to advancing age and personal needs.

X.   While in physical education certain psychic, social, and ethical results should be directly sought, the forms of exercise should always be arranged and controlled so that favorable physiologic values may be obtained. (379:85–90)

Over the next twenty years Wood worked out the details of the natural program in physical education, including the philosophy, content, method, measurement of achievement, role of the teacher, and evaluation. In 1927, with Rosalind Cassidy as co-author, *The New Physical Education* (381) was published. With Wood's 1910 *NSSE Yearbook* chapter cited above, these two works stand as the original documents of twentieth century-physical education. More than any prior work in English, *The New Physical Education* reflected the thinking and applied the work of philosophers, psychologists and educators to physical education. John Dewey, Edward L. Thorndike, Friedrich Froebel, Jean Jacques Rousseau, Charles Darwin, and William James were among the famous thinkers frequently cited and interpreted. Thus the work represented not only a turning point, but the coming of age of physical education as an endeavor having a relationship to the history of ideas. Physical educators had envisioned themselves as natural scientists—Wood enunciated a place for the profession within the broad realm of the social sciences, where it has since remained.*

* This is still, however, not reflected in the undergraduate professional preparation curriculums which require a full complement of courses in the physical sciences and a brief smattering in the social sciences.

Since Wood shifted the center of physical education from its singular focus on health, to the broader perspective of education, it is somewhat paradoxical that he originated the term health education, was the first Professor of Health Education so named, and played a large role in the initial development of that area of study. In 1927 he became Professor of Health Education, a position he held until his retirement five years later. Wood was active in the development of the American Child Health Association and served as an officer from 1923 to 1936; for over twenty-five years he was chairman of the Joint Committee on Health Problems in Education of the National Education Association and the American Medical Association, a committee he organized; he was chairman of the International Conference on Health Education of the World Education Congress in 1923; he was also chairman of the Committee on the School and the Child, at the White House Conference on Child Health and Protection, held in 1930 when Herbert Hoover was President.

Wood was the first to distinguish between physical education and health education, in terms of aim, content and administrative structure:*

> The Department of Physical Education has vitally important contributions to make to the School Health Program, but these correspond essentially to contributions to be made by teachers and departments of General Science, Biology, Home Economics, Nutrition, and other subjects, and also by physicians, nurses, dentists, nutritionists, social advisers, and in fact all members of the school staff, including very definitely the janitor or custodian of the building.
>
> Experience has clearly demonstrated that the desired cooperation and contributions from other departments and members of the teaching staff can be secured much more surely and effectively if health education, and the school health program in general, is quite independent administratively of the Department of Physical Education. (380:57–58)

His view of health education was comprehensive. Health, to Wood, was "the condition of the individual who is organically sound and who has the biologic basis for the attainment of completeness of body, completeness of mind, and completeness of character." (380:18) From this concept of health relating to the total being, he defined health education as "the sum of experiences, in school and elsewhere, which favorably influence [sic] habits, attitudes, and knowledge relating to individual, community, and racial health." (380:55) He advocated that every school have a school health program or division rather than a department, because of the variety of services he believed should be incorporated. Within the pro-

---

* That the profession was unwilling to accept his administrative distinction is evidenced by the preponderance of departments of health *and* physical education, the dual certification given to most graduates, and the continuous interchanging of roles while on the job. However, in recent years the Health Education Division has begun to consider a formal separation from the AAHPER. Refer to JOHPER, June, 1968, pp. 58–65, for a statement of their new position.

gram the following were included under the term "health services":  daily health inspection; periodic health examinations and weighing and measuring; correction by the school, home and through the cooperation of other agencies, of remediable health defects; maintenance of a sanitary environment; immunization; provisions for first aid and safety; and health supervision of teachers, janitors and others who came in contact with students. (380:50)  He also stipulated that follow-up health service by school or district nurses, and warm school lunches for those not eating them at home, be parts of the health program. (380:37)

In health education classes he stressed an interdepartmental program with teaching based upon the principles of psychology and pedagogy, and "knowledge that should be clearly worked out not only on each level or grade of education in the schools, but also in adaptation to the special needs of the individual school, and finally to the specific needs of the individual pupil." (380:52)  He believed the major goal of the classes to be "the appreciation and application of the scientifically approved measures for the promotion of health." (380:48)  He believed in placing "greater emphasis upon social than upon personal or individual aspects of hygiene.  The child . . . will get the best idea and habit in the care of his own health if he believes it important for social service and efficiency. . . ." (380:38)  He specifically rejected the teaching of anatomy and physiology, common to curriculums of hygiene classes since Edward Hitchcock included it at Amherst College:  "Systematic study of human anatomy and physiology is neither necessary nor desirable as a preliminary or accompaniment of health instruction.  This has been a common error in the past." (380:38)

Fundamental to his advocacy of health education was his belief that in a nation with compulsory education, schools were the agency best suited to teaching and directing the health habits and attitudes of a nation:

> The school in the United States, at least, is the universal, the officially accredited, and the strategic agency for leading in the educational program of health and for organizing and directing the health care of children of public-school age. Much of the actual work of health care of these children must be accomplished by the home, by health boards, and by other organizations both governmental and voluntary.  However, it is the peculiar privilege and province of the school to standardize the principles and methods of child nurture and training. (380:35)

Wood delineated a program for the care and teaching of health that involved not only the total school personnel, but the home and community agencies.  Though knowledge of the subject matter is more sophisticated at this time, the organization and scope of the program still functions along the lines laid out by Wood, primarily in the 1920's.  His books on health education included among others:  *The Child in School Care and Its Health* (1924) and *Health Education, A Program for Public Schools and Teacher Training Institutions* (1930).

His great contributions in the development of the new physical education and programs of health education, perhaps foreshadowed the work he did at Columbia University. In the 31 years he was at Teachers College, first as Professor of Physical Education and College Physician, and later as Professor of Health Education, he organized and conducted a department of physical education that became one of the most respected in this country. His writings and speeches to various groups did much to bring physical education to the attention and concern of school administrators. He was honored by selection as a Fellow of the American Association for the Advancement of Science, the New York Academy of Medicine, the American Academy of Physical Education, and the APEA, from which he was given an Honor Award with the first group in 1931. In 1925 he received the third Gulick Award. The citation, given by Jessie Bancroft, was a fitting tribute to his contribution:

> In the field of physical education you have been one of the outstanding philosophers,—a practical, constructive philosopher. . . .
>
> Through many committees of state and national scope, several of which you have served as chairman, and whose activities you have inspired and guided; through research and lectures and reports and publications of many kinds, you have been one of the most potent influences in the country to enlarge the field of physical education from mere gymnastics to a comprehensive health program. . . .
>
> Largely through your personal influence, the three great fields of medicine, and scholastic education, and physical education have been brought into a closer relation. (343:838–839)

# TEACHERS COLLEGE

Teachers College, Columbia University, was one of the most important institutions in the history of education in the United States. Both critics and supporters agreed that it was "far out"—i.e., a center for experimentation and innovative change in education. From Teachers College (T.C.) came the leadership of the progressive and the vocational education movement. Teachers College was the crusader for democracy in education as well as the champion of public education. In his work, *Columbia, Colossus on the Hudson*, Coon commented on its significance:

> Year in and year out for more than fifty years it has tried faithfully, sometimes in strange ways, to serve the poor as well as the rich, the stupid as well as the clever. Whatever may be said about the place, that must not be forgotten, for it is the key to this educational colossus which is the biggest professional school in the world. (77:212)

The school's involvement in social change sometimes caused it to be dubbed "radical" and even communistic, but it managed to weather such diatribes.

Besides being the world's largest teachers college, it probably had the most varied curriculum. Long before such subjects became a respectable part of academia, T.C. was offering majors in the "practical arts," including costume design and illustration, house decoration, household arts, industrial arts—and physical education. Within its portals were developed new teaching methods (such as William Heard Kilpatrick's "project method"), some of which ultimately became standard practice in American schools; in fact, T.C. may be credited with changing the whole character of teaching. During the 1920s and 1930s the school experienced a period of intense interest in research in which scholars sought to find facts upon which to base innovations. "Data was [sic] gathered on every imaginable subject, and published, of course, with elaborate charts. From these charts it was said to be possible to ascertain the average mark in Latin for the fifteen-year-old children of blond Presbyterians in the public schools of the Second Congressional District of Arkansas." (77:221)

The pride of Teachers College was its faculty. Students attending that institution had the privilege of studying with some of the most famous educational theorists of this century. In 1917, for example, a student could take courses from John Dewey, William Heard Kilpatrick, George S. Counts, Paul Monroe, and Edward L. Thorndike. In other years the faculty included Ruth Strang, R. Freeman Butts and Harold Rugg. The work of Thorndike, Dewey and Kilpatrick particularly, was espoused by students and faculty in the Department of Physical Education, who supplemented their professional work by taking courses and otherwise consulting with these famous professors. Physical education had its share of "greats" among the Columbia faculty, which at various times included Thomas Denison Wood, Jesse Feiring Williams, Harry A. Scott, Clifford Lee Brownell, Josephine Rathbone, Lillian Curtis Drew, Elizabeth Burchenal, Bird Larsen, and Gertrude Colby. Presiding over this array of genius was the Dean of Teachers College (1897–1927), James Earl Russell, and the noted President of Columbia University (1902–1945), Nicholas Murray Butler.

The relationship between Teachers College and Columbia University, from 1915 and thereafter, was one of close affiliation with institutional independence:

> Teachers College, founded in 1888, and chartered by the Regents of the University of the State of New York in 1889, became in 1898 part of the educational system of Columbia University. . . . The Faculties of Education and of Practical Arts in Teachers College are recognized as Faculties of the University. . . . The College is represented in the University Council by its Dean and two elected members of each Faculty. The College maintains, however, its separate corporate organization, its Board of Trustees continuing to assume entire responsibility for its maintenance. (360, 1917–1918:23)

A year after T.C. became part of Columbia University it began its first venture into training physical education teachers. In 1899 a summer session was inaugurated, consisting of a six-week course, with no requirements for admission. A single course, the Theory and Practice of Physical Education, was taught by five teachers to thirty-eight students (twenty men and eighteen women). (384:114)

In 1901 Thomas D. Wood was brought from Stanford to be Professor of Physical Education and College Physician. At that time the machinery for a four-year degree program was put into action, but it took two more years before it was formally listed as such. The *Announcement of Columbia Teachers College for 1902–1903* stated that:

> It is proposed to establish a course in Physical Education, similar to the course in Music, as soon as a gymnasium and working laboratories can be secured. In the meanwhile students may elect such courses as may be offered in the department with a view to meeting the requirements of the Bachelor's diploma when it becomes available. (384:92)

The requisite laboratory space became available as a result of a contribution in 1902 by Mrs. Frederick Ferris Thompson who donated $250,000 for a physical education building. Named for her late husband, Thompson Hall was formally dedicated on October 31, 1905 and was one of the finest structures of its time. In the 1903–1904 *Announcement* the physical education major curriculum was listed for the first time and five students were specified as degree candidates. (360, 1903–1904:99–100) Since each student was expected to complete two years of the Collegiate Course of General Education, professional courses were offered only for the junior and senior years. Although the Collegiate Course gave way in 1905 to a series of prescribed requirements, except for activities, the physical education program remained largely a two-year course.

Required theory course offerings were relatively unchanged for the approximately twenty-five years that a full undergraduate program was offered. Most of the requirements in the 1924–1925 *Announcement* could be found in earlier bulletins. For a Teaching of Physical Education diploma they were: applied anatomy, applied physiology, health examinations and anthropometry (replacing normal diagnosis and anthropometery), theory of the dance, kinesiology, personal hygiene, educational hygiene, foundations of health and physical education, principles and programs of physical education, educational psychology, history of education, and principles of teaching. (360:1924–1925:132–139) Practical courses for women included folk and clog dancing (the latter did not become part of the curriculum until the early twenties), natural gymnastics, athletics and games (including the dramatic game from about 1914), and individual gymnastics (correctives). (360, 1924–1925:132–139) For men the work was primarily in gymnastics, athletics, swimming, and games, although folk dancing was open to them. Few male students were enrolled in the program and in the summer session of 1920 a number of courses in the coaching of various team sports was offered for men only. This attempt to increase the male enrollment was apparently successful, for beginning in the early twenties there was a significant increase in the number of male students. (23:94–95)

Women had an opportunity to enjoy extramural competition, primarily against Barnard College and the Horace Mann School (one of the T.C. laboratory schools). While he was at T.C. from 1911–1916, Jesse F. Williams coached the women's teams in softball, swimming, basketball, and track and field. (23:65)

Course offerings in sports and outdoor education were strengthened by the purchase of Camp Mesacosa at Corinth, New York in 1919. The department conducted required camp classes there in June and September, beginning in 1920. The camp became known as Camp Saneo, a word formed from the last letter of each word in the phrase: *"mens fervida in corpore lacertoso"* ("a keen mind in a vigorous body"). In 1922 Camp Saneo was moved to Hinsdale, Massachusetts where it was operated for a few more years. In 1926 the four-year undergraduate curriculum at T.C. was abolished and skills courses, primarily on the graduate level, began to diminish in scope. In 1947 the Columbia College physical education staff took over the teaching of skills courses for students in the department at T.C.

The greatest change in activity offerings took place in the area of the dance. As early as 1905 some social and classical dancing was included in a course in gymnastics, and in 1907 a course in skills included work in dance dramas. In the next few years folk dances became an integral part of the curriculum. Dalcroze eurythmics and other courses in rhythm were introduced and in 1918 Gertrude Colby introduced her first course in natural dance. During the twenties and thirties the dance program flourished as an integral part of physical education. In 1947, by which time it was reduced to some courses in elementary rhythms, it became an interdivisional program within T.C. as a whole.

Also under the leadership of Gertrude Colby the dramatic game and dramatic expression became important courses. The former course dealt with fundamental play rhythms and music, interpretation through characterization and development of plot, dramatic and singing games, and simple folk dances, Indian dances, pantomimes, and ceremonies. The expression class aimed to develop understanding of the artistic side of physical education and its relation to music and literature. It demonstrated how motor activities such as sports, games, marches, and drills could be correlated to the curriculum through dramatization of poems, fairy stories, plays, and festivals. At one time these courses reached fad proportions at Teachers College because people were convinced they epitomized learning through interest and activity. These courses also complemented the newest curricular interest in 1914—play. A number of courses relating to play were added to the curriculum including one on the supervision of playgrounds, the theory of play and games, and play and playgrounds.

By 1924 a number of courses also had been added in supervision and administration, problems, principles, and methods. (360, 1924–1925:138–139) This trend continued throughout the next two decades.

In 1912 T.C. was divided into the School of Education and the School of Practical Arts. This organization continued until 1934 when the College regrouped into five divisions. Physical education was a major in the School of Practical Arts, but many courses in hygiene, play and "practical work" were offered to students in the School of Education. Furthermore, Thomas Wood was listed with both faculties, though in general each school had its own faculty. The School of Education retained control of all work leading to the B.S. degree and the T.C. diplomas in education. Therefore, students who wished to teach physical education took their first two years of work in Practical Arts and their last two in Education. However, it was possible to earn a non-professional B.S. degree in Practical Arts. In 1914 when the School of Education became substantially a graduate school, the

School of Practical Arts was authorized to control its own diplomas and a professional course within the school was provided.

Diplomas were earned in connection with degrees and were awarded to teachers and supervisors as evidence of potential professional success in the educational field, as opposed to the degree which represented scholarly ability: "Diplomas will be granted only to those who, besides qualifying for a degree, give promise of superior professional ability as evidenced by their personality, character, experience, and technical training. . . ." (360, 1917–1918:29) Teachers College diplomas were generally accepted in the United States and foreign countries as satisfying the legal requirements for certification.  To earn a diploma was a more important symbol of success than to earn a degree.  Physical education students had several diploma options:  Teacher of Hygiene and Physical Education, Supervisor of Hygiene and Physical Education, and Supervisor of Play and Playgrounds.  (The latter diploma was added in 1914.)  In 1922 diplomas for Teacher of Health Education and Supervisor of Health Education were added and in 1939 Leader of Recreation and Administrator of Community Recreation diplomas were also made available.  Supervisor's diplomas and degrees were only available to graduate students with prior teaching or work experience.  Special diplomas or certificates were granted to matriculated students after two years of study.  Although these were very popular —especially in New York City with the large part-time student population, and the multitude of teachers who attended summer sessions—by 1917 several departments, including physical education, excluded the certificate programs.

From the time the School of Practical Arts was formed until the early twenties when T.C. became largely a graduate institution, the department conferred an average of eighteen degrees and professional diplomas a year. Enrollment averaged 110 students each year and ranged from a low of forty-three in 1912 to a high of 208 in 1919. (23:55)  Almost all of the department's students were women.

From its inception, T.C. offered graduate work but until 1915 the M.A. and Ph.D. degrees remained under the jurisdiction of the Faculty of Philosophy through the Columbia University Department of Philosophy and Education.  In 1913 the School of Education began to offer only graduate work; in 1924 the School of Practical Arts dropped the freshman and sophomore years and in 1926 the whole undergraduate program was discontinued.  Nevertheless, a minimal number of B.S. degrees continued to be awarded to students who went to T.C. with a substantial background of work (two to three years in a normal school or liberal arts college) and completed requirements with some of the introductory courses. (82:61–80) The graduate program in the department of physical education began in 1901 when T.C., in cooperation wlth the Faculty of Education at Columbia University, established the first major in physical education leading to the master's degree. (287:22)  The first Master of Arts degree was awarded to Mary Reesor in 1910.*  It was 1916 before the first man, Jacob B. Grossman, earned a similar degree.  Between 1912 and 1920 an average of seventeen graduate students per year were enrolled, with an average of eight receiving their advanced degrees. (23:56)  In the next decade the graduate program in physical education grew to surpass all other departments in the School of Practical Arts.  By 1932, at its height, there were 304 students enrolled for advanced degrees in physical education and sixty in health education.†  The first Ph.D. in physical education was earned by Frederick Rand Rogers in 1925 upon completion of his dissertation entitled:  "Physical Capacity Tests in the Administration of Physical Education."  In 1926 Ethel Saxman became the first woman to receive the Ph.D. degree.  These were professional milestones because they were the first non-medical doctoral degrees in physical education in the United States.  In 1934 Columbia University began to offer an Ed.D. degree and in 1938 Thurston Adams received the first in physical education with a dissertation on "Motion Pictures in Physical Education: Teaching the Tennis Serve with Schoolmade Films."

The availability of the Ph.D. and Ed.D. degrees brought a marked change to advanced study in physical education.  Prior to 1925 a physical educator wishing to do doctoral level work generally earned an M.D. degree.‡  Appropriate as that was to the early programs run by men like Dudley Allen Sargent, it was not consonant with the physical education program emerging under the leadership of Jesse Feiring Williams who had been department chairman since 1923.  Candidates for the Ed.D. degree in all the departments in T.C. were required to complete at least fifteen points (credits) of work in the foundational fields of education—disciplines which could provide insight into the fundamental relationships between school, society and child.  This curricular innovation, later molded into a one-year, interdisciplinary course required of all master's degree students, was the first serious attempt to provide students with an understanding of the broad issues in education.  It cast teacher education in a whole new perspective.  However, despite the Ed.D.'s seeming potential for physical educators, the Ph.D. proved the more popular degree.  By 1940 only nine

---

* There is some evidence that a master's degree in physical education was completed as early as 1902.  The card catalog of the T.C. library indicates that in 1902 R. H. Bellows completed a master's thesis entitled "Physical Education in the Secondary Schools of the United States."  However, the registrar has been unable to verify the degree.

† In 1919, following a trend that had started earlier in the decade, the Department of Physical Education divided into two areas:  health education and physical education.  Thomas D. Wood led the former program and Jesse Feiring Williams assumed responsibility for the latter one.

‡ In 1941 when Clifford Lee Brownell was appointed department chairman he was the first in that role to hold a Ph.D. degree rather than an M.D. degree.

Ed.D. degrees had been awarded in physical education while twenty-two people had earned the Ph.D. degree. Almost twice as many men as women (twenty vs. eleven) earned the doctorate. (23:132) The Ed.D. degree finally became popular when, in 1944, the faculty voted to require a reading knowledge of two foreign languages plus University admission standards for all candidates for the Ph.D. By 1951 the number of students who earned the Ed.D. degrees was more than twice the number of those who earned Ph.D. degrees. (23:145–146) The height of the doctoral program at Columbia was in the late forties; in 1949 twenty-eight Ed.D. degrees were awarded to eighteen men and ten women; two men received Ph.D. degrees. (23:157) Since 1946 when the World War II veterans helped swell the enrollment to 530 students, departmental enrollments declined and at this time the program is comparatively small. Some idea of the size of the graduate program over the years is indicated by a survey of doctoral theses reported by Cureton in the *Research Quarterly* of March 1949; according to that survey Teachers College granted about one fifth of the total number of degrees awarded by the twenty-one institutions offering programs between 1930 and 1946. (23:167)

In 1938 the department recognized the growth of the health education curriculum by formally changing the name to the Department of Health and Physical Education. In 1939 it became the Department of Health and Physical Education and Recreation. In 1947 the curriculum was reorganized into areas of specialization. Students could specialize in administration, teaching or rehabilitation, in health education, physical education, dance or recreation; they prepared for jobs in schools and colleges, public health departments or voluntary health agencies, community recreation agencies, or rehabilitation centers. Thus a student could earn a degree preparing him to be an administrator or supervisor of health education in school or college. Or he could choose to be a teacher of the dance, or any other feasible combination of the elements listed above. (360,1952–1953:189) In later years the trend reversed, perhaps due to the decrease in enrollment, and at this time the department is again known as the Department of Physical Education, offering work only in physical education and dance.

The role of Teachers College in the growth of professional preparation in physical education was of extreme importance. An unusual professional faculty studded with figures of national prominence, supported at T.C. by some of the finest educational thinkers of the time, working in an atmosphere of experimental innovation in education, could not help but be influential. The early graduate program and the number of students who received advanced degrees and became famous in their own right helped Teachers College's philosophy concerning the broad social role of education and physical education to become one of the central forces in the development of physical education in the United States.

# CLARK WILSON HETHERINGTON

## 1870-1942

Clark W. Hetherington—scholarly, quiet, ascetic, perfectionist —was often referred to as the "modern philosopher of physical education." Yet the ambition of his later years, to set in writing his comprehensive theory of education through play, went unfulfilled because he strove for a perfection of expression that cannot be achieved. The work "Science and Education" which he was writing at the time of his death, and the series of volumes planned in fulfillment of the three-year foundation grant awarded him by the Playground and Recreation Association, were unfortunately never published. Two books, *A Normal Course in Play* (174) and the *School Program in Physical Education* (175), plus numerous articles, pamphlets, manuals, and speeches were the legacy of his lifelong research. He was reputed to have said: "I am not primarily a teacher, but by temperament and training a research man. . . . I have never uttered a sentence in the courses that I have given that was not based on at least two years of original research work." (69:24)

Although he was born in Lanesboro, Minnesota, his career in physical education began and ended in California, where his family had moved about 1874. As a youth Hetherington was extremely active in athletics and gymnastics and was characterized as a vigorous, dynamic individual— as an adult, however, he worked himself continuously, never played, and was considered placid. His education was interspersed with periods of working, and thus he was twenty-five when he received his A.B. with the "pioneer class" of Stanford University, majoring in education but with interest in biology and psychology. At Stanford he was inspired by Thomas Wood, for whom he worked as an assistant from 1893 (his junior year) until 1896. He was an avid gymnast, especially skilled in the art of club swinging, and in his senior year was president of the Gymnasium Club.

Following his Stanford experience, for two years Hetherington was Statistician and Director of Physical Culture at the Reform School in Whittier, California. He established play fields, organized games and teams and convinced the trustees of the need for a gymnasium. In their 1896 report it was mentioned that "great interest has been taken by the boys in football, handball and other healthy games—an interest which has proven alike beneficial to their moral and physical development." (54:15)

Fig. 72.    Clark W. Hetherington.

Charged with compiling records and statistics concerning the incarcerated boys, Hetherington did research on their past environment, attitudes and school work and administered a medical, physical, intellectual, and moral examination as each entered the institution.  His purpose, to discover individual differences and influences, and to determine the status of each boy so that proper treatment could be prescribed, was as pioneering an effort with reformatory work as was his organization of their recreation. From his statistics he concluded that the "personal data indicated that 75 to 80 per cent might have been saved an institutional career had they had a normal play experience." (172:633)

His work on individual differences and his belief that greater understanding of psychology could enable the construction of educational experiences that would help prevent the need for places like Whittier, led him to enter Clark University in Worcester, Massachusetts as a fellow and later also an assistant in psychology.  Clark University, under the leadership of G. Stanley Hall, was a center for the child-study movement.  Hall's interest in natural play activities made a strong impression on Hetherington who served as his assistant, and under whom he studied.  Although he spent two years at Clark and completed a thesis which was apparently not submitted, he was never awarded a master's degree.  His only other formal study was a year at the University of Zurich (1904–1905) where he studied anthropology, advanced human and topographical anatomy, and biological psychology.

Hetherington's next position was at the University of Missouri where he was Professor of Physical Training and Director of Gymnastics and Athletics from 1900–1910. His main contribution to physical education during his tenure at Missouri centered around his attempts to deal with the problems of intercollegiate athletics. Except for Amos Alonzo Stagg at Chicago, Hetherington was the only gymnasium director whose authority extended over athletics. In fact, his was the first totally centralized department, embracing under the leadership of one director men's *and* women's physical training, intercollegiate athletics, recreation, and all health programs and functions.

The work with men's intercollegiate activities was controversial and brought Hetherington great unpopularity. At that time professionalism was so rife in college athletics that teams contained players not enrolled at their schools. Hetherington's fight against such "ringers" and his insistence on placing a "clean" eleven on the field in 1902 were almost revolutionary. Enlisting support from faculty in other colleges, he founded the Missouri Valley Conference (1907); the existence of "conferences" in different parts of the country has been cited as an important factor in raising the standards of school sport. When the Intercollegiate Athletic Association (now the NCAA) was organized in 1906 Hetherington was appointed representative from the sixth district. But the organization through which he did most of his crusading was the Athletic Research Society of which he was founder and first president. This group, which focused on the subjects of amateurism and athletic administration, constructed a platform at its 1910 meeting which recognized the educational value of athletics when organized for *play* and called for efficient administration directed towards that end. It also called for a national federated committee on athletics and eventually succeeded in establishing the National Athletic Federation Committee and later the National Amateur Athletic Federation. In 1911 Hetherington cited the overall aim of the group's efforts:

> We believe the aim of all adult administrative effort in athletics should be the building of rational and wholesome play sentiments, habits and traditions among the masses of the youth of the land, the establishment of educational leadership, and the development of a general public opinion that will support an efficient and inspiring organization of athletics as play as distinct from athletics organized primarily as spectacle. (176:596, italics deleted)

His interest in athletics extended to girls' and women's sports. Hetherington introduced Play Days for high school girls in Missouri as a substitute for interscholastic sports and in other ways worked to limit competition for girls and women to intramurals or play days. His Athletic Research

14

Society started a movement to put interscholastic sport for girls and women out of existence. (54:29)

Hetherington also pioneered in bringing recreational activities and playgrounds to the people of Missouri. Through his efforts the Extension Division of the University employed a full-time instructor who travelled throughout the state consulting with school authorities in an effort to develop playgrounds and organize recreational programs in the public schools.

Underlying Hetherington's concern for athletics and recreation was his basic conviction that play was an educational endeavor. He used the term "play" in its broadest connotations: "We use the term general play to include plays, games, athletics, dancing, the play side of gymnastics, and all play activities in which the large muscles are used more or less vigorously." (172:629) Hetherington thought play and the educational process were fused in the most fundamental sense:

> Play is nature's method of education. Why? Because education, in its broadest sense, is identical with the process of living. More specifically, it is learning how to live through experience. But experience comes only as the result of activity, and play is the fundamental form of all developmental activity. It is spontaneous living. Out of the various reactions upon the environment that we call experience comes the development of the instincts and emotions and the experience that makes for knowledge, character and adjustment. (171:285)

To Hetherington, play as the primary form of activity was for the child both recreation and work: *"Play is the child's chief business in life.* In these internally impelled activities he lives and learns how to live. In them he should gain his primary development and life adjustment." (171:288) He argued that play was superior to work as a developer of the nervous and mental powers because "play is more intense, varied and of greater duration because of the sustaining power of enthusiasm which postpones the onset of fatigue and reduces the consciousness of effort which characterizes the volitional attention of work." (171:288) He concluded that "by realizing a progressive series of aims in play, the child learns how to work and to achieve life through work." (171:289, italics deleted) The influence of G. Stanley Hall was apparent in his comment that "better educational results in general and a broader and higher capacity to work are secured by organizing the child's natural self-sustaining activities than by forcing upon him those foreign to his nature." (171:290) His explication of the relationship between work (study) and play revealed the lack of antagonism between the two modes and was an attempt to dispel traditional biases against play. The lingering Puritan ethic still connected play with idleness, fooling or deviltry, and at best a luxury for little children. Hetherington sought to give it a philosophical basis in productivity, learning, and physical and character development.

Educational tradition separated the mental from the physical and Hetherington saw this dichotomy as engendering the growth of physical education as a special field designed to deal with the physical aspect of the child. Hetherington, however, viewed physical education not as a separate subject but as a fundamental part of *all* education:

> Physical education is discussed as though it were a subject of study in the curriculum, instead of one attitude in considering the whole educational process of which it is the basic part. Physical education, as a special field of educational effort, arose because of the twist in educational thought created by the rise of asceticism. It persists because of a survival of asceticism. (171:291)

In an earlier paper he had noted that "physical education takes over nature's means of education, organizes it to balance social conditions and directs it for the highest educational values." (172:635) This was consistent with his view of teaching as leadership—as the organization of the child's own "hungers" and expressions evidenced in play:

> Why not shift the problem from the organization of "subjects of study" that are selected products of racial achievement, to the organization of the child's own spontaneous active life; from the attitude of teaching primarily to that of leading (which includes teaching)? . . . Why not put our aims and our specialized adult interests in the background of our consciousness and enter into the child's life from his point of view, meeting his hunger for life and his desire for leadership with the resources of the adult? (171:292)

The opportunity to put his ideas into practice came with the establishment of the Demonstration Play School. Sponsored by the University of California, Berkeley, it was established on the university campus in 1913; it convened three hours a day for a six-week period corresponding to the regular summer session. In the first year the enrollment was 207 children, between the ages of four and twelve, and Hetherington was assisted by his wife and leaders recruited from public school teachers and students. Hetherington described his basic conception in a report to the Dean of the summer session.

> The play school is proposed as the next step in evolution of the elementary school. (1) It is suggested as the extra-home institutional center of child-life in which the school and the playground are educationally fused and their aims identified. . . . (2) It is proposed as a center in which children shall learn to live and to work with enthusiasm by living completely in their activities which include the whole physical and social environment and are organized to satisfy fully the child's hungers for experience and self-expression. (3) It is proposed as a center for complete leadership, where the interest is centered in the child, not in subjects of study. (171:380)

In stating the aims of the play school, Hetherington brilliantly wove the aims of education with the activity of play. The play school was a combination not only in title and fact, but in conception:

The aims of the play school may be summarized as follows:

1. To organize the opportunity for a complete play-life in order that the child may develop his powers, learn the meaning of his environment and discover himself.

2. To furnish leadership for the fundamental activities in order that organic, nervous and volitional powers for activity with enthusiasm and the capacity for work may be established.

3. To connect the play tendencies and interests with materials for activity that will feed and develop stable interests; and then connect these interests with the resources of society, especially literature.

4. To secure close observation, clear thinking, skilled execution and free linguistic expression in connection with all activities.

5. To mold the instinctive and emotional reactions in all activities in order that sound moral habits, moral judgement and social ideals may be established and come to control all developing powers for complete adult adjustment. (171:380)

In order to organize the child's activities in a manner that would provide a progressive educational curriculum, true to the child's nature, and satisfying his hungers and interests, Hetherington devised a classification system. There were seven categories of activities: big-muscle activities which included gymnastics plays, dancing, games, and athletics; manipulating and manual activities now termed arts and crafts; environmental and nature activities consisting of excursions and experimentations with physical nature; dramatic activities such as plays and pageants which dramatize social situations; rhythmic and musical activities including both body and vocal rhythms and the use of pre-musical instruments; social activities during which time leadership should stress acceptable democratic values; vocal and linguistic activities including story-telling and working with numbers; and economic activities such as banking, bookkeeping, buying, and selling. (171:430–436)

The demonstration play school of 1913 was a great success and was studied by educators and educational administrators from all over the country. Hetherington resigned as director in 1917 but his wife continued operating it until 1934 when lack of money forced the University to discontinue it.

In 1918 Clark W. Hetherington became State Supervisor of Physical Education for California, the second person to hold such a position in the United States.* His most important contribution in that position was to change the prevalent program of calisthenics and marching to a curriculum of natural activities. He prepared a syllabus of activities in which he recommended the use of formalized programs only when corrective measures were necessary or when facilities were restrictive; the primary focus was on natural activities. In *The School Program in Physical Education*, a work based on his manual for California schools, Hetherington said: "The

---

*The first was his Stanford friend, Thomas A. Storey, appointed in 1916 to hold the equivalent position in New York State.

natural physical-training activities arise out of children's play tendencies. . . . On the other hand gymnastic drills of calisthenic movements are pure adult inventions." (175:54)   He organized the curriculum into four programs:  the developmental program; training in character, morals and manners; hygienic behavior; and the control of health conditions or handicaps.  Since programs are only as good as those who staff them, he logically became involved in the teacher education and certification aspects of the California situation.  His attempt to promulgate regulations designed to insure a high level teacher preparation experience met with opposition and caused Hetherington to resign in 1921.

His next two positions were primarily centered around the development of professional preparation programs.  At New York University (NYU) where he accepted a professorship in 1923, he was charged with the responsibility of developing a department of physical education in the School of Education.  The professional curriculum which he formulated, regarded by many as his most important contribution to physical education, included a four-year undergraduate and three-year graduate program, similar to and based on programs he had previously developed at the Universities of Missouri and Wisconsin.*  (He was a professor at Wisconsin from 1913–1918.)  The NYU doctoral program began under Hetherington in 1926—about the same time as the one offered at Teachers College, Columbia University; they were the two earliest such programs in the country. The NYU program as it continued to develop under Jay B. Nash became highly respected, particularly by those interested in the recreational aspects of physical education.  Another NYU program which Hetherington inaugurated was the summer school camp on Lake Sebago in New York's Palisades Interstate Park (1927).  Originally intended to provide playing facilities for the city-based university, it functioned for almost forty years for over three thousand summer school graduate students who took instruction in physical education; it was also used as a family camping ground.  Hetherington's last position was at his alma mater, Stanford.  From 1929 to his retirement in 1938 he re-established the professional preparation program in the School of Hygiene and Physical Education which Thomas Wood had started.  (Refer to p. 375.)

Hetherington's professional life was marked by diversity of activity and employment within the confines of a single profession.  Besides the positions already discussed, he directed the Fels Foundation program for play and educational athletics (1911) and was research investigator at Teachers

---

* For complete enumeration of what Hetherington considered the functions of a physical educator and the courses needed to develop the abilities to perform those functions, refer to his articles "University Professional Training Courses in Physical Education" (177), and "Graduate Work in Physical Education" (173).  His suggestions bear a remarkable resemblance to current teacher education programs. Is it possible that so little change has occurred in half a century?

College, Columbia University (1921–1923). Some of his disappointments, particularly those connected with his failure to publish the quantity of original material he had written and organized from his research, were the result of recurrent sickness. Hindered from youth by weak eyesight, he was plagued throughout his life by somatic disorders and was forced to take months at a time to rest and recuperate. When he resigned or took a leave of absence from a position it was frequently because he lacked the stamina to continue working. Nevertheless, he made an important contribution to the philosophy of physical education. He formulated a theory of play; he delineated the idea of play as fundamental education, with its corollary view of physical education as guiding the educational development of the child through organizing and leading his play activities; and he designed a professional education program to prepare educators to meet such a responsibility.

He was honored by being made Fellow #1 of the American Academy of Physical Education, an organization which is generally considered to have been his brainchild. He served as chairman during the four years— 1926–1930—that the Academy was being organized. In 1939 the Academy awarded Hetherington a Creative Award for "the outstanding contribution to the foundation of a philosophy of physical education" (54:85), and in 1953 the Academy established the Clark Wilson Hetherington Award for scholarly achievement and service to the Academy. He was also made a Fellow of the APEA in the first group of persons receiving Honor Awards in 1931. In 1928 he received the Gulick Award and in 1935 was awarded an honorary Doctor of Pedagogy degree by the University of Southern California.

Clark W. Hetherington was one of the most scholarly of the American physical educators. His capacity to construct relationships and to formulate unified theories based upon scientific knowledge and logical thinking made him an invaluable innovator.

# JAY BRYAN NASH

## 1886-1965

Jay Nash extended the theories of Luther Gulick, Thomas Wood and Clark Hetherington to their furthest limit. Gulick and Wood clearly established that play had a place in physical education. Hetherington developed an expanded concept of play to include all internally impelled big-muscle activities and proclaimed it a fundamental aspect of the educational experience. Nash, viewing play in its broadest connotations of recreation, took it beyond the schools into the total life experience of children and adults. Gulick and Wood focused on physical education as it concerned activities natural to the individual; Hetherington's work centered on the individual as learner; and Nash's ultimate concern was with the individual's happiness and adjustment to life.

Nash's orientation was at least partially the result of association with Hetherington. Born in New Baltimore, Ohio, he attended Oberlin College where he earned his A.B. in 1911; he studied philosophy and sociology and worked in physical education under the leadership of Delphine Hanna and Fred Leonard. From 1911 to 1914 he was a high school instructor at Oakland, California. He then became the Assistant Supervisor of Recreation at Oakland, from 1915 to 1918, following which he became the Assistant Supervisor of Physical Education for the State of California, under Clark Hetherington. In 1919 he returned to Oakland as Superintendent of Recreation and Physical Education and in 1926 left for New York where he accepted a professorship in education at New York University, again under Clark Hetherington. While on the NYU faculty he earned his M.A. degree (1927) and his Ph.D. degree (1929). In 1930, after Hetherington resigned, he was appointed Chairman of the Department of Physical Education and Health in the School of Education. Upon his retirement in 1953 he was named Professor Emeritus. He continued his professional career after retiring from NYU and served as a Fulbright professor in India (1953–1954), and for a term, as Dean of Brigham Young University in Provo, Utah.

Unlike his mentor, Hetherington, during the course of Nash's career he wrote a significant number of publications, including nine books about physical education and the related areas of recreation, outdoor education and health education. He also edited a five-volume series called *Interpretations of*

*Physical Education*, containing contributions by many of the noted figures in the profession, and he wrote numerous articles, particularly in the *Journal of Health and Physical Education*. The continuing relevance of his literary contributions is reflected in the recent re-publication of two of his earlier books: *Philosophy of Recreation and Leisure* (253) and *Physical Education: Its Interpretations and Objectives* (254). One of his most popular works was *Spectatoritis* (255) which stressed the need for participatory recreation.

Nash's philosophical disposition, evidenced throughout his writings, was toward the idea of the integrated man, prepared to use his leisure time wisely by participating in activities of his own choosing. Unlike some of his colleagues who proclaimed the inherent unity of man while contradictorily talking of his mental and physical aspects, Nash spoke only in terms of the total organism:

> The concept of wholeness precludes any utilization of the words "physical activities" or "mental activities." The very words "physical" and "mental" confuse thinking. There is no such thing as a physical activity apart from a thinking and feeling activity and the latter is not possible without its physical counterpart. Therefore, in this discussion, the word "organic" will be used instead of "mental." In every activity there are organic and interpretive phases which also involve emotional experiences. Activities, then, may be classified on a scale—some high on the organic level, where heat and energy are produced; others, high on the interpretive level, where thinking is required. (254:93–94)

Fig. 73.    Jay B. Nash.

Essential to the concept of the integrated man was his biological inheritance, which Nash believed provided a basis for future development:

> We are a part of the run, the chase, the hide, the seek and the dodge. We are a part of the great out of doors. We are a part of all this biologically. It is this biological heredity which has sustained the race. It further represents the only way upon which to base future development. . . .
> With this biological heredity as a base, we can mold these age-old activities into a social inheritance which can be passed on from generation to generation. As a means in this transportation "the game's the thing." (252:48)

Nash's view of physical education was somewhat unique in that he considered it inseparable from recreation and camping: "There is a vital relationship here between physical education and certain phases of recreation. . . . Recreation activities which take one camping and in the out-of-doors or which give one enjoyment in a game of tennis, badminton or swimming, form a real point of articulation with physical education." (254:278) He made the point that the congruence was due not only to similarity of programs but to the totality of an individual's life:

> What is time in physical education? Is it not more than the number of periods a child spends in class, the number of minutes in each period? Accepting the definition of physical education, how can a line be drawn between class time and the time spent in activity at noon, after school, or even during the long summer vacation? These are all times for physical education. They have not always been recognized as such, and consequently have not been given the leadership, space, and other factors necessary for good programs. Physical education, as defined by time, is all the experiences children have in neuromuscular activities which are directed to the desired outcomes. (252:223)

On that basis, Nash conceived of the school as a hub from which community and school recreation activities could emanate, with the school's physical education department at the center of the administrative organization:

> In the very center of the community planning group will be the school; and at the center of the school group, the department of physical education. The department's interest in health and fitness, in recreation for all, and in education for citizenship, places it in this position. The director of physical education becomes the community engineer. (252:117)

During the time Nash was Superintendent of Recreation and Physical Education at Oakland, California he helped to develop the Oakland Plan which put into practice the concept of school-community relationship. The city of Oakland and the board of education each put in 50 percent of the money needed to finance a year-round program which included usage of all the playgrounds, park areas and schoolyards. All areas were kept open from 3:15 to 6:00 P.M. every afternoon, Saturdays and all vacations. Every public and private recreation and health agency in the city was tied into one central office headed by Nash. While in Oakland Nash also helped found two family camps and the Industrial Recreation Association, both related to his understanding of the comprehensiveness of physical education.

Nash's lifelong concern was for the whole individual's well-being and happiness. Within this framework he noted that physical educators could help to secure this state-of-being by preparing the child to live a life of participation in recreational activity, which he regarded as a natural and essential aspect of man's heritage. He proceeded from the point of view that man's life could roughly be divided into two categories, play and work, or time devoted to earning a living and time devoted to leisure. He believed that "education must lay the foundation not only for work but also for recreation." (254:213) Furthermore, he considered this the responsibility of the entire school, not just of the physical education department:

> The development of wholesome leisure-time habits has been accepted as one of the school's responsibilities. This recreation must not be considered only a phase of the physical education department with its sports and games. Recreation as an objective must be considered in the offerings of social science, music, manual and communicative arts. (252:44)

Throughout Nash's writings he emphasized that "the skill-learning period from five to fifteen years may be termed the great golden decade." (254:171) He made some studies on the recreational patterns of adults related to the age at which they began their hobbies and concluded that:

> Skills in youth are basic to the recreation patterns of later life, a concept which has been mentioned many times. . . . It is my privilege to relate, although it was no surprise, that over 85 per cent of the interests could be traced to below the age of twelve. (253:187)

Nash concluded, therefore, that "leisure time needs should be a guide to curricular construction in our public schools. . . ." (250:125) He advocated an emphasis on carry-over activities:

> Sufficient opportunity for experience in a number of individual and dual sports is equally important at the secondary level. This is particularly true in the later senior high grades because of the recreational, coeducational and carry-over values. Activities such as tennis, track and field, archery, badminton, bowling, golf, and, for boys, combative sports (wrestling) are not limited to the recreational value alone. They make major contributions to organic fitness, neuromuscular skill and social development as well. (252:291)

Thus he constructed a framework for a physical education program that would be concerned with the inculcation of skills, knowledge and attitudes that would insure effective participation throughout life. Essential to this was the child's interests or "felt needs": "The real issue is neither that which the child needs nor that which he can do. Rather is it some felt need, some want 'half-formed in the dawning of his consciousness' that is the basis of attitudes which, in turn, become the all-determining factor." (252:195) The "felt needs" served both as motivation to learning and as guides to the kind of activities the child would later enjoy, for Nash believed that the urge to participate in certain types of activity was a combination of heredity and the social environment in which the child lived. He stated that all activities could potentially fulfill the objectives of physical education if the child's interests were the prerequisite to both curriculum and method.

Teaching methodology was not a subject that interested Nash and it was barely mentioned in his writings. But the few remarks he did make underscored his belief that physical education activities should be pleasurable and geared to use. In that context he reminded his colleagues that the focus should be on *doing* the activities, not learning skills: "There has been developed a worthy technique of teaching. The student is not taught about a skill; rather, he is taught to do the activity." (254:55) Possibly that statement was meant to counteract the growing tendency, still prevalent today, to regard the development of skill as the primary goal, with the activity merely a vehicle for practice. Obviously such a concept conflicts with Nash's conviction of the importance of learning activities for future, leisure time use.

The other objectives of physical education, such as education for democracy, development of physical well-being and the development of certain personality traits, were all embraced by Nash inasmuch as they contributed to the ultimate well-being, integration and happiness of the individual:

> The four objectives [of physical education]: organic power, neuro-muscular development leading to skill in performance, the ability to do interpretive thinking and the guiding of the emotional urges essential to group living provide a sense of wholeness for the individual. (254:59)

He defined health and fitness in very broad terms and considered them as means to an end, rather than ends in themselves:

> The individual who has kept fit greatly enlarges his range for the fullness of living. It is possible for him to do a day's work with ease; to meet emergencies should they arise, to extend his recreational opportunities to a second game of golf, to a hike on the trail, to do the carrying of a canoe across a portage; and in a hundred ways, to do the things he likes to do. . . . . Physical fitness which can be maintained through the years lays the basis for the full life. (254:154)

. . . . . . . . . . . . . . . . . . .

> Health is not an end in itself; it is a means. The end is a well-adjusted, wholesome, self-directed individual meeting his responsibilities in the society in which he lives. (254:225)

Nash's basic point of view can be summed in his own words:

> If recreation is to be an important part of a way of life, six premises must be recognized and education for leisure planned in the light of them: (1) integration and normality are achieved through meaningful recreational activity; (2) modern society tends to fragmentize life; (3) skills are an integrating force and must be learned early; (4) skills in recreational activities must supplement and, in some instances, replace the satisfactions formerly found in work; (5) education, broadly interpreted, must be planned in the light of recreational needs; and (6) recreation may be utilized to make democracy function. (253:200)

Nash was considered one of the leading figures in the physical education profession. (193)  He was president of the AAHPER in 1942–1943, the American Academy of Physical Education in 1945–1947, and the Eastern District Association of the AAHPER in 1933–1935.  He was Executive Secretary of the New York State AHPER.  As one of the five founders of the Academy, he was listed as Fellow #5.  He received the Honor Award of the AAHPER in 1932, the Gulick Award in 1940 and the Hetherington Award in 1955.  He was also awarded an honorary Master of Science degree by Springfield College. (127b:20–21)

His ideas were widely accepted during his lifetime; the concept of carry-over sports became a fundamental tenet of curricular development and recently received a new surge of life with the development of the Lifetime Sports Foundation.  Partially through Nash's efforts, school camping and recreation drew closer to physical education and departments in colleges and universities, like the national organization, became health, physical education *and* recreation.  Yet it cannot be said that Nash's recommendations were widely practiced.  Team sports form the nucleus of the school programs up to the college level.  Within the sports program focus has been on fitness and skill development with little emphasis on doing the activities themselves.  The child's "felt need" has been submerged in the enormous classes that are the result of a widespread physical education "requirement."  Jay Bryan Nash set forth a philosophy of physical education—it is a challenge to the profession which accepted it to find means to secure its implementation.

# CHARLES HAROLD McCLOY

## 1886-1959

C. H. McCloy was rather a unique physical educator in his era. While most of the professional leaders gave the bulk of their time to developing curriculum and methodology appropriate to the new physical education programs, McCloy's efforts centered around research. Their basic orientation was to *apply* the principles expounded by other disciplines, in particular, psychology and biology, but McCloy sought to collect the fundamental data. As he said, "the leaders in physical education . . . have for years utilized the experimental results of physiologists and psychologists; but it is but recently that they have begun in any large number to use the methods of research." (219:10) McCloy led the movement toward increased research, although it has not yet reached the "tide of interest" he envisioned. McCloy was also one of the few who focused his work on the term "physical" rather than "education." Furthermore, McCloy's professional experience was singular in that it included thirteen years of work in China.

McCloy, like Jay B. Nash and Jesse Feiring Williams, was born in Ohio in 1886. He grew up in his birthplace of Marietta and attended Marietta College from which he received his Bachelor of Philosophy degree, magna cum laude, in 1907 and his Master of Arts degree in 1910. As an undergraduate he pursued the Latin Scientific Course, supplemented by three summers at the Harvard Summer School of Physical Education from which he received his Certificate in 1907. He earned his M.A. "in absentia" by doing supervised reading in the areas of psychology of adolescence and human physiology, though his thesis was in social economy. (212b:91–95) In 1911 he enrolled at Johns Hopkins Medical School but did not complete the degree; he also studied at Ohio State University. Several years later he entered Columbia University and in 1932 was awarded the Ph.D. degree.

While a sophomore at Marietta College he was appointed Instructor in Physical Training. For a year after graduation he was Director of Physical Education and Acting Head, Department of Biology at Yankton College, Yankton, South Dakota. In 1908 he began a long career with the YMCA by serving as the Physical Director in Danville, Virginia. He was employed by the YMCA for thirteen years in China, during which time he served as Secretary, Department of Physical Education in the National

Council of the YMCA from 1913 to 1921, and as Director of the School of Physical Education, National Southeastern University, Nanking, from 1921 to 1926. He then returned to the United States where he continued his work for the YMCA by serving as Secretary for Research in Physical Education, National Council of the YMCA, in New York City, until 1930. He also held appointments as Senior Instructor in Health Education at the Detroit Teachers College (now Wayne State University), from 1926 to 1927, and as Lecturer at Teachers College, Columbia University, from 1928 to 1930. For the next twenty-four years he was Research Professor in Physical Education at the State University of Iowa, and upon his retirement in 1954 was named Research Professor Emeritus. (127b:12–14)

During these years McCloy also accepted several assignments from the government of the United States, as well as the governments of several South American countries. Among these were appointments as Chairman of the Civilian Advisory Committee for the United States Navy Physical Fitness Program, Physical Re-conditioning Consultant to the Surgeon General of the United States Army, and Consultant to the joint U.S. Army and Navy Committee of Welfare and Recreation.

Fig. 74.    C. H. McCloy.

McCloy spoke Chinese fluently and read French, German, Italian, Japanese, Portuguese, and the Scandinavian languages.   The findings of his research were published in professional journals throughout the world, including Brazil, China, Chile, France, Germany, Italy, Japan, Norway, Portugal, Spain, and Turkey.   He enjoyed an international reputation as a research scholar.   Included among his prolific writings were fourteen books written in Chinese.   In English his publications include six books, primarily in the area of tests and measurements, and numerous articles, most of which were published in the *Research Quarterly* or the *Journal of Health and Physical Education.*

He was active in professional associations and served as president in the AAHPER (1937–1938), the American Academy of Physical Education (1947–1949), the Pan-American Institute of Physical Education (1946–1956), and the Central District Association of AAHPER (1933–1934).

His work was accorded the following honors:   Charter Member of the American Academy of Physical Education, Fellow #27; Gulick Award, 1944; Hetherington Award, 1956; Honor Award of the AAHPER, 1936; and American College of Sports Medicine Award, 1958.   He was awarded four honorary degrees:   D.Sc. by Marietta College, 1947; D.Sc. by Grinnell College, 1955; Litt.D. by George Williams College, 1957; and D.P.E. by The College of Medicine, University of Toronto, 1958.

Through all of McCloy's writings and work a thematic emphasis on the importance of the physical characteristics of man was clearly displayed. From his viewpoint, the nature of man clearly demonstrated an organic unity in which the physical dimension was a significantly major aspect of the whole being:

> The psychological literature of late years has spoken much of the fact of body–mind unity, but this same literature has usually gone on thinking and writing as though the school child were all mind.   We in physical education, with our growing overemphasis upon the educational aspect of physical education, are apt to fall into the same error.   *Our organism is more body than mind,* and it is only through the adequate functioning of *all* of it that the most desirable functioning of even the brain occurs. (220:77–78)

Real evidence of his appreciation for this aspect of man is found in McCloy's willingness to accept physical health, the satisfaction of skilled performance, and the enjoyment and appreciation of things of the body, as ends in themselves:   "Most people want to be well developed.   Down in their hearts they would like to be strong and healthy—and the girls and women, beautiful as well," and "there are more persons who feel deeply the competitive and more 'physical urges' than there are who entertain the more highly cultivated appreciations." (220:157, 14)   The immediately preceding statements indicate the kind of respect he had for a person's need to develop and take pleasure in his own body and its movements.   Unlike

Williams, who saw no spirituality, and therefore no good purpose, in developing the rectus abdominus (refer to p. 412), McCloy thought that "it is just as 'natural' to desire a good body and to be willing to work for it even in artificial ways as it is to hit a golf ball. . . . In some institutions weight-lifting clubs organize around this desire." (220:97–98)  Furthermore, he contended that a skilled physical performance was, in and for itself, a cultural activity:

> I believe that *any worth-while activity executed skillfully enough to give the doer exquisite sensory pleasure* is cultural. . . . I think that we do not need to borrow all our physical education culture from music, art, and other disciplines—we have a rich cultural field of our own.  Perhaps not more than a small percentage of our people will ever achieve culture in the humanities, at least as culture is defined by the humanists; but a very large percentage *can* achieve such culture in the motor field, for these skills reach far down into phylogenetic depths and touch a cord to which our beings easily respond. (220:91–92)

With these concepts of the worth of physical activity and the importance of the physical in the nature of man basic to his thinking, McCloy emphasized that the role of physical education within education was to deal in particular with the physical objectives.  In 1940 he published *Philosophical Bases for Physical Education* (220), a collection of speeches and articles which he wrote and considered significant enough to re-publish.  These assembled articles reveal two important factors about the thinking of C. H. McCloy.  The first is that his ideas underwent a considerable change in their emphasis in the period between 1930 and 1938.  In the later articles his conception of the role of physical education seems more highly developed in that it exhibited a consistent theme:  the stress on physical considerations.  "The Forgotten Objectives of Physical Education," "How About Some Muscle?" "In Quest of Skills," and "Are There any Fundamentals in Physical Education?" were all titles of articles calling for more emphasis on the physical objectives.  He repeatedly made the point that he was not in favor of eliminating the other educational objectives of the profession, such as the development of character traits, but he stressed throughout these articles the point of view that development of the physical was the objective that should be of most concern to physical educators:

> We need better-developed muscular systems than most of the current literature in our profession is demanding. . . . Therefore, I should like to propose that as a profession we rethink the whole problem of our more purely *physical* objectives, and that we emphasize them more.  I yield to no one in our profession in my belief in the educational importance of physical education when it is adequately organized and taught; the health-education procedures are also of great importance.  But the basis of all physical education—developmental, educational, corrective, or any other—is *the adequate training and development of the body itself*; that should be thought of as a fundamental prerequisite. (220:80–81)

Within McCloy's stress on the physical objectives he sought to delineate those which were of greatest importance to the physical development of the child. Thus he stated that: "We need . . . more emphasis upon the sensuous and the muscular in physical education. . . ." (220:102) He most vigorously advocated the pursuance of motor skill as a primary objective: "Skills must be mastered to the point where in these and subsequent situations the pupil may perform with such joy and satisfaction as to get from the activity its maximum educational effect." (220:9)

McCloy believed that if those objectives were to be accomplished, programs would have to have more class time, a different organization than was then popular, and teaching methods which emphasized the mastery of subject matter:

> I believe that we need, particularly at this time, a better organization of our programs. Too many times I have seen project types of organizations which, while possibly educational, certainly wasted much valuable time. I have repeatedly timed many pupils in gymnasium programs who, in the twenty-five or thirty minutes of so-called activity, engaged in no more than three or four minutes of vigorous muscular work. Biologically at least, this is certainly a minor. Until we obtain more time than we have now, I think we should compromise with "education" and obtain a little more for biology. (220:72)

In terms of teaching methodology, he was particularly critical of the progressive educators who advocated student-centered approaches arising from "felt-needs" (e.g., Nash—refer to pp. 400–401) and utilized discussion techniques for learning and program development:

> How long would it take children themselves, discussing, to evolve the game of basketball? or the crawl stroke? or the modern dance? One answer is that those things were not evolved even by teachers for more than 2,500 years after the physical education of Greece. (Sometimes one wonders if the children might have done better!) (220:241)

.    .    .    .    .    .    .    .    .    .    .    .    .

> If we are going to teach her tennis at all, we must *teach* it sufficiently well so that she will develop maximum skills in the shortest possible time, so that she may derive the maximum pleasure and satisfaction from her playing. Mechanical drill on mimetic tennis skills is not the answer—but neither is the make-the-equipment-available, wait-for-a-felt need, unhampered trial-and-error process. Not only must we decide *what* we are going to teach, but we must *teach* it *as well as we can* (not just permit the pupils to learn as best they can), keeping our instruction geared to the potentialities and present abilities of our pupils, coaching the motor morons so that they may progress to the limits of their abilities and have as much satisfaction as it is humanly possible for them to have, but not depriving the motor geniuses of the extra finishing touches and opportunities that their added brilliance craves and needs. (220:113–114)

Measurement, according to McCloy, was fundamental to all he advocated in terms of physical education programs and teaching. In order to promote the development of skill and strength, the educator had to know exactly what an individual child could and should be able to do. "We need an adequate measurement program which will give the educator more specific information about the pupil plus a scheme of studying this information and interpreting it. . . ." (220:13):

> The use of motor tests corresponds to the use of the best intelligence tests in mental education. It makes possible the determination either of the general development of motor function or of the relative innate strengths and weaknesses. Before a teacher can serve a pupil to the best advantage, he should know the innate capacity of the pupil. (221:4)

He advocated that "in addition to teaching, there should be standardized objective tests of proven validity to measure performance." (220:50) To McCloy, measurement was a key to individualizing instruction, not only by providing insight into each student's capacities and potentialities, but by making it possible to have homogeneous sections and a graded curriculum:

> Observation leads us to venture the opinion that relatively few teachers of physical education in the schools utilize more than thirty-five per cent of their potentiality as educators. Most of the programs are ungraded; there is far too much duplication of teaching material from year to year; classes are badly sectioned or not sectioned at all; there are few widely used standards of achievement; and most existing standards are not correlated with the individual differences in the innate capacities of the pupils; there is poor motivation of the program; there is almost no diagnosis of the causes of individual deficiencies; the grading and promotion systems are largely subjective and inadequate; and most of our progress is by trial and error. (221:3)

McCloy suggested, therefore, that one of the major purposes of tests and measurements is "to assist in the adequate organization, administration, and supervision of instruction. . . ." (221:4) He claimed that tests, properly administered, would yield information about the innate motor capacity and present motor ability of students, which in turn would aid in classification, grading, motivation, diagnosis of difficulties, and program evaluation.

The other general purpose of measurement cited by McCloy was for research, an essential factor in a "scientific" physical education program. Much of McCloy's own research centered around problems such as the testing of general motor capacity and the measuring of different components of strength and motor ability. His books, *Appraising Physical Status: The Selection of Measurements* (1936), *Appraising Physical Status: Methods and Norms* (1938), *The Measurement of Athletic Power* (218), and *Tests and Measurements in Health and Physical Education* (221), dealt with those subjects, as did numerous articles which he published in the *Research Quarterly* between 1934 and 1940. His most valuable contributions in these areas lay in the establishment of norms for a large variety of tests and the development of test groups yielding representative scores. He proposed that "we use *quotients of ability relative to capacity* rather than raw scores of ability alone." (221:4) To this end he developed an Athletic

Quotient. Based upon a Classification Index of age, height and weight factors, and scores for each of several track and field events, a formula was evolved to yield an Athletic Quotient for boys. In like manner he developed a formula for an Athletic Strength Index and a General Strength Index. Using several standard tests, e.g., the Sargent Jump, the Burpee Test and the Iowa revision of the Brace Test, he calculated formulas that yielded General Motor Capacity Scores and General Motor Achievement Scores. Dividing the latter by the former yielded a General Motor Achievement Quotient, which was an expression of the relationship between an individual's developed ability and his innate capacity. By dividing the General Motor Capacity Score with the norm for individuals with the same Classification Index, a Motor Quotient was derived. "The quotient is the motor analogue of the Intelligence Quotient in the mental field. It gives his motor capacity relative to his size and general maturity rather than his absolute motor capacity." (221:126)

McCloy's books and numerous articles reporting the results of his research, as well as setting forth procedures and methods for the conduct of measurement programs, were attempts to interest the profession in these matters, as well as to bring to it the tools and methods of researching problems and implementing techniques he considered important to the development of good, scientifically-based programs of physical education.

Charles Harold McCloy believed the primary objectives of physical education to be the development of skills and organic vigor. He criticized the manner in which programs were then conducted because they did not lead to the fulfillment of those aims. That they were designed to fulfill objectives of a different nature was of no interest to McCloy, who considered it fallacious to de-emphasize the physical aspect of man. His advocacy of research, particularly measurement, was closely allied to his concepts of program. He believed research was vital to knowing the child in order to prescribe appropriate activities, validated by scientific inquiry rather than authoritative pronouncements. His was a vital influence on physical education; under his impetus tests and measurements began to be more widely applied. Professional preparation programs heretofore interested only in the anthropometric type of measurement and the measurement of strength and lung capacity, broadened their approach. Skill testing, for example, became recognized as a fundamental aspect of measurement. Yet it is doubtful how successful were the majority of teachers in applying McCloy's careful techniques when measuring large groups of children. Imperfect measurements carried out in situations where variables were not controlled, resulted in invalid and confounding data and have led to a great deal of legitimate criticism of tests and measurements programs. Perhaps McCloy's vision of every teacher as a practical researcher is not feasible. Nevertheless, the contribution of Charles Harold McCloy to physical education was substantial in the decades between 1930 and 1960.

# JESSE FEIRING WILLIAMS

## 1886-1966

The ideas of Jesse Feiring Williams dominated physical education in the period between 1930 and 1960. His enormous influence may in part have been made possible by the congruity of the objectives he set forth for physical education with those of general education of that time. The physical educator espousing Williams' philosophy was more completely a part of education than at any other time since the utopia of Plato's *Republic*. The acceptance of programs was widespread because to question their value implied questioning the value of education with its identical purposes.

Williams' ultimate concern was with the development of the individual in relation to his social environment. Reiterated throughout his voluminous writings was the belief that it is the function of education and the role of physical education within it, to prepare the child for life in the democratic society of the United States:

> Physical education should devote itself to expressing the dominant ideas, needs, and purposes of the American people and should help them to acquire sounder ideas, to recognize more pertinent needs, and to hold higher purposes. (376:177)
>
> .   .   .   .   .   .   .   .   .   .   .   .   .   .
>
> Education must give respect for law, teach the citizen to take his place in government, and show him how to apply in his whole life those moral principles of democracy that underlie the concept of government by free men. Such moral education must center its efforts on the activities of the young who can learn by experience the meaning of equality of opportunity, dignity of the human personality, individual responsibility for outcomes, and other moral concepts of democratic life. Some of these concepts will arise and must be taught in physical education. Four of these, equality of opportunity, personal worth, individual responsibility, and self-achievement, relate directly to physical education. (376:57)

He believed that education must prepare citizens who are adequately equipped with both the knowledge and attitudes necessary to *adjust* to the society in which they live. Physical education with its team activities was a particularly valuable medium for teaching individuals to adjust to the group:

> In addition to the objectives in motor techniques, there are specific ends in adjustment of the individual to the group. A sense of belonging to a working

group is valuable to every personality. It comes from planning and working together for a common purpose, a goal that is recognized and accepted as valuable and desirable. The necessity for adapting one's own movement to synchronize with that of others and of conforming to a particular design carries with it a strong feeling of responsibility to the group. (376:337)

Fundamental to his conception of the individual's relationship to society, was the element of service—it was the duty of each citizen to prepare himself to *serve* society. His definition of health as "that quality of life that enables the individual to live most and serve best" (377:4, italics deleted) illustrates that point. Williams was more interested in the use to which health was put, than in the attainment of health itself: "The emphasis in education upon health . . . results from the conviction that the first concern of the individual is to live and also the great need for him and for society that he live well." (373:5) In that context he stressed not only physical, mental and emotional balance, but also the holding of certain values, such as self-discipline and control: "It should be pointed out, therefore, that the emphasis upon health in education carries with it a fine idealism, a disciplining of self, a training of one's powers, a regimen of preparation for worthwhile causes. . . ." (373:5)

Williams recognized the theories concerning the original nature of man and was concerned that education should make use of instinctive drives and the learning potentials that accrued to "satisfyers and annoyers," but he advanced the concept that education should guide the child's nature into patterns of socially approved conduct. Thus, the child's interests, needs, drives, and inherent abilities were not necessarily to be satisfied, but used as facilitators to reach other ends.

Williams' conception of the physical educator was that of a man who used games and sports and the other activities of the profession as tools through which the child might learn the socially approved values of his society. "Education takes place by helping individuals to develop through activities and not by presenting subject matter to them." (378:38) Formal drill as a method of teaching was inimical to this approach: "In a democracy, where initiative, self-discipline, and ability to take charge of oneself, are educational goals, then formal drill for the general development of the citizen is a mistake and a waste of time." (376:62–63) He advocated, instead, the use of the project method to involve individuals more fully in the activity, and discussion to insure thoughtful consideration of values:

> Discussion is considered highly valuable as a method of instruction in mental learning. . . . Its use in physical education has been extremely limited in the past.
>
> Suppose for example that it is honestly desired to achieve in football the values that are so often claimed for those who engage in this activity. The qualities mentioned are "subordination, loyalty, ability to lose without sulking, to win without boasting, alertness, self-confidence and self-control," and many others. Now if these purposes are to be secured by the football players they must do some thinking about them. (378:45–46)

Williams therefore recommended that more class time be devoted to discussion, even at the expense of activity:

> The emphasis given by physical education teachers to questioning and to discussion should be increased. The time is past when a physical education period is adjudged good or bad depending upon the amount of physical activity obtained during the period. A period is good or bad to the extent of desirable, useful and pertinent intellectual knowledges, skills, and control obtained. (378:81)

Willingness to evaluate a class in the manner just described was characteristic of Williams' whole approach to physical education. He had no interest in physical activity per se and in fact disparaged the idea that muscle development might be a desired objective:

> What then, is to be said of the efforts of certain persons to develop large and bulging muscles or to pursue certain odd skills that have no useful function in life? The satisfactions derived from such exercises serve only whimsical values such as exhibitionism; at times they are outlets for maladjusted personalities. For example, the yoga devotees may finally acquire unilateral control over the *rectus abdominus*, but the evidence is lacking that this in any way deepened spirituality. (376:186–187)

> Cultivation of the body for the body's sake can never be justified. All strength and power developed that is not used to further mental and spiritual values are parasitic forces consuming the earth's bounty.... It is easy to forget and to think of strength and power as ends instead of considering them as means. (375:286)

Fig. 75.  Jesse Feiring Williams

Nevertheless, he was not totally opposed to the learning of skills. They could be justified as appropriate subject matter for education provided that they were either utilitarian or recreational:

> The human individual is skill-hungry. . . . He may be taught all sorts of skills but only those that are functional contribute to his education. Functional skills are either utilitarian or recreational. The utilitarian skills are walking, running, sitting, standing, lifting weights, climbing stairs, carrying objects, and other neuromuscular coordinations employed in daily life. The recreational skills are innumerable coordinations that function in games, sports, athletics, dance, and self-testing activities. These illustrate the functional use of skills and suggest their educational contribution as the individual enters into recreational activity at various age levels. (376:45)

Of course, "athletic sports and games furnish very desirable material because of the instinctive appeal in such plays and the opportunities they present for the development of moral and social values." (374:61) This was consistent with his statement of the aim of physical education:

> Physical education should aim to provide skilled leadership and adequate facilities that will afford an opportunity for the individual or group to act in situations that are physically wholesome, mentally stimulating and satisfying, and socially sound. (375:287)

Williams' whole position was predicated on the basis of his philosophical belief that man was a unified organism. To overplay the physical aspect was an "ugly distortion" of the balanced, harmonious human being first conceptualized by the ancient Greeks. To relegate education of the body to physical educators, and education of the mind to teachers of academic subjects, would have been an acknowledgement of dualism. It followed, then, that physical educators, dealing as they were with the whole child, must teach for outcomes reflective of this unity:

> The basis for the determination of principles of physical education has swung from the consideration of man as composed of so many muscles to a point that views man as a unity of mind and body, with spirit or soul as an essential element of the whole. This modern basis holds that for educational purposes man cannot be dissected, the organism must be the object of our study; and that for physical education, too great a reliance on physiologic principles with resulting neglect of the social, moral, and spiritual elements in life produces the "crude, vulgar, self-seeking individual" so obnoxious in human relationships and so dangerous to the state and the nation. (374:16)

In summation of Williams' philosophy of physical education, was his famous statement showing the progression of physical education from a subject the concern of which was education *of* the physical to one which purported to educate *through* the physical:

When mind and body were thought of as two separate entities, physical education was obviously an education *of* the physical; in similar fashion mental education made its own exclusive demands. But with new understanding of the nature of the human organism in which wholeness of the individual is the outstanding fact, physical education becomes education *through* the physical. With this view operative, physical education has concern for and with emotional responses, personal relationships, group behaviors, mental learning, and other intellectual, social, emotional, and esthetic outcomes. Although important and not to be neglected, it is quite insufficient to develop strength of muscles, bones, and ligaments, to acquire motor skills, and to secure physical endurance. (376:8)

There was nothing in Jesse Feiring Williams' early background that foretold his future convictions. Born in 1886 in Kenton, Ohio, he attended the Kenton public schools and Oberlin College, where he received his A.B. degree in 1909. He also attended the Chautauqua Summer School of Physical Education and was awarded his diploma in 1907. His formal education was completed at Columbia University, College of Physicians and Surgeons, where he earned his M.D. degree in 1915.

His first job was as Tutor, Director of Athletics, and Coach at Oberlin Academy from 1907–1909, while he was still an undergraduate. From 1910 to 1911 he was Instructor in Physical Education at the New York Institute for the Education of the Blind. In 1911 he was appointed to Teachers College, Columbia University as Instructor in Physical Education and in 1913 was raised to the rank of Assistant Professor. From 1916 to 1917 he was Professor of Hygiene and Physical Education at the University of Cincinnati. He then served a year with the United States Army as a lieutenant in the Medical Corps, following which he worked a year with the American Red Cross, holding the rank of major. In 1919 he returned to Columbia University as Associate Professor of Physical Education and from 1923 until his retirement in 1941 he held the rank of Professor and Chairman of the Department. Upon retirement from Teachers College he was named Professor Emeritus. During his tenure at Columbia University he received an appointment from 1935–1936 as visiting Carnegie Professor, accredited to Universities of Latin America. After his retirement he served as Professor of Health and Physical Education at the University of North Carolina, from 1942–1944. (190:351)

During the course of Williams' long association with Teachers College, he apparently was strongly influenced by the theories of his colleague John Dewey. There is an apocryphal tale that Williams wrote *The Principles of Physical Education* (375) with a pen in one hand and a work of Dewey's in the other. Certainly the ideas of Williams were a direct application of Dewey's philosophy to physical education. Dewey introduced the concept that the "whole child" attended school; Williams insisted on the idea of organismic unity and made it the core of his approach. In explicating the purposes of physical education as involving the development of socially useful conduct, with an emphasis on training in judgments about persons and human nature, and of character development, Williams was employing Dewey's theory that the purpose of education is to transmit and form through the interaction of the group, the cultural values of a society.

Social theorists of the time were paying a great deal of attention to the implications of the theory of evolution. The original tendencies or natural instincts of man were seen as important considerations in the educational process. Dewey proposed modifying or adjusting these instincts to benefit the social structure: "The natural or native customs of the young do not agree with the life customs of the group into which they are born. Consequently they have to be directed or guided. . . ." (87:39) Williams was aware that "man presents in the racial patterns of his nervous system certain underlying predispositions to function in well-defined motor activities characterized in type and quality by his motor experiences over thousands of years," and recommended that "under proper guidance, such expressions may be made to serve high causes and noble ends. . . ." (376:185)

Finally, Dewey's theory of how man learns, how he is directed and what influences his being, is tightly interwoven with his theory of social control. He believed that knowledge does not come from a man's merely existing in an environment and perceiving sensations from it—in other words, from contact with the physical world—but rather that behavior is modified in reference to another's behavior. Williams viewed the play field as the place in the school best set up to provide maximum social pressure and influence, pressuring the individual to meet the standards set up by society.

Williams' recognition of and interest in Dewey, and other formulators of the new theories of his time, such as Edward L. Thorndike (also at Teachers College) who structured S–R bond psychology, William James who engendered pragmatism, and G. Stanley Hall the great psychologist, is evidenced by the footnotes appearing in his writings. Early editions of *The Principles* carry many references to those men. That Williams was able to draw these theories together and use them in the construction of rational principles for physical education, was in part the reason for the respect accorded his work.

The importance of Williams' work was further magnified by its volume. Incredible as it may seem, between 1916 and 1964, forty-one different book titles were published under his name, either alone or in co-authorship. Seven books were published in multiple editions, the total number being forty-two editions. *The Principles of Physical Education* not only numbered eight editions between 1927 and 1964 but was also published in Japanese and Spanish translations. Since Williams was a medical doctor he was particularly qualified to write in the field of health, and the great bulk of his books were in health-related areas. He also wrote a large number of articles, many of which were for the *Journal of Health and Physical Education*, the *Teachers College Record* and *School and Society*. One of the most famous articles was "Education Through the Physical" published in the

*Journal of Higher Education* (371).  It is impossible to calculate the influence of one man's ideas when they are communicated to the large number of people that read Williams in one form or another.

Furthermore, his years at Teachers College, then one of the most famous institutions for graduate study in physical education in the country, brought him into contact with the best of the young professionals as they were doing advanced degree work.  This magnified the impact of his work even more.

Williams was active in the profession at large; he served as president of the American Physical Education Association (1932–1933), the College Physical Education Association (1928), and the Eastern District Association of AAHPER (1929–1931).  He was a charter member of the American Academy of Physical Education (Fellow #16) but he later resigned and his membership is sometimes recorded as "cancelled."  He was among the first group of recipients of the Honor Award in 1931, and he received the Gulick Award in 1939.  He was awarded honorary degrees by Rollins College (D.Sc., 1939) and Oberlin College (D.Sc., 1956).  Schwendener, one of his former students who wrote *A History of Physical Education in the United States,* summarized Williams' contribution:

> His touch upon physical education was one of absolute genius through which he imparted his vitality to the field.  A leader in the greatest sense of the word, a master of dialecticism, a superb champion of the cause, a student of unusual ability, and a gifted teacher, the professional career of Jesse Feiring Williams is synonymous with that of the functional development of American physical education. (330:153)

In the time of Williams' greatest influence the aims of education and of society in general seemed clearly ordered.  They included the belief that the preservation of democracy lay in inculcating society's values in the young.  The social system took precedence over the individual in that the latter was expected to adjust to the amorphous whole.  The central purpose of education was to prepare good citizens by preserving and transmitting the knowledge, attitudes and purposes of the society.  Williams was able to explicate physical education in terms of these beliefs.  He demonstrated the value of a subject the activities of which were a microcosm of society and therefore formed an excellent laboratory for social learning.  His writings convinced the profession that the best purpose physical education could serve was the development of desirable character traits, skills and values suitable for the individual's life in a democratic society.

# BIBLIOGRAPHY

1. "Adolf Hitler Speaks on Physical Education." Translated by E. Thoma. *Mind and Body*, 40 (November, 1933), 150–152.
2. "Affiliation of Normal College, A. G. U. and Indiana University." *Mind and Body*, 39 (November, 1932), 161.
3. Ainsworth, Dorothy S. *The History of Physical Education in Colleges for Women*. New York: A. S. Barnes and Company, 1930.
4. American Association for the Advancement of Physical Education. *Proceedings of the Second Annual Meeting*. Brooklyn, New York, 1886.
5. ————. *Proceedings of the Third Annual Meeting*. Brooklyn, New York, 1887.
6. ————. *Proceedings of the Fourth Annual Meeting*. New York City, 1888.
7. ————. *Proceedings of the Fifth Annual Meeting*. Cambridge and Boston, Massachusetts, 1890.
8. ———— *Proceedings of the Sixth Annual Meeting*. Boston, Massachusetts, 1891.
9. ————. *Proceedings of the Seventh Annual Meeting*. Philadelphia, Pennsylvania, 1892.
10. ————. *Proceedings of the Eighth Annual Meeting*. Chicago, Illinois, 1893.
11. ————. *Report of the Ninth Annual Meeting*. Connecticut, 1894.
12. ————. *Report of the Tenth Annual Meeting*. New York City, 1895.
13. Anderson, Lewis Flint. *Pestalozzi*. New York: McGraw-Hill Book Company, 1931.
14. *The Anderson Normal School of Gymnastics*. Catalogue for 1893–4.
15. Anderson, William G. "The Early History of the Association." *Journal of Health and Physical Education*, XII (January; March; April; May, 1941), 3–4, 61–62; 151–153, 200–201; 244–245; 313–315, 340.
16. ————. *Gymnastic Nomenclature*. New Haven: O. A. Dorman Company, 1896.
17. ————. *Light Gymnastics*. New York: Maynard, Merrill and Company, 1898.
18. ————. "Physical Training for Women." *Outing*, XV (January, 1890), 265–268.
19. ————. *Second Annual Report of the Director of Physical Education of the Adelphi Academy, Brooklyn, N. Y.*, 1886.
20. Arnold, Thomas. *The Miscellaneous Works of Thomas Arnold, D.D.* First American Edition. New York: D. Appleton & Company, 1845.
21. Association for the Advancement of Physical Education. *Proceedings at its Organization*. Brooklyn, New York, 1885.
22. "Athletic Sports as a Factor in European Life." *The Review of Reviews*, X (August, 1894), 208.
23. Averitte, George W. "A History of the Department of Health Education and Physical Education." Unpublished Ed.D. dissertation, Columbia University, 1953.

24. "Awards for Outstanding Service Presented by the American Association for Health, Physical Education, and Recreation." *Journal of Health, Physical Education, and Recreation*, 31 (April, 1960), 98–99.

25. Ballin, Hans. "Biographical Sketch of Friedrich Ludwig Jahn." *Mind and Body*, 1 (October, 1894), 1–7.

26. ————. "Gymnastics in the Bible." *Mind and Body*, 2 (September, 1895), 129–132.

27. ————. "Johann Heinrich Pestalozzi." *Mind and Body*, 2 (February, 1896), 221–227.

28. Bamford, Thomas William. *Thomas Arnold*. London: Cresset Press, 1960.

29. Bancroft, Jessie H. *Games*. Revised and Enlarged Edition. New York: The Macmillan Company, 1937.

30. ————. "Pioneering in Physical Training—An Autobiography." *Research Quarterly*, 12 (October, 1941, Suppl.), 666–678.

31. ————. "The Place of Automatism in Gymnastic Exercise." *American Physical Education Review*, VIII (December, 1903), 218–231.

32. ————. *School Gymnastics Free Hand*. New York: E. L. Kellogg & Company, 1900.

33. ————. "Some Educational Aspects of Physical Training." *American Physical Education Review*, XV (April, 1910), 233–240.

34. ————. "Some Essentials of Physical Training in Public Schools." *American Physical Education Review*, III (December, 1898), 281–287.

35. Barr, Stringfellow. *The Will of Zeus*. New York: Dell Publishing Company, 1965. (First published in 1961: New York: J. B. Lippincott Company).

36. Baskin, Wade, ed. *Classics in Education*. New York: Philosophical Library, 1966.

37. Bassett, John Spencer. "The Round Hill School." *Proceedings of the American Antiquarian Society*, 27 (April, 1917), 18–62.

38. Beck, Charles. *A Treatise on Gymnasticks, Taken Chiefly From the German of F. L. Jahn*. Northampton, Massachusetts: Simeon Butler, 1828.

39. Beecher, Catharine E. *Calisthenic Exercises*. New York: Harper & Brothers, 1870.

40. ————. *Physiology and Calisthenics*. New York: Harper & Brothers, 1870.

41. ————. *Treatise on Domestic Economy*. Revised Edition. New York: Harper & Brothers, 1854.

42. Beecher, Catharine Esther, and Stowe, Harriet Beecher. *The American Woman's Home or, Principles of Domestic Science*. New York: J. B. Ford, 1869.

43. Bennett, Bruce L. "Contributions of Dr. Sargent to Physical Education." *Research Quarterly*, 19 (May, 1948), 77–92.

44. ————. "The Life of Dudley Allen Sargent, M.D. and his Contribution to Physical Education." Unpublished Ph.D. dissertation, University of Michigan, 1947.

45. ————. "The Making of Round Hill School." *Quest*, IV (April, 1965), 53–63.

46. Berlin, Isaiah. *The Age of Enlightenment*. Vol. IV of *The Great Ages of Western Philosophy*. 6 vols. New York: George Braziller, 1957.

47. Blaikie, William. *How to Get Strong and How to Stay So*. New York: Harper & Brothers, 1879.

48. Blundell, John W. F. *The Muscles and Their Story, From the Earliest Times*. London: Chapman & Hall, 1864. (Free translation of *De Arte Gymnastica* by Hieronymous Mercurialis.)

49. Bonnamaux, Charles. "The Contributions of Baron Pierre de Coubertin to Physical Education." *American Physical Education Review*, XXIII (February, 1918), 91–98.

50. *Boston Normal School of Gymnastics. Third Annual Catalogue, 1893–1894.* Boston: Geo. H. Ellis, Printer, 1894.

51. Bowen, H. Courthope. *Froebel and Education Through Self-Activity.* New York: Charles Scribner's Sons, 1906.

52. Boykin, James C. "History of Physical Training." *Report of the Commissioner of Education for 1891–1892.* Washington, D. C.: U.S. Government Printing Office, 1894.

53. "Brief Outline of the Life and Work of Dr. Delphine Hanna." *Research Quarterly*, 12 (October, 1941, Suppl.), 646–652.

54. Bronson, Alice Oakes. *Clark W. Hetherington Scientist and Philosopher.* Salt Lake City: University of Utah Press, 1958.

55. Brosius, Geo[rge]. "The Rise and Growth of the North American Normal School of Gymnastics at Milwaukee." *Mind and Body*, 3 (November, 1896; January, 1897), 165–168; 220–221.

56. Brown, Margaret C., and Beiderhase, Josephine. "William G. Anderson." *Journal of Health, Physical Education, and Recreation*, 31 (April, 1960), 34, 126.

57. Brubacher, John S., and Rudy, Willis. *Higher Education in Transition.* New York: Harper and Row, Publishers, 1958.

58. Bukh, Niels. *Primary Gymnastics.* Translated by F. Braae Hansen and F. de H. Bevington. New York: E. P. Dutton & Company, n. d.

59. ————. "Primary Gymnastics." *Mind and Body*, 38 (November, 1931), 633–634.

60. Burchenal, Elizabeth. "A Constructive Program of Athletics for School Girls: Policy, Method and Activities." *American Physical Education Review*, XXIV (May, 1919), 272–279.

61. ————. "Does Training in Dancing Contribute to General Grace of Carriage and Posture?" *American Physical Education Review*, X (June, 1905), 101–106.

62. ————. *Folk Dances from Old Homelands.* New York: G. Schirmer, 1922.

63. ————. "Folk Dancing as Social Recreation for Adults." *Playground*, XIV (October, 1920), 404–416.

64. ————. "Reviving the Folk Dance." *Journal of the National Education Association*, XV (November, 1926), 241.

65. ————. "The Use of Folk Dancing as Recreation in a Health Program." *Playground*, XII (September, 1918), 228–232.

66. Burger, Ed Wolfgang, and Groll, Hans. *Leibserziehung.* Vienna: Österreichischer Bundesverlag, 1959.

67. Burgess, William C. "The Life of Thomas Denison Wood, M.D. and his Contributions to Health Education and Physical Education." Unpublished Ed.D. dissertation, Columbia University, 1959.

68. Burr, Hanford, and others. "Dr. Luther Halsey Gulick, 1865–1918: A Symposium." *American Physical Education Review*, XXIII (October, 1918), 413–426.

69. Butler, George D. *Pioneers in Public Recreation.* Minneapolis: Burgess Publishing Company, 1965.

70. Cahn, Joseph L. "Contributions of Plato to Thought on Physical Education, Health, and Recreation." Unpublished Ed.D. dissertation, New York University, 1942.

71. Carkin, Janice Williams. "Biographies of Five Women Gulick Award Recipients." Unpublished Ed.D. dissertation, Stanford University, 1952.

72. Chamberlain, Arthur H. "John Swett—Teacher—Author—Man." *Sierra Educational News* (May, 1913), 6.

73. Cogswell, Joseph Green. *Life of Joseph Green Cogswell as Sketched in His Letters.* Arranged by Anna Eliot Ticknor. Cambridge: Riverside Press, 1874.

74. Comenius, John Amos. *Comenius.* Translated, edited, and introduction by M. W. Keatinge. New York: McGraw-Hill Book Company, 1931.

75. ————. *The School of Infancy.* Translated, edited, and introduction by Ernest M. Eller. Chapel Hill: University of North Carolina Press, 1956.

76. Cook, Mabel Cathryn. "The N.A.G.U. Normal School." *Mind and Body*, 11 (November, 1904), 268–269.

77. Coon, Horace. *Columbia, Colossus on the Hudson.* New York: E. P. Dutton & Company, 1947.

78. Cottrell, Leonard. *Realms of Gold.* Connecticut: New York Graphic Society, 1963.

79. Coubertin, Baron Pierre de. *The Evolution of France Under the Third Republic.* New York: Thomas Crowell & Company, 1897.

80. ————. "The Olympic Games of 1896." *The Century Magazine*, LIII (New Series XXXI) (November, 1896—April, 1897), 39–53.

81. ————. "The Re-establishment of the Olympic Games." *The Chautauquan*, XIX (September, 1894), 696–700. (Translated from *Revue de Paris*.)

82. Cremin, Lawrence A., Shannon, David A., and Townsend, Mary Evelyn. *A History of Teachers College, Columbia University.* New York: Columbia University Press, 1954.

83. Cross, Barbara, ed. *The Educated Woman in America.* New York: Teachers College Press, Teachers College, Columbia University, 1965.

84. Cubberly, Ellwood P. *A Brief History of Education.* Boston: Houghton Mifflin Company, 1920.

85. *Delsarte System of Oratory.* Fourth Edition. New York: Edgar S. Werner, 1893.

86. Descartes, René. "Second Replies to Objections." *Philosophers Speak for Themselves: From Descartes to Locke.* Edited by T. V. Smith and Marjorie Grene. Phoenix Books. Chicago: The University of Chicago Press, 1957.

87. Dewey, John. *Democracy and Education.* New York: Macmillan Paperbacks Edition, 1963. (First published in 1916.)

88. ————. *Interest and Effort in Education.* Boston: Houghton Mifflin Company, 1913.

89. ————. "My Pedagogic Creed." *Classics in Education.* Edited by Wade Baskin. New York: Philosophical Library, 1966.

90. Dorgan, Ethel Josephine. *Luther Halsey Gulick 1865–1918.* New York: Bureau of Publications, Teachers College, Columbia University, 1934.

91. Dulles, Foster Rhea. *America Learns to Play.* Massachusetts: Peter Smith, 1963.

92. Eastman, Mary F. *The Biography of Dio Lewis, A.M., M.D.* New York: Fowler & Wells Company, 1891.

93. Eastman, Max. *Heroes I Have Known.* New York: Simon and Schuster, 1942.

94. Eby, Frederick. *Early Protestant Educators.* New York: McGraw-Hill Book Company, 1931.

95. "Editorial Note and Comment." *American Physical Education Review*, IX (June, 1904), 151–152.

96. Ellis, George E. "Recollections of Round Hill School." *Educational Review*, I (April, 1891), 337–344.

97. *The Eurythmics of Jacques-Dalcroze.* Introduction by M. E. Sadler. London: Constable & Company, 1912.

98. Fairs, John R. "The Influence of Plato and Platonism on the Development of Physical Education in Western Culture." *Quest,* XI (December, 1968), 14–23.

99. Faust, A. B. "Commencement Address at the Normal College of the North American Gymnastic Union, at Indianapolis, June 22, 1912." *Mind and Body,* 19 (November, 1912), 358–365.

100. Felshin, Janet. "Changing Conceptions of Purpose in Physical Education in the United States from 1880 to 1930." Unpublished Ed.D. dissertation, University of California, Los Angeles, 1958.

101. ————. *Perspectives and Principles for Physical Education.* New York: John Wiley and Sons, 1967.

102a. Fisher, George J. "Clark W. Hetherington, Pioneer, Indefatigable Worker, Student, Idealist, Organizer, Fighter." *American Physical Education Review,* XXXIII (March, 1928), 165–169.

102b. ————. "Jessie H. Bancroft, Educator—Author—Pioneer—Philanthropist." *American Physical Education Review,* XXIX (October, 1924), 476–480.

103. Fitz, George W. "American Society for Research in Physical Education." *American Physical Education Review,* IX (March, 1904), 60–62.

104. ————. "Conditions and Needs of Physical Education." *American Physical Education Review,* IV (December, 1899), 337–339.

105. ————. "Editorial Note and Comment." *American Physical Education Review,* XI (March, 1906), 35–36.

106. ————. "A Micrometer for Pure Culture and Microchemical Work." *Science,* 79 (March, 1934), 233–234.

107. ————. "Play as a Factor in Development." *American Physical Education Review,* II (December, 1897), 209–215.

108. ————. "A Practical Photometric Method for Case Record." *American Physical Education Review,* X (October, 1905), 292–306.

109. ————. "Problems of Physical Education." Reprint from *Harvard Graduates' Magazine* (September, 1893), 1–6.

110. ————. "A Simple Method of Measuring and Graphically Plotting Spinal Curvature and Other Assymmetries by Means of a New Direct-Reading Scoliometer." *American Physical Education Review,* XI (January, 1906), 18–23.

111. Forbes, Clarence A. *Greek Physical Education.* New York: The Century Company, 1929.

112. Frame, Donald M. *Montaigne: A Biography.* New York: Harcourt, Brace & World, 1965.

113. Frederick, Mary Margaret. "Naturalism: The Philosophy of Jean Jacques Rousseau and its Implications for American Physical Education." Unpublished D.P.E. dissertation, Springfield College, 1961.

114. Froebel, Friedrich. *Autobiography.* Translated and annotated by Emilie Michaelis and H. Keatley Moore. Syracuse, New York: C. W. Bardeen Publisher, 1889.

115. ————. *The Education of Man.* Translated and annotated by W. N. Hailmann. New York: D. Appleton and Company, 1896.

116. ————. *The Mottoes and Commentaries of Friedrich Froebel's Mother Play.* Translated and with an introduction by Susan E. Blow. New York: D. Appleton and Company, 1909.

117. ————. *Pedagogics of the Kindergarten.* Translated by Josephine Jarvis. New York: D. Appleton and Company, 1900.

118. Gardiner, E. Norman. *Athletics of the Ancient World*. Oxford: University Press, 1930.

119. Gardiner, Rolf. "Rhythmic Gymnastics in Germany." *Mind and Body*, 32 (December, 1925), 776–780.

120. Gaulhofer, Karl. *System des Schulturnens*. Edited by Hans Groll. Vienna: Österreichischer Bundesverlag, 1966.

121. Gaulhofer, Karl, and Streicher, Margarete. *Grundzüge des österreichischen Schulturnens*. Vienna: Deutscher Verlag für Jugend und Volk, 1922.

122. ————. *Grundzüge des österreichischen Schulturnens*. Vienna: Verlag für Jugend und Volk, 1950.

123. ————. *Kinderstunden-Erste Schuljahr*. Vienna: Deutscher Verlag für Jugend und Volk, 1930.

124. ————. *Natürliches Turnen I*. Vienna: Verlag für Jugend und Volk, 1949.

125. ————. *Natürliches Turnen II*. Vienna: Verlag für Jugend und Volk, 1949.

126. Gaulhofer, Walter. "Aus dem Leben Karl Gaulhofer." *Leibesübungen und Leibeserziehung*, V (October, 1951), 2–5.

127a. Gerber, Ellen W. "Learning and Play: Insights of Educational Protagonists." *Quest*, XI (December, 1968), 44–49.

127b. ————. "Three Interpretations of the Role of Physical Education, 1930–1960: Charles Harold McCloy, Jay Bryan Nash, and Jesse Feiring Williams." Unpublished Ph.D. dissertation, University of Southern California, 1966.

128. Gilbert, M[elvin] B[allou]. "Classic Dancing." *American Physical Education Review*, X (June, 1905), 145–154.

129. Goodsell, Willystine, ed. *Pioneers of Women's Education in the United States*. New York: McGraw-Hill Book Company, 1931.

130. Green, Robert Montraville. *A Translation of Galen's Hygiene*. Illinois: Charles C Thomas, Publisher, 1951.

131. Grisar, Hartmann. *Martin Luther*. Adapted from the Second German Edition by Frank J. Eble. London: B. Herder Book Company, 1935.

132. Groll, Hans. "Dr. Margarete Streicher zum 60. Geburtstag." *Leibesübungen und Leibeserziehung*, V (March, 1951), 49–52.

133. ————. "Gaulhofer-Gedenkpeier." *Leibesübungen und Leibeserziehung*, XV (December, 1961), 1–5.

134. Guimps, Roger de. *Pestalozzi His Life and Work*. New York: D. Appleton and Company, 1890.

135. Gulick, Luther Halsey. "Academy of Physical Education." *American Physical Education Review*, XV (May, 1910), 342–344.

136. ————. "Athletics from the Biologic Viewpoint." *American Physical Education Review*, XI (September, 1906), 157–160.

137. ————. "The Ethics of Sport." *Physical Education*, V (July, 1896), 43–46.

138. ————. "Exercise Must be Interesting." *American Physical Education Review*, XII (March, 1907), 60–63.

139. ————. *The Healthful Art of Dancing*. New York: Doubleday, Page & Company, 1910.

140. ————. "The Pentathlon." *Physical Education*, I (March, 1892), 26–30.

141. ————. *A Philosophy of Play*. New York: Charles Scribner's Sons, 1920.

142. ————. *Physical Education by Muscular Exercise*. Philadelphia: P. Blakiston's Son & Company, 1904.

143. ————. "The Place and Limitations of Folk Dancing as an Agency in Physical Training." *American Physical Education Review*, XIII (October, 1908), 377–382.

144. ————. "Prof. T. D. Wood, A.M., M.D." *Physical Education*, I (March, 1892), 24–26.
145. ————. "Rhythm and Education." *American Physical Education Review*, X (June, 1905), 164–169.
146. Guts Muths, Johann Friedrich. *Gymnastics for Youth*. London: J. Johnson, 1800. (On the title page authorship is incorrectly attributed to C. G. Salzmann.)
147. Hackensmith, C. W. *History of Physical Education*. New York: Harper & Row, Publishers, 1966.
148. Haglund, Patrik. "About the Reorganization of the Gymnastika Central-institutet." *Mind and Body*, 29 (April, 1922), 24–26.
149. Hall, Edward T. *The Silent Language*. New York: Doubleday & Company, 1969.
150. Hanna, Delphine. "Championship Skating as One of the Events of a Women's Athletic Association." *Mind and Body*, 11 (April, 1904), 56.
151. ————. "Gymnastic Lessons." *American Physical Education Review*, XVI (November, 1911), 515–520.
152. ————. "Present Status of Physical Training in Normal Schools." *American Physical Education Review*, VIII (December, 1903), 293–297.
153. Hanna, Delphine, and Spore, Nellie A. "Effect of College Work Upon the Health of Women." *American Physical Education Review*, IV (September, 1899), 279–280.
154. Hansen, Emanuel. *Sports in Denmark*. Copenhagen: Det Danske Selskab, after 1955.
155. Harris, H. A. *Greek Athletes and Athletics*. London: Hutchinson & Company, (Publishers) 1964.
156. Hartung, Henry. "The Present Condition of Gymnastics and Athletics in the North American Gymnastic Union." *American Physical Education Review*, VIII (December, 1903), 273–279.
157. Hartwell, Edward Mussey. "Book Notices and Bibliography." *American Physical Education Review*, II (September, 1897), 193–196.
158. ————. "Peter Henry Ling, the Swedish Gymnasiarch." *American Physical Education Review*, I (September, 1896), 1–13.
159. ————. "On Physical Training." *Report of the Commissioner of Education for 1897–1898*. Vol. I. Washington, D. C.: U.S. Government Printing Office, 1899.
160. ————. "On Physical Training." *Report of the Commissioner of Education for 1903*. Washington, D. C.: U.S. Government Printing Office, 1904.
161. ————. *Physical Training in American Colleges and Universities*. Circulars of Information of the Bureau of Education. No. 5, 1885. Washington, D. C.: U.S. Government Printing Office, 1886.
162. ————. *Physical Training Treated From American and European Points of View*. Boston: Geo. H. Ellis, 1890. (Reprinted from the *Baltimore Sun*.)
163. ————. "Report of the Chairman of Section on History and Bibliography of Physical Education." *Physical Education*, II (March, 1893), 127–130.
164. ————. *Some Aspects of Athletics and Gymnastics at Home and Abroad*. New Hampshire: Republican Press Association, 1891. (Reprinted from the *Proceedings of the American Institute of Instruction*, at the Annual Meeting, July, 1891.)
165. Harvard University, Lawrence Scientific School. *Description of the Four Years' Course in Anatomy, Physiology, and Physical Training*. Cambridge: By the University, 1894, 1894–95, 1896, 1897–98.
166. Harveston, Mae Elizabeth. "Catharine Esther Beecher Pioneer Educator." Unpublished Ph.D. dissertation, University of Pennsylvania, 1931.

15
2

**424 BIBLIOGRAPHY**

167. Heafford, Michael. *Pestalozzi*. London: Methuen & Company, 1967.
168. Henderson, Robert W. *Ball, Bat and Bishop*. The Origin of Ball Games. New York: Rockport Press, 1947.
169. Hergl-Gottlieb, Kathe. "Gaulhofer-Streicher." *Leibesübungen und Leibeserziehung*, XX (September, 1966), 11.
170. Hetherington, Clark W. "Athletic Research Society." *American Physical Education Review*, XV (April, 1910), 262–263.
171. ————. "The Demonstration Play School of 1913." *American Physical Education Review*, XX (May; June; October, 1915), 282–294; 373–380; 429–445.
172. ————. "Fundamental Education." *American Physical Education Review*, XV (December, 1910), 629–636.
173. ————. "Graduate Work in Physical Education." *American Physical Education Review*, XXX (April; May, 1925), 207–210; 262–268.
174. ————. *A Normal Course in Play*. New York: Playground Association of America, 1909.
175. ————. *School Program in Physical Education*. New York: World Book Company, 1922.
176. ————. "A Statement of Principles for a National Athletic Platform." *American Physical Education Review*, XVI (December, 1911), 593–599.
177. ————. "University Professional Training Courses in Physical Education." *American Physical Education Review*, XXV (May, 1920), 185–197.
178. Higginson, Thomas Wentworth. "Gymnastics." *Atlantic Monthly*, VII (March, 1861), 283–302.
179. Hitchcock, Edward. "Athletic Education." *Journal of Social Science*, XX (June, 1885), 27–44.
180. ————. "The Gymnastic Era and the Athletic Era of Our Country." *Outlook*, 51 (May, 1895), 816–818.
181. ————. *A Part of the Course of Instruction Given in the Department of Physical Education and Hygiene in Amherst College*. Massachusetts: Gazette Printing Company, 1878.
182. Holmberg, Oswald. "The Expanded Chest—Hjalmar Ling's Opinion in the Light of Modern Ideas." *Mind and Body*, 40 (February, 1934), 270–277.
183. ————. "Was Swedish Gymnastics Dull?" *Mind and Body*, 42 (October, 1935), 92–100.
184. Homer. *The Iliad*. Translated by E. V. Rieu. Baltimore: Penguin Books, 1950.
185. ————. *The Odyssey*. Translated by E. V. Rieu. Baltimore: Penguin Books, 1946.
186. Hughes, James L. *Froebel's Educational Laws for All Teachers*. New York: D. Appleton and Company, 1901.
187. Hughes, Thomas. *Loyola*. New York: Charles Scribner's Sons, 1892.
188. Hughes, Thomas. *Tom Brown's School-Days*. Philadelphia: Porter & Coates, n. d. (First published 1857.)
189a. Hunter, Adelaide Meador. "R. Tait McKenzie: Pioneer in Physical Education." Unpublished Ed.D. dissertation, Columbia University, 1950.
189b. Hussey, Christopher. *Tait McKenzie A Sculptor of Youth*. London: Country Life, 1929.
190. Ingram, Dorothy. "Jesse Feiring Williams: His Life and Contributions to the Field of Health, Physical Education and Recreation." Unpublished Ph.D. dissertation, Texas Woman's University, 1963.
191. "In Memoriam [Baron Nils Posse]." *Mind and Body*, 2 (February, 1896), 231–232.

192. James, William.  *Talks to Teachers*.  New York:  W. W. Norton & Company, 1958.  (First published in 1892.)

193. Jessup, Harvey M.  "Jay Bryan Nash:  His Contributions and Influence in the Fields of Physical, Health, Recreation, Camping and Outdoor Education."  Unpublished Ed.D. dissertation, New York University,  1967.

194. Johnson, A. H., ed.  *The Wit and Wisdom of John Dewey*.  Boston:  Beacon Press, 1949.

195. Johnston, Johanna, and Steffensen, James L.  *Reformation and Exploration*. Vol. VIII of *The Universal History of the World*.  Edited by Irwin Shapiro. New York:  Golden Press, 1966.

196. Joseph, H. Ludwig.  "Medical Gymnastics in the Sixteenth and Seventeenth Centuries."  *CIBA Symposia*, 10 (March-April, 1949), 1041–1053.

197. Juvenal.  *Satires*.  Translated by Jerome Mazzars.  Ann Arbor:  University of Michigan Press, 1965.

198. Kandel, I. L.  *History of Secondary Education*.  New York:  Houghton Mifflin Company, 1930.

199. Knudsen, K. A.  *A Text-Book of Gymnastics*. Translated by Ruth Herbert and H. G. Junker.  Philadelphia:  J. B. Lippincott Company, 1920.

200. Koch, K.  "Folk and Child Play."  Translated by Anna L. von der Osten. *American Physical Education Review*, XIII (June, 1908), 325–334.

201. Kroh, Carl J.  "The German System of Gymnastics."  *Proceedings and Addresses of the National Educational Association*, 36th Annual Meeting. Milwaukee, Wisconsin, 1897, 880–883.

202. Larkin, Richard A.  "The Influence of John Dewey on Physical Education." Unpublished M.A. thesis, The Ohio State University, 1936.

203. La Salle, Dorothy.  "Thomas Denison Wood."  *Journal of Health, Physical Education, and Recreation*, 31 (April, 1960), 61, 118.

204. Lee, Mabel, and Bennett, Bruce.  "This is Our Heritage."  *Journal of Health, Physical Education, and Recreation*, 31 (April, 1960), 25–33, 38–47, 52–58, 62–73, 76–85.

205. Leonard, Fred Eugene.  "The First Introduction of the Jahn Gymnastics into America."  *Mind and Body*, 12 (September, 1905–February, 1906), 193–198; 217–223; 249–254; 281–287; 313–319; 345–351.

206. ————.  *Pioneers of Modern Physical Training*.  Reprinted from *Physical Training*.  Published by the Physical Directors' Society of the Young Men's Christian Association of North America (No date given but published in 1910).

207. Leonard, Fred Eugene, and Affleck, George B.  *A Guide to the History of Physical Education*.  Third Edition.  Philadelphia:  Lea & Febiger, 1947.

208. Lewis, Dio.  "The Health of Our Girls."  *The Atlantic Monthly*, IX (June, 1862), 722–731.

209. ————.  "The New Gymnastics."  *The Atlantic Monthly*, X (August, 1862), 129–148.

210. ————.  *The New Gymnastics for Men, Women, and Children*.  Eighth Edition.  Boston:  Ticknor and Fields, 1864.

211a.————.  *Weak Lungs, and How to Make Them Strong*.  Boston:  Ticknor and Fields, 1864.

211b.*Lewis's Gymnastic Monthly and Journal of Physical Culture*, II (January, 1862, Extra), 24 pages.

212a.Little, James R.  "Charles Harold McCloy:  His Contributions to Physical Education."  Unpublished Ph.D. dissertation, University of Iowa, 1968.

212b.————.  "Charles Harold McCloy:  His Professional Preparation and Early Work Experiences."  National College Physical Education Association for Men.  *Proceedings of the 72nd Annual Meeting*.  Durham, North Carolina, 1969.

213. Locke, John. "Essay Concerning Human Understanding." *Philosophers Speak for Themselves: From Descartes to Locke.* Edited by T. V. Smith and Marjorie Grene. Phoenix Books. Chicago: University of Chicago Press, 1957.

214. ————. *Some Thoughts Concerning Education.* Introduction and notes by R. H. Quick. Cambridge: University Press, 1913. (First Edition 1880.)

215. Lucas, John Apostal. "Baron Pierre de Coubertin and the Formative Years of the Modern International Olympic Movement 1883–1896." Unpublished Ed.D. dissertation, University of Maryland, 1962.

216. Luther, Martin. "Letter to the Mayors and Aldermen." *Classics in Education.* Edited by Wade Baskin. New York: Philosophical Library, 1966.

217. Lynn, Minnie L. "Delphine Hanna." *Journal of Health, Physical Education, and Recreation,* 31 (April, 1960), 51, 110.

218. McCloy, Charles Harold. *The Measurement of Athletic Power.* New York: A. S. Barnes and Company, 1932.

219. ————. "Methods of Research in Physical Education." *American Physical Education Review,* XXXIV (January, 1929), 10–16.

220. ————. *Philosophical Bases for Physical Education.* New York: F. S. Crofts & Company, 1940.

221. ————. *Tests and Measurements in Health and Physical Education.* New York: F. S. Crofts & Company, 1939.

222. McDowell, Hilda. "Denmark and the Ollerup High School for Adult Students." *Mind and Body,* 29 (July, 1922), 155–161.

223. ————. "Ollerup Gymnastik Folkhojskole." *Mind and Body,* 28 (July, 1921), 668–670.

224. McIntosh, Peter C. *Physical Education in England Since 1800.* Revised and Enlarged Edition. London: G. Bell & Sons, 1968.

225. ————. *Sport in Society.* London: C. A. Watts & Company, 1963.

226. McIntosh, P. C. and others. *Landmarks in the History of Physical Education.* London: Routledge & Kegan Paul, 1957.

227. McKenzie, R. Tait. "Annual Address by the President of the Society of Directors of Physical Education in Colleges." *American Physical Education Review,* XV (February, 1910), 71–78.

228. ————. "The Athlete in Sculpture." *Journal of Health and Physical Education,* III (November, 1932), 41–46, 54–55.

229. ————. *Exercise in Education and Medicine.* Second Edition. Philadelphia: W. B. Saunders Company, 1917.

230. ————. "The Expression of the Face in Violent Effort." *Outing,* 39 (November, 1901), 190–197.

231. ————. "Memorandum on Life of William Gilbert Anderson, M.D., M.P.E., D.P.H." *American Physical Education Review,* XXXIV (October, 1929), 494–498.

232. ————. "Physical Education at the University of Pennsylvania—from 1904 to 1931—and the Gates Plan." *Proceedings of the Society of Directors of Physical Education in Colleges,* Thirty-fifth Annual Meeting, New York City, 1931, 19–26.

233. ————. *Reclaiming the Maimed.* New York: The Macmillan Company, 1918.

234. ————. "The Regulation of Physical Instruction in Schools and Colleges from the Standpoint of Hygiene." *Science,* 29 (March, 1909), 481–484.

235. ————. "The Relation of Physical Education to the Business of War." *American Physical Education Review,* XXII (December, 1917), 525–528.

236. Maclaren, Archibald. *A Military System of Gymnastic Exercises and a System of Fencing.* London: Her Majesty's Stationery Office, 1868.

237. —————. *A System of Physical Education*. Oxford: The Clarendon Press, 1869.
238. MacVannel, John Angus. *The Educational Theories of Herbart and Froebel*. New York: Teachers College, Columbia University, 1905.
239. Marrou, H. I.: *A History of Education in Antiquity*. Translated by George Lamb. New York: The New American Library, 1964. (First published in 1956, New York: Sheed and Ward.)
240. May, Jonathan. "The Bergman-Österberg Physical Training College," in Peter C. McIntosh. *Physical Education in England Since 1800*. London: G. Bell & Sons, 1968.
241. Mayer, Frederick. *A History of Ancient and Medieval Philosophy*. New York: American Book Company, 1950.
242. —————. *The Great Teachers*. New York: The Citadel Press, 1967.
243. Mercurialis, Hieronymous. *De Arte Gymnastica*. Libri Sex. Amstelodami: Andreae Frisii, 1672.
244. Metzner, Henry. "A Brief History of the North American Gymnastic Union." Translated by Theo. Stempfel, Jr. *Mind and Body*, 20; 21; 22 (May, 1913; November, 1914; December, 1914; April, 1915; May, 1915), 94–101; 358–364; 403–408; 610–613; 654–656.
245. Miller, Kenneth D. "Stearns, Hitchcock, and Amherst College." *Journal of Health, Physical Education, and Recreation*, 28 (May-June, 1957), 29–30.
246. Montaigne, Michel de. *The Complete Essays*. Translated by Donald M. Frame. California: Stanford University Press, 1948.
247. Moolenijzer, Nicolaas Johannes. "The Concept of 'Natural' in Physical Education: Johann Guts Muths-Margarete Streicher." Unpublished Ph.D. dissertation, University of Southern California, 1966.
248. —————. "Implications of the Philosophy of Gaulhofer and Streicher for Physical Education." Unpublished M.S. thesis, University of California, Los Angeles, 1956.
249. Mulcaster, Richard. *Elementarie*. Edited, with an introduction, by E. T. Campagnac. Oxford: The Clarendon Press, 1925.
250. Nash, Jay B. *The Administration of Physical Education*. New York: A. S. Barnes and Company, 1932.
251. —————. "The Gulick Award, 1946 [Ethel Perrin]." *Journal of Health and Physical Education*, 17 (September, 1946), 405, 448–449.
252. —————. *The Organization and Administration of Playgrounds and Recreation*. New York: A. S. Barnes and Company, 1928.
253. —————. *Philosophy of Recreation and Leisure*. Iowa: Wm. C. Brown Company, 1960. (First published in 1953: St. Louis, The C. V. Mosby Company.)
254. —————. *Physical Education: Its Interpretations and Objectives*. Iowa: Wm. C. Brown Company, 1963. (First published 1948: New York, A. S. Barnes and Company.)
255. —————. *Spectatoritis*. New York: Sears Publishing Company, 1932.
256. Nash, Jay B., Moench, Francis J., and Saurborn, Jeanette B. *Physical Education: Organization and Administration*. New York: A. S. Barnes and Company, 1951.
257. Nash, Paul, Kazamias, Andreas M., and Perkinson, Henry J. *The Educated Man: Studies in the History of Educational Thought*. New York: John Wiley & Sons, 1965.
258. "News Notes." *American Physical Education Review*, IX (June, 1904), 153.
259. "News Notes. North American Turnerbund." *American Physical Education Review*, IX (September, 1904), 219–220.

260. *Nine Pioneers in Physical Education.* Great Britain: The Physical Education Association, 1964.

261. Nock, Albert Jay, and Wilson, C. R. *Francis Rabelais.* New York: Harper & Brothers, 1929.

262. "Normal College Notes." *Mind and Body,* 25 (April, 1918), 92–93.

263. "Normal Physical Training." *Physical Education,* I (November, 1892), 165–166.

264. Norris, Kathryn. "Normal College North American Gymnastic Union, Indianapolis, Ind." *Mind and Body,* 24 (November, 1917), 339.

265. "Notes from Normal Schools." *Mind and Body,* 16; 22 (April 1909; December, 1915), 76–77; 861.

266. "Notes from the Posse Gymnasium." *Physical Education,* III (June, 1894), 68.

267. Oktavec, Frank L. *The Professional Education of Special Men Teachers of Physical Education in Prussia.* New York: Bureau of Publications, Teachers College, Columbia University, 1929.

268. Oliphant, James. *The Educational Writings of Richard Mulcaster.* Glasgow: James Maclehose and Sons, 1903.

269. Osborne, Barbara J. "An Historical Study of Physical Education in Germany and its Influence in the United States." Unpublished M.Ed. thesis, University of North Carolina, Woman's College, 1961.

270. Panzer, Henry. "Progress in Physical Education." *Mind and Body,* 36 (January, 1930), 297–302.

271. Pawel, Jaro. "Sports in the English College." Translated by W. C. Schaefer. *Mind and Body,* 2 (June; July; August, 1895), 71–73; 94–96; 108–109.

272. Perrin, Ethel. "Athletics for Women and Girls." *Playground,* XVII (March, 1924), 658–661.

273. ———. "Confessions of a Once Strict Formalist." *Journal of Health and Physical Education,* IX (November, 1938), 533–536.

274. ———. "A Health Issue in the School Today." *Journal of Health and Physical Education,* III (January, 1932), 15–17.

275. ———. "Methods of Interesting School Children in Good Postural Habits." *American Physical Education Review,* XIX (October, 1914), 503–506.

276. ———. "Outdoor Recreation as a Factor in Child Welfare," *Playground,* XVIII (July, 1924), 240–242, 246, 266.

277. ———. "Win or Lose—But Play!" *The Nation's Schools,* 20 (September, 1937), 22.

278. "Personals." *Physical Education,* IV (August, 1895), 86.

279. Pestalozzi, Johann Heinrich. *How Gertrude Teaches Her Children.* Translated by Lucy E. Holland and Francis C. Turner. Syracuse, N. Y.: C. W. Bardeen, 1915.

280. Phillips, Madge. "Biographies of Selected Women Leaders in Physical Education in the United States." Unpublished Ph.D. dissertation, State University of Iowa, 1960.

281. Phillips, Paul C. "The Eurhythmics of Jaques-Dalcroze." *American Physical Education Review,* XVIII (March, 1913), 142–145.

282. *Physical Training, A Full Report of the Papers and Discussion of the Conference Held in Boston in November, 1889.* Reported and edited by Isabel C. Barrows. Boston: Geo. H. Ellis, 1890.

283. Piccolomini, Aeneas Sylvius. "De Liberorum Educatione." *Vittorino da Feltre and Other Humanist Educators.* William Harrison Woodward. New York: Bureau of Publications, Teachers College, Columbia University, 1963.

284. Plato. *The Laws*. Translated with an introduction by A. E. Taylor. Everyman's Library. New York: E. P. Dutton & Company, 1960

285. —————. *Phaedrus, Ion, Gorgias, and Symposium, with Passages from the Republic and Laws*. Translated by Lane Cooper. London: Oxford University Press, 1938.

286. —————. *The Republic*. Translated by Benjamin Jowett. The Modern Library. New York: Random House.

287. Poindexter, Hally Beth (Walker). "Graduate Professional Preparation in Physical Education in Selected Colleges and Universities With Implications for Teachers College." Unpublished Ed.D. dissertation, Columbia University, 1957.

288. Pollard, Hugh M. *Pioneers of Popular Education*. London: John Murray (Publishers), 1956.

289. Posse, Baron Nils. *Handbook of School-Gymnastics*. Boston: Lothrop, Lee & Shepard Company, 1891.

290. —————. "Modifications of the Swedish System of Gymnastics to Meet American Conditions." *Physical Education*, I (October, 1892), 169–174.

291. —————. *The Special Kinesiology of Educational Gymnastics*. Boston: Lee and Shepard Publishers, 1894.

292. "The Posse Gymnasium." *Physical Education*, IV (July, 1895), 63–67.

293. *Proceedings of the California State Teachers' Institute*, San Francisco, 1863. Sacramento: Department of Public Instruction, 1863.

294. Quick, Robert Herbert. *Essays on Educational Reformers*. New York: D. Appleton and Company, 1929. (First edition revised, published in 1890.)

295. Quintilian. *Institutes of Oratory*. Translated by John Selby Watson. The Library of Liberal Arts. New York: Bobbs-Merrill Company, 1965.

296. "R. Tait McKenzie." *Journal of Health and Physical Education*, 15 (February, 1944), 49–104.

297. Rabelais, François. *The Works*. Nottingham: Printed for Private Circulation. (No translator or date of publication given.)

298. Ray, Harold Lloyd. "The Life and Professional Contribution of William Gilbert Anderson, M.D." Unpublished Ph D. dissertation, The Ohio State University, 1959.

299. *Report on the Lingiad 1949 and Idla Gymnastics*. Edited by Vello Pekomäe and Gunvald Häkanson. Translated by Albert Lynden. Stockholm: AB Seelig & Company, 1949.

300. "Reports from Sections, States and Local Societies [The Gulick Medal and the Contribution of Luther Halsey Gulick to Physical Education]." *American Physical Education Review*, XXVIII (September; October, 1923), 336–340; 378–384.

301. Rice, Emmett A., Hutchinson, John L., and Lee, Mabel. *A Brief History of Physical Education*. Fifth Edition. New York: The Ronald Press Company, 1969.

302. Riemer, Bernhard. "The Grandfather of German Gymnastics." *Mind and Body*, 1 (May, 1894), 1–3.

303. Rinsch, Emil. *History of the Normal College of the American Gymnastic Union of Indiana University—1866–1966*. Bloomington: Indiana University Press, 1966.

304. Robinson, Rachel Sargent. *Sources for the History of Greek Athletics*. Ohio: By the Author, 439 Ludlow Ave., Cincinnati, 1955.

305. Rogers, Frederick Rand. *Physical Education in Institutions of Higher Learning*. United States Office of Education. Pamphlet No. 82. Washington, D. C.: U.S. Government Printing Office, 1937.

306. Roper, R. E. "Systems of Gymnastics: Their Origin and Evolution." *Mind and Body*, 36 (May, 1929), 60–64.

307. "Round Hill School." *American Annals of Education*. 1 (July, 1826), 437–439.

308. Rouse, W. H. D.   *A History of Rugby School*. New York: Charles Scribner's Sons, 1898.

309. Rousseau, Jean Jacques. *Émile, Julie and Other Writings*. Selections edited by R. L. Archer,  New York:  Barron's Educational Series, 1964.

310. Runes, Dagobert D.   *Pictorial History of Philosophy*. New York: Bramhall House, 1959.

311. Santayana, S. G.   *Two Renaissance Educators:  Alberti and Piccolomini*. Boston:  Meador Publishing Company, 1930.

312. Sargent, Dudley Allen.   *An Autobiography*.  Edited by Ledyard W. Sargent. Philadelphia:  Lea & Febiger, 1927.

313. ————. "Competition and Culture." *American Physical Education Review*, XV (November, 1910), 579–585.

314. ————. *Health, Strength and Power*. New York: H. M. Caldwell Company, 1904.

315. ————. *Hygienic Institute and School of Physical Culture*. Brochure announcing opening, 1878.

316. ————. "Interest in Sport and Physical Education as a Phase of Woman's Development." *Mind and Body*, 22 (November, 1915), 830–833.

317. ————. *Physical Education*. Boston: Ginn & Company, 1906.

318. ————. "The Physical State of the American People." *The United States of America*. Vol. III. Edited by Nathaniel Southgate Shaler. New York: D. Appleton and Company, 1894.

319. ————. "The Physical Test of a Man." *School and Society*, XIII (January, 1921), 128–135.

320. ————. "Physical Training as a Compulsory Subject." *School Review*, 16 (January, 1908), 42–55.

321. ————. "The Place for Physical Training in the School and College Curriculum." *American Physical Education Review*, V (March, 1900), 1–17.

322. ————. *Sanatory Gymnasium*. Brochure published between 1891 and 1894.

323. ————. "Useful Dancing from the Standpoint of Physical Training." *Mind and Body*, 16 (September, 1909), 217–221.

324. Sargent, D. A., Seaver, J. W., and Savage, Watson L. "Intercollegiate Strength-Tests." *American Physical Education Review*, II (December, 1897), 216–220.

325. Savage, Howard J. *Games and Sports in British Schools and Universities*. Second Edition. New York: The Carnegie Foundation for the Advancement of Teaching, 1928.

326. Schmidt, Albert-Marie. *John Calvin and the Calvinist Tradition*. Translated by Ronald Wallace. New York: Harper and Brothers, 1960.

327. Schrader, Carl L. "Rhythmical Exercises Based on Dalcroze Eurythmics." *American Physical Education Review*, XXXI (February, 1926), 667–668.

328. ————. "Our Tribute to the Late Mr. Gilbert." *Mind and Body*, 17 (June, 1910), 142.

329. Schroeder, Louis C. "The Gymnastic School at Ollerup, Denmark." *American Physical Education Review*, XXXII (January, 1927), 54–62.

330. Schwendener, Norma. *A History of Physical Education in the United States*. New York: A. S. Barnes and Company, 1942.

331. Senkeintz, Ernest. "The Cologne Turnfest." *Mind and Body*, 36 (April, 1929), 1–5.

332. Shattuck, George Cheever. "Centenary of the Round Hill School." *Proceedings of the Massachusetts Historical Society*, LVII (December, 1923), 205–209.

333. Shaw, Albert. "Baron Pierre de Coubertin." *American Monthly Review of Reviews*, XVII (April, 1898), 435–438.

334. Skarstrom, William. "Life and Work of Amy Morris Homans." *Research Quarterly*, 12 (October, 1941, Suppl.), 615–627.

335. Smith, T. V., and Grene, Majorie, eds. *Philosophers Speak for Themselves: From Descartes to Locke.* Phoenix Books. Chicago: University of Chicago Press, 1957.

336. Snider, Denton J. *The Life of Frederick Froebel.* Chicago: Sigma Publishing Company, 1900.

337. Spiess, Adolf. "Pedagogical Gymnastics." *Mind and Body*, 1 (January, 1895), 1–8.

338. Stanford University. *Register.* California: By the University, 1891–92, 1892–93, 1893–94.

339. Stanley, Arthur Pehrhyn. *The Life and Correspondence of Thomas Arnold, D.D.* Boston: Field, Osgood, and Company, 1870.

340. Stebbins, Genevieve. *Delsarte System of Dramatic Expression.* New York: Edgar S. Werner, 1886.

341. Stecher, William A. "Foreign Items of Interest." *Mind and Body*, 37 (November, 1930), 221.

342. Steffensen, James L. *The Renaissance.* Vol. VII of *The Universal History of the World.* Edited by Irwin Shapiro. New York: Golden Press, 1966.

343. Storey, Thomas A., and Jean, Sally Lucas. "Presentation of the Luther Halsey Gulick Award to Dr. Thomas D. Wood, Professor of Physical Education, Teachers College, Columbia University." *American Physical Education Review*, XXXI (April; May, 1926), 782–786; 837–839.

344. Stowe, Lyman Beecher. *Saints, Sinners and Beechers.* Indianapolis: Bobbs-Merrill Company, 1934.

345. Streicher, Margarete. "Göttingene Rede." Original Manuscript, 1961.

346. ————. *Natürliches Turnen III.* Vienna: Verlag für Jugend und Volk, 1950.

347. ————. *Natürliches Turnen V.* Vienna: Verlag für Jugend and Volk, 1959.

348. ————. "Das Schulturnen." *Handbuch der Pädagogik.* Langensalza: Verlag Julius Beltz, 1929.

349. ————. "Systematik und Bewegungslehre." *Festschrift Diem.* Vienna: Limpert Verlag, 1962.

350. Streit, W. K. "Normal College of the American Gymnastic Union." *The Physical Educator*, 20 (May, 1963), 51–55.

351. Sumption, Dorothy. "Danish Gymnastics." *American Physical Education Review*, XXXI (November, 1926), 1089–1094.

352. ————. *Fundamental Danish Gymnastics for Women.* New York: A. S. Barnes & Company, 1927.

353. Swett, John, ed. *The Bookseller*, I (August, 1860).

354. ————. *History of the Public School System of California.* San Francisco: A. L. Bancroft & Company, 1876.

355. ————. *Methods of Teaching.* New York: American Book Company, 1880.

356. ————. "A Plea for Amusement and Physical Culture." *The Bookseller*, I (September; November, 1860), 41–44; 130–133.

357. ————. *Second Biennial Report of the Superintendent of Public Instruction of the State of California, 1866–1867.* D. W. Gelincks, State Printer.

358. ————. *Thirteenth Annual Report of the Superintendent of Public Instruction of the State of California, 1863.*

359. Taylor, Margery F. S.: "An Historical Study of Professional Training in Hygiene and Physical Education in the Boston Normal School of Gymnastics at Wellesley College." Unpublished M.A. thesis, Wellesley College, 1938.

360. Teachers College. *Announcement.* New York: By Columbia University, 1903–1904, 1917–1918, 1924–1925, 1934–1935, 1944–1945, 1952–1953.

361. Thulin, J. G. "The Application of P. H. Ling's System to Modern Swedish-Ling Gymnastics." *Mind and Body*, 38 (November, 1931), 625–631.

362. Tileston, Mary Wilder. *Mary Hemenway.* Boston: Privately Printed, 1927.

363. Tucker, Anna P. "Delsarte and his Contribution to Physical Education." *Proceedings and Addresses of the National Educational Association*, 36th Annual Meeting. Milwaukee, Wisconsin, 1897, 880–883.

364. Ulich, Robert. *History of Educational Thought.* New York : American Book Company, 1945.

365. Van Dalen, Deobold, B., Mitchell, Elmer D., and Bennett, Bruce L. *A World History of Physical Education.* Englewood Cliffs, New Jersey: Prentice-Hall, 1953.

366. Van Wyck, Clarence B. "Harvard Summer School of Physical Education 1887–1932." *Research Quarterly*, 13 (December, 1942), 403–431.

367. Vendien, C. Lynn, and Nixon, John E. *The World Today in Health, Physical Education, and Recreation.* Englewood Cliffs, New Jersey: Prentice-Hall, 1968.

368. Wacker, Hazel Marie. "The History of the Private Single-Purpose Institutions which Prepared Teachers of Physical Education in the United States of America From 1861 to 1958." Unpublished Ed.D. dissertation, New York University, 1959.

369. Welch, J. Edmund. *Edward Hitchcock, M.D. Founder of Physical Education in the College Curriculum.* North Carolina: By the Author, P. O. Box 2043, Greenville, N. C.  27834, 1966.

370. Weston, Arthur. *The Making of American Physical Education.* New York: Appleton-Century-Crofts, 1962.

371. Williams, Jesse Feiring. "Education through the Physical." *Journal of Higher Education*, I (May, 1930), 279–282.

372. ————. "Fundamental Point of View in Physical Education." *Journal of Health and Physical Education*, I (January, 1930), 10–11, 60.

373. ————. "Health, an Objective of Education." *Journal of Health and Physical Education*, IV (March, 1933), 5–6.

374. ————. *The Organization and Administration of Physical Education.* New York: The Macmillan Company, 1922.

375. ————. *The Principles of Physical Education.* Second Edition. Philadelphia: W. B. Saunders Company, 1932.

376. ————. *The Principles of Physical Education.* Eighth Edition. Philadelphia: W. B. Saunders Company, 1964.

377. Williams, Jesse Feiring, Brownell, Clifford Lee, and Vernier, Elmon Louis. *The Administration of Health and Physical Education.* Sixth Edition. Philadelphia: W. B. Saunders Company, 1964.

378. Williams, Jesse Feiring, Dambach, John I., and Schwendener, Norma. *Methods in Physical Education.* Philadelphia: W. B. Saunders Company, 1932.

379. Wood, Thomas Denison. *Health and Education. The Ninth Yearbook of the National Society for the Study of Education.* Part I. Chicago: University of Chicago Press, 1910.

380. ————. *Selections from Addresses*. Privately Published, 1932.
381. Wood, Thomas Denison, and Cassidy, Rosalind Frances. *The New Physical Education*. New York: The Macmillan Company, 1927.
382. Woodward, William Harrison. *Vittorino da Feltre and other Humanist Educators*. New York: Bureau of Publications, Teachers College, Columbia University, 1963. (First published 1897: Cambridge University Press.)
383. Woody, Thomas. *Life and Education in Early Societies*. New York: The Macmillan Company, 1959.
384. Zeigler, Earle Frederick. "A History of Professional Preparation for Physical Education in the United States." Unpublished Ph.D. dissertation, Yale University, 1950.
385. Zwarg, Leopold F. "A Study of the History, Uses and Values of Apparatus in Physical Education." *Mind and Body*, 38 (April; May; June; September; November, 1931), 429–438; 481–490; 556–565; 594–601; 637–650.

# INDEX

Page numbers in *italics* refer to illustrations.

**435**